THE DIARY
OF RICHARD L. BURTSELL

*This is a volume in the
Arno Press collection*

THE AMERICAN CATHOLIC TRADITION

Advisory Editor
Jay P. Dolan

Editorial Board
Paul Messbarger
Michael Novak

*See last pages of this volume
for a complete list of titles.*

THE DIARY OF RICHARD L. BURTSELL PRIEST OF NEW YORK
The Early Years, 1865-1868

Edited by
Nelson J. Callahan

ARNO PRESS
A New York Times Company
New York • 1978

Editorial Supervision: JOSEPH CELLINI

First publication 1978 by Arno Press Inc.

Copyright © 1978 by Nelson J. Callahan

THE AMERICAN CATHOLIC TRADITION
ISBN for complete set: 0-405-10810-9
See last pages of this volume for titles.

Manufactured in the United States of America

Library of Congress Cataloging in Publication Data

Burtsell, Richard Lalor, 1840-1912.
   The diary of Richard L. Burtsell, priest of New York.

   (The American Catholic tradition)
   1. Burtsell, Richard Lalor, 1840-1912.
2. Catholic Church--Clergy--Biography. 3. Clergy
--New York (State)--Biography. 4. New York
(State)--Biography. 5. Catholic Church in
New York (State)--History--Sources. I. Callahan,
Nelson J. II. Title. III. Series.
BX4705.B946A33   1978   282'.092'4 [B]
ISBN 0-405-10813-3   77-89146

EDITOR'S PREFACE

It is my hope that the publication of the first three years of the Diary of Richard Burtsell will make more readily available for scholars a source of Nineteenth Century American Church History which, I believe, is of greater significance than has been heretofore noticed. I did not discover the Burtsell Diary; it was known to several New York priests over the past fifty years. It was also seen by Ellis and quoted by him in his Life of James Cardinal Gibbons. Trisco quoted from the Diary in his essay in The Catholic Priest in the United States : An Historical Perspective and Dolan consulted the first year of the Diary in his Immigrant Church.

The Burtsell Diary, written in ledger books and numbering nearly 5000 pages was not always so easily accessible. It was stored in the attic of the rectory of Dr. Daniel Burke, one of Burtsell's former assistants, at The Church of St. Philip Neri in the Bronx until Burke's death in 1931. It was then transferred to the Corrigan Library Archives of the Archdiocese of New York where it is still housed today along with five ledger books of Burtsell letters. In the Diary, Burtsell makes reference to his scrap books and to his personal papers; I am not aware that these scrap books and personal papers exist anywhere any longer.

There are phases to the Diary. The first three years are filled with extensive and reflective entries. It ceases abruptly in Feb., 1868, with Burtsell, having finished his period of assistantship at St. Ann Parish, commissioned to found the parish of Epiphany at Second Ave. and Twenty-second St. in Manhattan and living in a boarding house.

When Burtsell resumed writing his Diary on Jan. 1, 1872, Epiphany Church and rectory had been built; Burtsell had two assistants; he was concerned very much about the details of the life of a city pastor. The First Vatican Council was over and Burtsell's reactions to it are altogether unrecorded. The diary was continued with gaps in 1894-95 and again in 1905-07 until Burtsell lapsed into pneumonia and died in Feb., 1912. But after 1872, while the Diary is often discoursive, and frequently full of detail, it seems to lack the freshness of speculation that one finds in the first three years which are published here.

Richard Lalor Burtsell was born in New York City, April 13, 1840. His father, John, was somewhat successful as a merchant in New York, but died while his son was a student in Rome. The Burtsell family had been in America since 1640 and traced its roots from Wales to the Catholic colony of the Calverts in Maryland in the 1600's, and finally to New York where they were living by the time of the Revolutionary War. They owned property at the corner of Broad and Wall Sts. in lower Manhattan which they sold to the Drexels of Philadelphia in 1872 for $675,000. Eventually, Richard Burtsell inherited this money, much of which he gave to the Archdiocesan Seminary of St. Joseph at Dunwoodie New York in 1907.

Burtsell's mother was Dorothea Morrogh. She was born in Cork Ireland; she came to New York prior to the Great Famine in spite of the fact that the Morroghs and their cousins, the Russells, were and still are a landed family of wealth in Ireland. Here Mrs. Burtsell taught music at the Convent of Mt. St. Vincent after her husband's death and died in New York at Epiphany Rectory in 1875. She had a sister who was married to the Garabaldian general, John Avezzena, who lived in Italy; another sister was married to a New York jeweler, Peter De Coppet. She had a brother a physician; a second brother was a priest; he was Dr. William Plowden Morrogh, who was pastor of the Church of Immaculate Conception on E. 14th St. during the period covered by this excerpt of the Diary.

Richard Burtsell had a brother, John, who was married and living in San Francisco during the first three years of the Diary, and one sister, Ann, who died while Burtsell was studying in Rome.

Burtsell's education began at the school of St. Peter on Barclay St. He attended the Jesuit school attached to St. Francis Xavier Church on 16th St. in New York, and at age eleven, was sent to study the classics at the Sulpician Seminary in Montreal. In 1853 when he was thirteen, Burtsell was sent to study in earnest for the priesthood at the Urban College of the Propaganda in Rome by Archbishop John Hughes. The boy made the journey from New York to Rome alone. The Diary recalls occasional reference to his student days in Rome. Burtsell's uncle, Dr. William P. Morrogh, was a professor of Theology at the Urban College when Richard was a student there; Burtsell was, according to Don Philip Tansioni, Rector of the College, an excellent student. Propaganda archives indicate that Burtsell earned a Doctorate in Philosophy in 1858 and a Doctorate in Theology in 1862. He was ordained in Rome on Aug. 10, 1862, by Archbishop Clemente of Damascus. The young priest now twenty-two returned to New York in Nov., 1862, and was appointed by Archbishop Hughes assistant to Fr. Thomas Preston at the Church of St. Ann at 8th St. and Astor Place in lower Manhattan. He remained there until Dec., 1867, when he was appointed founding pastor of Epiphany parish. It is the last three years at St. Ann that this edition of the Diary embraces.

In the portion of the Diary published here, one notices

already several themes which would effect much of Burtsell's whole life.

1) Burtsell had a profound sense of loyalty to his friends. These friends were, however, almost all Alumni of Propaganda. Their names constantly appear in the Diary; most significant was the gifted Edward McGlynn who was Chaplain of the Army Hospital in Central Park when the Diary commenced, but who was appointed to succeed Dr. Jeremiah Cummings as pastor of St. Stephen on 28th St. when Cummings died in January of 1866. Dr. Patrick McSweeney was an assistant at St. Patrick Cathedral on Mott St. between 1865 and 1868. Fr. James Nilan was assistant at the Church of the Holy Cross on 42nd St. during this period, and Fr. Thomas Farrell, probably the most significant of the men to whom Burtsell gave his friendship, was pastor of St. Joseph Church in Greenwich Village.

2) Cummings, who was a Propaganda alumnus, had organized an "Ecclesiastical Society", (the term is Burtsell's), which seems to have been a loosely bound species of clerical secret society. From the beginning, it was concerned for scholarship and study which focused on theology. At the same time there was also an emphasis on how genuine Catholic doctrine might be accomodated to the developing cultural uniqueness of the American experience. With the death of Cummings, Farrell, who had really been its primary mover, became the president of the Ecclesiastical Society. The meetings became more regular and rather disciplined; a wide range of speculative and positive theology was discussed. At the same time there was considerable criticism of current church policy. Often visitors to New York who were Propagandists, were invited to the meetings, men like John Moore of Charleston South Carolina who would become bishop of St. Augustine, Edward Fitzgerald of Cincinnati who would become bishop of Little Rock, and James O'Connor future bishop of Omaha.

3) From the beginning, the Diary reveals Burtsell's special concern for the problems of law; for a change in the language of the church to the vernacular; for the abolishment of the temporal power of the Papacy; for the poor and for the cause of abolition. Burtsell simultaneously favored exposure of the newly freed black people to American Catholicism and at the same time the preservation of the values of the cultures of immigrants who were arriving daily in massive numbers from Europe at New York. But, Burtsell and his friends wanted these new Americans who were Catholic to begin to become part of the American process rooted in liberty and democratic processes as soon as possible.

4) Burtsell and his friends examined in great detail the discipline of celibacy for the secular clergy in the United States. They were dismayed when they found that it was imperfectly observed, but concluded that its sign value for the Kingdom warranted its continuance. Those who could not keep it however, were to be permanently suspended and allowed to marry.

5) The parochial school system was also examined. Here the conclusion was that at best it was a luxury which the immigrant church, rooted in poverty, could ill afford. Moreover, Burtsell felt that if such a school system were legislated, (it was not legislated until the Third Plenary Council in 1884 although it had been urged by provincial councils as early as 1851), it would be staffed primarily by religious women. Burtsell saw this as a great mistake since he believed that should such a system be introduced, within two generations, there would develop two versions of Catholicism in the United States. The one he felt would be rooted in true theology; the other in convent piety.

6) At the core of all of this, one finds the unique

hope of Burtsell and his friends for America. As Propaganda alumni, they returned to the United States with the intention of being missionaries in their native land. They understood clearly the distinction between Church doctrine and church discipline. They ardently wished to adapt the discipline of the Church to the emerging culture of a new country. They believed, as did Johnathan Edwards before them, that America had a great destiny. They wanted to convert this country to Catholicism to which they were incredibly loyal and which they believed gave the only true meaning for the life to all men. But they knew that if non-catholic Americans perceived the Roman Church to be alien to American institutions, then it would have little appeal for anyone but the Catholic immigrant. Certainly there was something of Orestes Brownson and Isaac Hecker, both of whom Burtsell's Diary mentions, in all of this. But the Brownson-Hecker vision was not quite that of Burtsell and his friends. One suspects that in the case of Brownson, they felt that he had lost his force for good because of his harshness and lack of pragmatic understanding of the newly arriving immigrants. In the case of Hecker, it would seem Burtsell was sympathetic but suspicious as he wondered whether Hecker would be willing to risk much if the opprobrium of radicalism should be leveled by church authority against his small and vulnerable Paulist community.

      7) By mid-1867, however, the Diary shows that Burtsell had discovered so much anti-catholic bigotry in the Protestant churches of New York, and such a need for the catholic minority to defend itself against this bigotry, that Burtsell appeared to have pretty well abandoned his great hope to evangelize the country from the base of a Church which was uniquely American. Perhaps the intransigence of the Second Plenary Council of Baltimore in 1866 was also partially responsible for this change

of heart on the part of Burtsell and his friends; in any case, the issue is not urged again.

When on Jan. 1, 1872, Burtsell resumed his Diary, the reader finds a man subtly changed. Burtsell, who in 1867 had proposed his own agenda for the First Vatican Council and who had opposed any definition of personal infallibility for the Pope which would go beyond the general infallibility assigned by theology to the Church, made no record of his reaction to the Council. One suspects that he regarded the magisterium of the Church as sufficient to end all speculation. The Diary does note as early as 1867, that the only way Burtsell saw that the definition of the doctrine of the Immaculate Conception by the Pope in 1854 could be justified would be for the Council to declare the Pope's personal infallibility retroactive.

But by 1872 many other things had changed for Burtsell. His friends, James Nilan and Patrick McSweeney had been made pastors in rural parishes; Nilan in Pt. Jervis, N.Y., a mining town two hundred miles from New York City and McSweeney at Poughkeepsie almost one hundred miles up the Hudson. Here in 1874, Burtsell notes that McSweeney inaugurated the Poughkeepsie School Plan. It called for the rental of the existing parochial school to the State of New York for a dollar a year. The state, in turn, would assume the cost of maintaining and operating the school, of supervising the teachers and was to allow Catholic children attending the school to receive religious instruction on released time in the parish building adjoining the school. One notes that this plan predated Archbishop John Ireland's similar plan at Fairbault and Stillwater, Minn., by almost sixteen years.

As has been noted, Burtsell's mother died in 1875; her loss was a cause of profound sorrow for her son. Still, that same year, he took great delight in the elevation of New York's archbishop John McCloskey to the Cardinalate, the first Cardinal from the United States. In 1876, Burtsell took a prolonged vacation in Europe; he visited Rome for the first time since he had left for America after his ordination in 1862. In Rome he had a special audience with Pope Pius IX who was by then badly besieged by the policies of the new Government of Victor Emmanuel. Burtsell and Pius IX talked briefly of events they had shared in Burtsell's days as a student in Rome, and the Pope, who had less than two years to live, sent through Burtsell his special blessing to the people of Epiphany parish.

In 1880, the Diary records the death of Fr. Thomas Farrell, the mentor of Burtsell, McGlynn, McSweeney, Nilan and many other young New York pastors. The final years of Farrell's life were filled with some sort of bitterness; his goals for an American church were unachieved; and he had been prohibited from preaching, even in his own Church, by Cardinal McCloskey. One wonders why. But Farrell's will of which Burtsell was an executor left a large sum of money in Alabama bonds to be used for the establishment of a church for black people in New York and for a country home for black children on Long Island. Burtsell alone saw to the execution of Farrell's will; he established the Church of St. Benedict the Moor in lower Manhattan in 1883; he acted as the temporary pastor of the church until it was able to stand on its own merits and sent one of his assistants, Fr. John Burke to be its first pastor. Then Burtsell transferred the whole operation of St. Benedict to the Archdiocese, free of debt and in a flourishing condition. There was much of Burtsell's heart and his money in this mission parish which exists to the present day.

Meanwhile in 1880, Michael Corrigan, a contemporary of Burtsell and McGlynn at Propaganda, was promoted from Bishop of Newark to

Coadjutor to McCloskey in New York with the right of succession. Burtsell and his friends were saddened by this appointment; it proved to be the beginning of a tragic confrontation in New York between Corrigan, who assumed the archbishopric with the death of McCloskey in 1885, and Edward McGlynn, Burtsell's closest friend.

All during the 1870's and early 1880's, Burtsell found himself more and more called upon by aggrieved priests to act as their canon lawyer in litigations against their bishops. By 1886, Burtsell had acquired the reputation among the clergy of the country as one of the foremost defenders of the rights of the clergy, surely a position which hardly endeared him to the American bishops. In nearly all of the cases Burtsell counseled his clients to appeal to Rome for justice and mercy; in nearly every case Rome heeded their appeals and ruled in favor of the due process for which Burtsell asked.

Burtsell, who was disturbed that neither he nor his friends were invited to the II Plenary Council of Baltimore in 1866, was a participant as theologian to Bishop John Moore of St. Augustine at the Third Plenary Council of Baltimore in 1884. At the Council, Burtsell served on the Commission on the rights of Pastors and almost as an afterthought, he and Fr. De Concilio of Newark composed the Baltimore Catechism.

But late in 1886, Burtsell suddenly became involved, much against his will, in the great crisis of his life. In September of that year, Edward McGlynn became actively involved in the political campaign of Henry George for Mayor of New York. George espoused, as the primary plank of his platform, the single tax theory. This theory, considered revolutionary in its time, was fully developed by George in his book, Progress and Poverty, which he published in 1879. In the book, George argued that just as all the people owned all the air which they were free to breathe, so, all the people owned all the produce of the land of any given nation. He applied the theory at first to Ireland which George visited in 1881. There he hoped to offer a peaceful solution to the awful plight of the farmers of that devastated country. He suggested, one suspects rightly, that the tenant farmers in Ireland had a right to the profits made from the produce of the land which they worked. At the same time George held that landlords who owned the land in Ireland but who lived, generally, in England, had no right to the profits which came from the land they owned in Ireland. Rather, George held that profits from Irish land belonged to all the Irish people to be shared evenly.

But by 1882, McGlynn saw that George's theory of land reform in Ireland had little chance of success in that country without Parliamentary cooperation, a thing for which Charles Stuart Parnell was campaigning with far greater success than George. But McGlynn saw also that in the United States where free elections and proper representation of all people was at least a possible reality, George's theory might be promoted as a political base in city, state, and even national elections. Moreover, McGlynn saw that George might be the political champion of a third party in American politics, a party that might unite the poor in a great crusade against laisez faire capitalism. It was McGlynn who urged George to run for the office of Mayor of New York City and it was McGlynn who nominated George. His candidacy, supported by McGlynn who was probably the most influential priest in the country at that time, was not lost on the leaders of Tammany Hall. They controlled, for the most part, the traditionally Democratic Irish vote for all offices in New York municipal elections. These leaders saw that George's candidacy would diminish and divide their power; they knew that George would draw few votes from the established Republican party in New York. But a divided Democratic vote would give the election to the Republicans.

The Burtsell Diary does not say so specifically, though it strongly suggests that Burtsell believed that the Catholic leaders of Tammany Hall went to Archbishop Corrigan and urged him to denounce McGlynn and the George Single Tax theory as socialism bordering on Communism. Both had already been denounced by Papal documents as incompatible to Catholic belief, and hardly causes which might be supported by a Catholic priest.

Corrigan's motives in what followed are not at all clear. Perhaps he truly believed that the George theory was socialistic or somehow contrary to papal teaching; perhaps he was moved merely by the political pressure of the Tammany leaders. In any case, he acted suddenly and with all the decisive force of his office. First he warned McGlynn not to make the speech nominating George. But Corrigan delivered the warning to McGlynn the day before the speech was to be given. McGlynn, for his part, replied with a compromise. To cancel the speech would, he felt, embarrass the Archbishop in the eyes of the poor; hence, McGlynn chose the lesser of two evils. He replied to the Archbishop that he would give the nomination speech, but promised to take no further part in the political campaign of George. Corrigan found this solution unsatisfactory; indeed he saw McGlynn's action as direct disobedience to his warning. So the day following McGlynn's nomination speech, Corrigan secretly suspended McGlynn from all priestly functions at St. Stephen's for two weeks. Then the Archbishop referred the case to Rome.

At this point the whole event becomes a bit difficult to

unravel. McGlynn, feeling that Corrigan had violated his part of the bargain suggested by McGlynn, but to which Corrigan had never agreed, felt free to campaign for George throughout much of the Fall of 1886. Corrigan continued to extend the period of McGlynn's suspension through January of 1887, waiting for Rome's advice on the matter. When Rome did reply, it was to urge McGlynn, as a loyal alumnus of Propaganda, to come to the Eternal City and discuss the George theory and his support of it. McGlynn refused, pleading poor health and a genuine reluctance to go to Rome as a suspended priest, a position which rendered him at least partially guilty without having had benefit of a hearing. This struck McGlynn and Burtsell, his canon lawyer, as a total violation of due process. Corrigan reacted by removing McGlynn from the pastorate of St. Stephen and giving him no other assignment until he would go to Rome. The Archbishop maintained he had no power to remove the suspension since the case was in Rome on appeal. Finally Rome ordered McGlynn to come over to talk about the whole affair under pain of excommunication. McGlynn refused while he was suspended unless, and until, he was reinstated; on July 4, 1887, he was formally excommunicated by Rome.

After the excommunication, McGlynn sought to revive the George forces, (which had been beaten in the election of Nov., 1886), seeking to continue the momentum of the third party in New York. McGlynn renamed the party "The Anti-Poverty Society." For more than two years he lectured this society nearly every Sunday evening at the Cooper Union or at Chickering Hall in New York. But there was an air of desperation about the whole aspect of these meetings. For his part, McGlynn was an excommunicated priest; he had lost his pastorate, and to a great extent, he had lost the great influence he had enjoyed while a functioning priest with people of all classes, but especially with most Catholics, even the poor. For his part, Henry George was no longer interested in politics and he saw the Anti-Poverty Society as a fruitless exercise by his disappointed followers.

Between 1887 and 1892 the Burtsell Diary records the exhausting, but in the end, successful struggle of McGlynn's friends to get him reinstated with the Church. At first, the efforts, led primarily by Burtsell himself, were rooted in appeals to the Congregation of the Propaganda in Rome. Cardinal Gibbons and Archbishop John Ireland tried to help when they were in Rome in 1887 but were made ineffective by some of McGlynn's rather bitter slurs upon Archbishop Corrigan and upon Roman Institutions as well during his lectures to the Anti-Poverty Society. Later, McGlynn's old classmate at Propaganda College, Bishop John Moore of St. Augustine, Florida, hit upon a new tactic. Going over the head of Propaganda, he appealed to the Vatican Secretary of State, Cardinal Rampolla, asking that an apostolic Delegate be sent by Pope Leo XIII to the United States to make a thorough investigation of Bishop-priest difficulties in this country. Rampolla strongly favored just such an opportunity as, it would seem, did the Pope himself. In 1889, Archbishop Francisco Satolli was sent by the Pope as his Delegate to the dedication of the new Catholic University. Satolli sought to speak to McGlynn but found him absent from New York on a lecture tour. The Delegate returned to Rome. Then, in 1891, Pope Leo issued his radical social encyclical, Rerum Novarum, which moderated to a striking degree, the previous position of the Church toward Socialism, the rights of laboring men and their power to strike for living wages. At the same time the Encyclical placed great stress on the duties of Capitolism.

In 1892, through his Secretary of State, President Benjamin Harrison asked Cardinal Gibbons to obtain on loan, maps from the Vatican Library which indicated the route taken by Columbus in his discovery of America. They were to be displayed at the Chicago World's Fair the following year commemorating the four-hundredth anniversary of Columbus' Discovery. The Pope seized upon the invitation as an occasion to send Archbishop Satolli to this country once again as his Delegate. Satolli arrived in October, 1892; he went to Washington to establish a temporary headquarters at the Catholic University. The week before Christmas of that year, the Delegate asked a few faculty members at the University to examine the George doctrine which McGlynn had espoused at such great cost, for doctrinal error. These faculty members found no such errors in George's work and McGlynn, with Burtsell acting as his lawyer, was absolved by the Delegate in time to offer mass on Christmas of 1892.

Burtsell in the meanwhile had run into his own problem with Archbishop Corrigan for his advocacy of McGlynn's case. In January of 1890, Corrigan wrote Burtsell that he would be removed from the pastorate of Epiphany parish by June of that year because he was having a harmful effect upon the younger clergy of the Archdiocese. Burtsell appealed to Propaganda by mail. He was invited to come to Rome to defend himself, but for reasons which are simply never stated in the Diary, Burtsell remained in New York during the six months of his appeal. Propaganda sustained Archbishop Corrigan in the case and in June of 1890, Burtsell was transferred to the pastorate of St. Mary's Church in Rondout, New York, one hundred miles up the Hudson River. Burtsell went to Rondout making no protest at all.

Only after McGlynn's reinstatement did Burtsell make

an effort to prosecute personally his own grievance. He went to Rome in
October, 1893, remained there nearly a year, and finally came home without
ever having had a real hearing. The Diary described his extensive dealings
with high Vatican officials, both at Propaganda and the Secretariate
of State, including the future Pope, Benedict XV, but Burtsell never was
vindicated. He returned to Rondout and remained until his death in 1912.

    Burtsell's Diary reveals many contacts with Archbishop
Satolli who seemed often to have relied upon Burtsell for legal clarifica-
tion in ongoing Bishop-priest difficulties, but Burtsell never seemed to
speak to Satolli about his own case. One wonders why. In any case, after
the death of Archbishop Corrigan in 1903, Burtsell was made a Monsignor
by the new Archbishop of New York, John Farley, in 1904. In 1905, he was
made Dean of Orange County; and, while accompanying Farley to Rome in
1911 when Farley received the Cardinal's Hat, Farley's request that
Burtsell be named a Protonotary Apostolic was granted by the Papal
Secretariate of State.

    This summary of the life of Richard Burtsell as it is
revealed in his Diary is not intended to be a biographical sketch, nor
is it intended to cover all the major issues contained in the Diary. It
is intended to give some skeleton to the life of the man whose first three
years of Diary writing are here being published.

    My own feeling is that the issues which dominate the
life of Richard Burtsell, issues for which he suffered greatly in espousing,
are to be found, at least in embryo form, in the text of the Diary's first
three years. There are several premeses which I feel substantiate this
belief.

    1) The fundamental ideas which moved Burtsell's whole

priestly life are discoverable in the first three years of his Diary. No doubt he went through a remarkable degree of growth and developed great sophistication as he grew older, but one notes his basic attitudes did not find their source in his priestly work at St. Ann, at Epiphany or at St. Mary, Rondout. One is strongly inclined to believe that he formed his ideas at Propaganda College. There he found students who represented countries from all over the world. Contact with them opened Burtsell to the wide variety of disciplines which existed in the Church in his time and to the amazing adaptability of Church law and discipline to the unique culture of each nation which was represented in the student body of the Propaganda College.

2) It is precisely this point that I believe gives the Burtsell Diary such great significance. Up to now, it would seem that American Church Historians have traditionally noted two major parties in the nineteenth-century American Church.

The first one might term the Americanists. They are usually depicted as being led by Cardinal Gibbons, Archbishops John Ireland and John Keane and to some degree, by Bishop John Lancaster Spalding. These men more or less ignore the non-english-speaking immigrants, leaving them to the care of their ethnic enclaves until they can achieve full status as Americans. The Americanists feel this is to occur as quickly as possible. These Americanists display little sensitivity to the value of middle and eastern European culture and show even less concern for the fear of so many of the clerical leaders of these people who might be deprived of the opportunity of contact with the language, culture, custom and faith as they knew it in their place of origin in Europe. Should this deprivation occur, these immigrant peoples might well lose that faith altogether.

The second party in the nineteenth century American Church which historians traditionally describe might be termed the nationalists or Europeanizers. They were led by Archbishops Fred Katzer and Michael Heiss, by Bishops Seidenbuseh and Juncker and much of the German and Polish clergy who rarely found representation in the hierarchy of the United States. Their concern was for the preservation of the faith, language, culture and custom of their people. They saw the Gibbons-Ireland approach as an effort to force their people into territorial parishes which were perceived as Irish parishes. One suspects that they were at least half-right; the territorial parishes of the last century were usually dominated by Irish pastors who had little understanding of their own culture, and understood that of the new arrived non-english speaking immigrant from Europe even less. The Europeanizers were very well represented both by Peter Paul Cahensley and by Peter Abbelein. Both protested to Rome in the 1880's as they sought to effect a tolerance in the American hierarchy for the nationality parish in the major urban centers for at least one generation after immigration. One suspects that these Europeanizers also felt that their homogenous European culture was superior to the heterogenus culture they encountered in the United States. Hence there were established nationality parishes in major American urban centers and these understandably saw few converts to Catholicism in the true non-english parishes until these parishes were at least two generations old. In many ways the Europeanizers, at least initially, sought to do all they could to preserve the faith of their people and to oppose any tendency that might force them to Americanize too quickly.

It is my hope that the first three years of the Burtsell Diary may be seen to reveal a third party in the American Church of the last century. I should like to call this party the Americanizers. As I have already pointed out, this group was, by the very nature of the seminary training of most of its members, rooted in the transcultural experience gained at the Propaganda College. These men, (Burtsell, McGlynn, McSweeney, Nilan, and Farrell were prominent in their leadership), valued highly the culture of the United States. They saw in this culture great hope for the future of the Church. But they also saw the value of the culture the European immigrant brought with him to this country. They had no desire to suppress that culture, for like the Europeanizers, they knew that culture and faith were closely linked. They were perfectly content to allow the immigrant to pursue the faith in the congregation in which he felt most comfortable. But at the same time, the Americanizers dreamed of a day when the immigrants would melt into one great and new Church which would reflect the free institutions of the United States. They differed from the Americanists in the following ways:

      a) They did not urge a super-patriotism from the immigrant as the Americanist did. They did believe in a gradual assimilation of the immigrant and saw a protest of this assimilation in terms of loyalty or super-patriotism as demeaning to the immigrant.

      b) They saw the Americanists as representing basically an Irish model of Church, a thing which they saw equally as foreign to American institutions as was the Europeanist model. In the last third of the last century, generally foreign-born Irish pastors had charge of the territorial parishes in the urban centers and ran them according to what they recalled from Ireland. More often than not, the Irish-born pastor was totally undemocratic in his decision making; the Europeanist surprisingly was quite democratic. Too, the foreign-born Irish pastor was usually extremely Roman in his outlook; his language was always latin in liturgy and English in homilies. The Europeanist pastor was latin in his liturgical language but homilies and para-liturgical functions were done in the vernacular of the country of origin of the immigrant.

c) The Americanizers sought no power base in the large urban dioceses. This was not the case with either the Irish-born Americanist pastors (and bishops), or with the Europeanist pastors (and bishops). Both struggled for power; the reasons why they did are not at all clear. Perhaps the Europeanists were fearful lest they be made extinct by the opprobrium of inferiority that was attached to their congregations by the Americanists and therefore they fought the Americanists as the enemy. This could have caused the Americanists to fight back, somewhat mindlessly, setting up the Irish-German hostility that existed for so long in the nineteenth-century church. For their part, the Americanizers saw all culture as good and yet knew that a new culture was sure to emerge in the United States. Their concern was to prepare the Church in the United States to be able to evangelize all men within the context of this new culture; they felt they had time to wait for it to emerge. But they were extremely impatient with the superficial and somewhat immature struggle for power in the Church of the United States which they felt impeded the evolution which was sure to come.

In any case, the Americanizers, who so desperately hoped an American Church to develop here were at least partially responsible for the event that caused their hope to flounder in conflict and in the end, to become all but forgotten right up to our time. The whole event revolved, one suspects, around the McGlynn case. Justice from Rome was such an integral part of Burtsell's early creed that, no matter what his hopes may have been for an uniquely American Church, and whatever may have been his opposition to Roman centralization, when McGlynn was deprived of due process by his Archbishop in the United States, Burtsell seems to have abandoned these positions to achieve this justice. His only hope was to appeal to Rome for an Apostolic Delegate. Burtsell must have known full well what the presence of a Delegate in this country could do to his hope of preparing the United States for a conversion to Catholicism; so did Burtsell's friends know this. So did many Americanists including Cardinal Gibbons and Archbishop Ireland realize this. Still, to gain justice for McGlynn, Burtsell and Bishop Moore invited a Delegate to come. And when the Delegate arrived, Burtsell was able to urge him to secure justice for many aggrieved priests, including McGlynn. But Burtsell became exasperated with Archbishop Ireland, as the Diary reveals, for Ireland's extremist attitude toward the Europeanizers and for his ill-disguised efforts to try to get Archbishop Satolli to espouse Ireland's views. On October 16, 1896, the day before Satolli left the United States to be replaced by a new Apostolic Delegate, Burtsell visited Ireland in New York. Burtsell wrote in his Diary for that Day, "I visited Abp. Ireland at the 5th Ave. Hotel; he says that C. Satolli has gone completely over to the Germans. I suggested that in his plain talk he must not antagonize C. Satolli so as to force him into the arms of the enemy. We talked more than an hour. . ." This enigmatic entry seems to defy interpretation.

That the Germans should be seen by Burtsell as the enemy is hardly consistent with the tolerance which he had always urged for their gradual assimilation into American culture. But in 1896 there were issues that were being debated in the American Church which went far beyond the simple tolerance of German congregations in American Dioceses. The extremism of the position of Ireland and Denis O'Connell, (a position which their fellow-Americanists, Gibbons and Keane had never held nor agreed with), was being fought out in the politics of the Catholic University. There the Germans were demanding proportionate representation on the faculty for men who would occupy what we would call today, chairs of German language and culture. Ireland sought to thwart these German hopes. Archbishop Corrigan and Bishop McQuaid of Rochester, both of whom resented Ireland on ideological grounds, sided with the aspirations of the Germans. Corrigan and McQuaid were, one suspects, really the eney in the mind of Burtsell.

In any case, Satolli returned to Italy. From the deck of the steamer which was to take him home, the departing Delegate was asked by a newspaper man what he thought of the United States. Satolli responded: "I saw little of the supernatural in that country." Back in Rome, Satolli must have discoursed at length with Pope Leo XIII on this same theme, and is generally suspected by United States Church Historians as being one of the primary authors of the Pope's devastating letter to the American bishops in 1899, Testem Benevolentiae. This was the letter which condemned what the Pope called "Americanism." In his Diary, Richard Burtsell never makes a single reference to the Americanism issue, nor to the controversy which followed its publication. One can only guess about his reaction. Surely the letter put to an end, once and for all, Burtsell's hope for an American Church, loyal to Rome but reflecting American culture in its discipline. Burtsell was, himself, as his silence concerning the Papal Infallibility decree of the First Vatican Council seemed to indicate, to much of a theologian to argue about an issue already decided by the magisterium of the Church. Roma locuta, causa finita probably summed up his position. But

Burtsell surely must have seen the irony of the whole event. It was he who wanted a Delegate in the United States to protect the rights of priests. It was he who worked closely with the Delegate when he finally did come, to this end. Yet it was, it would seem, the first Delegate who was instrumental in the condemnation of Americanism and who, subsequently, cautioned Roman authorities to view with some suspicion the movements in the American Church toward a concilliation with American civil institutions.

Indeed, one suspects that so powerful was Cardinal Satolli's representation in Rome after his return from the United States that it was not until the middle of this century that Rome reluctantly began to take seriously the contribution that the American Church could make to the style of the Universal Church. This task fell upon John Courtney Murray at the Second Vatican Council. It appears he succeeded ably, for he acted as one of the periti of Cardinal Spellman at the Council. Yet Spellman, who liked Murray and gave him genuine support in Rome, was opposed his whole lifetime to any attempt to promote the thesis of religious liberty espoused by Burtsell, McGlynn and their friends. Murray had taken up the cause of Burtsell and McGlynn (though one wonders if he had ever even heard of them), and carried it to a relatively successful conclusion after heroic effort, half a century after the death of the two New York priests.

The paradox -- indeed the irony -- seems startling. Yet to substantiate the probable connection between Burtsell and Murray with regard to religious liberty, I should like to quote at length from a letter Burtsell wrote in his own defense to the Holy Office in 1890. Fr. Thomas Preston, Burtsell's old pastor at St. Ann's in the 1860's, was still Vicar General of the Archdiocese of New York in 1890. For reasons which are not quite clear, Preston took it upon himself to write to Rome, without the knowledge of Archbishop Corrigan, to accuse Burtsell, McGlynn and their friends of constituting the nucleus of a clique or secret society of priests who were, Preston said, seeking to Americanize the Church in this country. Moreover, Preston accused Burtsell, McGlynn and the others of opposing the temporal power of the Pope and of refusing to build parochial schools. Burtsell was asked by Rome to reply to the charges which he did. He began by stating:

> 1) "I am a liberal with both God and man. The name liberal does not frighten me. By God's grace, I shall always be liberal in regard to others and in regard to God inasmuch as I shall recognize in others their worth, even if they have not the gift of faith. I shall ever seek to make known to them the reasonableness of our Church, being aware that only reasonable homage is acceptable to God. I am liberal inasmuch as I love liberty. I love very earnestly political liberty which insists that Society shall protect the poor and the weak. I love freedom of discussion with regard to the arrangement of our social concerns, guaranteed to us by our American institutions. I love also, in the sphere of the Church, the full freedom of discussion in all things wherein God allows us liberty because this seems to me most fitted to promote the good of souls and the extension of the Church in the United States.
>
> 2) The charge of a clique is imaginary. Abp. Corrigan's expression, uttered through Msgr. Preston, that 'Dr. Burtsell shared and partook, more or less, of the liberal ideas of a clique' is so elastic that I do not know how to answer. The idea of a clique is mere fancy. My friends were never at one with me in the opinions left to free discussion nor I with them, in matters left by the magisterium to free discussion. It is ridiculous to call a clique the meetings of friends that differed from one another in many things but who knew how to legitimately discuss questions which are speculative about theology and philosophy in accord with the training we received at the Propaganda College in Rome. . . .
>
> 3) With regard to Parochial Schools, I was never in sympathy with those who attacked the system of public schools in this country which, while it eschews the teaching of religion does not do so out of hatred of religion, but precisely so as not to violate the rights of citizens and not to force them to hear instruction contrary to their religious convictions. I always hate the fanaticism that dares to calumniate these schools as well-springs of iniquity. And it never pleases me, in consideration of the small number of Catholics here, to endeavor to make support of parochial schools a matter for

suffrage because the request of Catholics (for public money) for their separate public schools always arouses hatred of the Church and does more harm than good. . . .

4) I was charged with wishing to further the use of the English language in liturgy. This came from priests' conversation among priests about the utility of extending the English language in the liturgy and in the ritual, but subject always to the legislation of the authority of the Church. These same ideas today appear in the Catholic papers of England, even in the Tablet of London and also in the excellent periodical, "The Catholic World" without the suspicion that the writers of these articles in England form with me and my friends a clique. It will never seem to me to be contrary to the spirit of the Church to talk in a legitimate way with other priests of whatever might promote the welfare of souls, even though some persons may wish to attribute to this talk a false meaning.

5) I have also been accused of wishing to promote the use of secular dress by the priests at the celebration of Mass. This is simply gross calumny. Some of my friends suggested, again in private conversation among priests, that priests should dress as simply as possible when they celebrate mass in the tenement houses of the poor immigrants of this city. I find this a reasonable hope, subject of course, to the legislation of the Church. . . ."

Does this not sound like Courtney Murray in the 1960's?

I include this lengthy statement here because I believe it represents the mature judgement of Burtsell about the course of action taken by his friends and himself for close to twenty-four years in the Archdiocese of New York. The fact that the letter was written to Cardinal Rampolla rather than Cardinal Simeoni would seem to corroborate the theory I have already developed that by 1890, Burtsell had lost all confidence in Propaganda and in Cardinal Simeoni and as a consequence was writing to the Papal Secretary of State suggesting that a Delegate from the Pope be sent to look into the affairs of the U. S. Church.

Three years later, on Oct. 28, 1893, Burtsell arrived in Rome to pursue his own case. On that date, he made one of his more significant entries by writing:

"I arrived at the San Paulo Station, Rome, at 7 a.m. and reached the Minerva at 8. I took breakfast and called on Msgr. Denis O'Connell, Rector of The American College. He received me very cordially and entered in medias res at once. He told me that in my dealings in Rome, I must take cognizance of the fact that everything, even my little case, hinges upon the political policy of the Pope who favors France and the republican United States, while Card. Ledochowski is on the side of the Triple Alliance. O'C. says the Pope has broken the latter's strength. I must not trust Propaganda of which the Cardinals belong to the Holy Office; they will not have diverse opinions in diverse rooms. Propaganda is against me because it is against Msgr. Satolli and favors Abp. Corrigan as his opponent. . . .He told three Archbishops, however, that asking for a Delegate was like the fly asking the spider to pay him a visit. . . .I must deal frankly with Card. Rampolla as also with the Pope, but not in a yielding spirit. I showed him my last signed document to the Holy Office and he thought I had already involved myself in a doctrinal dispute, wherein if I were condemned, the Jesuits would hold me always as an incipient heretic endorsed by Msgr. Satolli whose mantle would fall on the Pope who had not followed their advice given through Card. Mazzela. Msgr. O'Connell thinks I should ask the Pope to remit the whole matter to Msgr. Satolli. . . .I called upon Card. Rampolla who received me cordially, but, though he had read Msgr. Satolli's letter, asked me whence I had come. I told him that in my case, I wished to deal with the Pope whereas I had been the intermediary for the reconciliation of Dr. McGlynn through Msgr. Satolli, Abp. Corrigan had sought to persecute me, even using the Sacred Congregation of Propaganda to carry out his designs. Card. Rampolla mentioned that Dr. McGlynn was fieri. I told him that as a collegian, he had been exceptionally meek, though remarkable for learning and piety, and that as a priest, until this agitation began, he was distinguished as a model of sacerdotal life. Hardships heaped upon him, however, had hardened him. . . .Card. Rampolla asked me about Msgr. Satolli's mission. I told him that Msgr. Satolli was very welcome to the priests (he said 'si sa') and to the American people, both Catholic and Protestant. . ."

All of the above, I would suggest, indicates Burtsell quickly grasped the forces at work in the Roman Curia at the time of his visit. But it also indicates the strong feeling at the level of the Secretariate of State, to calm the whole reaction to the McGlynn case. It would seem that as much as anything else, it is the McGlynn story which is most clearly described in the Burtsell Diary and which requires research and publication so that we might more clearly comprehend the dynamics of the Church in the United States in the late nineteenth century.

In publishing the first three years of the Burtsell Diary I have copied the original text verbatim. I have included his grammar as he wrote it and his spellings as he wrote them without noting any of his spelling or grammatical errors. To do so, would, I suspect, detract from the freshness of the text. Also, I have left blank in the text, spaces which are blank in the Diary. These generally are proper names Burtsell failed to recall when writing.

I am extremely grateful to all who have aided and encouraged me in this work. There are several persons who helped in special ways however, and I should like to mention them particularly. I am indebted to Fr. John Tracy Ellis who constantly urged the publication of this work, showing to an often confused editor the great value of the Burtsell Diary; to Msgr. E. Harold Smith whose insights into the history of the Archdiocese of New York and the lives of its great priests has been invaluable to me; to Fr. Aldo Tos, who as a priest of the New York Archdiocese, reflects its greatness and its traditional urbanity and hospitality; to Fr. Richard McBrien who frequently clarified for me the theological and ecclesial meaning of the vision of Richard Burtsell; to Dr. Richard Braeden and Mr. James Mahoney of the Corrigan Library at Dunwoodie Seminary for their constant cooperation in aiding my research in the Archives of the Archdiocese of New York; and Msgr. Francis Costello, Pastor of Epiphany Church in New York for sharing with me his knowledge of his predecessor, Richard Burtsell.

I am indebted to Prof. Jay Dolan of the University of Notre Dame for creating the opportunity for me to publish the Burtsell Diary and for his genuine concern that this work be made available to students of American Church History. Likewise, Dr. Harry Browne was frequently consulted about the social and ecclesiastical background of New York into which the Burtsell Diary must be placed. His insights have proved invaluable.

Finally, I cannot sufficiently thank Joanne Stuimer and Mary School who spent much of the winter of 1977 typing this manuscript, often in the face of what seemed to be an impossible editing deadline.

In the end, I do not claim to be any kind of an expert on the history of the Archdiocese of New York. I am however, very much convinced, because of my research into the life of Richard Burtsell and his friends, and from my knowledge of the history of other dioceses, that few American Dioceses have so rich a heritage as does New York. I can only hope that priests of New York today would research as deeply as possible into the history of the forces that have formed them and their Church. I suspect that such research, honestly done, would reward both the researcher and whomever he might touch with an understanding of the meaning and the true identity of the New York Clergy and of the Church that Clergy serves.

> Nelson J. Callahan
> Bay Village, Ohio
> April, 1977

1865

January

<u>Tue., 31st</u>   I visited the Library and gallery of the Historical society with a Mr. Van Ellen, a sufficiently intelligent Protestant. The chief picture was 'Ladies of the court of Louis XIV'. In the evening I was present at the meeting of the Xtian Unity Association of Dr. Montgomery's church in Madison Ave. Cor. 35th St. Rev. Sheldon Davis gave a poor lecture on the Moravians whose quality most interesting to him was their having preserved the Episcopal succession : in which they were of equal authority with the P. Episcopal Church. Therefore, this is the admirable conclusion to which he came, the Episcopal Church could use Moravian ministers for the poor. The Episcopal church giving the money, the Moravian the labourers. A Moravian bishop Dr. Schulty was present to accept the proposition. A Slavonian 'Orthodox' monastic priest from Athens sent by Dr. Hills of the P.E. church was announced as seeking after Greeks and Slavonians, who wanted a priest of their communion. He had found 70 Greeks and 20 Russians in N.Y. and in Boston four Greek families and some 70 Russians. He is to celebrate in St. John's chapel. Dr. Prescott was president. Dr. Montgomery gave the service, assisted by Rev. Mr. Young of Trinity Chapel. I met the Rev.   the exiled secretary of the Abp. of Mexico.

<u>Wed., 1st</u>   I heard confessions at St. Stephen's. I visited Mrs. Daschauer, our organist's wife, who has just returned from Europe.

<u>Thurs., 2nd</u>   I visited Miss McKnight, who is seriously ill. Preston blessed the candles.

February

<u>Fri., 3rd</u>   I visited Father Hussey, who is sick of typhoid fever : and met Dr. McGlynn who gave me an interesting account of a discussion had by him with the Abp. at St. Joseph's on slavery, churches for blacks, churches for whites, etc. To-day Anderson dined with us and explained his new project of editing the N.Y. Tablet with Dr. Ives under the ecclesiastical supervision of Father Preston. Dr. Anderson is so excessively careful never to use a harsh word of even anyone's intellect that the journal will be rather weak in its answer to calumnies on the Catholic Church. He is over-cautious about his political predictions.

<u>Sat., 4th</u>   I took a walk with Dr. McGlynn to Wall St. : his conversations are always replete with most interesting matter. He dined with us. We still discussed some of the topics which had been brought up at St. Joseph's the Thursday before. I was vaccinated by my uncle Dr. Thos. Burtsell : the small pox has been prevalent of late : for caution's sake, I wished this preventive of it.

<u>Sun., 5th</u>   I preached on 'Faith' : In the evening I went to Uncle James Morrogh's : where I find great pleasure. He is a sharp lawyer and delights in discussion. For love of arguing he takes the opposite side from me in any question that may be brought up. Mrs. Morrogh is a very good woman and a perfect lady. They have lost all their children : four boys of very good parts. I met there Dr. Archibald Morrogh and his wife. He is talented, but very reserved in speech. She is a Protestant of the Anglican Episcopal Church. I took a walk with Dr. McSweeney and had a long discussion again about the Abp's statements expressed at St. Joseph's on last Thursday. McSweeney takes quite opposite grounds from Dr. McGlynn who's very progressive in his theories and detests old fogyism.

<u>Mon., 6th</u>   I visited Father Nilan, a student of the American College

February 3

in Rome, who is now stationed at the Church of the Holy Cross. He is sufficiently talented and made a name for himself at Fordham College : but to me he seems a follower more of others' than his own ideas. He took tea with me. Our conversation principally fell on the American college of Rome, it's students, and it's rector Rev. W. McCloskey, whose character we agreed was small, since he endeavors to bring all others to imitate his own conduct exactly : otherwise there is no goodness had in the student. McCloskey is a good priest for his own character : but by no means popular or engaging with those, who know him for any length of time.

Tues., 7th   I remained in the house all day : in the morning studying Moral Theology and Colenzo's and Walworth's ideas of Scripture inspiration : in the evening reading Hawthorne's 'Old Home' and 'Scarlet Letter'. After tea I went to the Mercantile Library Reading rooms, to read some of the Prot. Church papers that thunder most terribly against the most reasonable propositions of the Pope's late Encyclical letter : which is a protest against the doctrines in vogue principally in Italy, France, and Germany at the present day.

Wed., 8th   I visited the corpse of Father William Hussy, who died last night, in the Immac. Conception parish, 2nd, assistant to Dr. Morrogh my uncle. Father Hussy died of typhus fever, caught at a sick call. He was a good, humble, zealous priest; only 6 weeks a priest, of the first ordained of our new seminary at Troy! I met Dr. McGlynn with whom I went to visit the outside of the Spring St. church, near Varick St., which he has been looking after to Catholicise it. In the evening, I met the altar-class, and literary society : to each of which I give an hour every Wednesday. It gives me great pleasure to meet the

February

parish boys often : knowing their characters I can do a great deal of good to them.

Thurs., 9th   I assisted as subdeacon at the funeral of Mrs. Butler at the Immac. Conception. I gave her the last sacraments : and afterwards visited her. On this occasion the Irish custom of giving donations to the priest without any delicacy came out so awkwardly, that I got disgusted with the custom, and the persons who followed it on this occasion. I declined going to see her any more. On further consideration I believe they intended no insult : but I have made up my mind long ago not to accept offerings at sick-calls, lest the more ungenerous generation that is rising up in our country should be deterred from sending for the priest, by fear of incurring extra expense. It is to be feared that a people given intensely to the worship of the mighty dollar will think that the clergy are only seeking a livelihood by the administration of the sacraments. For this reason I believe that the orders in this country that have the vow of absolute poverty will do most good in this country : by their renouncing this world's riches. In the evening Emc and I paid a visit to Mr. Booth, the celebrated actor, who is during this season playing Hamlet. He acts grandly : and is a model speaker.

Fri., 10th   I assisted to-day at the funeral of Rev. W. Hussey. The High Mass was celebrated by Rev. W. P. Morrogh DD. Propagandist, deacon, Rev. Tandy, procurator of Troy Seminary, and ordained six weeks ago with Father Hussey. About 25 priests were present : the Archbishop performed the absolution. Rev. McGean, a college companion of Fr. Hussey, made the funeral oration : in which no particulars of Fr. Hussey were distinctly given. Fr. Hussey was only 23 years old when he died. He was buried in a vault of St. Patrick's cathedral. R.I.P.

February 5

In the afternoon Dr. McGlynn and I went to Fr. Malone's in Williamsburgh. He is a whole-souled man : generous, unprejudiced on everything but the slavery question on which he is constantly harping : though on the right side. Dr. McGlynn and I there had a sharp discussion on the separation of Church and State. He maintained the possibility and utility of total separation, so that the state in his opinion, is to take no cognizance of revealed law. I upheld 1: the impossibility of totally separating them : 2: I maintained such separation, if possible, to be injurious to God and to society.

Sat., 11th   In the morning I made my confession to Rev. Daubresse a Jesuit in 16th St. college : a good man, apparently petty in outward ways, but having a good mind.

Sun., 12th   I sang High Mass : Fr. Preston preached a nice sermon on correspondence to the calls of God. Mr. Daschauer our organist dined with us : he has almost recovered from a severe illness 'Bright's disease of the kidneys' which was on the point of taking him to eternity. He is a good, talented, well-informed and polite man. His musical taste is excellent : he plays the organ magnificently. In the evening, I went to Dr. Morrogh's : where I had a discussion with C. Farrell on scapulars, and attrition.

Mon., 13th   I commenced a tour to induce the children of the parish to come to our Sisters' day-school. My first visit to Mrs. Dogharty's was successful : she a good Irish woman apologized for not sending her girl, whom she was forced to keep home during her own illness. I then went to Mr. Vergnes. He is a Frenchman, who thinks that the pure Christian morality has disappeared from Christian sects, and has been at last reached by himself after mature study. His two girls had been

February

sent to the Sisters' school during his absence in Europe : on his return
he withdrew them. He intends impressing his own views on them : and
obstinately declined allowing them to return, where they would be
treated to notions about an outward form of Christianity : which, he
says, he belongs to the spirit and is not to be shown outwardly. I
visited also a Mrs. McElroy, a very respectable lady now a milliner,
who has in her employ a girl, Mary Finnegan : after whom I was looking,
thinking that she lived there. In the evening I visited the McKnights :
after which I went to Mr.   , concert given at Niblo's saloon,
where Mme. Katon, a Russian, made her first debut in playing on the
violencello : she played grandly. Mr. Wehli also for the first time
gave a public exhibition of his piano playing : which pleased me very
much. Miss Huntley, the soprano singer of our church, was at first
tame, then sweet in her singing. Mr.   the basso sang pretty well.

Tues., 14th   I continued my tour for school children. I gained
at once one child, Mary Ann Brady : for three others, Burns by name, I
had to talk for about an hour before I gained my point. The mother's
impression seemed to be that at the sisters' school they might get religious instruction but not as good civil education : and as she said,
the family was poor, and therefore the children had to make as rapid
progress as possible before they were sent to work. In the evening I
went to hear Miss Anna Dickinson's lecture entitled 'A glance at our
future'. Her discourse was a criticism on our attempts at reconciliation
of North and South : especially on the conference of President Lincoln at
Hampton with three Southern commissioners, Stephens, Hunter &   .
She rejoiced that it had failed : thus a battle lost is a victory won :
in other words our defeat at peace conference was a victory for freedom :

February

for now 4,000,000 slaves are irretrievably made free. She desires no amnesty to the rebel leaders. She wishes confiscation of Southern property that thus 1. the southern whites not land holders may have a chance to get a portion of it : which would induce them to lay down their arms : 2. the European immigrants may leave our crowded Eastern cities with chance of property in the South. 3. Our soldiers may have part of those lands, as reward of their services. 4. that the blacks may have a portion of the land, which their labour has made so productive. We are not to let the rebels go unscathed and untaxed, in the troubles which their treason has caused. She hoped that the franchise would be given to the blacks to counteract the disloyal vote of the brutalised Irish. She said that there was no American disloyal party. The rebel sympathisers in the North are foreign. America, she concluded, is progressing : and history standing as sentinel demands of her the countersign. She proclaims it : 'Liberty for all' and is allowed to pass on, for the countersign is correct.....Miss Anna Dickinson in her speaking is graceful : but oftentimes has the air of a school girl : I think that she is used by the ultra republican party to put forth their views : which, coming from a woman, will not hurt the persons' fellowship against whom she speaks : whilst at the same time the ideas make an impression, which can easily be made deeper by subsequent discourses of others. She passed on eulogy on Butler, whom she considers the greatest man of the country : 'out of faults greatness is built' this is an idea of Shakespeare's so Butler has committed faults but his greatness shines through them. Butler has lately fallen into disgrace, on account of the failure at Fort Fisher.

<u>Wed., 15th</u>   It snowed the greater part of the day : & this kept me in the house. In the evening I went to Cooper Institute to hear

February

Bishop Bayley's lecture on the 'power of prejudice'. This is the last subject that he should have chosen for no one is more under the control of petty prejudice, especially about Puritans, than he is. He is a very poor speaker : and never prepares the discourse. He is constantly heming and hawing. He quoted a protestant divine who gives the Puritans a greater antiquity than they claim since they are the first born of the devil. He spoke about the London fire ascribed to Catholics, and the whole plot of Titus Oates' to illustrate how wantonly Catholics were belied. Achille, the Italian apostate, was described as a man who understood how fond John Bull is gullible (sic) against Catholics or anything else, of which he does not wish to perceive the good qualities. An hour and three quarters were spent not uselessly, because they displayed how brazen a speaker Bishop Bayley is, and with what little dignity a man of his station can act. He is otherwise a good & intelligent person.

Thurs., 16th   Dr. McGlynn and I visited Father Thos. Farrell, who is a very intelligent practical man, and truly zealous for the good of souls. Emc and I had a lively discussion on the Encyclical of the pope lately come out : I considered it necessary, expedient, and timely. He argued against it, as opposed to the 'defacto' advancement of the age.

Fri., 17th   I gave the usual Friday instruction to the children of the sisters' school. We hear the confessions of some of the girls for an hour every Friday morning. We also have confessions for grown up people every Friday evening from 7 to $9\frac{1}{2}$ o'clock. Dr. McGlynn and I took a walk to Mr. Cavanagh's real estate office (42nd St. & 6th Ave.) to see about the late Jewish Synagogue in Greene St. near Bleecker St. which is for sale.

Sat., 18th   I visited my mother, who lives with her brother Rev.

February

Dr. Morrogh. They had just received news of a new cousin of theirs : an Alexander Russell, who had enlisted in the Union service, and near Savannah, had his arm taken off in an Artillery duel. Mrs. Lynch of Janesville, Wisconsin writes that he is presently in the Central Park Hospital. I bade farewell to my barber, in 3rd Ave. because he had given my tender beard over to the mercy of a stripling son of his : and left my arms, to one of the barber's firm.

<u>Sun., 19th</u>   I preached at the $10\frac{1}{2}$ o'clock mass, on the 'word of God', the subject of this (Sexagesima) Sunday's gospel. The boys had no Sunday-school, their room in 7th St. near Hallplace being closed, on account of the janitor's absence. In the evening I preached an old sermon on the practical utility of the confessional in the church of the Immaculate Conception, Jersey city, by invitation of Rev. Dr. Brann, who is second assistant, but likes to act as boss there. The church was well filled : their vespers were devout with plain music, and at $7\frac{1}{2}$ o'clock. The sermon took place after the Magnificat : and it was followed by the Benediction of the B. Sacrament. The Doctor thought that my voice had considerably 'improved'. He had never heard me preach. Father DeConcilio is first assistant there. Father Lenez, the pastor, was absent on a mission at Cleveland, Ohio. I went up to Lawyer Morrogh's in 26th St. N.Y. : after I got through in Jersey city.

<u>Mon., 20th</u>   I sang Requiem High-Mass for a Miss Prudence Muldoon a servant girl in the Dinsmore family at 122, 10th St. The family Dinsmore, though Protestant, was present : I made a few remarks about the deceased. In the evening Emc and I paid a visit to the Academy of Music : where Don Sebastian was being exhibited. Ligro Carozzi Zucchi was soprano, Massimiliani, Bellini, and Weinlict were the other principal

February

singers. I was very much pleased throughout the performance. I love
music : though I have no ear for singing. My mother and I visited
Alexander Russell at Central Park Hospital. He is an intelligent young
man, and quite pleased to find friends. Dr. McGlynn accompanied us
back to the city.

<u>Feb., 21st</u>	We had Requiem High Mass to-day for Mr. Burke, an
old acquaintance (in misfortune, more than otherwise) of my father's.
Fr. Preston sang the mass, I acted as deacon, Dr. McSweeney as subdeacon; Fr. Preston made a few neat remarks. Mr. Burke was a clerk in
Mr. Roosevelt's establishment, and married his daughter (against her
parents' wish). By her he had several children : who inherited the
mother's property and gave a pension to him, even after he took a second wife on their mother's demise. He was a counsellor-at-law : his
funeral was attended by Judge Roosevelt, Judge Clarke, Charles O'connor
etc., etc. who acted as pall-bearers. I accompanied the funeral to
Calvary : in the carriage I had only Mr. Walsh, the undertaker and sexton of St. Joseph's church, to keep me company. I found him pleasant
and intelligent. In the afternoon Dr. McGlynn and I went to Adam's
express Company : where he paid $1.00 to have $55.00 expressed to
Cleveland Ohio.

<u>Wed., 22nd</u>	I left my card at Mrs. Burke's. I visited Mr. Tiers
with whose wife principally I had a long talk about Dr. Forbes with whom
they were on friendly terms, and whose failing, they agreed, was pride
and love of respectability : which caused him to leave the Catholic
Church to return to Episcopalianism. I visited Mrs. Hubbard, a very
good lady (residing at Gramercy park house) who spoke very sharply on
the little influence that religion has presently on the lower classes,

February

servants especially, of the Catholic church, and showed more zeal in this way than our Church authorities. I dined at Mr. Daschauer's : he gets up his dinners in grand French style : as one of the principal qualities of them is a great variety of wines, I not drinking wine am deprived of the power of appreciating them fully. In the evening I attend the altar and literary classes.

<u>Thurs., 23rd</u>   I attended a Mr. Gaffney : whose daughter-in-law was a servant in the   family and knew me as a child. I also continued my tour for the school children : and immediately obtained that Mary Stines should be sent, as well as Annie Mehaney. In the afternoon I went to the Paulists' : I had an hour's conversation with Fr. Huot, especially on the inspiration of Scripture : we both agreed that it was not necessary to believe that the inspiration of Scripture extends to any further matter, than the infallibility of the Church : viz : to faith and Morals. I afterwards passed another hour with Fr. Hecker, with whom the talk fell on, principally, the new review, entitled 'the Catholic world' : which Mr. Hassard under his supervision is to give forth shortly, and is to select the best dissertations of the European reviews, magazines etc., etc. I took tea with them : their diet was plain. The Paulists are quite gentlemanly, and cordial to a visitor. I met at table Fr. Baker, Walworth, and Young, besides the two Hecker & Huet. Fr. Hecker accompanied me to hear Dr. Draper's lecture 'on the force of political ideas'. The Doctor illustrated his subject especially from the advancement of Mohametanism. He considered Mohamet to have been deluded by cerebral excitement, which brought apparitions before his eyes, in consequence of a melancholy at the variety of the world's goods. As an earthquake that shook the earth from Norway to Morocco, from Poland to

the West Indies : so his dogma. 'There is one God and Mohamet is his prophet' thrilled the hearts of men from Arabia to China : from Europe to India. His system soon gave birth to it's philosophers in Bagdad : from the controversies these held on man's free-will and predestination, fatalism especially became a favorite. It's extension to Spain concerns us most : since from there it had great influence on European society. It gave rise to the different systems on predestination adopted by the Franciscans and Dominicans : both orders commenced their careers during the Moorish domination of Spain. Columbus seems to have preserved his confidence in his theme for the discovery of America, by a tinge of fatalism, whence he derived his mission to discover unknown regions. Mr. Draper is a celebrated physiologist : and when speaking of Mohamet's visions announced that anyone given much to mental prayer and to rigorous fasting would have similar delusions.

Fri., 24th   In the afternoon Dr. McGlynn and I had an interesting talk on Captain Beale, a Confederate officer, who was to-day executed as a spy by the U.S. government's authority. Emc visited him and spoke on religious matters: finding him quite a gentleman, very good, and ready to listen to any most pious talk : He was an Episcopalian. Yet Emc gave him absolution, requiring from him a generally-expressed confession of his sins, directed toward the exercise of the absolving power. He was attended to his last moments by a Dr. Weston, of St. John's P. E. Church.

Sat., 25th   Dr. McGlynn and I had another interesting conversation on Beale's execution : the account of whose trial we bought at Appleton's. A Mr. and Mrs. Stuart with her mother introduced themselves to me. He is a convert : the ladies are of an old Baltimore Catholic family.

Sun., 26th   I sang High-mass. Our boys' Sunday-school had no

February

session : the janitor of the 2nd Regt. Armory having disappeared. In the evening I was at Lawyer Morrogh's with whom I had a discussion of civil marriage in France : which he approved, of which I sought to show the impropriety. He approved of it merely as a public registry of the marriage. John Avezzena and Mr. and Mrs. McLaughlin (once Miss Josephine Avezzena) were there with Mrs. Burtsell, my mother. The Avezzenas are my cousins : their mother being my mother's sister. John Avezzena is a soft, naturally good-hearted soul. Having General Gino Avezzena for his father, who is a good man but an infidel, and presently deputy of the Italian parliament, John has been made vice-consul of Italy. When a young boy he was always given to novel reading. He married a Jewess to legitimatise a child she had of him, though he was already engaged to a Miss Anderson. Active cause of this step was a good drubbing which he had received from the Jewess' brothers. The marriage first took place before an Alderman : Dr. Cummings managed to get her consent to be baptized, and though now she doesn't think that the sprinkling of water did her much good, it was then deemed sufficient to take away the impediment for the acknowledgement of the marriage in Italy : of which the ceremony was repeated before Dr. Cummings. The Doctor undertook also to give her religious instruction : but she gives an account of her own of why he failed. She is a pretty, fascinating girl : though her husband supposed once that he was somewhat slighted. A temporary separation took place : the business was patched up soon, though now hot water seems to be plentiful in their house. John now reaps the fruits of what he sowed.

<u>Mon., 27th</u>   Dr. McGlynn and I visited Cavanagh, the real estate agent, who said that the Greene St. church might be bought with the adjoining house for $40,000. On our way, we met Dr. McSweeney taking his

February

systematic walk.

<u>Tues., 28th</u>   I despatched an important letter to Francioni, rector of the Propaganda, about the destitution of the N. Y. diocese, which I ask him to represent to Card. Barnabo. Fathers Killeen, C. Farrell, Doctors McGlynn, McSweeny & Corrigan took tea with me before going to 16th St. debating society. I heard the discourse of John Murphy, whose declaration was smooth but devoid of animation : his subject was Logic and Philosophy. Edward Kane of N. Y. spoke quite animatedly on Religious instruction. Michael Nevin of Brookly gave out some very nice ideas in neat language on History and Political Economy, but his declamation was monotonous. The chairman John Cohalen of London, England, decided in a very impassionate manner. The Archbishop made some neat remarks on education, about which the debate principally treated. There was some fine singing by the college choir : and Weinlich sang two basso-solos.

March

<u>Wed., 1st</u>   I blessed the ashes : for the day is Ash Wednesday. Fr. Preston and I and Dr. Corrigan (who had remained with us overnight), placed the ashes on immense numbers of the congregation. I visited two destitute families : in one I found three children alone, whose mother did her best to get work, and was out washing. The girl of eight seemed as wise as one of seventeen. She took care of two of five and six : whom she taught to read. In the other family, a poor girl had a child, unlawfully, and was inclined to give it over to the corporation. I induced her to give up such a thought. I visited Mrs. Burtsell, my mother, who resides with her brother Rev. Dr. Morrogh and the Burtsells of 4th Avenue. Miss Anastasia Burtsell, my father's sister had been laid up for a month with boils. I met in the evening the altar and literary

March 15

classes. Dr. McGlynn came in to see me as I got into bed.

Thurs., 2nd   At the meeting of the Theological society, Dr. Cummings stated that the discussion was to be on Colenzo's views of the inspiration of the Holy Scriptures : he gave the history of Colenzo's cause. Dr. Brann gave a tolerably good idea of the various opinions held in the church on the inspiration of Scriptures. He loves to be florid even when writing a Theological essay. I endeavoured to give the Society an insight into the inconsistencies into which Protestantism fell by declaring the Bible, the only rule of faith : and then giving private interpretation a similar supreme authority. Dr. McGlynn thought that all the objections raised against the Pentateuch and Joshua's book, could be admitted by a Catholic. That being an Anglican, with those objections he might become a rationalist. Had he been a Catholic, his idea of the inspiration of the Bible would have not been repugnant to the 'minimum' idea of inspiration that a Catholic can hold without being a heretic. Fr. Malone sent the solution of the moral case about the corruptions of representatives of the people. He thought that a representative was bound to make restitution of any money, which he received for his vote. Several priests differed from him widely. Fr. Donnelly of St. Michael's church dined at our house : our conversation fell principally on the Theological Society. This Society was not formed in the right way. Dr. Brann originated it, and appointed Dr. Cummings president : who returned the compliment by asking Dr. Brann to be vice-president : but he declined this honour, to which is annexed correspondence of great extension, especially to Archbishops, bishops etc., etc. **Rev. George McCloskey; and Rev. Thos. Farrell** were made vice-president and treasurer. Many of the clergy will have nothing to do with the society because so formed : the self-constituted officers are not at all inclined to resign their places. Fr. Donnelly has just been appointed one of a committee to inquire into the state of the Blind's asylum, which has been lately complaining of great mismanagement in it's affairs. He was once president of St. Joseph's (Fordham) seminary. There a squabble arose between the native and Irish elements : he sided with the natives : and henceforth was not liked by either party. He has just built the church of St. Michael : arranged, one would think, for the glory of hide-and-seek. Having lately returned from a tour through Europe, he declares that he has not, in the least, lost his liking for the plans of his own church : which is, by the by, the creature of his own architectural taste. He lectured 'on Europe' after his return. In the evening Dr. McGlynn and I went to the Christian Union meeting at St. Paul's M.E. Church Cor. 4th Ave. and 22nd St., where Dr.   presided. Letters were written of Bishop McIlvaine of Ohio, and Dr. Bacon of Connecticut encouraging the cause. Dr. Vermillyea (Dutch Reformed) thought the spirit of exclusiveness to be the great obstacle to Union amoung Protestant churches : he cared not for uniformity but for union, on the basis of receiving all who received Christ. Mr. Weston of the Baptist Madison Ave. church required unity of faith and uniformity. One Lord all have, one faith all are getting, one baptism is still of the future. He thought true progress consisted not in yielding any good already obtained, but in accepting all the good proposed by anyone. Dr. Cone, Episcopal Bishop co-adjutor of Western New York, said that the meeting was most important, as it sought to organize all Christian sects against Popery and infidelity. The true basis of unity was the Nicene creed, admitted according to Dr. Schench, a Presbyterian divine of this city, by all Trinitarians. This united them also with the Greek church : of which he lauded the

March 17

constancy in rather undergoing the yoke of the Turk than bowing before the ambition of the Papacy. The claims of the Papacy were the first to divide the church. Nicolas 1st excited the Greeks to a separation. Infidelity is growing in America because there is no organised opposition to it by the Protestant churches. Popery is making rapid strides because of it's organisation. The Jesuits' present it's best phalanx : and rejected from Catholic countries they come here : and Protestants send their children to be cared by them! In a village Western New York he met five churches and no residing minister. The village could afford to support one minister but not five : therefore in the competition none gained the point of residence. In one of the five churches, services were had on Sundays by a Baptist minister of a neighbouring village. He was told that other thirty similar villages were found in that and the neighbouring counties. The Catholic Church had a steady congregation : for he had been told that the priest forced the labourers to pay their tax for his and the church's support : and often struck for higher wages, thus forcing his men to strike for higher wages, whence a new increase of income should accrue to him. The Pope wished nothing better than to see the disorganisation of Protestantism : for it gave him the advantage of warring against separate guerilla bands. Catholic governments reject his late dirty bull : but it was received and read by McCloskey (sic) to his congregation.... Dr. Cone is a coxcomb or as Fr. Brady called him, a bantam. He is not earnest or sincere, to all appearance, in what he says. He once was an intimate friend Father Preston's and had made great advance towards the Catholic Church : but one day informed Fr. Preston (still a Protestant minister) that he and Williams (now Episcopal bishop of Connecticut) had determined to go on the back track. Since that he

March   18

has become a very low churchman : and hardly has the ways of a real
gentleman..... Dr. Vermillyea protested against an union with the
Russian dead Church (a favourite project with the Episcopal church in
this country and in England). The union should be among the live
Christian churches.

Fri., 3rd   I bought a razor at Saunders' for $1.75 : I met there
Mr. Saunders and Miss Saunders. I visited the McKnights. Dr. McGlynn
and I agreed on some good ideas thrown out by Colenzo in his work on the
inspiration of Scriptures as to the possibility or improbability of certain facts about the history of the Jews under Moses.

Sat., 4th   To-day was appointed as a public holiday to celebrate
the late victories at Savannah, etc., and the taking of Charleston etc.
by the U.S. troops. The weather was so unpropitious that it was postponed.

Sun., 5th   I preached for the first time without having written
out my sermon, on the gospel of the day. I felt no embarassment. I
preached in the afternoon at the Sunday school of boys. This being the
first Sunday of Lent, we had the stations of the cross : before which
Father Preston gave the first of a series of discourses on the passion :
on our Lord's agony. He described the agony beautifully : and showed
how the chalice which our Saviour desired to pass from him was not his
passion, which he had desired most ardently to come, but the pain he felt
at seeing how many would not use, and would abuse his passion for greater
offences of God. Christ directs those words : 'Watch with me' to all
Christians, who are expected to meditate during lent especially on his
sufferings. In the evening I went to Lawyer Morrogh's where I found
my mother and Mrs. McLaughlin : the topic was the fast of Lent.

March

Mon., 6th To-day the celebration of the lately-gained victories took place. A grand procession which passed down Broadway and up Bowery was quite conveniently seen from our residence or our school-house. The first part was of soldiers : the second was a novel feature, viz : an exhibition of the various articles of trade, of sewing-machines, hats etc. This would have been quite nice, had not the Yankee instinct induced some of the owners to make this a means of advertising their wares : this took off much of it's dignity : the third and last part of the procession was composed of firemen with their engines. In the evening there were fine fire-works : the most admirable piece which I noticed was an engagement of fireworks between the Monitor and the Merrimac in memory of their encounter on the 9th of March, 1862. I preached in the evening on the Sacraments in general. This is the first of a series on the Sacraments : which I am to give during this Lent. The church was not filled : I suppose on account of the holiday's attractions elsewhere. Emc visited me.

Tues., 7th Fr. Malone came to our house. We had a long talk on the nation in general, abolitionism in particular, and on the Church promiscuously. We visited Fr. Farrell's where the same miscellany of subjects was digested. In the evening the altar and literary classes met.

Wed., 8th I took a walk with Dr. McSweeney : during which we had a heated discussion on the practical extent of episcopal authority over priests : I contended that a priest on his own personal responsibility could do as much good as he chose : by being a priest, he does not lose the liberty of doing good, that he would have as a layman : if the priest did anything extravagant, the bishop could restrain him if the extravagance injured the Church, in the same way as the priest or bishop could

March

20

restrain a layman : that as a father could justly deprive a son who married a prostitute, of his inheritance, so the bishop could suspend justly a priest that did wilfully something seriously detrimental to the church's honour : but as the father would committ grievous injustice in disinheriting the son without just cause, so the bishop would sin grievously by restraining the priest's power to do good, or suspending him without a grievous reason. Dr. McSweeney thought I was giving myself over to the too liberal ideas of certain liberal clergymen : he would stick to his old ideas of consulting authorities (even with the risk of being discouraged and prevented from doing good) on any important step to be taken. I gave an example : I could rent a house and begin to instruct the ignorant of catechism, without saying anything to the bishop. He thought otherwise. He meant by the liberal clergy, the Paulists, Malone, McLaughlin, Cummings, McGlynn, Fr. Farrell etc. Dr. McGlynn and I held a confab on the necessity of showing earnestness in the acquisition of the Greene St. church. Father Tom Quin of Connecticut called with Emc. And he took off an umbrella of mine. R.I.P. He was formerly U.S. chaplain and was present at many engagements with the rebels. Some of his experiences, as chaplain, are very interesting. Burnside received and wore an agnus Dei, given him by Fr. Quin. Fr. Preston spoke in the evening on the enormity of sin, and the necessity of repentance. This was the regular Lenten discourse, preceded by the Rosary and followed by Benediction of B. S.

Thurs., 9th   I heard confessions of boys at St. Joseph's in the morning : to my surprise Fr. Farrell asked me if I didn't think the boys went to confession too soon. They were between 12 and 16 years of age. At dinner Dr. McGlynn and I discussed the propriety of the state taking

March

cognizance of the revealed law for it's own regulation. He denied... I affirmed it's propriety. In the evening I heard Burnett's declamations of various pieces of quite various characters : he is truly a good declaimer of any, but the sentimental pieces. He takes off a variety of characters, and changes from one to almost it's contrary, with different tone of voice etc in an admirable manner.

Fri., 10th   I attended Mrs. Kennedy, who was dangerously ill : she resides at 165, 12th St. In the evening I confessed to Fr. Miguard in 16th St. basement. In my walk I met Fr. Neligan who agreed with some of my expressed views as to Colenzo's not being an out and out rationalist. Dr. McGlynn took tea with us and spoke to Fr. Preston about the Greene St. Church : the getting of which is now still less probable than before. Preston thinks that insisting with the Archbishop will only be lost ammunition. Fr. Preston is anxious to get a position for Dr. McGlynn for Archbishop Hughes removed Dr. McGlynn from St. Ann's to give a place to Preston.

Sat., 11th   I had a long talk with Dr. Anderson, the present editor of the N.Y. Tablet : about an article of mine on P. Episcopalianism. He declined taking it, unless modified to suit the wishy-washy style of the Tablet : which the Dr. thinks most conducive to good. He fears that it however excites no sympathy among friends and appears weak to it's enemies : and perhaps in time this compromising style will have to be abandoned. I told him, my vanity would not allow me to modify my article.

Sun., 12th   Fr. Preston preached on Hell : whose torments are required by the justice of God to be eternal, and in which the pain of sense afflicts every sentiment in it's own way, and the pain of loss is truly a burning pain to the soul : He used the gospel of Lazarus and Dives, as

March 22

his text. I sang High-mass : I talked on prayer at 9 o'clock mass : and preached to the boys on the '2nd article' and began at the girls' Sunday school a system of running through the catechism by explaining page by page. In the evening Fr. Preston gave a very effective sermon holding up the Iscariot, as a type of the usual downfall of sinners, who begin by small things and end in great crimes. No less than Judas, is the sinner a traitor, who sells his Lord for the gratification of a passion, who under cover of hypocrisy offends God, who receives a sacrilegious communion, who betrays his neighbour by a kiss, who despairs of salvation.

Mon., 13th   Dr. McGlynn and I visited Cavanagh, the real estate agent, who thinks that he can get the Spring St. Church for $50,000. Mr. Con Devon is to act as intermediate for Dr. McGlynn : the property is to be bought for manufacturing purposes but for raising up souls from death to life, and leading them to heaven. We went to the church of the Imm. Conception in Jersey city to hear confessions : Dr. Brann had invited us. In the evening I preached on the matter of form of Penance and on Contrition more especially. Afterwards we criticised Brann's lecture on inspiration, in which he falsely accuses Colenzo of denying all inspiration of the Holy Scriptures.

Tues., 14th   I visited R. O'Gorman to get knowledge of the whereabouts of a Mr. Coppinger a cousin of Alexander Russell, the union soldier, who under Sherman lost his arm near Savannah is now in the Central Park Hospital : and is a second cousin of mine on the Mother's side. He is brother of Mr. Russell, of Mount Russell in Limerick. O'Gorman could not give me the desired information. This is the first time I spoke to O'Gorman. He is rough looking but polite : having a lawyer's

March   23

way of dispatching business. I visited also John Avezzena, my cousin, who is vice-consul of Italy : and gave him a little religious talk, derived from a few remarks on Spiritualism. I visited Lawyer James Morrogh No. 4 Pine St. : I gave my essay on the way in which P. Episcopalianism seeks to effect Christian Unity, to McMasters, editor of the Freeman's Journal, to read and publish if he has no objection to it. McMasters told me that Dr. Cone, who is therein spoken of, was turned out of school, because he was a liar : and also stated a year before McMaster's entering the church, that he (Dr. Cone) had taken the back track because he did not wish to be known as a Catholic especially in America. I visited Mrs. Burtsell, my mother, and at the house had quite a talk with Fr. Donnelly (alias St. John) about the exposure of chaplains at the war. He said that but seldom are they much exposed. Fr. Farrell accompanied homewards, and gave me some items of his prefecture at Fordham in which he says he was very severe on the boys but never reported them to their superiors. In the evening I met the altar and literary classes : after which I went to hear Burnett repeat his caricatures of various characters. On my return I found Dr. Anderson who showed anxiety to have again the composition which I wrote on P. Episopalianism.

<u>Wed., 15th</u>   I took a Russian bath in 4th Street, for a perfect cleansing of my body. In the evening I preached 'on Confession'. Dr. McSweeney recited the rosary instead of Fr. Preston, whose chest is sore.

<u>Thurs., 16th</u>   I took a walk with Dr. McSweeny : in the afternoon Fr. Donnelly called to get confessionals for St. Patrick's day. He is to give 'papal blessing' on Sunday and takes the occasion to get as many as he can to Confession and Communion to gain the indulgence. I preached in the evening 'On Confession' at Fr. Malone's church Williamsburgh. He

March 24

expressed great satisfaction. Fr. Killeen called for a moment.

<u>Fri., 17th</u>   I assisted at P. High-mass by the Abp. at the Cathedral in honour of St. Patrick. Fr. Dealy the Jesuit preached the panegyric of which one third was about St. Patrick : the rest was flattery of the Irish nation. I had at dinner Dr. Malone, & McGovern of Williamsburgh, and Mr. Berryane. I read them my essay on P. Episcopalianism : it pleased them hugely. I missed seeing the entire procession : a sick call pretended to be urgent prevented me from seeing the beginning : what I saw of it, presented quite a number of fine, sufficiently intelligent men : boys' cadets also filled the ranks.

<u>Sat., 18th</u>   Dr. McGlynn called, and gave me quite a flattering account of the Hartford people, to whom he had spoken about St. Patrick on the day before. Fr. Hughes is a good priest that makes his people go to their confession regularly. They are now celebrating the jubilee in Hartford.

<u>Sun., 19th</u>   Sunday. 3rd of Lent. I preached at H. M. on the gospel, at Low mass on the word of God & spoke at both Sunday schools. Fr. Lancake, the Jesuit sang H. mass. With him I had quite a discussion on spiritualism : I held that the table-movings, wrappings might be the effect of magnetism : whilst the spirit-seeing and talking were cretures of the fancy : which the spiritualists believed to be real visions. He thought that both the table-movings and the visions proceed from the evil one. I had been with him at Jesuits' school in 3rd Ave. bet. 12 & 13th Sts. about 13 years ago. In the evening Fr. Preston took the flight of the apostles and the denial of St. Peter as the type of our ingratitude when we offend God. Dr. Cummings had a grand concert in his Church by the whole corps of opera singers : I got there in time only to hear the

March

last screech of the soprano. I then went to Lawyer's Morrogh's, where I found the McLaughlins and my mother.

Mon., 20th   McMasters persuaded me to cut off part of my essay on P. Episcopal. some of which, he said, was too pious for his readers. I left out the rejection of their orders. He says 75 percent take his paper for it's political sympathies : 25 percent read the religious part. He does not wish to attack Episcopalians, Presbyterians, Methodists, among whom he has many readers : but he does not touch them with a soft glove when they attack Catholicism. He sent all his messages to me through Berryane. In the afternoon I visited the Burtsells at 145 4th Ave. I explained to the people the ways of confession.

Tues., 21st   I entended a hunchback, 30 years old, 3½ feet high with a face apparently one foot long. Dr. McGlynn took dinner : and gave Fr. Preston an idea of how authorities here had treated him, when sending him to Central Park from St. Ann's of which he was pastor, and removed to give place to Preston by Abp. Hughes who sought to put at St. Ann's a convert in place of Forbes, the apostate priest, who returned to P. Episcopal. We afterwards commented on Mgr. Manning's discourses on Card. Wiseman on the occasion of the latter's funeral. I read Fabiola at least five times always pleased : and saw Wiseman frequently at Rome. I also heard Manning preach many times in Rome. He spoke without any motion of the body, except the tongue; his ideas were fine. I have several sketches of his discourses. Emc. and I discussed how far a priest may go without the consulting the bishop : We find our centralisation system clog immensely the energies of every individual priest.

Wed., 22nd   I visited the Gallaghers at 111, 32nd St. who are my cousins. With them are living Miss Ann Burtsell, my father's sister, and Mrs. Decoppet also my father's sister who is married to a Swiss protestant. They have a little doll of a child. Fr. Preston gave a lively, somewhat too severe a discourse on the proximate occasion of sin. His text were the words addressed to Lot and his family, on their leaving Sodom : Arise, take thy wife etc. **save** thy life : look not back, neither stay thou in all the country about : but save thyself in the mountain, lest thou also be consumed. Gen. XIX. 15. 17. I wrote two letters to John Burtsell, my brother, and Emma his wife, who is an Episcopalian, both living in San Francisco. I answered objections made in theirs about the necessity of belonging to the Catholic Church for their salvation.

<u>Thurs., 23rd</u>   With Dr. McGlynn, I went to Fr. Malone's at Williamsburgh. He was out, but we met Fr. McGovern an unfortunate though really good priest, who however lost his position for excessive drink, and Fr. Campbell, who is a stubborn ignorant fellow. In the evening we went to Cooper Institute where Mr. Hewlett had engaged to lecture 'on the shades and lights of Irish character' but the committee of the M. E. Lexington Ave. Church begged him to treat on a more congenial subject, and he delivered a rigmarole on what he said was uppermost in our minds : the destiny of our country.

<u>Fri., 24th</u>   I found a poor man dead whom I went to **anoint** : I had heard his confession and gave him the Eucharist. His name was McGarr. I met Scannell's father : who is a carman, but quite intelligent. Scannell is the best of my altar boys, good and talented : whom the father and I would wish to have ordained priest, but he does not show inclination to the priestly state. In the evening I preached on Confession at the Imm. Conception.

March

Sat., 25th I sang High-Mass at 9 o'clock, this being the feast of the Annunciation : I gave a short discourse on the nature of the feast.

Sun., 26th 4th Sunday of Lent. Fr. Preston preached on the gospel of the Magdalene's conversion. I sang High-Mass, preaching on the necessity of charity to our neighbours, at the 9 o'clock mass. I explained the 3rd article to the boys and the catechism's page to girls. At evening service Fr. Preston took for his text the words of the Jews : 'His blood be upon us and upon our children' and described the passion till those words were pronounced.

Mon., 27th In the evening Fr. Malone, and Drs. McGlynn and Freel visited me together. Dr. Freel told that his bishop said that he would suspend any priest going to hear a Protestant minister preach in a Prot. church : and also held that anyone dying out of the visible communion of the Catholic Church was sure of damnation. Fr. Nilan came in afterwards : and I induced him to admit that half of our Irish population is Catholic merely because Catholicity was the religion of the land of their birth. This is owing to the neglect in which their instruction is left. I preached on satisfaction and indulgences to the children : for not many others seem to understand that these instructions are for them.

Tues., 28th A Fr. Caraignon of Stamford-Hamilton diocese, Canada East, slept with us. He accompanied me to St. Joseph's where I preached on 'The day of justice, and the day of Mercy'. He is a good listener and generally assents to whatever is told him. He is a friend of Fr. Preston's.

Wed., 29th Fr. Killeen visited me : as also Dr. McSweeny. We three visited Dr. Cummings : whom I never remember having met, without being insulted by him. He has no delicacy towards anyone. He thought and

March

expressed the thought that we had gone expecting that he would offer to us his late work on Spiritual progress. I accompanied Fr. Killeen to Erie railroad depot on the Jersey side. In the evening Dr. McGlynn called. I preached the same sermon to our people that I gave to St. Joseph's congregation yesterday.

Thurs., 30th   I visited the Burtsells, who entertained me by the treatment Peter is receiving at the hand of the Jesuits : as he is good, they are making him bear all the penances, that the worst in his class deserve. If they show severity to him (who, they think, will bear it unresentingly) they will impress the bad ones with an idea of what they may expect and never get. The Doctor has taken to asceticism : at least he does not mix with the community. Dr. McGlynn called : we discussed Dr. Moriarity's speech on last St. Patrick's day, in which he suggested that Ireland might become one of the United States. I argued that Colenzo did not prove any of his objections, especially from Exodus XII. We agreed that a different spirit is to be brought into the church's legislation. We have the country whence a new activity may spread throughout the whole Xtian world. A little more democracy would be of use. We agreed also that the most oppressive mystery of our faith is the promise of never-ending happiness. Eternity oppresses the mind, accustomed to the variety found in time. We can hardly look forward to an eternal existence with pleasure. Annihilation seems almost desirable.

Fri., 31st   It rained the whole day. I paid a visit to my mother : I found Dr.Morrogh quite recovered from an illness from which I helped much to rouse him.

April

Sat., 1st   I spent the morning writing my sermon. My barber

April   29

actually told me that Petersburgh is very much fortified and that we should have some difficulty in taking it.

Sun., 2nd   Passion Sunday. I preached on the gospel at H. Mass : a new tenor, Dr. Gluck, sang for us. Errani our former tenor accepted an offer of $600 (in gold) a month and expenses paid to go to the West Indies to give concerts. He sang beautifully : Dr. Gluck has a poor voice. I preached on 'the Holy family' to the boys explaining the 3rd article. To the girls I spoke on the nature of God : which is the greatest of mysteries, and if we once admit his existence, no other mystery can be hard of belief. Fr. Preston in the evening took for his text : 'And bearing his own cross he went forth to that place which is called Calvary' John XIX. 13. and described the passion till Christ reached Calvary.

Mon., 3rd   Dr. McSweeny called to see me. We during a walk discussed again the zeal of our Church Authorities for the salvation of souls. He said that I should be heroic if not caring for the good esteem of authorities here or in Rome, I should do all in my power to save the souls, neglected by them. In the afternoon I went to Mr. Avezzana the vice-consul of Italy to interest him in a case of Mrs. Alberganti, whose husband has left her after two weeks' living with her. I married them three weeks ago. He seems to have run off to Italy : where he has some property. She was an Episcopalian, Puduly by name : I got dispensation for them. Downtown there was intense excitement produced by the news of the taking of Richmond. I paid my subscription for the 'Catholic World', a new eclectic magazine, edited by Mr. Hassard, to cull the best articles of Catholic reviews of Europe. I subscribed also for one year for my brother John M. Burtsell, living in San Francisco.

April

Mr. Kehoe the agent, spoke to me like an auctioneer selling his goods and trying to sell his purchaser. I met in the park J. Roche who was formerly a student of the American College of Rome : who gave me his idea of Con. Callaghan, of the two schools' strict and lenient among the Jesuits, of the Irish priests' contempt for the North, and of Ambrose O'Neill, who did not appear to him as one from whom counsel was to be taken in his troubles, though Ambrose lately has offered himself to him as spiritual adviser. I bought some articles at Saunders' and with Miss Saunders discussed the reasons why the poor do not go to Protestant Churches. Her relatives on both sides are Protestants. I preached to the children etc on the B. Eucharist. Mr. Preston, Fr. Preston's father, came to N.Y. this evening from Hartford. I had to entertain him for an hour: a hard thing to do! but the day's news gave ample matter for a rattling conversation.

Tues., 4th   I wrote a long letter to Cardinal Barnabo, prefect of the Congregation of Propaganda, on the wants and state of New York, the diocese. I kept a copy of it in my own hands for future contingencies. Emc & I in the evening visited Mr. Forrest who is acting the part of Richelieu (from Bulwer's novel) at   . He acted the old man splendidly : but the piece is not well adapted to call out Forrest's powers. I met both the altar and literary classes.

Wed., 5th   Miss Anastasia Burtsell visited me. I visited the Burtsells in 4th Ave. Fr. Preston & I went to the Paulists to condole with them on Fr. Baker's death. I said Mass for him in the morning : when the news came upon us like a shock. He had however been sick about a week. Fr. Preston in the evening took for his text : "The sin against the Son of man will be forgiven : but the sin against the Holy Ghost will not be

April   31

forgiven in this world or in the next" and preached on the presumption of those who delay their repentance, till it is made final impenitence, which is the sin spoken of.

Thurs., 6th   I went to Fr. Baker's funeral. Fr. Hecker sang the Mass. Fr. Huet told us how Baker and he were companions for 23 years. They had met in the Baltimore P.E. seminary. Before that Baker had been over-pious : the death of father, mother, and two elder brothers sobered him. He was respected by all who knew him. He was received into the church in 1853 by Abp. Kenrick. He was an eloquent speaker : and very devout of the B. Sacrament. The Church was packed : about 40 priests were present. The Abp. gave the absolution. The corpse was taken to the Cathedral. R.I.P. I had a very lively discussion with a priest from Utica, a sympathiser with the South, and who said he detested abolitionism in any form or shape. He said that the negroes could not be retained as Catholics. After a Catholic master's death they would all be easily led to Methodism. Fr. Killeen and Orsiengo dined with us. I found Fr. Doane of Newark educated in the Roman seminary at dinner with Fr. Preston. In the evening I went to see the Unitarian social gathering at the Academy of Music : I paid a dollar to see them eat. I remained a whole hour occupied thus. I had heard Dr. Hewer pray, and Peter Cooper read for about 3 minutes each. Afterward they had more speaking : I had left.

Fri., 7th   Dr. McGlynn called to see me. He believes that Devereux to whom he has given the charge of getting the Spring St. church knows more than Cavanagh, who imprudently offered $50,000. We discussed Clericus' (probably Walworth's) second article about the late debate of the Theological Society on Colenzo. It's better than the first: but weak in several parts.

April   32

Sat., 8th   In a walk up 5th Ave., I met Fr. Quin of St. Stephen's.
We discussed Dr. Cummings' late work on Spiritual progress. He noticed
that the Dr. never quotes Scripture or the Fathers : and is never dogmatical, but moral and practical in his discourses : and even that is merely
natural morality. We discussed the needs of New York diocese. He feared
that the Abp. would use high-handed means to quiet any one complaining of
his diligence. I thought that complaining would arouse his vanity, which
is great, to do for human respect what zeal would not cause him to do.

Sun., 9th   Palm Sunday. We had solemn blessing of the palms at
High Mass, which I sung. Fr. Preston took the sacrifice of Isaac as the
type of Christ's Sacrifice on Calvary, and compared the two in his sermon.
I spoke at 9 o'clock mass. I explained the 4th article to the boys and the
2nd to the girls. Instead of Vespers we had Rossini's Stabat Mater sung
beautifully by our choir. The Church was filled. In the evening Fr.
Preston gave an explanation of the seven words of our Blessed Lord on the
Cross.

Mon., 10th   I visited the Burtsells in 4th Ave. and gave the last
instruction to the children - on the dispositions for communion.

Tues., 11th   I walked to Central Park : where I met Mr. O'Connor
on horseback. He is John McLaughlin's second cousin. His father is a
builder and become quite wealthy. He has given his son a thorough education.

Wed., 12th   In the evening we had confessions : and the Tenebrae
were sung by our choir. The lamentation by Miss Gormienne was beautifully given : the other two were devoid of sympathetic effect.

Thurs., 13th   Holy Thursday. We had High Mass en regale : The girls

April 33

of sisters' school mingled in the procession, carrying flowers. The repository was in the porch of the church and very tastily arranged. Mrs. Hassard adorned it. Dr. McGlynn called : and we visited Fr. Clowry of St. Gabriel's to break an engagement that Dr. McGlynn had made with him to preach on a day when he had another engagement. I got the new Oils at the Cathedral. I met the McKnights. In the evening the Choir again sang Tenebrae, with the same perfections and imperfections. The children sang the Stabat Mater at the repository.

Fri., 14th Good Friday. We performed all the ceremonies. I read the passion in English, whilst the celebrant, Fr. Preston read it in Latin. Why is not more of the service given in English for a similar reason, if not the whole of it? The grace of Unity does not force us to deprive the people of understanding the sense of the prayers, gospels etc which were originally introduced for the edification and instruction of the people. In the afternoon Dr. McGlynn called : we went to the Cathedral, where I assisted at the Matins of the Tenebrae sung by the priests. I like the community style of priests singing much more than merely having the service sung by the choir. In the evening we had our Tenebrae, and after them the Stabat Mater. I cannot comprehend how the people show an intense in a ceremony of which they understand very little. Why cannot we have the service in English? This is my 25th birthday anniversary! I paid a visit to my mother on account of the day and ransomed myself from the 25 whacks.

Sat., 15th Holy Saturday. We performed the ceremonies as fully as possible. To-day we got the news of Lincoln's assassination. It shocked me. He was a noble hearted and noble minded man. What a terrible thing for assassination enter into our political annals! The idea of a Southern assassin, crying : 'Sic semper tyrannis' when every Southern

April 34

slave holder should receive a similar fate, if such a thing could ever be justified! Seward, we hope, though severely stabbed, will survive. Johnson who becomes ipso facto president is a man known as talented but considered a drunkard. The calamity seems to be as great for giving power to such a man! If he had sense to give Grant, dictorial powers, a great danger would be averted! Dr. McGlynn heard confessions for a time instead of Fr. Preston.

Sun., 16th   Easter Sunday. I preached on the gospel. We had solemn High Mass. At dinner were Mrs. Hassard, Miss Denning of Litchfield, Mr. & Mrs. Daschauer, Col. McMahon, Capt. O'Bourne, J. Hassard, Mr. Regnaud the Jesuit Scholastic. In the evening we had a grand sacred concert in the church : under the direction of our organist Mr. Daschauer. The church singers, Sig. Remi, Mlles. Gormienne and Huntley had the principal solos : Made. Paulitre too had a solo. The singing was all Italian music by Verdi, Gordigiani, Rossini, and a Regina caeli by Daschauer. We had also a union of Piano, Organ and Horn, and again of the two first with the violin. Daschauer played the organ, Schubert the piano, Schmidtz the horn. The music was exquisite. The seats were all occupied. After it we had a little supper prepared for the Abp. and other clergymen present. The Abp. showed his cautious temper by expressing approval of Abp. Kenrick's dislike for priests who figured in newspapers. Fr. Quin was rude, asking out of time for brandy and water. Five Jesuits showed community impoliteness by taking off immediately after the concert without taking a snack. Dr. Neligan came to concert and supper uninvited.

Mon., 17th   I visited my mother and Rev. Dr. Morrogh and the Gallaghers, Decoppets, and Miss Ann Burtsell all living together in 32nd St. near 6th Ave. and all relatives of mine.

April   35

Tues., 18th   I paid the subscription of $16.00 for Rev. J. Adam
of Visalia Tulare Co. California for the Spanish Journal La Cronica. I
visited the Burtsells of 4th Ave. : where the Dr. was unwell from excessive earnestness in the affair of Lincoln's assassination. He had imbibed too much of the spirit of the times. I visited Miss Waters, to
get her services at the organ for to-morrow.

Wed., 19th   We had the funeral mourning for Abraham Lincoln. We
had L. mass and the psalm miserere for the occasion. I made an eulogy
of Abraham which is to be found in the papers. In the evening I visited
Central Park; and with Dr. McGlynn strolled down Broadway to see it in
it's sombre attire. Great scrrow has been shown for the assassination
of Abraham Lincoln, whose name will ever be glorious as the emancipator
of the slaves, and restorer of the Union. We met on our way Rev. J. Woods
who too had imbibed too much of the spirit of the times and with a
Mr. McGirke and a Mr. Kelly of the Bloomingdale Catholic Association had
initiated an Irish wake over the death of A. Lincoln. I blundered about
the day of Miss L. McCormick's wedding : and paid her a visit of congratulation a week before the event. I had a very pleasant conversation
with her and her mother.

Thurs., 20th   Dr. McGlynn and I visited Fr. Malone's where we found
a number of priests gathered. Emc & I discussed the last order from
Stanton, ordering W. Booth (when caught) to be court-martialed. I held
that it was not a crime against a military law, and therefore not amenable to a court military. But Gov. Fenton is commander-in-chief of the
state militia, and yet an offence against him is not a military offence.
Political assassinations in Europe in time of war are not military
offences.

April   36

Fri., 21st   I visited the Burtsells in 4th Ave. Mrs. Tiers called on me (Fr. Preston not being home) to suggest that a letter written to A.T. by young Dr. Hassell should be sent back to this young man who had rather boldly written of an 'affinity feeling' which he had not been able to overcome towards A.T.

Sat., 22nd   I was visited by Miss Anastasia Burtsell, who gave an account of the Dr.'s last night's doings at home. Typhus fever two years ago weakened his system : stimulants easily excite his brain : and he is very rough at times.

Sun. 23rd.   Low Sunday. I sang High Mass : spoke at 9 o'clock mass and to the boys on the 5th article, and to the girls on the 3rd article. In the evening I visited Lawyer Morrogh's : where the letters from the Avezzana girls in Italy were discussed.

Mon., 24th   Miss Fleming announced to me to-day that she intended to become a Catholic. She had been at Fort Hill for one year : where the Sisters gave her as much instruction as she desired but declined having her admitted to the church, without her parents' consent, whilst under their charge. She wishes to place herself under Fr. Preston's guidance, who, she supposes, will as a convert be able to direct her better than others. Her parents are Episcopalians. Her uncle's goodness influenced her to become Catholic. I told her she must attend to the change at once. With Dr. McSweeny, I went to visit Abraham Lincoln's remains exposed in the City Hall. As clergymen, the police brought us to Supervisor Fox, who gave us a pass. The brow of the president was very prominent : his cheeks were much sunk. I liked the countenance more than I expected. I had no time to look at the surroundings : we were expected to pass by instantly : and thus my whole attention was concentrated on

April   37

the face. When animated, it must have shown great benevolence & intelligence. The crowd on the Broadway side was not very great and we were not delayed long. On the other streets the crowd is said to have been immense. In the evening I visited the McKnights : but strangers came in and prevented me enjoying the evening. The McKnights are good hearted and intelligent people. Mary McKnight was educated at Mount St. Vincent's with my sister Mary : and as a great friend of hers, she insisted upon being introduced to me by Fr. Preston. I became still more acquainted with the family at a fair of St. Ann's held last December in the Assembly rooms. She is a favourite with many priests : whose society she courts almost exclusively. She married a clerk in her father's business : but never lived with him, as her father disapproved the match and persuaded the young man (by money) to give her up. Adelaide took a fancy to me at the fair, and was sure to have a bouquet in my hands each evening. She is bashful, and not very bright, but good-hearted. They have another sister who is still an Episcopalian and a younger one about 11 years old. The father is engaged, I believe, merely in renting his own houses. He owns the whole block on Bleecker St. between Mott and Elizabeth Sts. The mother is a good, quiet woman, very patient and intelligent.

<u>Tues., 25th</u>   To see the crowd waiting for Abraham Lincoln's funeral procession, I made my with difficulty to Broome Street. I saw the procession pass by eleventh St. & Broadway. It was truly a grand affair. The military made a grand display. Now they have learned to march magnificently : and present a finer appearance than the French army : of which I saw a great part in Rome. The funeral car was superb, drawn by 16 horses, cared by 16 darkies, and all the greatest men of the city joined in the procession. Abp. McCloskey walked the whole way in the procession.

April 38

It took 4½ hours to pass by one spot. I was present also at the meeting in Union Square. Dr. Tyng gave the prayer of entrance. I never liked his tone or manner : it is too sanctimonious-looking. Hon. J. Bancroft gave a nice address, 1. making personal eulogy of Abraham Lincoln, 2. calling upon us to preserve the monument he raised for himself by his emancipation proclamation, and 3. showing that Johnson would be a good successor, and that though the president is dead, the republic lives. Bancroft gave dark argument in favour of the Constitutional amendment abolishing slavery. The slaves formerly owed allegiance to the States and through them to the federal government. The States forfeited their allegiance : which thus is direct towards the federal goverment which can therefore free them. Rev. Mr. Bosle read a psalm. Dr. Thompson read Abraham Lincoln's last inaugural, a document showing forth his great mind and charitable spirit. Dr. Osgood read an Ode by Cullen Bryant. Dr. Isaacs (a Jewish Rabbi with his hat on) read a passage of Scripture. Dr. Hitchcock gave benediction, in default of Abp. McCloskey, for whom the plea of fatigue was given to account for his absence, but who declined because though he thought that it was not what is technically termed 'communicatio in sacris,' yet it would not look well for him to be praying where Prot. clergymen were present! Oh bright Theology! O cowardice! Does the Catholic church forbid us to bless our countrymen! This blessing would have been effective! I & Dr.McGlynn visited Fr. T. Farrell's where we found Malone and McLaughlin etc etc. We discussed the Archbishop's attitude as to the procession and meeting. The people would receive the excuse.

Wed., 26th   Fr. Preston & I paid a complimentary visit to Mr. & Mrs. Donnelly (Lizzie McCormick) who had a grand reception. She belonged

April 39

to our parish : but is now to go to Montreal with her husband. She is
not handsome but accomplished. He is not over-bright : and says he will
come to Yankee land when we have settled our troubles. I met her at the
fair in December last. There were many priests at the reception. Dr.
Brann dined with us. Fr. Preston & I gave him some plain talk as to the
organisation of the Theological Society, which, I said, would not live a
whole year unless it's defects were remedied, by admitting all the priests
for the election of officers. Dr. Brann intends awaiting the year's
course. Miss McKnight came to select several articles for the Sisters'
of Mercy fair, from articles left over from St. Ann's. In the evening
the boys of the literary class played the first scene of Hamlet.

Thurs., 27th   I went out to New Rochelle to Fr. Thos. McLaughlin's.
He is pastor there. There were several priests of the B. republican
stamp and Mr. Berryan. We discussed especially the killing of Booth by
Boston Corbett, and concluded that it was the best way for the assassin
to be taken off. We discussed also how far the Church prohibits the
'communion in sacred things' with heretics. I maintained that it is
first to prohibit any union with a meeting designed for heretical purposes, or at least in a place generally used for such purposes, where
the ministers act in the name of the heretical congregation. Fr. McCarthy
thought it extended to any prayer-union even of a private kind. In the
evening I went to the Immac. Conception's fair, where I patronised almost
every article set up for raffle.

Fri., 28th   I visited the Burtsells in 4th Ave. in reference to
the Dr.'s conduct yesterday, when he was quite uproarious and acted as if
ready to go to an asylum for lunatics. I was there told that the Dr.
had said that all that ever ailed W. P. M. was delirium tremens and that

April

C. F. was now suffering the effects of misbehavior.

Sat., 29th   I went to the Burtsells in 4th Ave., intending to lecture the Dr. but he was not home. I saw him at a store Cor. Bway & 13th St.

Sun., 30th   I preached on the gospel at High-Mass : on the month of May at L. mass and on the 6th article to the boys and on the 4th to the girls. In the evening I visited the Lawyer Morrogh's : where I found Dr. Archibald Morrogh & wife, Mr. McLaughlin & wife, and my mother. The principal topic of conversation was Gn. Walker's letter to Gen. Wallace saying the South would be infamous forever if with 300,000 men she still resisted, and that rather it would sacrifice all for independence as illustrating the 'braggadoccio' of Southerns still kept up even when soundly whipped.

May

Mon., 1st   We commenced the month of May services. Each evening in our church, we have the Litanies, a short instruction, and a hymn. I have undertaken to explain the Magnificat, under Paslo Legueri's guidance, during the instructions which it will be my turn to give. Emc and I visited Mr. and Mrs. Keane, who are now playing at Bway theatre. Henry the VIII was played : in which Mr. Kean played Wolsey and Mrs. Kean played Q. Catherine. Mr. Kean is not a first class player. He does not enter into the character fully : oftentimes very important sentences are flung out without attention to their sense. The great sentence of Wolsey that he wished 'he had served his God as well as his king' was spoken almost unnoticed. In a farce of the 'jealous wife' Mr. Kean was very good, Mr. Kean acted the husband well. Neither of them has right to be termed first class.

May   41

Tues., 2nd   In the afternoon Dr. McGlynn and I went to Staten Island : on the beach of which we had a long confab. We agreed that celibacy was the great characteristic of the C. clergy and should be maintained even in spite of many individuals' frailty. I had in view poor C. F.'s sickness. It has it's disadvantages of rendering unsocial, and melancholy, one who has not cultivated a large spirit of Christian charity and unselfishness. Marriage cramps and narrows the clergyman's mind to the petty wants of his family : the celibate takes a wider view of the needs of the human race. The Dr. was fatigued : and he confessed to me that both at college and now it is the exception for him to have a night's rest in his bed. He generally sleeps in a chair : and in college whilst walking fell flat to the ground overcome with sleep. He has a feeling that 63 years is about his appointed time for death : though at any time he would be ready. In the evening Emc & I went to see Mr. Kean who played Louis XI (translated by Boucicault from French). He entered very well into the spirit of this character. Louis XI was a great lover of life : and killed everyone in his way : and died dreading death and tortured with life.

Wed., 3rd   I visited the Burtsells in 4th Ave. where I gave the Dr. a long talk on his wayward ways. I spoke very plainly : and he promised that he would not touch drink. He spoke funnily and falsely about his wife and children : and said that A. B. had injured her mother's skull : had ejected P. B. her brother, had caused J. B. to become a drunkard. I met both the altar and the literary classes : and gave the month of May instruction.

Thurs., 4th   I went to the meeting of the Theological Society : 14 members were present. Dr. McSweeny read a dissertation on Renan's 'life of Jesus' : showing how flippantly he rid himself of the facts of Christ's miracles, and how he hardly believes his own explanations. Furfur and Dr. Cummings praised his style : Fr. Nicot thought little of it : I have read it, and the style quite attracted me. I never felt annoyed even when he showed very poor critical ability, but yet it has no great strength. Dr. Cummings imprudently read an essay, which he said he had written as a boy for another boy-priest to teach him 'how to prepare a sermon'. Dr. Cummings never respects anyone's feelings : he insults everyone he meets. We discussed a moral case whether the old oils can be used for the blessing of the font, and for a baptism : till the new ones are had. The answer for the first was negative : but that the infusion of the oils could be supplied privately : for the second a decree of a council of Lyons, was generally considered to permit only for a case of death danger. During the discussion restiti in faciem Furfuris, who had most ungentlemanly interrupted me several times. In the afternoon I called at the Burtsells in 4th Ave. to give them the result of my confab with the Dr. who does not seem to have mended his ways. In the evening I went to the Sisters' of Mercy's fair at the Palace gardens : well got up by 12 churches and five private parties but not well attended. The Sisters gave out statistics to prove their good works : but are over sanguine of the impression made. Their season tickets cost $2, their family tickets 1$, and single admission 50 c. which are considered too much. The McKnights have furnished our table : Miss A. Burtsell assists them : and also the O'Reillys were present. These latter are immensely talkative and speak trash and nonsense. I cannot bear them. They were lauding Booth to the skies. Miss McKnight is very charitable : having ambition is an excellent one to be at a fair.

May

Fri., 5th I visited my mother : had a long talk with Fr. St. John about Abp. Kenrick of St. Louis whom he described as a very independent and reserved man : that keeps at a distance from the clergy. In St. Louis there are about 22 churches : each attended by two priests. The city contains about 60,000 Catholics. The Americans are all secessionists : the Germans both infidel and Unionists. In the evening I again went to the fair, where I met Fr. Healy of St. Peter's, who has little brains and uses them for little purpose. He accompanied me to a few tables and played the generous by paying down $1 at one table, because I had resolved not to spend anything this evening.

Sat., 6th It rained almost all day : and in the evening had a thunderstorm : but the confessions were abundant as usual.

Sun., 7th Sunday. I sang H. Mass : spoke on the patronage of St. Joseph at 9 o'clock : explained the 7th article to the boys and the 4th to the girls. Fr. Preston took occasion from the feast of the patronage of St. Joseph to speak of the church triumphant in heaven : He explained how the soul of the saints wings it's quick flight to heaven, how there, it's joy is to love God : how even there it does not forget those left on earth, but does honour to God by praying him to help us : how they hear our prayers even though they be not ubiquities. My spirit, he said, now is in the torrid zone of Africa, now is near the dome of St. Peter's in Rome, now returns to this altar. How much more can a spirit when freed from this body, travel from place to place to listen the prayers directed it to it. Beside do they not see God, in whom all things are reflected : and from the motion of whose grace our prayers take rise? Can they not see our prayers in him, as in a mirror. And they know they give honour to God, when they pray to him for us. St. Joseph is the second

May 44

greatest Saint : who was honoured on earth, and will be honoured in
heaven. In the evening I visited Mr. Plowden Morrogh, the lawyer, my
mother alone was there with me.

Mon., 8th   I went to Yonkers to Fr. Lynch's funeral. He was
pastor. Fr. McNierney sang solemn High-Mass. Fr. Starrs gave the absolution. Fr. Donnelly of St. Michael's gave a neat discourse, stating
that he had known Fr. Lynch 15 years : had first met him in Fordham
College : that he was always of a marked class of associates that are
never forgotten. His talents were good : his affability great. He left
as a memory of himself the improved church and a magnificent school-
house. He was intensely loyal : and had rejoiced that before his death
the great spot on his country had been wiped away. He had prepared himself well for death. A dinner was spread for us in the school-house which
is quite large, and well designed : about 35 priests were present : the
ladies of the place waited upon us, and, seemed to be quite proud of the
chance. Fr. Oram is left in charge for the present. I have only known
Fr. Lynch since he has been unwell, of lingering consumption. He never
showed much animation since my acquaintance with him : I presume he was
no scholar but gained popularity in Yonkers by his gentlemanly ways. In
the evening at the funeral procession were present three Protestant
ministers and the town bells tolled all the time. The Catholic priests
and boys marched in cassock and surplice till the body was placed in the
cars, to be taken to Syracuse. R. I. P. Going to Yonkers I was with
Fr. Malone : a monomaniac on (loyalty and abolitionism) which are one
thing for him. Coming down I was with Fr. McKenna of St. Andrews :
born in Savannah, ordained when about 45, and a petty minded fellow :
little brains but good enough heart. In the stage I was with Fr. Farley

May   45

of Jamaica & Rockaway, a man of no ability. In the evening Dr. McGlynn called at our place and slept with us.

Tues., 9th   The whole day was rainy : Dr. McGlynn and I talked on almost every subject imaginable : especially of the necessity of his setting to work at the erection of his new church, lest he should be called a loud-mouthed declaimer without doing his share of the work. Mr. Berryan called in and dined with us : of course the conversation fell on Italy, where all three of us had been for many years. Dr. McGlynn and I went in the evening to Fr. Tom Farrell's where he commenced a subscription for Mrs. Gen. Sherman's table at the Chicago fair. Dr. McGlynn & McSweeny & I went to the Sisters of Mercy's fair : where I believe 2 thirds of the money taken in this evening was given by ten or twelve priests who were there. The fair has not prospered. The Sisters expect 30,000 dollars : but will not probably get more than one fourth of this sum. Dr. McGlynn had presented a nice church to the fair : but it was hidden from sight.

Wed., 10th   I was present in the morning at the meeting of the Anti-slavery society : where a debate was held whether the society should dissolve. Rev. Mr. Spalding gave a long discourse against the dissolution. He measured every word, and spoke at such length, that after several interruptions, he was voted off the platform by the whole audience. Mr. May and Purvis spoke confusedly. Fred. Douglass (the negro) spoke magnificently on the necessity of having a guide in the Anti-slavery Society to maintain the rights of the freed slaves. He has a very intellectual face, and speaks very purely. Miss Anna Dickinson also spoke beautifully against the dissolution. She has a pleasing face, and fine forehead : earnestness gives her great influence and she has great command

May   46

of thought and language. She gave a hard rap to Gen. Sherman : on
account of his late treaty with Joe Johnston. A   told her in
Baltimore that she a Northern woman and Garrisonian abolitionist would
dare to tell the people, that the abolition of slavery was for their
own interest.

Mr. Forrest accused President Johnson of saying that he would rather see
the black race ten fathoms under water, than see the union dissolved.
This was contradicted : but Wendell Philips read a letter to prove it.
Fred. Douglas thought it a rhetorical flourish to show his love for the
white in preference to the blackman. Harmony was restored by it being
proved, too that Johnson had asserted that he was prepared to give the
ballot to the negro. Garrison argued for the dissolution because the
Society had made no report since 1861, because it had no treasury, no
agents, no accession of members, no object. I left the meeting whilst
he was speaking. He sought to make Wendell Philips plead in favour of
dissolution by quoting his speeches of 1861. Philips thought it cruel
to inflict the speaker's words on him twice and spoke in favour of the
Societ's continuance. The vote being taken, 48 voted for and 140 a-
gainst dissolution. Garrison declining the nomination, Wendell Philips
was chosen president. In the evening I visited Dr. Morrogh's. I called
W. P. M. to account for drink : and told of my suspicions about C. F. In
the evening I gave the May instruction : besides attending to the altar
and literary classes. In the latter session, Foster, J. Burke and J.
McCabe acted the first act of Hamlet. Fr. Caro dined with us. He said
there would be a revolution in Europe before Preston returned. I bet
there would not be. The wager is a dinner.

<u>Thurs., 11th</u>   Dr. McSweeny and I walked to the Central Park. The

May

Dr. told me of a 'spat' he had with the 'dulcinore', Starrs' housekeeper who refused to sew a button on his shirt or make his bed. I laid down my plans for not being prevented from doing good even by the Abp.'s carelessness : nor do I care for his esteem or that of the Roman authorities, if it is to prevent me from doing good. The Abp. was 'huffed' at the Dr.'s expressing 'approval' of a discourse of his on the Church's body and soul : in which he admitted the possibility of a heretic being saved. In the afternoon I walked with Dr. McGlynn to see lots on the corner of Vestry and Hudson Sts. for his new church project. We thought the ground admirably situated. They were clearing the ground of houses, to make it fit for lease or sale. I was told to-day of the fate that awaits Brennan of St. James : the Dr. may probably get his church. Preston told me that there was a rush for Yonkers. The Dr. supped with us : and gave Preston some clear views on the bright projects of the Fenians. We went to the Sister of Mercy's fair : which was tolerably patronised. Quin has decided peremptorily that it will not be kept up beyond Sunday : because a mission commences at his church on that day. He is opposed by several priests. Brennan of St. James' was 'soft' at the fair. Fr. Andrew of 31st St. (Dutch) was doling out at various tables his contribution to the fair. Fr. Doran of Albany was present under the auspices of Quin. Miss McKnight and the O'Reillys gave signs of mutual jealousy.

<u>Fri., 12th</u>   Bish. Bayley of Newark said mass at our church and breakfasted with us. He talked a long time on his travels in Italy especially : then on the wants of the church in New York city in the knowledge of which he showed more interest than our Ecclesiastical authorities generally do. I gave him a good deal of information : but he seemed to have studied the matter himself. He spoke too on Dr. Forbes for whom he still

May 48

showed anxiety, but called him selfish and proud. In the evening I went to the Sisters of Mercy's fair.

Sat., 13th   In the morning during walk I met Fr. Quin of St. Stephen's who told me that Don Giov. Orsenigo was delighted to go to Croton Falls. The dignity of pastor has made him stout : Fr. Coyle of Yorkville is to take his place at St. Stephen's. Preston remarked that he did not consider Slevin having enough energy to improve Yonkers, where he has been removed from Croton Falls which he did not improve at all. He uttered some threat that if he were not soon taken from the Falls, which he disliked he would quit the diocese. He had been assistant to Fr. Mooney at St. Bridget's who once wet him and was put under the hose in return : incompatibility of temper forced them apart and sent Slevin to 'Croton' Falls.

Sun., 14th   I preached on Indulgences at H. Mass, at 7 o'clock, to the boys and to the girls : in view of the Jubilee to commence here in the city of New York on the 15th May to last till the 15th June. The Archbishop's pastoral was tolerably got up : no startling idea was manifested in it. My mother and I visited the Morroghs of 26th St.

Mon., 15th   Fr. McNeirney dined with us : he stated that the Archbishop had already received $35,000 'in promise' of which $8000 were in hand. The building of the Cathedral is not proceeding on account of a discrepancy between Hall and Joyce the architects : the Abp. has right to break the contract, they not proceeding when ordered. Hall is more faithful : Joyce wishes to be bought off. The latter is a Catholic. The Abp. fears to reject him lest the Irish should say he preferred the Protestant. Asking about Dr. McGlynn's building projects, McNeirny seemed to doubt whether Fr. Thos. Farrell wished his parish divided : having once opposed the division of St. Mary's parish. I assured him the Thos. Farrell was most zealous in assisting Dr. McGlynn to get a new place. I informed him too very significantly that the church in Greene St. which the Abp. could have bought for Catholics, was again occupied as a Jewish synagogue : and that the Presbyterians had created an Irish church for evangelisation purposes in the same street. The Abp. had objected to this neighborhood because not respectable. In the afternoon Fr. Preston started for Hartford for a 4 day stay. Mr. Kellogg commissioner of charities refused to take a baby by name Riordan for six months at Randall's island, though without support. Dr. McGlynn assisted me at hearing confessions which we have every evening for the two ensuing weeks for the jubilee.

Tues., 16th   A Fr. Monahan of New Orleans dined with Dr. McGlynn and myself. We afterwards took a ride to High Bridge. Fr. Monahan is a native of Cork Co.; says in New Orleans he was considered a great Cecessionist : is glad that the negroes are freed for their moral amelioration, though their physical condition will not be improved : says Butler gave the poor people much work and therefore was popular, yet was fond of an escort of cavalry in New Orleans. Banks was a more plain and capable administrator. A great fruit from the war is the extirpation of the creoles, who were rich, and proud, and irreligious, treating priests as servants. A Creole man is happy with a horse, a gun, and a pretty woman. Fr. Monahan said that to gain the reputation of a preacher with the Irish was sufficient to denounce the heretics. The Irish are factious. New Orleans in his eyes is nothing compared with New York. Around New Orleans there are no hills : all is alluvial ground. He was much taken with Dr. McGlynn. He starts on the 17th for the old country : has been

May   50

in New Orleans for 18 years, where he has a brother too a priest. His
church there is only lately built of stone : his house is a frame
building. I gave the Month of May exercise and heard confessions afterwards. In the evening Dr. McSweeny called : he published his essay in
the Tablet, and thinks that the publication has been an important step
to overcome human respect. For the jubilee at the Cathedral they have a
sermon every morning and evening and confessions during the day. Two
Jesuits preach and hear confessions.

Wed., 17th   Dr. McGlynn dined with me, and afterwards we went to
Fr. Malone's of Williamsburgh : but only Fr. Campbell was home who told
us of Fr. Farley of Jamaica coming to Malone's quite 'high'. They were
stirring up the house for spring-time. I remarked at dinner that our
cook is not anxious to please me in eatables, as she is to please Fr.
Preston : things were badly cooked. In the evening after confessions I
went to Sisters' of Mercy's fair to be present at the fair's close. Mr.
Devlin, jr. told me that about $20000 is the result of the fair. The
articles of our table were raffled off with pretty good profits. Miss
McKnight thinks she will never put a hand to a fair again : I am afraid
that life will not last long enough to allow her to break the promise
often. All the McKnight family is delicate.

Thurs., 18th   In the morning I went to St. Peter's
where I heard a Redemptorist preaching on confession. He said no historical fact was known of breaking the confessional seal. I am afraid that
I have known some. Fr. Mooney of St. Bridget's whipped and published the
theft of a boy told in confession alone. The Redemptorist told a fact
that happened in Belgium (?) where a priest let his own brother die hanged
and his mother die of chagrin rather than say a word to let the real

malefactor be known, who had told all in confession. Also a priest in the French revolution was shot by an unknown hand, whilst threatening to publish a confession of a girl, who upbraided him for associating with Jacobins. The redemptorist spoke familiarly and animatedly, though a German. A mission is held in the church by the redemptorists. The church was only 3 fourths filled. I visited afterwards the Cathedral to fulfil the conditions of the jubilee. The redemptorist preacher had also stated that Luther was constantly asked by his nun-wife to tell of certain sins confessed by her companion nuns : which he always declined to do. I believe that the seal is broken frequently through imprudence, perhaps even through malice : but still the law holds good : and the Almighty has chosen to require this severe condition from us even with the risk of public shame attached to it. I met Mr. W. Coddington, clerk of Dr. Ives and sexton of St. Michael's. The reformatory has procured a farm near Westchester of 160 acres for $40000. It will have it's house of reception with a few buildings there and an office in the city to get the city appropriations : which have been refused till now because not a permanent institution : having only hired buildings. The boys are often bound out but frequently run away not only for bad-treatment but for love of excitement. Fr. Killeen of Red-Bank took one of the best boys but failed to keep him on account of the boy's rowdiness.

I met Fr. Orsenigo : who is elated at the prospects of Croton Falls. The people there has been delighted to find that he intended to live in their midst. Fr. Slevin had not lived with them : nor had he improved the place at all. At Dover Plains, one of the stations, there was only a borrowed altar stone. Fr. Slevin has been promoted to a good place, notwithstanding his sluggishness, because he said he would leave the

May 52

diocese. Fr. Crsenigo received $120, from the servants of Bellevue H. with a testimonial. He replied that he had preferred preaching to them than to a fashionable audience. The report was published in the Herald. The parish gentlemen will present a souvenir to him though opposed by Dr. Cummings.

Fr. Preston told me of a disagreement between Fr. Hecker and Mr. Hassard about the Catholic World. Fr. Hecker objected to two passages of book notices about works on the B. Virgin because he wishes to have the essential Catholic doctrines impressed on the Protestant mind. Fr. Hecker's brother gives the money for the review : the Abp. wished Fr. Hecker to be responsible editor : he declined omitting the two passages. Probably Mr. Hassard will retire, prompted I believe in great measure by Fr. Preston who objects to the Paulists' school of Theology. I met Major Cassidy at the Burtsells in 4th Ave. He is brother to Mrs. Dr. Burtsell. He was wounded in the leg in the U. S. Service. He has now a position in the audit-office annexed to the Custom-house. I visited my mother, who told me that Fr. Quin had roughly handled a drummer who with others was playing at the Sisters' fair with the consent of the ladies, St. Peter's excepted who had not been asked by mistake : and to a lady that accused him of unfairness in the disposition of the tables, confining St. Ann's table to a corner when it had drawn another position, Fr. Quin answered 'she was a liar' to which she replied 'I thought Fr. Quin was a gentleman and am now undeceived'. Some men had got drunk over three demijohns of wine innocently presented to the fair by the Sisters' and a regular fight took place. Dr. Morrogh showed anxiety not to hold conversation for fear I should trouble him with more stories of C. F.

Fri., 19th   I visited in the afternoon Mr. Tiers, who by paralysis

May 53

is confined to his bed : his tongue is half dead and he cannot talk freely. I was pleased with Miss Agnes Tiers, who has quite a gay disposition, and is very pious, being at mass every morning. She thought the 'Providence table' at the Sisters' fair did not succeed, because held to be the aristocratic table being attended by Mrs. Gen. Meagher, Mrs. Gen. Kearney, and Pardows and Tiers etc. The Tiers family is quite pleasant in conversation. The young boys are quite lively too : I never met the older ones. On my return I found Dr. Freel and Fr. Nilan. I got no news from Dr. Freel who is always non-committal in his speech. We walked to Canal St. and Fr. Nilan and I walked back to 42nd St., in which is the church of the Holy Cross where Fr. Nilan is assistant to Fr. McCarthy. Fr. Nilan gave some good ideas about the childish manner in which Roman seminaries are conducted : and how Fr. W. McCloskey of the Amer. college is small-minded, and using his authority to prevent Northerners from speaking in favour of the Union, because he sympathised with the South.

Sat., 20th   Mr. Hassard dined with us : I told him that the second number of the Catholic world was not as pleasing to me, as the first. Fr. Mignard had reversed the case to him.

Sun., 21st   Fr. Preston spoke on the Sacrifice of the Altar : as the everlasting prayer, by which we are sure to gain what we wish. He took his text from the gospel of the day. I spoke on the jubilee at 9 o'clock : and to the boys on the 8th article. In the evening I went to the Morroghs of 26th St. with my mother. We discussed the right of trying by military tribunal Jeff Davis etc. We all thought that he should be tried by civil tribunal because the assassination was not committed by anyone connected with the confederate army. Rev. Dr. Morrogh had a

May 54

stroke of apoplexy yesterday but is well.

<u>Mon., 22nd</u>   I visited the Decoppets, Gallaghers and A. Burtsell at 111, 32nd St. all relatives of mine : we discussed the success of the Sisters' of Mercy's fair, which is said to have realised fully $20,000. Dr. Cummings had promised to give as much as the gains of the highest table : which was St. Francis Xavier's, it having made $2600. This surprised the Doctor. Fr. G. McCloskey of Nativity promised to give as much as the lowest table : our's did not make more than $400. Miss Anastasia Burtsell with Maggie B. called to see me to-day. I gave the month of May exercise in the evening. We continue to hear confessions every evening during this week to afford all an opportunity of going to confession.

<u>Tues., 23rd</u>   In the morning I took a walk in 5th Ave. In the afternoon we heard the confessions of the girls of our school who are preparing to make their first communion. They have been well prepared by the Sisters.

<u>Wed., 24th</u>   I heard the confessions of the girls of St. Joseph's who are preparing for confirmation. In the evening I had the altar class, and I drilled the girls for the procession and gave the month of May instruction and heard confessions.

<u>Thurs., 25th</u>   Ascension day. We commenced the devotions of the 40 hours : for the first time practised in this diocese. Dr. McGlynn assisted us at the solemn High Mass : we had a procession in which the girls joined. In the afternoon we dined at St. Joseph's where we had several discussions with the Archbishop. 1st on indulgences; when the Abp. maintained that there is a decree quoted by Gury of the Congregation of Indulgences declaring the Jubilee communion to satisfy the Easter duty

May 55

if received in the Easter time : whilst a decree of the Congregation of regulars states the contrary in 1841, a year after the former decree. 2nd. We maintained that in countries where the clandestine decree of the Council of Trent is published, the parish-priest ought to be present at the marriage of protestants if these chose to come before him, lest their marriage should be invalid. The Abp. maintained erroneously that the marriages of Protestants in those countries was held to be valid. He maintained too, for a time at least, that the priest is minister of matrimony : who therefore should not use his spiritual functions for the spiritual good of heretics. We said however that Fr. Edward Purcell marries Protestants, acting as civil minister : the state holding any gospel minister as such for marriage. 3rd. The Abp. maintained that in New York there are presently only 300000 Catholics, that the Catholics cannot support more priests, or build churches more rapidly, and that we have more Catholic church-room in proportion than Catholic Paris. Dr. McGlynn and I maintained that there are in New York at least 500000 Catholics, that the Catholics would support more priests too willingly if we only had priests to rake up those who by neglect have grown careless, that 50 more churches could be easily supported, each one having a full congregation : We know more of numbers of Catholics than he who never mixes with the people, knows nothing of the East side of the city where Catholics are most populous : We told him that the Church was not built to enable priests to live luxuriantly as all the priests of New York do now. Each one has at least $800, besides his support from salary and masses. The perquisites average $1000 for each priest besides said amount. The board and house-keeping are paid out of the perquisites : but an average $2000 in each parish remains after the expenses of the house : which is divided fairly between the two priests. In St. Ann's and one or two other churches the purguisites not sufficing to support the house, are taken by the priests. The perquisites here amount to about $900. Dr. McGlynn had from Fr. Preston that 3 years ago there were 21,00 baptisms in New York diocese : which being multiplied by 25 (the lowest average number) would show that in New York we had at least 525,000 : which number must have increased since. The Abp. sought to elude this argument by saying that our population is a floating people : and that many had left since : but it was replied that as many and more had come into the city since. Fr. McNierney in defense of the Archbishop said that our assertion was the same as D'Arcy McGee's against Abp. Hughes : that is, that hundreds of thousands of souls are perishing without anyone to care for them : the blame was Abp. Hughes'. We thanked Fr. McNierney for having brought forward so able a witness as D'Arcy McGee for the truth of our assertion. I showed that last year in a parish where three churches are wanted $20,000 were expended on building a steeple, and painting the church. Why could not that money be spent in building other churches, if no other money could be had? The Abp. quoted Judas' saying 'could not the money be spent for the poor' instead of squandering ointment on the Saviour's body. Dr. McGlynn retorted by quoting the words 'Vae vobis qui aedificatis sepulchra prophetarum' as an argumentum ad hominem against the Abp. who is building the Cathedral. The Abp. thought us optimists : and therefore sarcastically asked why instead of eating grand dinners and drinking champagne, we were not helping some poor man dying in a hovel. I and Emc replied that we were engaged in a more important work - in opening the eyes of an Archbishop to the wants of his diocese. Fr. Starrs when the Abp. had retired

May

for a moment spoke authoritatively to Dr. McGlynn saying : you ought not to speak so boldly : the Dr. asked Fr. Starrs if he desired him to suppress the truth as Starrs had done all his lifetime. Starrs said the Dr. was half-crazy, intemperate and impertinent. The Dr. replied that their respective estimate of each other was nearly equal. Afterwards we met in Fr. Farrell's room, where we joined all around in jokes and pleasant talk.

Fri., 26th   Dr. McGlynn assisted us again at the solemn H. Mass 'pro pace'. We got the purple dalmatics from the Imm. Conception. We agreed that our last evening's conversation with the Abp. would tend to stir him up : and make his two defenders be in an awkward position. We went in the afternoon to Duncan, the agent of Trinity church who says that the six lots on Vestry Street and Hudson would not sell for less than $100000, and neither there nor in Varick St. would they sell for churches, because churches interrupt the business of a street. The Trinity Corporation is waiting till those streets are improved : at present they sell property at 25 percent more than other estates. Almost all their ground is lease property. They are considered old fogies : preventing the improvement of their own property.

Sat., 27th   We had solemn High Mass. Dr. McGlynn assisted. We had also a requiem H. Mass for Stephen Boyle : a very good and generous man of our parish. With Fr. McGean who assisted at the requiem mass Dr. McGlynn entered into details about the Cathedral. Fr. Starrs prevented McGean from collecting boys together, lest they should hack the benches of the school : the boys will not go to the basement : notwithstanding that Starrs defines it to be the best basement in the city. Starrs about two weeks ago took up McGean for being too positive in his

May

Theological decisions : Starrs 'did not like to see young men, so decisive in their opinions', when Starrs himself was in the wrong.

<u>Sun., 28th</u>   Mr. & Mrs. William Preston and George Preston with little Tommy Preston came down from Albany to stay two days with us. William Preston is very pleasant and intelligent : likes to discuss legal and religious questions. Mr. Berryan was present at dinner and made me tell the spicy sayings of ours to the Abp. and Starrs. George Preston is taciturn. Mrs. Preston is a very nice lady, open and good-hearted. Fr. Preston bade adieu to the Congregation asking their prayers : and spoke then on the glory of Heaven, which is expressed to us by Christ's ascension. In the afternoon the premiums were distributed to the sunday school children, 17 to the girls and 16 to the boys. In the evening I preached at St. Theresa's church on the Sacrifice of the Mass. Fr. Boyle had been present and approved our stand with the Abp. Fr. Farrell who had been removed from St. Mary's and barely allowed to go to St. Teresa's 'propter potum' was glad to see somebody show the wants of the diocese to the Abp. He walked homewards with me : and expressed great admiration for Dr. McGlynn. John Preston told me that Fr. Ambrose O'Neil was a good preacher. He had published one on the papacy by request of several gentlemen of the city directed against a Prot. Dr. Clarke who had said "now we have got through our war let us stop the encroachment of popery". Mr. Preston told me that Abp. McCloskey had said it was easier to convert pagans than Protestants, and said we had not enough priests to give lectures merely for the benefit of Protestants.

<u>Mon., 29th</u>   Dr. McGlynn called in the evening and after tea we went to Fr. Thos. Farrell who recommended the Dr. to be more calm and dispassionate in his arguing the good cause, lest it should be lessened

May

in respect by the defects of those who defended it. The Dr. read his letter directed to Mrs. Gen. Sherman, in the name of several priests giving a donation to the Chicago Sanitary Fair. It approves of the tables being under the various churches, that a rivalry may be engendered of well-doing : also because the churches are the best authorities to sanctify obedience to civil law, and the abolition of slavery. Fr. Preston had told me at dinner that McNierney gave him quite an excited account of the discussion with the Abp. thinking that the Dr. had passed all bounds : McNierney has but selfish motives for giving this colour to the picture.

Tues., 30th   We had quite a sweet may-festival by the children of our school; all the compositions displayed good taste, the recitation was excellent, the singing was also very good. With Dr. McSweeny I walked to 50th St. and back. I read to him by letters to Francioni and Card. Barnabo about the wants of N.Y. diocese : he approved of the matter, and style of both. Fr. Nilan called also to see me. Fr. McGuire had advised Dr. McSweeny to tell Dr. McGlynn not to be so imprudent again in addressing the Abp. Dr. McSweeny approved of Dr. McGlynn's course : and hoped to see him one day with full authority (episcopal) to carry his schemes into effect. Dr. McSweeny had declined an offer from the Abp. to go to St. Stephen's, saying that if sent he would have no objection to go. The Abp. thought him wise in not going, if his health would not keep up under the duties of said parish : this reason was adduced by the Doctor for not going unless sent. He had been sent on Sunday to say 1 mass, but was asked to say two masses : in the first he took the ablutions which provoked Dr. Cummings. We read Dr. Brann's lecture at the laying of a cornerstone of a German church in Jersey city. He accused "Protestant ministers north &

May

south of exciting to war : whilst the Catholics kept aloof altogether".
Catholics did so through cowardice : because we ought to have spoken in
favour of the Union and the abolition of slavery. Dr. McSweeny liked the
discourse : I disapproved of it's tirade against Protestants.

<u>Wed., 31st</u>   I went to Fordham to hear speeches at St. John's college.
The subjects were Enterprise, Free Institutions, Military Glory, Literary
Exercises, Power of Religion. The speeches were poor, devoid of logic
or good language : the recital was without animation. The music was pleasing, except that Mr. Colliere pronounces Italian like French. Fr. Starrs
announced as usual his approval of the compositions & of the music both
vocal and instrumental : but.... he thought the speeches were recited too
fast and not distinctly. Everyone was astounded at this new idea that
changed for once the tone and words of his approbation of public exhibitions : and no one else thought that the boys spoke fast. The Jesuits
are very hospitable, preparing a hearty dinner for the guests : I went
to Fordham with Fr. McGean who had to buy Fr. Starrs' ticket : and who
gave a history of some of his meannesses. Fr. Starrs refused to let him
have the school-house for instruction of the public school boys because
they might hack the benches : not caring much for the boys' souls. At
dinner I was alongside Fr. Nilan, who agreed with me in criticising the
discourses of the morning, as containing too much unreal respect for the
Church as the civiliser of the universe. Their constant effusions about
the church appear almost hypocritical. I made the acquaintance of Mr.
Byrne and Charley Burne whom I had known as Sally Byrne when at the
Jesuits' day college in New York city some 15 years ago. Coming home
we took the Fordham horse-cars : the trip was quite a pleasant one in
the midst of nice farms. I gave to Fr. Donnelly an account of our dis-

May

cussion with the Abp. on last Thursday. He approved of it : and was surprised beyond measure to think that the Abp. had said that our people could or would not support more priests. He hoped that no excessive display of zeal should damage the good cause. Fr. Preston showed me the flattering letter which he received from Loyzance S. J. describing him as a patron of the Society to Fr. Becks the general of the Order and also to the Society at large. Mr. W. Coddington praised Fr. Donnelly's way of collecting money, by the St. Michael's society where each member pays 5 cents a week : he employs a collector of this fund. He is severe on withdrawing the pew of even the most aristocratic, if not paid for in advance. 3 cents are asked for entry to the church at mass : 10 cents at 9 o'clock, the children's mass. It is very hard to have to ask money when the people go to mass but the necessity of the church seem to require that those willing to pay are admitted in preference to those who are unwilling : we have not enough church room for all.

June

Thurs., 1st   I gave Dr. Thos. Burtsell a serious lecture on his deranged ways for some time : he took it quite coolly, but I fear it will not have great effect. At tea we had present Dr. Bayard a homoeopathic physician who actually recommended Fr. Preston to take no less than seven powders in connection with his sea-voyage : to prevent sea-sickness or remedy dyspepsia consequent on the sea-trip. He disapproved of asparagus, as injurious to the stomach : and laid down that no one needs stimulant drink till the age of 65, when it is useful. Mrs. Hassard & Son were present also. Dr. Morrogh was half-soaked to-day.

Fri., 2nd   Edward Preston came from Hartford to-day : to whom Fr. Preston recommended to get through with his first confession before

June

returning. Edward is very good hearted and has given his attention to the matter of religion. He is an Episcopalian and will soon become a Catholic. He and I agree pretty well : and he remarked to his father that he could argue with me and yet could never get angry. I visited Mrs. Boyle to condole on the death of her husband. She bore his death well : she received communion two days afterwards for him. He was in the liquor business and she thinks the constant trying it brought on apoplexy.

Sat., 3rd   To-day Fr. Preston with Mr. Daschauer and family left on the steamer Hansa of the Bremer line bound for Southampton : He is to make a few months' stay in Europe, travelling about. He was in great glee. Mr. Lancake heard confessions in his stead. The Hansa is a fine steamer : but the company was principally German. He will not be pleased with their society. He has longed to see Europe, and will appreciate the grand things to be found there.

Sun., 4th   Fr. Lancake sang solemn H. Mass; a Dutch Jesuit scholastic assisted as subdeacon. I as deacon and preached on the gospel, this being Pentecost. I preached also at the rosary-meeting : besides at 7 o'clock mass, and to the boys and girls. At dinner I argued with the two Jesuits that they acted wrongly in giving so many scholastics to teaching grammar etc. whilst being ordained they could assist on the mission. They argued that their rule directly gave them the care of education : I argued that the circumstances of this country required their attention to missionary labour. It was argued on both sides in good humour. I was at Lawyer Morrogh's with my mother and the McLaughlins, where we talked on the easiness of getting to heaven, whilst the greater part of people form a very gloomy idea of it's difficulty.

June   63

Mon., 5th   Miss A. Burtsell gave me a sad account of the M. D.'s
state from drink : he had spoken harshly of me after my lecture to him.
In the evening I visited the McKnights, with whom I enjoyed myself very
well. Our conversation fell on sea trips where I gave my experience on
the Asia, Cunard line, which lost it's paddle-wheel, rudder wheel, four
boats, four engineers who were scalded, all the chronometers, it's
captain was knocked senseless (he was a Capt. Shannon) : the first cabin
was filled with water : the excitement on board quite terrific. I had
kept cool, and not feeling alarmed could enjoy the scenes of fright.
One poor Irishman thought I would never be a good priest to pity others,
because I laughed at his fright, whilst asking of the ladies whether they
thought there was any danger and they consequently were much more alarmed.
I met a Dr.   , whom I suspect to be in love with the P. E. sister,
who returns the feeling. He was a pleasant man. They went out to walk
before I left. Adelaide showed me that when she became a Catholic she
did not understand the doctrine itself of transubstantiation. She wondered too why Fr. Lancake had broken the communion particles. I gave
an account of Dr. Coxe's sermon for Xtian union against popery, preached
in a Methodist church : and how Dr. Potter the P. E. bishop of New York
condemned his conduct principally in his late pastoral : all on account
of Fr. Agapius the Russo-Greek priest declaring his abandonment of the
Greek church : whilst Dr. Potter had given him the use of a Trinity chapel
for Greek service. Dr. Potter seeks to prove that lending the church
was not encouragement of the Greek church : for union without unity of
faith could not be allowed with the Greek, nor with the radical protestant sects.

Tue., 6th   All the morning I heard confessions of the boys of the

June

Immaculate Conception parish : and dined there. Fr. Thos. Farrell called at our house and engaged Dr. McGlynn and myself to go begging for the Chicago Sanitary fair. Dr. Morrogh and Fr. Farrell declined giving anything: which was mean considering that two priests asked it, and to whom they are indebted for frequent assistance at hearing confessions, preaching etc. We visited Fr. Farrelly, who has just left Rondout to take charge of St. James' parish in the city. Fr. Brennan it's late pastor was relieved of all duty : because habitually drunk and neglectful of the dying etc. etc. He foolishly told the people that he had expected to live at St. James' always : and cried because obliged to leave. He asked pardon for scandals given. Had he pretended to travel for health, no one would have been the wiser. Yet he received presentations. More still : a deputation waited on the Abp. to have him recalled : to this the Abp. would make no answer. Fr. Farrelly is not pleased to come to St. James' : He preached shooting over the heads of his audience : next time Dr. McGlynn remarks he must fire at their hearts. Fr. Farrelly asked the Dr. to give his ideas of the parish's wants. Dr. McGlynn had been assistant to Fr. Brennan. We visited Fr. Trainor, who had some good California wine, who gave $5 for the Chicago fund : and promised to give Dr. McGlynn two collections in his church for the Dr's. new one not yet born. Fr. Trainor thought the Protestants were not safe guardians of the fair-money. Fr. Keegan of Brooklyn gave $5 for the Dr's. sake : but had given a collection in his church for the Brooklyn sanitary fair. Dr. Cummings a priest from Ireland was there too; who knows a good deal about fast horses; and said that in Ireland the respectable families when dying have always H. Mass and office, with 6 priests, each receiving 10 shillings or 1£ sterling. He is stationed at Brooklyn. A lank stiff priest from

June

Boston O'Reilly by name was there also, to preach in the evening. We visited Fr. McCurran who gave $10; Fr. Larry McKenna his assistant at St. Andrew's gave also $10. Fr. Briady gave for the Dr.'s mother's sake $5. In the evening I assisted for the first time at the conference of St. Vincent de Paul : which in our parish finding no poor, takes care of the Sunday-school children. They can be organised into a committee for promoting other interests of the Church. M. Kelly is president : Mr. O'Neil is secretary, and Mr.   , treasurer. They read the reports of the French and Irish conferences. I walked to 47th St. with Dr. McGlynn.

Wed., 7th   In the morning we visited Fr. Healy of St. Peter's : who besides $5 volunteered advice as to where Dr. McGlynn ought to build his church. Fr. Shanahan, a blind old priest, gave $2, because he wouldn't trust more in the hands of Protestants. Fr. Con. O'Callaghan of St. James' gave $10, but called Dr. McGlynn a niggerhead (in play). He told us that Fr. Farrelly wished to turn out all the grog-shops from his parish : he and Dr. McGlynn thought the best way was to promote the welfare of the Temperance Society. Fr. Farrelly almost thinks it a sin to sell liquor. Abp. Connolly of Halifax playfully declined to give Fr. Hecker a glass of wine after a mission sermon against liquor-dealers, whom he accused generally of sin. Fr. P. Ferrell gave $5. Fr. Egan $3. We met Dr. McSweeney on our return home who told us that Fr. Starrs has lately spoken very emphatically on the necessity of more churches in N. York where almost a church on every corner would be filled, and two priests should take care of them. Fr. McGean pretended to oppose him : and Starrs argued the case manfully, using other people's thunder. By and by, Starrs (lucus a non lucendo) will maintain that he always said so.

June

We dined at Fr. T. Farrell's where were Fr. F. Malone and McCarthy : with whom we discussed the impropriety of the pope's taking Lincoln to task for being at a theatre on Good Friday : whilst in Rome the theatres are open on Sunday which would shock American Protestants. In this country I asserted that priests look on bishops, as demi-gods' as if not one of themselves. The people has the same opinion of priests : and yet all this influence is not used to promote good. The people would be politically subject to the bishop : if he chose to use this political power for the good of the church, we could have everything our own way here. In the afternoon I took a walk with Dr. McSweeny with whom the changes of priests was a topic of conversation. In the evening I had the altar-class : but adjourned to give the boys a chance of seeing the fire works in Astor-place erected to do honour to Gen. Grant who was to be present at a mass meeting to approve Johnson's administration. I went into Cooper institute, but hearing nothing and suffocated by the heat retreated. Such a packing I had never met with.

Thurs., 8th   I visited Mr. Tiers who with family are going to the country - Buttermilk falls - on Saturday. We again talked on Msgr. Bedini's stay in America : in which I know his mission was considered a failure by the American authorities. They speak highly of the Nuncio, who visited them frequently. In the evening I went to hear Gerrit Smith who argued against punishing the leading-rebels for treason 1st because by acknowledging them as belligerents we implicittly promised to deal with them according to the laws of war between two distinct nations. 2nd because when a rebellion is upheld with all the organisation of a separate nation, it can only be dealt with as a separate nation. So said Vattel one hundred years ago. Shall we now be less humane than those of the last century?

June

Hallani also condemned the execution of Charles I, because he was waging war under perfect national organisation. Macaulay endorsed Hallani's opinion. Both these died in 1859 : and are great men. Their authority must weigh heavily in the balance of Mercy. G. Smith is old : fumbled too much with books and papers for his authorities : and I grew tired and left. I visited our singing school of about 20 girls and 5 boys under the direction of Miss T. Waters : who takes a great interest in teaching the children, and has improved them very much. I was also present at the Christian Brothers' Manhattan college's concert, which was very entertaining : the boys played the piano, and band, and fiddle soloes : and sang also with great effect. I was at the Burtsells in 4th Ave. : where Maggie's 11th birthday was being celebrated. Peter B. took tea with me and carried back for me to Maggie $11 : for a summer-hat. They are rather limited in means through the Dr.'s extravagances. I met Mr. Durenberg, a Jew anxious to join the Church, whose attention was called to it by Miss Doran to whom he is engaged to be married when a Catholic. Fr. Orsenigo slept in our house.

<u>Fri., 9th</u>   Fr. Orsenigo told me that he wishes to have his parish divided : that his people are most generous in their donations : that one part of his parish is 38 miles from the other extremity, that he had to say mass at Patterson in a room 12 feet square with 50 persons present, that he intends spending $700 for repairing churches, that he will do without salary this year. The parishoners of St. Stephen's are collecting for him. Dr. Cummings expressed discontent at this, because it takes from the church building fund. The Dr.'s infirmities have made him peevish and unsympathetic with others. With Dr. McGlynn, who dined with me, I visited Manhattan College, directed by Brother Patrick : who is very

June 68

intelligent. We spoke to him about the wants of the Church : he felt them fully. He is anxious to have his boys come in familiar contact with priests : because otherwise they get estranged from priests, as beings of a different class and then if they go astray, have not courage to seek their guidance to return to the right road. Brother Patrick is anxious to beat new paths for showing the progress of his college. Thus he had yesterday's exhibition : which was a success. And at the yearly examination He wishes to have extemporaneous debates by his boys. He asked Dr. McGlynn to supervise their debates. Brother Patrick observed that the brothers had great difficulty in getting their school-boys in the city to confession. What must it then be with the public-school boys? The reason alleged was that the priests could not give more time? Therefore there is absolute need of more priests. B. Patrick coated the idea that the people would not support more priests. Dr. McGlynn gave him an account of our discussion with the Archbishop at St. Joseph's. We visited Fr. Brien, pastor of Manhattanville; who came from Chicago for troubles with the resigned (half-deposed) bishop Regan. He is a good priest : he engaged Dr. McGlynn to preach for him on Sunday of the Octave of Corpus Xti. He brought up a voluminous work of Theology by   to prove that one could gain the priviliges of a jubilee by fulfilling other obligations, such as fasting on the Ember days, receiving the Easter communion etc etc. It did not take cognizance of particular decrees on the subject.

Sat., 10th   I went to confession to Fr. Mignard : whom I found reading a newspaper, who therefore found it necessary to tell me that till just then 11 o'clock he had not gone to his room, having been engaged in the confessional, and called my notice to the ordinary plainness of a Jesuit's room : and hurried away on some sudden business. Why must a

June   69

Jesuit always apologise even for his most innocent amusement? I called at the Imm. Conception : where I saw my mother and the French priest who is to act as 3rd assistant there. In the afternoon at 5½ o'clock Fr. Aubier came to hear confessions. He speaks English pretty well in conversation. He apologised for coming late. Fr. G. McCloskey was anxious to get one of us to say a 9 o'clock mass for him. But Fr. Aubier did not come in time to enter on any engagement. Fr. McCloskey had searched the city to get a priest to say an early mass. He has been laid up for 4 months with rheumatism but has had no one to assist his assistant. This proves again the necessity of more priests. Fr. Aubier at tea always spoke of the Jesuits of Rome or elsewhere.

Sun., 11th   Trinity Sunday. Fr. Aubier went away immediately after 7 o'clock mass, asking to be excused from coming on Thursday the feast of Corpus Xti, if I could possibly get on without him. Fr. Juan, who was a teacher when I was at St. Francis Xavier's, preached at H. Mass a fine sermon on the B. Trinity, in which he called the sublimiest mystery of our faith, which we could not unfold in a clear way to our reason. Our reason tells us that God is one, unchangeable, eternal. But faith opens to us a new treasury of knowledge of God's nature : it shows Him to Us, One in Nature and Three in personality. This neither the human nor the Angelic nature could know without revelation of God. The Fathers have sought to explain it : by saying that the Father seeing himself inwardly produces the image of himself within himself : every act of God is subsistent, whence this image subsists or is a 2nd person. The Father loves the Son : the Son loves the Father : this act of reciprocated love is again a subsistence, viz the Holy Ghost. St. Augustine once trying to find a method of explaining it saw a child on the sea-shore trying to confine the sea in a hole made in the sand : and calling the child foolish for this attempt, was told in return that he was guilty of equal folly in seeking to comprehend the B. Trinity. He then showed the Trinity to be the model of the unity and harmony to be held among men. I was pleased with Fr. Juan's delivery and enonciation, though to be a German : I suspected that the sermon was too well written to be his : this may however be a rash judgement. I preached at 9 o'clock mass, sang H. Mass & Vespers : preached to the boys on the 'Communion of Saints' and to the girls on the 6th article; and to the altar society on the B. Trinity. I regret having allowed a Protestant lady to act as sponsor to a child of Mrs. Meade : I allowed because another Catholic lady held the child and it was but a compliment to the Protestant lady on the part of Mrs. Meade. I think I acted imprudently & wrongly. A girl by name Annie Gibbons with lock jaw was anointed, & confessed & communicated by me : though a protestant Mr. Harris told her that only the Lord Jesus could do any good for her. I went to L. P. Morrogh's.

Mon., 12th   Mr. Durenberg received his first instruction from me : Miss Doran had called to explain to me that he had need both of instruction and of controlling his temper. I had to rebuke a Canadian girl for getting married to a Protestant by a Protestant minister, in Cana., where she thought it was under penalty of excommunication. She came to the house by recommendation of Mrs. Tiers to know whether I should absolve her if she came to confess to me. I told her that she should return to confession in Canada, where she goes in a week. The real reason was because I believed her indisposed, careless of the excommunication, and proud under a gentle rebuke. In the evening I visited the Burtsells : where I met Ambrose Cassidy, who passes his evenings with his sister,

June   71

Mrs. Dr. Burtsell. He boards cor. 8th St. and University place. Our talk was commonplace about the heat and about the dullness of Albany compared with New York. I went to visit Fr. Nilan of 42nd St. church but he was in the confessional. Mr. Berryan took tea with me and asked me to write introducing him to John Avezzana, vice-consul of Italy, asking him to procure for Mr. Berryan an Italian passport : which is less costly, and as good as ours. Mr. Berryan in the name of Mr. Wheaton recommends Fr. Orsenigo to live in Dover Plains, which is more central to his mission : but the Abp. told Fr. Orsenigo to live in Croton Falls. Fr. Orsenigo slept at our house. He received a present of $300 from the conference of St. Vincent de Paul of St. Stephen's parish.

<u>Tues., 13th</u>   A Fr. McGrath, of the Oblates of Mary, of Ottawa said mass and asked me to let him sell some lottery tickets for a church of his city through our sexton. I recommended him also to Mr. Coddington, the Catholic bookseller. Fr. McGrath is intelligent : and versed in Theological matters though he thought the Council of Trent on clandestinely not to bind Protestants. He recommended to me a pamphlet by Mgr. Bouget bishop of Montreal on the impediments of marriage for this country. He spoke of the good done by his order in Liverpool, where 4 think they are killed by the care of 9000 souls. What must it be when here 2 priests as in at least seven parishes of New York have 20 000 or 25 000 souls to look after? The oblates give missions and take care of seminaries. In America they have a house in Ottawa, Buffalo and Plattsburgh. He hoped to have one established in this diocese. The Oblates have missions in America and Africa. Mr. Durenberg the Jew convert shows great anxiety about what Protestants say with regard to the Catholic Church, especially about confessing sins to the priest, about reading heretical books etc. A Miss

June 72

lately a convert showed me that she did not understand the doctrine of indulgences, the workings of God's grace, the authority of the church in matters of faith, or the power of making laws, when she became a Catholic. She could not understand why she should not go to Protestant churches, where Christ is worshipped in a good way. I visited the Imm. Conception where besides Dr. Morrogh, Fr. Farrell and Abbe I met Fr. O'Reilly of Newburgh who asked me an account of our discussion with the Archbishop on the needs of the diocese. Fr. O'Reilly is considered a smart priest. Fr. O'Reilly speaking once of the Abp. said he was false from top to toe : false hair, false teeth, false attitude, false gait etc. I was present at the conference of St. Vincent de Paul which now counts 33 members. I exhorted them not to tire of well-doing. Their conference was a representative of the Christian spirit of charity. We should strive to emulate each other in doing good. If one member grows cool, the others imitate him : if all are diligent, improvement is the consequence : & one good action is a step to a better one.

Fri., 14th   Fr. O'Reilly of Newburgh called to see me : we had a discussion on the good to the negroes from the war : he thought no good would come to them. Dr. McGlynn called whilst he was with me. He told Dr. that his sermon two weeks ago at Newburgh had delighted the people : though at the time Fr. O'Reilly had said that it was too discursive and not animated. The people had not liked as much the flowery sermon of Fr. Farrelly of Rondout the following Sunday. Fr. O'Reilly left by neglect Sizer's phrenological description of his head. His brain is 22 inches : The greater part of the qualities were placed at no. 6. Spirituality was a no. 4 : I'm sorry to say that on this day his spirituality was no. 6 : he was in consequence in libero pede. Dr. McGlynn and I hunted up some of

June

Brownson's reviews at the Mercantile library, to which we are both associated : to give matter for a debate to the students of Manhattan college on the perfectibility of human nature by reason or by grace : which the Dr. at the request of Brother Patrick is superintending. Fr. McGrath said mass and breakfasted with me : He told me that the diocese of Sandwich under Bishop   , receives a great many suspended priests and is therefore always in hot water. He agreed that from Ireland we could easily get many young and smart and good priests : but in Ireland there is an impression that they are not wanted. I heard confessions all the afternoon.

Thurs., 15th   Corpus Christi. I sang High-mass, assisted by Fr. McGrath and a Jesuit Scholastic M. Regnaud. We had solemn procession and benediction. I preached on the B. Sacrament. Fr. McGrath and Mr. Berryan dined with me. The conversation fell on the Fenians : who argue against Maynooth students that they take an oath to defend the B. government. I asked why must B. American bishops and especially U. S. bishops act as British spies in denouncing the Fenians? Dr. McGlynn took me down to visit a man by the name of Reilly in St. James parish who is dying, who did a great deal for the children's improvement. He told how Fr. Brennan had frequently desired not to be bothered by the children's confessions. He had taken all the St. James' parish children from Mr. Van Meter's proselytising school-house, and had initiated a custom of providing daily dinner of meat & soup for poor Catholic children. Dr. McGlynn told me how Brennan had been accused of keeping a married relation away from her husband and living with himself frequently, perhaps not cum commersio, though it was suspected.

Fri., 16th   Fr. Killeen visited me. He is building a house for

June   74

himself at Redbank : it will cost $3500. He uses his own money : but
will be paid back by his parish. He could get no mortgage in New York,
where no one wishes to mortgage property out of the state. His parish
embraces Long Branch and Sandy Hook. He told me of a Mrs. Garrick who
is a parishioner of St. Ann's who knew Brennan well, and wished to have
nought to do with him because constantly getting drunk at her house.
Fr. Killeen told me too that a brother and sister of a girl with whom
Brennan had a malpractice had asked Fr. Starrs to stop it, whilst Abp.
Hughes was in Europe : but Fr. Starrs declined touching the case till
the Abp.'s return. Fr. Killeen told me too that Abp. Hughes with other
priests had engaged a girl to kiss Dr. Cummings in the public street, to
ruin him : this was told by the girl on her death-bed and Fr. Thos.
Farrell got a note from her testifying to this fact, lest any harm should
ever come to Dr. Cummings from it : because she did her part. Dr. McGlynn
called in the afternoon. A Mr. Gamble of St. James' parish had told him
that he was the accuser of Fr. Brennan : that Starrs reproached Fr. Con.
O'Callaghan of not having told of Brennan, (though Starrs knew all about
Brennan's doings) and advised Gamble not to bring the complaint to the
Archbishop. But Gamble has been threatened of his life in an anonymous
note : which is suspected to come from a hanger-on of St. James' church
who was peculating there : and making love to the servant girl. Dr.
McGlynn and I took a look at a church in King St. for sale : It will hold
about 600 persons; & can be bought for $18 000. It was a D. Reformed
church. We strolled to the battery : where the barracks have been lent
in part to the Christian commission for poor Union refuges.

Sat. 17th   I went to the Burtsells in 4th Ave. to recommend a Miss
McCarthy grand-niece of Bishop McCarthy of Killarney and recommended by

June   75

Bishop Moriarty of Killarney, as good and very well educated. Bishop Moriarty's brother is married to a Morrogh, second cousin of mine : but the Morrogh family has a much higher position in the County of Cork : in fact is the principal Irish family of the place. In the afternoon the confessions were very straggling : I suppose because they were heard on Wednesday evening.

<u>Sun., 17th</u>   I preached at 7 o'clock, at 10½ o'clock and after Vespers to the Sodality on the B. Eucharist : and to the boys on the 10th article and to the girls on the 7th. Fr.   teacher of Belles Lettres at St. Francis Xav.'s college heard confessions and sang H. Mass. At dinner I had a discussion with him on Slavery. He thought that the negroes' condition would be made worse by emancipation. I thought the war would damage them as the whites of the South. But the South alone is accountable for the war. Freedom would improve the negroes. He though that the South should have prepared them for freedom by degrees, and the Church's influence should have first been extended to them. I replied the South was extending slavery, with the help of many Northerners : and the Church had no prospect of reaching the negroes for a very long time. Therefore we should not keep the negro in bondage till the conversion of the South, and it would be better for the negroes to be Methodists with a sprinkling of Xtianity than to be idolators. I pointed to how Catholic Cuba treated the negroes : how this was in great measure the fault of the priests. He then vindicated the priests by saying that Fr. and Fr. Delawine and Meagher who had lived in Spanish America found a great many good priests and not many bad ones. I brought up incontestable evidence that in Mexico many had concubines not in the cities but in the villages. He said that the spoliation of the church would be a practical good to the church in Mexico.

June 76

In the evening I visited the McLaughlins. John had been very ill the last week : I visited also Dr. Morrogh's and the Morroghs of 26th St. with my mother.

<u>Mon., 19th</u> With Dr. McSweeny I took a morning walk : and in the afternoon we went to visit Drs. Freel and Gardiner, both of whom we found not home. We then visited Fr. Fitzpatrick of the Amer. college of Rome who is at St. Patrick's : where we found Dr. Freel. Fr. Fagan the pastor was unsettled in mind by drink : he is vulgar in look, and is known as a hater of the negro. The conversation of us Romans fell on the letters that appeared in the Herald accusing and vindicating Fr. W. McCloskey of the Amer. college of Rome of secession sympathies. The attack was by a Protestant who seemed to have learned some of the secret history of the college : for Fr. McCloskey had actually abolished the 4th of July holiday not to hurt the feelings of the Southerners : and had also thought anarchy to be the necessary consequence of Lincoln's assassination. He had forbidden 35 Northerners to speak on politics, lest 6 Southerners fed by Northern money should have their feelings hurt. And he always praised the Southerners very highly : saying nothing of the Northerners. All the Northern students disliked him. The subject of politics was continually discussed however. Dr. Corrigan of Seton Hall wrote a poor vindication calculated to make the charge more grievous, saying that far from being a rabid secessionist, Dr. McCloskey deplored the war. What a contraposition! He said that he did not approve of the exterminating theories of Americans travelling abroad rather than performing field service at home. That Bishop Lynch was received in the college to examine his Theological students. That the rector of the college did not influence the education of the students, because they attended the lectures of the

June

Propaganda where Catholic theology was taught rather than transmarine secession. He agreed himself 'unus ex proto alumnis.' I expected better English and more common sense from Dr. Corrigan : whom I formerly esteemed but whom I find to have been despised by the 'American' students as too girlish, and narrow-minded. Dr. McSweeny spoke disrespectfully to Freel of B. Laughlin. Dr. Freel is suspicious, ever intriguing, thinking that no one ever acts honestly. I never liked him since I knew him. I was his prefect in Propaganda where he wanted to force me to show favour to him in preference to other students. I declined and a rupture ensued. He is so anxious not to compromise himself that no news can be had of him. He praised B. Laughlin for anxiety to learn : and for his zeal. B. Laughlin is stupid, ignorant, and petty in his ideas. He was once scandalised that Dr. McSweeny said Christ could have chosen a more rapid means than confession of pardoning sins! Dr. Freel is not liked by anyone whom I know. Fr. Nilan had called to see me but I returned too late to see him. In the evening I went to hear Miss A. L. Durgon's literary recitations. She read a dialogue from Murphy's "Three weeks after marriage" very poorly. She recited Lewis' Maniac with animation, and Mrs. Norton's 'Binges on the Rhine' very well but from Shakespeare's Romeo and Juliet very poorly.

Tues., 20th We went (Dr. McSweeny and I) to visit Fr. Conron of New Brighton, who gave us a lunch. We discussed the question of education. Fr. Conron said that he would not send a boy destined to the priesthood to any college in the U. States : Ireland was better to preserve the boy's innocence. He had known many who had lost their vocation in even our Catholic colleges. I said : that happened because no zealous priest kept an eye on them. I mix in with St. Ann's boys and could find out of 30 boys at least seven who would become good priests, if I had the means and time

June   78

to attend to them. Fr. McGean had thought the St. Ann's boys were more
forward and independent than Irish boys or than was good for them. I
differ from him : because I know more of them, I can with reason deny
his assertion. I declaimed against Italian customs such as hand-kissing,
foot-kissing etc. being made a part of the universal ceremonies of the
church : just as Parisian customs would not be made holy, or beautiful if
Paris were the centre of unity. Dr. McSweeny remarked that Dr. McGlynn &
I who once were over zealous of obedience to authority were now approaching
the other extreme. I replied that we upheld obedience, but required
authority to be reasonable in it's dictates. A diocese or the Universal
church is not to be governed as a large friary or college. Fr. Conron
has taken a dislike to his neighbour Fr. Lewis, a German, who is generally
considered as mean. He corrected Fr. Conron before many laymen for a
presumed inaccuracy in this title for a Society 'a mutual benefit and
benevolent Soc.' He had originated a company to get coal cheaper : and
backed out of it, because coal was offered him for nothing on this condition.
He lives with his niece and her husband, whom the people says to be dressed
and fed by their money, and in grand style. He calls his people to a
strict account for their Easter dues. He speaks of Fr. Conron as being
too young not to need his guidance. It rained before we got home: where
we had an evening dinner. I attended the conference of St. Vincent de Paul :
whose members I advised to be kind and charitable when they had to refuse
assistance to anyone : making profession of charity they were to be delicate
in it's exercise. I visited afterwards the Burtsells, who are doing what
they can for Miss McCarthy : whom they like for her goodness, and whose
pronunciation of French they deem good, whilst her English is mixed with
Irish idioms. Her nervousness prevented her from displaying skill in music.

June

She had not been properly taken care of at the Sisters of Mercy, who sent her to a place where she had to sleep with four other girls in one bed : who were lazy and impudent and fond of talking with men.

Wed., 21st   Dr. McGlynn dined with me. We went to Fr. Thos. Farrell's where we discussed which Ave. was the best place for the Dr.'s church. Mr. Price the Stuart-Estate agent offers two place 1 Cor. Hudson & Vestry Sts, 115 by 75, the other Cor. Hudson & Watts Sts, 115 by 100, without mention of price. We met Cavanagh who said that $10 000 a lot was not too much. The church in King St. was not to be let, though Cavanagh offered five years rent in advance. I went to Mrs. McGlynn's where Mary her daughter sang for us. She is a good girl of about 17 years, her education was neglected in her childhood by the mother who thought health better than instruction : the mother gave me an account of Dr. Cummings' building. He had bought 7 lots on 27th St. & 4th Ave. for $14,000 for which he got $45000 from the H. R. R. Co and then built his present church : where he paid $3000 a lot. The McGlynns were among the first contributors. Frank McGlynn a former co-student of mine in Propda is married in California and has a child : Andrew too who had been in Propda and then tried the Jesuits is principal of a public school in S. Francisco. I brought Dr. McGlynn to see St. Ann's literary class play Hamlet : Tessier as Horatio and J. Burke as Ghost spoke well.

Thurs., 22nd   Mr. Durenberg, the Jew-convert, desires me to get him another place where he will not be tantalised by Protestants for his being led by his lady-love to join the Catholic church. He spoke highly of the Passionists, of Hoboken whom he supposed to have been once wicked men now doing penance. He asked whether he would be received among them : he thought then he would be saved from the mockery of his friends. I visited

June

Miss T. Waters 177, 10th St. to arrange about the children singing High-Mass in August : she fears the children will not be steady in coming for the rehearsals. Dr. McGlynn dined with me : then we started for Coney Island and being caught in a thunder-storm started for Dr. Morrogh's : whose ideas we asked concerning a church to be built between his and Dr. Cummings. He thought it would stop his church altogether : but has no good reason for such belief. Not more than 6000 persons out of at least 20000 in his parish can get in his church on Sundays to hear the 5 masses there said. In the evening Dr. McSweeny called to see me. He says that Fr. Starrs now advocates the experiment of a coloured church, and also the increasing the number of priests and churches in the city.

<u>Fri., 23rd</u>   I heard the confessions of the children of the church of the Holy Cross (Fr. McCarthy, pastor) during the morning. I went to 27 Park Avenue to see Bishop Rosecrans, who was not staying at Mr. Grace's as I had heard. We saw Mr. Grace, who is a Dutchman and presented himself in shirt-sleeves. Dr. McGlynn and I talked about a variety of subjects, rehearsing for the future debates with the Abp. about Ecclesiastical matters. At Fr. McCarthy's we denounced the Chancery office, where Mr. O'Connor, a layman grants dispensations of the banns, filling up blanks where Fr. Preston's name is printed or Fr. Starrs' is previously signed. What a mortification for a man asking a dispensation in consequence of a committed sin, to be scanned by a layman, who has known the story from the priest's letter directed to the Rev. chancellor! Why make money the sole reason for dispensing from the law of the banns! It is thought by some priests that Mr. O'Connor gave dispensations from the invalidating impediments! The whole system of church government in this country is disordered. The E. authorities give the care of orphan asylums reforma-

tories etc. to laymen, whilst the clergy that has to collect the monies has no voice in their direction. Mr. J. B. Nicholson gave a permission of entry to the orphan asylum for two half-orphans to a Michael Connolly, whom he mistook for the judge, at the same time that he declined giving admittance to an orphan child just taken from a Protestant institution, who had no one by whom to be taken care of : and was recommended most pressingly by Fr. McCarthy : and refused 'for want of room'. Dr. McGlynn was never refused at any application that he made, and he thinks it all came from J. B. Nicholson knowing Mrs. McGlynn. The Authorities fear being questioned on the Calvary Cemetery monies. Fr. Starrs once told Fr. Farrell that it was an improper question to ask what revenue came from Calvary cemetery. Fr. Preston said that at least the revenue is equal to $30000. The Abp. gets $1, for every paying interment of an adult in the cemetery. Thus he gets $5000 for salary : at least $4,000 from the cathedraticum and at least $5000 from Calvary besides the perquisites for marriages, baptisms, funerals etc. to which he is frequently called. And he says that we cannot support more priests!

Sat., 24th   I went to Astor-house to see Bishop Rosecrans, he had left the hotel. I bought to-day an alapaca coat for $5 and a panama straw hat for $15. In the afternoon Fr. Lancake assisted me to hear the confessions : but the people came in very stragglingly. Our 10½ o'clock congregation has principally gone to the country, and taken their help with them: This accounts for the falling off of confessions : Fr. Preston too had a system of putting off people with even venial sins or imperfections : which made the confessional be repeatedly crowded. Sometimes he put off servant girls for four or five weeks running : which I have heard denounced as an intolerable inconvenience by families whose help they were. I spoke with

June 82

Fr. Lancake in favour of negro-emancipation. He thought that slavery was wrong : but that the Church alone could properly prepare the negro for freedom. I said the Church was doing nothing for him : why should he wait so long to attain a partial good.

Sun., 25th   Sunday. I sang H. Mass. Fr. Johan preached at 10½ o'c. on 'presumption and despair' with the day's gospel as his text. Showing them to be two dangers equally to be avoided by a Christian. I afterwards had a long talk with him on the Germans. He said that in Missouri the Germans are infidels who will laugh at a priest that speaks to them on religious matters : they never go to Church. In Cincinnati diocese they build fine churches but care not for the support of the priest : for which he accounted by the fact that in Germany priests are supported by the government and they have not been made to understand the different position of the clergy here : otherwise they would contribute quite liberally. He reproved the anxiety of German priests in New York to get the Irish to their church instead of the Germans : because the former pay most to the priests. The Germans become jealous and don't go to church in consequence of the preference shown to the Irish. A Fr. Raffeiner a flighty-genius was formerly vicar-general for the Germans : but since his death several years ago no one has been appointed in his place : though it be necessary for them to have somebody to superintend the Germans of the diocese. Our ordinary authorities almost ignore their existence. The German priests deplore the neglect in which their people are left. I told him of my experience of Fr. Ludolget lately dead who was pastor of the church on 31st St. near 6th Ave. who once gave me the B. Sacrament in the worst pix that he had : that I might give communion to a dying man, but suspecting me to be an imposter he would not trust with me a precious pix. A man who acted as German pastor during 4 years at Poughkeepsie left suddenly and is now suspected not to have been a priest. He allowed a child to carry the B. Sacrament for him, and refused to assist any dying person, who had been to his Easter communion, saying this to have been sufficient. I attacked Fr. Johan on the abolition question : he thought a serfdom should have been made a step to perfect emancipation. I said that total emancipation would more rapidly ennoble the blacks. He thought that the cruelty of the whites would exterminate the race. I praised the abolitionists for their intelligence and good motives : he thought that it was merely a struggle between commercial and agricultural interests. I said slave labour was the curse of the South : free-labor will push it onwards, in the way of civilization. He thought that white labour alone would be employed : the blacks think freedom to be an exemption from work. I replied : the blacks will work not to starve; That we shall have a police system to prevent vagrancy and stealing and murder (which he said would be quite frequent in the South) and that if this gave us great trouble, we deserved it on account of the inhuman way in which the blacks have been treated. Fr. Johan is a German from Breslau, who was obliged to give up his Prussian citizenship when he went to Rome to study. There he spent two years of novitiate in the Jesuit order, three years of study of Theology, and taught for two years Mathematics in Modena, whence he was expelled as a Jesuit in 1848 by the Piedmontese : his bishop declined to receive him till the Prussian obnoxious law was repealed and he came to America, where he says he is proud of American citizenship and would now fearlessly return to Prussia as an American citizen : (though during the war he sympathised with Secession). I preached on SS. Peter and Paul at 9 o'clock, on the resurrection of the body to the boys, on the

June   84

Holy Ghost to the girls, and on St. John the Baptist to the Sodality of
men after Vespers, giving them the Baptist as their model in the spirit
of prayer, and of self-denial. In the evening I refused to marry Lucian
Conterno to Annetta Cannatta because when I asked Mr. Conterno whether he
had gone to his confession, he replied that this was not his religion. I
told him that dispensation of the banns did not suffice to let him be married : with such a profession, he should get a dispensation as a heretic.
He said that he would go either to a Protestant minister or another priest :
I replied that sin would be against his soul in his going to a Prot. minister : as to the dispensation, it was directed to me; I should not give it
to him to be used by another priest. I would give him a note to-morrow
to have the dispensation-fine returned to him. They thought that I would
be much chagrined at the loss of the marriage-fee. I am sorry for the
girl who is really good. I would have let the man's sin in receiving the
sacrament unworthily fall on his own head, that she might not suffer from
his sinfulness : but they spoke so that I could not compromise the matter
without lowering myself, as if anxious to get the marriage-fee : which
they expressly offered as an inducement. In the evening I visited the
Morroghs of 26th St. stopping on my way at the McLaughlins. I saw Dr.
Archibald Morrogh & wife : and Charline Philipsee, daughter of Mrs. Jas.
Morrogh by a former husband. She is a Protestant and quite prejudiced
against Catholics. I manage to keep on the peaceful side with her by
speaking favourably of the talents of Protestant ministers and others whom
I know, and also by clinging to the ultra American ideas. She is to be
married shortly. I sent up my 'cartes de visite' of the Morrogh family
in Ireland to them, and pointed the various persons whom I had seen but
three years ago on my way through Ireland to America from Rome.

June   85

Dr. Archibald is sure to muddle his brain by drink : and his tongue is thick so that his conversation is very limited. His wife is chatty, but not at all interesting.

Mon., 26th   Fr. Cornell presented himself quite abruptly to enjoy the hospitality of our house, because I had invited him to dinner. He quartered himself on me without invitation for the next week previous to his departure for Europe. He is a friend of Fr. Preston's, once belonging to the Redemptorist order which he left without permission of the Superiors or the Holy See, and had been received into the Newark diocese where he was discontented with S. Amboy, his parish, and then taken to the Boston diocese. He is a musician, and his taste in music is considered quite refined. Fr. Malone called to see me : he invited me to preach at his church on Sunday evening but he let me off that I might be present at Fr. McCarthy's dinner with the Abp. Fr. Donnelly came to have translated certain indulgences affixed to a medal gotten out by himself in Rome with St. Michael on one side, and the pope on the other. I showed him the translation in the Sodality book : they were the usual indulgences granted to medals : which the pope granted to his newly coined medal by special request. Mr. Conterno of last evening's adventure returned to get a note demanding the restitution of the dispensation money. He had gone to St. Stephen's hoping to find Dr. Cummings but saw Fr. Gambeville, who refused to marry him because out of the parish : he then went to a Methodist minister who married him. He explained that he did not profess Catholicity, and had no objection to be called a Protestant : he had wished to accomodate himself to the young lady's taste. I had told him before that I would get for him the dispensation 'mixtae religionis'. I pity the poor girl who was good. Dr. McGlynn called to see me and we talked a great

June   86

deal about the good we can do by declaiming against church abuses. He
approved my conduct with Mr. Conterno. We agreed that Abp. McCloskey's
vanity would not allow him to imitate Abps. Spalding and Purcell who have
shown great energy in correcting abuses and providing more priests. Abp.
Spalding requires each parish to educate several young men for the priesthood. Here we have no other female order to supervise every work but the
Sisters of Charity : and no other male order but the Jesuits : both are
old, fogyish. We agreed that Cavanagh is not the best real-estate agent :
he has not half the sharpness that Americans generally show. We agreed
that Fr. Cornell's conduct with me was excessively boorish, almost author-
ising me to refuse hospitality to him. We took an ice-cream in a Broadway
store Cor. of 12th St.

Tues., 27th   The O'Reillys visited me, before starting for New
Rochelle where they will stay for the summer. They told me that the Jesuits visited them very frequently : and pretended that they belonged to the
16th St. congregation though they came to St. Ann's. They live in 17th
St. near 6th Ave. At breakfast I spoke to Fr. Cornell strongly in favour
of the Abolitionists, whom I said to be men of good intentions, and smart
minds : and are to be distinguished from the Republicans who are politicians. V. Philips, G. Smith, L. Garrison etc. are earnest men, Regmous &
Summer etc. may trim their sales according to self-interest. Slavery was
a curse on the country. He expressed great dislike to New Englanders :
and said the church never spoke against slavery but it's abuses : and
St. Paul required the obedience of Onesius to his master : I replied :
among New Englanders hypocrisy is the only vice that is conspicuous : thus
to be respected, one had to put on the semblance of virtue : which shows
that virtue is held in respect there. The Church compromised often, where

June

87

it shouldn't have done so. To-day the Church compromises and we criticise the action of old-fogy and cowardly men who presently represent the church. The Church even to convert from paganism did not require civil laws against it, when it could and perhaps should have had them passed. St. Paul required obedience to civil authority : and yet rebellion was at times lawful. And if any people ever had the right to rebel, the blacks south have a right to rebel : and consequently any nation has a right to help them to gain their freedom. We parted on very friendly terms. Yet I saw nothing of Fr. Cornell after this. He took his bag from the house without saying good-bye. In the evening I took tea at the Decoppets who had just returned from a three weeks residence at Stratford near Bridgeport, Connecticut, which they described as a most lovely place. Mr. Decoppet is a protestant of very little talkative powers : and he and I come generally to a dead lock in conversation. Mrs. Decoppet thinks that I don't like to speak to Protestants. She is greatly mistaken. She is 55 years old : he about forty : they have one daughter, a doll of 7 summers : with no brains, but pretty. The conference of St. Vincent de Paul met as usual : but I said nothing : not considering their meeting as an occasion for preaching. We hardly have anything in our parish that comes under the direct object of the conference : Their business-meetings are dull and of stale routine. We have no poor. The 1st Secretary of the general council hoped that we should have some poor to be taken care of in the winter. I think they could be made good use of for the care of the Spanish children : except that they look too much to the letter of their rules : almost having a superstitious reverence for the decrees of the French council. I think too that influence could be made to bear on them for carrying through Catholic ideas of a school-system in political voting. I was called to see Miss Mary

June

McKnight who was taken with cramps in the stomach : and is in great danger of dying. Eventually consumption will take her life. These attacks have been frequent and each time increase in bad effects.

<u>Wed., 28th</u>   I went to Seton Hall to see the exhibition. The speeches were very poor. Two of the Philadelphia Tiers spoke. Another young man spoke on self knowledge : the speech consisted in cutting up every one and every thing but self. Fr. McQuade spoke to the people in a most tedious and mountebank way, holding up Seton Hall as the model of colleges. The music was tolerable only, by the college boys. We met there Fr. Jas. O'Connor formerly of Pittsburgh now President of the Philadelphia Seminary. He stopped for the night at the S. Orange house, a mile from the college. He is quite unassuming. We had a long talk with him on church-matters and bishops : He had been obliged to leave Pittsburgh seminary by calumnies of his bishop Domeneck : the smallest man that could be found in the country. He was accused of being frequently absent from the seminary, and thus not giving class : and of giving many general holidays. He had given 3 holidays, and been absent seven days : so the Seminarians voluntarily testified. B. Domeneck accused Dr. Keogh of bad administration of the monies. A committee appointed by the bishop acquitted Dr. Keogh who required an apology of the bishop, who was even ready to sign one : and made it before his council. The bishop sought an excuse to bring in the Lazarists; he had belong to their order : but the priests of the diocese opposed this design. In the evening I left Fr. Jas. O'Connor with the understanding that he should take up his headquarters at St. Ann's in New York. I attended the altar and literary classes : the last I adjourned till September.

<u>Thurs., 29th</u>   With Fr. Jas. O'Connor I went to St. John's college's

exhibition at Fordham. The discourses of the graduates were well written but with nothing to relieve the monotony. A Wm. Daintz speaking on modern republicanism, allowed that no other nation especially of Southern Europe & America was fit for a republican form of government but the United States. He spoke especially of the South American people as 'irreligious, at church in the morning and in the evening brandishing the stilletto, disorderly, fit only to be ruled by the iron hand of authority.' I found out afterwards that it was merely the outpouring of hostile sentiments had against the Spanish-American students in the college : other graduates asked in surprise 'how could the Spanish-American boys be kept in order without being thrashed, or treated as the United States' boys. Dr. Ives gave the address to the graduates, in which he warned them that now they were to go on unknown seas : but that they had a steady pilot, the Catholic faith, to guide them to a safe port, if they did not reject it's guidance. He recommended them to be careful to select a good wife to accompany them on their trip : and to remember that they were called upon to perform duties to God, to Society and to themselves : they would have to answer for their superior training, if they did not bring forth fruit corresponding to the care taken of them. The Archbishop congratulated the young men in the delight and pleasure and gratification which they showed themselves so able to afford himself and the rest there present. The exhibition was held on the lawn in front of the college. The Jesuits entertained us afterwards with a sumptuous dinner. Dr. McGlynn accompanied us home : and Fr. Jas. O'Connor gave us a description of the state of society in Propaganda when he was there in 1848. The Jesuits ruled the college, and Fr. Bresciani was superior : deceit and calumny were constantly used against the students. Fr. Jas. O'Connor was accused of having insulted the professor of

June 90

dogma, Sottovia, and called to account by Mgr. Barnabo, who first grew angry with him but was soon convinced of his innocence. Fr. Bresciani pretended not to know anything of the accusation but had been the accuser himself to get Fr. Jas. O'Connor turned out of the college, but failed. Fr. Jas. asked himself then to be ordained in his 3rd year, lest they should devise more cunning plots against him. He does not speak harshly of the Jesuits : but thinks them a good society, too zealous and not honest in their means of doing good : hence they attain a rapid popularity and as rapidly lose it.

Fri., 30th   In the morning I heard confessions of the children at the church of the H. Cross. Many children about 13 were making their 1st or 2nd confession, 1st communion and receiving confirmation at the same time. In the afternoon Drs. Morrogh & McGlynn & Fr. Jas. O'Connor & I took a ride to H. Bridge of which the height is 120 ft and is about 2000 ft. long. It is the aqueduct bringing the Croton water to the city. We visited Manhattanville, where our discourse fell on the Ives' family, of which one member being a priest married a protestant, who left him when converted to the true church. She fell back to sin with him, but now he has been persuaded by Fr. Duranquet the Jesuit to bury himself in a Carthusian monastery. Fr. Jas. O'Connor knew him in Propaganda : his manners were charming and very easily attracted the everyone's sympathies. He had led a poor life : was ordained at Munich by recommendation of the Jesuit's for B. Henni's diocese. He had led a sensual life beforehand, and Fr. Jas. O'Connor had stated that he would turn out 'in resurrectionem vel ruinam multorum'. Dr. McGlynn took Fr. O'Connor to his mother's and both slept at our house.

July   91

Sat., 1st   I visited Miss McKnight who is much better. I had Fr. Lancake S. J. to assist me in the confessional. I showed him an attack in the Tribune against Mr. Dainty's speech on Modern republicanism insinuating that the Hispano-Americans were kept unfit for republicanism by Catholicity. Fr. Lancake showed no anxiety about the article : as he had half made up his mind not to read newspapers anymore. He thought that they distracted him too much. Fr, O'Connor told me that B. Rappe of Cleveland forbade his clergy to keep brandy in their houses, which makes them hypocrites, for they keep it, but pretend never to drink. A priest visiting Pittsburgh refused to drink wine, pretending teetotalism, when afterwards found drinking, gave this as the reason of his former conduct : 'that he might be told on to his bishop'. He obliges all his priests to give up all their perquisites, except the $300 salary from the church. They consequently falsify their accounts. The bishop really has no right to make them give up their perquisites : though it be to enable him to build more churches. A Bishop Young of Erie, though crack-brained is liked for his straightforward honesty. Even B. O'Connor prohibited his priests from keeping brandy at home, because he saw a pastor of a church which he was dedicating fall into the foundations from drink. But he when cooled down did not enforce the prohibition. What right has a bishop to prescribe what a priest may or may not retain in his own house. Bishop O'Connor, Fr. Jas.' brother, was a Propagandist, but ever since on the mission anxious to be a Jesuit. The appointment to the bishopric prevented this for many years. Now he is a Jesuit : He went through his novitiate in Munich : unknown as a bishop to all but the superior and one other who heard him once say 'Pax vobis' at mass.

Sun., 2nd   I preached at 7, on the Visitation : and at 10½ on the

July

Primacy of St. Peter. Fr. Lancake sang H. mass. Mr. Harrison the organist dined with us. The conversation fell on music. Fr. Lancake admired Busch's 'Stabat Mater', preferring it as sacred music to Rossini's, though Rossini's far surpassed it as music. I called Busch's abominable, from what I had heard from others. I must say that my ear is not acute enough to be a judge of music : generally I enjoy, sometimes it is so dead as not to distinguish one piece from another. I prayed fervently in my college-life that I might be enabled to sing at H. Mass with sufficient dignity and tone : I am afraid my prayers were not heard. In the evening Fr. Jas. O'Connor and I were present at a dinner given to the Archbishop by Fr. McCarthy after confirmation. The Archbishop spoke very forcibly against excursions to Jones' Woods : which have become scandalous on account of the bad characters that crowd in it. Lately at Fr. Trainor's excursion a man was killed. Eustace, a Catholic detective, has brought the best proof that the best girls have fallen into fornication at these excursions. The conductors of the 3rd Ave. cars have ordered out passengers from them, saying their cars were not to be turned into brothels. The proprietor gains ten times more than the church, by selling liquors : and Mr. Somers a Jew, the proprietor most disinterestedly was ready to affirm that no harm was ever done at these excursions. Abp. Hughes had prohibited them : but the prohibition was eluded by having the excursions no longer in boats to places outside the city as formerly but to Jones' Woods. Fr. Starrs luminously distinguished between excursions and picnics : these might be allowed, though the former were prohibited. Frs. Mooney, McCarthy and Boyce thought the excursions could be conducted decently. But the Abp. maintained that practically the abuses were inseparable from them. Fr. Jas. O'Connor approved of the Abp.'s views : saying that in the western dioceses the same

July

evils were found in excursions. The Archbishop, I think, is preparing the priests for a prohibition of excursions.

Mon., 3rd   Fr. O'Connor and I visited the Academy of design : in which the most noticeable picture was a Union Soldier dying attended by a Southerner. Two landscapes of the Wyoming Valley by Cropsey were very fine too. In the afternoon we attended the exhibition of the Sacred Heart Manhattanville : where the girls spoke most charmingly in a French piece entitled 'La Bohemienne,' their French pronunciation was very good. They also had composed a play named 'The Sicilian Vespers' in which they acquitted themselves with exceeding good taste. Everything, literature and singing, and playing bore testimony to the real progress of the pupils and the education of the teachers. I really was moved to tears by the play of the Bohemienne : in which the gipsy-girl turned out to be sister of the children that received her to partake with her their delicacies of food. They have a system of distribution, which I fear does away with emulation. Hardly anyone goes without a premium : and in public all the members of each class receive the same ornaments of wreaths and ribbons. The Archbishop, who had presided, said that since he was there, this academy had changed as if by enchantment : he was not afraid of telling the young ladies that they had succeeded, because they had a right to hear it, and this would stifle vanity, though they were young ladies. They had given a show of knowledge and virtue far more estimable than outward beauty : and the grace with which every thing proceeded had surpassed the utmost expectations. We had lunch afterwards. Then we went to Manhattan college : where the exhibition was interesting on account of the examination of one class in Persius (of whom by the by I hardly known the name in college), and of the Philosophy class in Logic and Metaphysics. The boys

July   94

spoke in Latin : of course they stammered a little but they showed of
what stuff they were really made. An extemporaneous debate too gotten
up under Dr. McGlynn's direction was very interesting. The question was
whether 'man can reach natural perfection by the power of nature alone' :
and the boys spoke very sensibly on both sides. We got home about 11
o'clock.

<u>Tues., 4th</u>   Fr. O'Connor left for Saratoga with Dr. McGlynn. Fr.
Thos Farrell visited me for a few minutes. Miss A. Burtsell called to see
me. I wrote an answer to Fr. Preston's letter written from Paris on the
16th June, in which he stated he had visited London on his way. He had
a trip of 10 days, 19 h. across the Atlantic : in good health. He had
been pleased with the Cathedral and a Corpus Xti procession at Amiens. He
stopped in the Rue St. Honore at Paris having very good quarters. In the
evening I went to see the fire-works at Madison Square : the principal
pieces represented stars of red, white and blue : the large piece represented Grant & Sherman with a motto of Victory after the figure of liberty,
and underneath the words 'A tribute to the Brave'. I afterwards visited
the Burtsells, where I criticised Peter for taking only 1 medal and 6 distinctions. They showed me the article of Sacerdos in the Herald confirming
the charges against Fr. W. McCloskey and refuting 'Unus ex proto alumnis.'
He denied that there were any alumni of the Amer. college of Rome : because
they were all graduates of other colleges. He asserted that Fr. W.
McCloskey sympathised with secessionism etc. He showed that his opinions
were not to be laid to the account of the Catholic Church. They showed
me a sermon of Fr. McQuade's at the Paulists lauding them (after a panegyric of SS Peter & Paul); they could not in modesty praise themselves.

<u>Wed., 5th</u>   I wrote to a Mrs. Ward in Boston that I could not comply

with a request made to have a pew engaged in St. Ann's for her, because
there is no vacancy. In the evening Dr. McSweeny took a walk in 5th Ave.
and afterwards went to 15th St. exhibition (of St. Franc. Xav's college).
There was very fine music. A Mr. Nevin spoke a good piece on Philosophical
teachings but with a very monotonous voice. Mr. Murphy ridiculed skepticism because it established for certain that we can be certain of nothing;
metempsichoses of Pythagoras and Empiricles. The first died because he
would not eat what once belonged to a human soul that had passed into a
lower order of creatures. The 2nd through himself into the Etna volcano.
Pythagoras was first a son of Hercules (so he said) then a warrior at the
siege of Troy, then a peacock, then a rooster, and afterwards a philosopher.
To a fly he might have had a blood relationship : and the fly might say :
with the formula of a negro at the present day : 'My friend and brother'
to Pythagoras expelling him from history. He cut up Mormonism, and Spiritism : all these were condemned as the vagaries of the human mind. Mr.
Loughran in very florid language, spoke of the language of nature, and drew
down immense applause by citing the 'immortal Shamrock' as a principal
witness of God's power of creation. A Mr. O'Connor in the master's oration
denounced Socialism for destroying the right of property, though his theme
was 'The efficacy of principle'. The delivery was good. Fr. McGean gave
the address to the graduates reminding them that the difficulties encountered in college compared with those to be found outside it's walls were
as a mound to a mountain : that they were to lead the masses by right principle, and not to be led astray by others less educated in morality than
they were; that each one owed a duty to Society proportioned to his talents,
and they consequently should be good citizens : however that religion should
be the mantle of their intellect, and morality and citizenship. The Arch-

July 96

bishop congratulated them on the discourses well written and well spoken : as also on the fine music which had diversified and relieved the entertainment. He felt that these young men were to take the van of Catholic Society : and were to leave on it the impression which they had received from their education. The Jesuits gave all the clergy present in great numbers a substantial lunch before dismissing them.

Thurs., 6th   With Frs. Nilan & C. Farrell I went in the Steamboat N Haven to the fishing banks, where an immense number of fish were caught. There was another steamboat and a schooner already there for the same purpose. The fish caught are called pogies. We started from pier No. 4 North R. & landed at Broome St. We were about 2½ hours going. I amused myself principally reading Harper's magazine and newspapers, and talking on the improvement made by the present generation in giving education to the people. Of course this was to Fr. Nilan. Fr. C. Farrell loves to be loaferish in his ways, picks up acquaintance with any and every body, dislikes all serious talk, and has a most disgustingly drawling way of telling a story. The captain & bar-tender of the boat had a rather loud talk on the proper position of the boat for fishing : the captain hardly commanded the pilot to steer properly, merely hesitatingly requested him to do so. In the evening I attended the singing-class which is preparing for H. mass in August.

Fri., 7th   I felt an excessive gloom come over me : it proceeds from want of confidence in myself. I tried to work as much as possible : and thus keep my mind from thinking of the lonesomeness which I felt. I heard the girls' confessions in the morning. I preached to the girls in the afternoon. I heard the boys' confessions in the evening : but few came : and I paid a visit to my mother.

July 97

<u>Sat., 8th</u>   My fit of melancholy continued. I went to Devlin's at the Park to buy pants ready made for which as clergyman I paid $18 : whilst otherwise I should have paid $20. I went then to Devlin's near Grand St. to have two cassocks fitted for me. They have imported a taylor from Italy for this precise purpose of making cassocks. I visited Miss M. McKnight who had recovered from her late severe attack. I found with her Fr. St. John (or Fr. Donnelly of St. Louis) who is now stationed at St. Mary's church : where he says he finds less sickness than at the Imm. Conception and far less confessions : though the parish contains more people. At St. Mary's he averages 3 sick-calls : at the Imm. Conception he averaged 10 aday. We discussed the merits of the assassin Stors' of Lincoln's case. They thought that Mrs. Surratt should not have been hanged, because a woman : I thought that should not exempt from the penalty to which the others were condemned. I went to the Burtsells in 4th Ave. : where I was told that the Dr. though milder continues to drink, and avoids me since I spoke to him; and that his grocery-bill just sent in amounted to $700, of which nothing was paid, and many other bills are due. He also at times mimics the children saying their prayers : and tells them to say Hail Columbia instead of Hail Mary! Fr. Lancake came to hear confessions, but neither of us heard more than three hours : the warm weather has caused a great falling off. Our 10½ o'clock congregation has in great measure gone to the country : they have taken with them their servant girls. Some of these generously give up their places rather than go to a country-place, where they will have no opportunity of going to mass.

<u>Sun., 9th</u>   Fr. Lancake at the 7 o'clock mass preached near 25 minutes on prayer. He had the misfortune of letting a few drops of the Precious blood fall on the corporal and through it on the altar linens. I

July 98

had to wash these and through the water into the vestry baptismal font. I said the 9 o'c. and sang the 10½ o'c. mass. Fr. Jonin preached on the necessity of forgiving our enemies : showing that nature teaches us to love our neighbours : and grace adds it's law. Even in our enemies we must recognise human nature : and the love of Christ for him. This is the mark of Christ's faithful : and in the Our Father we ask God to measure his forgiveness to us, as we give it to our neighbour. We must act in a friendly way even to him who wronged us : we need not treat him intimately. We can refuse to speak to him if his morals are corruptive : but not through dislike for him. I preached to the boys on hell : and told them to excuse themselves during the vacations from Sunday-school, but to sanctify them as St. Aloysius did, so that he was ready to die whilst playing at the hour appointed by the rule. Mr. Lovejoy assisted at H. Mass in cassock & surplice. He had been a S. school teacher two years ago in this parish. He had been also in the Jesuit noviciate : and two years ago had been accepted into Halifax diocese. He is not very brilliant : has a tendency to insanity : but yet now is very good. He was in Montreal seminary during the last year : where he found the Sulpicians very severe. The professor of Moral Theology Pere LaRue, always followed the rigid opinion where there was a discussion on a point, though he left the young to chose for themselves. In Montreal, the churches are under the control of the Sulpicians who have only one parish-church, the others being chapels : all other clergymen act by sufferance of the Sulpicians. Bishop Bouget sought to have this altered when he last went to Rome. He likes to Romanise the ceremonies, and every thing about the churches. In the evening I visited M. White an altar-boy who is sick : and also the Morroghs of 26th St. with the McLaughlins and my mother. I met there Mr. Belcher the intended of

July 99

Charline   , Mrs. Morrogh's daughter by a former husband, and still a P. Episcopalian with no prospect of becoming a Catholic.

Mon., 10th   I said Low-mass and the funeral service over Lucian Costar, and made a few general remarks on him at 9½ o'c. I suspect that the body is to be taken to Greenwood cemetery : I forgot to ask. It is prohibited in this diocese to have any funeral service over any one that is to be buried in any but a Catholic burying ground. Dr. McSweeny called to see me : and we took a ride to the Central Park, where we visited the collection of wild-animals and the statuary in the old arsenal. There were two camels, a peccary, and a few wolves, a bear and raccoons and monkeys. I noticed one raccoon kindly devouring the insects that he found on an elder one. I saw a beaver for the first time : it had a tub of water in which to swim and a platform on which to repose. American eagles were there in abundance, very poor types of American activity. The principal piece of statuary represented the States in their power of education, and invention and agriculture. I believe that the greater number are models of Crawford's. We took a lunch in the cottage and afterwards had a sail in a row boat around the lake, having a very stubborn and uncommunicative guide. Our conversation principally fell on Fr. McGean's self-assertion, who though his father and mother are of no high-class is always speaking of the circle in which he moves : and patronises every one. He has offended the Sisters of Mercy by declining to do more than was done by Fr. McNeirney when chaplain of the convent : though when he first began, he like every new broom was quite ready to do far more work and with great zeal. Fr. Maguire preached on Sunday against anger (every one mentally saying : medici, cura teipsum) and denounced all who called their neighbour a wretch : except, and this was wedged in in the Cicero pro-domo-sua style, in just indignation.

July   100

In the evening I attended the singing glass, and promised a picture to all the children who should persevere in their attendance at the rehearsals and at the singing of High mass in August. I attended a poor girl, who almost despaired of salvation because of neglect.

Tues., 11th   This morning I commenced teaching J. Burke Arithmetic and English grammar. My fit of melancholy still lasts, I endeavor to keep myself constantly engaged. I believe that bashfulness is the most prominent ingredient of my trouble : and a too unsympathetic nature, which with the help of God, I shall overcome. It impedes from entering the position of my neighbour as I feel bashful even in the company of children. I feel as if they were constantly criticising me : though in reality I know that many are much attached to me. If I live for my own enjoyment, I shall never enjoy myself : and yet I do good to others merely for the sake of enjoyment, I can gain no merit for my good deeds. In the afternoon I walked to 42nd St. to see Fr. Nilan. We talked over Gioberti's opposition to the Jesuits. Whilst I was in school with the Jesuits, I thought that they were the leaders of the age. But now I find them wishing to fossilize us with the habits of the middle ages. Especially in this New York province, the superiors are Frenchmen of very cramped minds, who denounce our institutions as they would denounce the revolution of 1793. I read a few pages of Gioberti's apology of his 'Gesuita Moderno' which gave me an appetite for more of his writings. Nilan told me of a good thought of his that the Catholic religion is like the human race, adaptable to every climate and form of government : whilst the sects are like the brute creation, only fit for a limited number of climates and forms of government. We spoke also of Galileo : of whose condemnation Bellarine was a principal agent. One Jesuit told a friend of Galileo's that had he kept friendship with the Frs. of the R. College

July 101

he would have been free to teach anything even his system of the motion of the Earth. So writes Galileo. The sentence expressly condemns Galileo's opinion of the mobility of the Sun as false in philosophy and formally heretical in Theology, as contrary to Scripture : and his opinion as to the motion of the earth as 'at least erroneous in faith' and opposed to Scripture. The text from Scripture is that : 'Terra in aeternum stat'. The Fordham Jesuits thought to quibble by saying that at that time the word 'heretical' was used to mean anything erroneous, but the words of the judgement are too clear to admit this interpretation. Fr. Nilan gave a lecture on Galileo before their literary society. To save the church's infallibility, we must say that the matter was not a fit subject of it's definitions of faith. But was it not a dogmatical fact? I shall give this subject greater attention. We both agreed that probably the pope will have to give up his temporal power : it is better then that we should prepare the church to do without it. In the evening I assisted at the conference of St. Vincent de Paul : where I proposed a new census of the parish for the beginning of September that I might know where to find the children of Catholics for our Catholic schools. I went afterwards to see Miss Adelaide McKnight who was taken with a sudden fit from which her father feared that she would not recover. I met there Frs. C. Farrell & St. John. I was reminded by the conduct of Fr. C. Farrell of the exhortations that an old missionary to china, P. Hurpiere's who lived in Propaganda, gave to English speaking students of never going to tea-parties, where young ladies were present. He joked about her beau (neck-tie?) not being pleasing to her, and said that priests had the power of administering the ring which always cured damsels of the disease of the heart, of which she complained. Pretending to be off sooner, he used it as a ruse to have a

July   102

downstairs confab with Miss Mary.

Wed., 12th   I have been using artificial engagements to get over my melancholy fit. Mr. Fairbrother called in the evening and gave me an account of how he got a Fr. Hudson a priest of a village near London, to undertake the task of getting more churches for London : and how they began at the lowest neighbourhoods of the city. He proved that 193,000 persons were not able if willing to go to church on Sundays or to confession. The first bishop to whom Fr. Hudson made this known died two days afterwards, Mr. Fairbrother thinks, of heartbreak at this news. Dr. Walsh said he would never have gone to London as bishop had he known such awful responsibilities to be connected with it. Dr. Wiseman exhorted Fr. Hudson to commence remedying this state of affairs at once. Mr. Fairbrother is writing a letter to the Archbishop showing that we are in a similar condition. He calculates our having 58 active priests and 505,000 people in New York. Mr. Fairbrother is a poor mechanic, but of a surprisingly large mind, and immense zeal. I felt abashed at my melancholy mopings inwardly, whilst his whole soul seemed to be taken up entirely with good that he seeks to do for his neighbour. He was eye-witness of a shameful act in the Cathedral, where the sexton a quarter of an hour before six on Sunday morning deliberately locked all the open pews to prevent the poor people from occupying them : and two persons died without the priest, a stone's throw from the Cathedral though the priest arrived both times after the persons' death. Mr. Fairbrother has been seeing about the letting of a school-house near Canal & Varick Sts., to be gutted for a Catholic church. It belongs to Trinity Corporation whose agent stated that he had a positive permission to let for a Catholic church, if asked for : the rent would be $3000 a year : It is 84 by 107 : 8 years of lease will be guaranteed : but

July

not a cent paid for improvements. He was anxious to communicate with Dr. McGlynn, who is out of town. In the morning I taught Mr. Derenberg his catechism; J. Burke arithmetic and Eng. grammar : visited a Mrs. McGee who has a cancer of the womb and is anxious that I should have an eye on her two sons, one 19 yrs who is dishonest, the other 17 yrs who is giddy. I went to a Mr. Cummings in 3, 3rd St. who has been drinking but would not be persuaded to give up drink till he saw me again on Friday evening. I recited the funeral service over a coloured child at 158, 10th St. and visited Ade. McKnight, who had relapsed into several fits during the day, in which she bit her lips and sought to injure others. I visited Dr. Morrogh's where I met a Mr. Dunn who is a relative of Fr. C. Farrell and is going on a three years trip to Nevada. Mrs. Dunn seemed quite an amiable lady : she is to be left at home. My mother showed great anxiety to go to Rockaway, where the sand bar has been united to the rest of the land, giving thus excellent surf bathing. I have been to Rockaway about a week of the two years since I returned from Europe. I found the Society rather poor in intellect : the well-ado lower classes abound there. Last year the bathing being wretched disgusted me with the place. I gave a grand lunch of cakes and fruit to the altar-boys, and literary-class : at which they showed their usual good humor. Fr. Jas. O'Connor and Dr. McGlynn arrived from Saratoga : with which they had been well-pleased, not having found the imagined whirl of fashion, where they did not wish it. The waters are purgative : Dr. McGlynn gained 5 pounds in a week. They had heard Bishop McFarland preach a plain sermon with good delivery but no original idea, or style. They returned disgusted with Troy Seminary, which is unfit for the purpose : 2 students sleep in one room : other rooms are hardly fit for one bed. The whole building required patching to suit it to it's new

July 104

destination. The class rooms are not airy. The chapel is a square room, without ornament. A seminary must have a fine chapel where the ceremonies will be carried out with pomp : hence the priests derive their love of ceremonies and a desire to see them well performed in their mission-churches. Fr. O'Connor remarked that Ecclesiastical blunders about buildings are the history of Sacred Architecture in the United States. Fr. Tandy the procurator, led them through the building : and impressed them that he was an obstinate self-asserting man, without brains for theories of school, or for practical management.

Thurs., 13th   We were present at the exhibition of the girls' school at Holy Cross Ch. Fr. McCarthy was detained at New Rochelle, till too late to be present more than a few minutes. The girls acquitted themselves remarkably well. A nice drama, by C. Oakely, on Wiseman's Fabiola gave the children an opportunity of displaying their declamatory powers : They took the scene of Fabiola inflicting on Lisa a wound with the stiletto : introducing Agnes, anxious to buy Lisa from Fabiola. A comic piece entitled 'Aunt Twiggle' showed their powers of acting. The music was sacred and patriotic. One piece was on the "Celtic Tongue," gave Dr. McGlynn in his congratulatory remarks an opportunity of speaking highly of Irish generosity and Irish faith, saying how now they should give to the harder enunciations of the conqueror's (English) tongue, a share of that warmth of heart which ennobled the Irish. Here in this country they had a mission from Providence to warm by the fire of divine love, those who have not the same faith : and their power must not be stiffled by selfishness even as material fire always is expansive. As fire moulds iron and steel, so their charity must mould their fellows' hearts to noble ideas. These children of Celtic blood must ever cherish the gift of faith received from their sires : as the best legacy that they could have left after them. The premiums were distributed by Fr. McCarthy at the end : the other priests absenting themselves : which I did not like for they ought to have patience & encourage the children by their presence. At dinner Fr. J. O'Connor opposed the suffrage being given to the negroes : not because he is black but ignorant. He deprecated universal suffrage, even for the whites. We condemned emphatically Stanton for having restricted Fr. Walter in his serving Mrs. Surratt, requiring that he should say nought about her innocence. He consented lest she should be deprived of the Sacraments : though he solemnly protested against the restriction. Fr. O'Connor thought Stanton to be an honest, though too impetuous man. Fr. O'Connor left during dinner for Philadelphia. In the evening Dr. McGlynn and I took a walk in which the Dr. gave me some items about B. Dominec he had from Fr. J. O'Connor viz : that a young lady worked constantly in his room, that he boasted to a private family of having cheated his order of $3000, that he wilfully accused the Fr. J. O'Connor & Dr. Keogh of peculating at the Seminary, after the committee appointed by himself declared the charge unfounded : that the priests of his Cathedral talk disparagingly of him : that 5 shop-keeping ladies form his board of consultation : that his society is detested by the families that he visits etc. etc.

<u>Fri., 14th</u>   With Dr. McGlynn I went to visit the Trinity Corporation school to see how adapted it may be for a Catholic church. It is 67 by 57 : has three floors and a garret : by gutting it, the two lower floors may be a church about 30 feet high. The walls are very solid. Mr. Fairbrother acted as our guide. Three persons called on him offering $3000 a year for it. The highest floor can be used as a Sunday-school, St. Vincent's conferences or Adult boys' dormitory. The Dr. seems anxious to have something of this last description. Mr. McCready who studied in Maynooth 4 years,

July

and not ordained because too taciturn, and 1 year in Mt. St. Mary's where he taught Mathematics, dined with us. He said the system of the seminary teaching and being prefects at the college gave them no time to study. At least one half of the seminarians were lately from Ireland : those more fourth Irish-born though some years in this country : the rest were natives. Dr. McCaffrey has a large mind : but is a secessionist. Fr. J. McClosky is very hesitating even about letting a boy buy a neck-tie : is Northern in sentiment. Fr. McMurdy the rector of the Seminary and teacher of both Moral and Dogmatic Theologies and attends sick calls is a secessionist. Dr. McCaffrey wrote a letter to Dr. McGlynn saying that Mr. McCready is smart and good : but not sufficiently well-known to be recommended for the priesthood : and reminded the Dr. that the superiors of Mt. St. Mary's always are above selfish motives in approving candidates for Holy Orders. Our day school ended to-day for this year without exhibition.

Sat., 15th   Fr. Lancake arrived at $6\frac{1}{2}$ o'c. to hear confessions. Dr. Brann and a seminarian Mr. Walsh called to see me. The latter smoked my cigars, without permission. The former asked me a loan of $50, which, taught by Dr. McSweeny's experience, who was insulted by him for a like kindness, I declined. He thought that at the next meeting of the Theological Society, an election of officers must be proposed : he thought Dr. Cummings would not consent to it. He said that Abp. Spalding had inaugurated a similar society in Baltimore : and there was one too at Cincinnati. I visited Ade. McKnight who is still sick and gave communion to Michael White.

Sun., 16th   We recommended very strongly the helping the reformatory schools : of which the corner-stone is to be laid on next Sunday 23rd inst. Fr. Lancake stated that Christ would repay a hundredfold interest for the capital that we should lend him, by giving to the poor. And again he is the only absolute owner and master of all things : we are only the administrators for him and the poor. He spoke at H. Mass on the Scapular : instituted by Simon Stock superior of the Carmelites, whose beginning dates back to the Apostles, and they were always remarkable for devotion to the B. Virgin. The B. Virgin promised that none should perish eternally who wore the scapular at the hour of death : he said that one who was to be damned would lay aside the scapular at that time, or before it. He had read of a man who sought to commit suicide by drowning, and after 5 attempts succeeded only when he took off the scapular. In the afternoon to the Sodality I spoke on the subject, giving Gaume's ideas as expressed in the 8th book of the Catechism of Perseverance. Fr. Lancake speaks well : and has a very good delivery : and descriptive power. He described Simon Stock in his tree, and partaking of herbs and spring-water, quite graphically : as also the suicide, who was once pious, afterwards steeped in vice, drinking vice etc. etc. Mr. Harrison and Mr. Lovejoy, dined with us. Our conversation fell on French ceremonies : and the Romanising tendencies of French bishops, which I thought of no great utility. Mr. Lovejoy found the Sulpicians severe against Secret Societies under which class they held the Fenians to be considered. I gave him my notions that they were not plotting against religion nor a lawful government and therefore not technically a secret society. We had no Sunday-school. I sang H. Mass and Vespers and in the evening went to the McLaughlins and to my mother's where Fr. Profillet told me that the Haytians forced him to leave the island because he sought to reform abuses. There had been a Schism in Hayti. The president of the republic appointed the priests, who were of course bad ones, and sought only money, and had children publicly recognised as such. The Haytians are all negroes : some of whom are well educated and

July 108

smart men : but the government is too weak to stop abuses. The people are outwardly religious, give as much money as the priest wants if he obeys them implicitly, have High Mass sung (if the priest is sick or too drunk to appear, have grand processions in Holy Week, where immoralities are plentiful since they last till midnight : and once surrounded Fr. Profillet's house to kill him, because he refused to sing Mass on Christmas night, whilst prostitutes etc. etc. were carrying on in the Church. He was obliged to fly by night-time : accompanied by two men armed to the teeth. The Haytians speak a patois French and childishly. In church they kiss their hands to every image or picture : go to confession and Communion frequently : but are an immoral set. Mr. Lancake told me that only by strict economy, and because the individual Jesuits did receive no money, the 10th St. college was made a paying establishment.

<u>Mon., 17th</u>   Mrs. Burtsell visited me and told me that Dr. Morrogh had been in bad humour for the last few days, the result of the usual cause of his troubles. He has to collect soon $60000. Dr. McSweeny and I took a long stroll in Central park. We talked on Abp. McCloskey's fairness, when as pastor of St. Joseph's he vanquished the trustees his opponents, by never speaking ill of them. Bishop Dubois used to receive commands from the trustees' wives about the subject to be chosen for his Sunday sermon. The seminary of St. Joseph's fell under our censure : on account of the seminarians' immorality who with Fr. O'Brien their professor visited often the low dens of Mercer St. : and this professor in Moral class proposed the most obscene queries. So says Fr. Maguire. In the evening Dr. McIntyre a Propagandist, of Kingston, C. W., diocese, took tea. I had never known him before. He is broken down by drink and I fear, has gone further. I declined allowing him to sleep on our parlor-sofa or in our house : I gave

July

him $4,50. He left Propaganda in 1843 : could have commanded sufficient respect, by a good head : but drink has lowered him!

<u>Tues., 18th</u>   Dr. Sweeny and I took a trip to Green Wood Cemetery, where we walked around, finding it to be a finely laid out villa, but not having the appearance usual to cemeteries. We hoped that Calvary cemetery would preserve a more religious aspect. From this we descended to consider where the revenues of Calvary were stowed away : they are supposed to be $60000 per year. Why not educate with this money more priests and build more churches! Where does the dispensation money go in the Chancery? Fr. Preston has the reputation of being the most charitable man in the United States : is it a wonder when he can give in charity the immense sums had for dispensations? for they have no other established object for which to be disposed. It is a crying shame that for money a dispensation is at once given. Fr. Starrs never asks any condition : nor did Fr. Preston. Fr. Starrs pockets the money that he gets. I attended the conference of St. Vincent of Paul where the question arose whether members of the Sodality should go to St. Patrick's on Sunday for the quarterly communion of the conference, or receive as the Sodality in our church. To gain the Conference indulgence, presence at the mass for the conference is necessary. Fr. Preston had established that in the conflict, the Sodality's ordinance should be maintained even at the risk of losing one of two plenary indulgences to be gained on that day. I confirmed this rule, because established.

<u>Wed., 19th</u>   Dr. McGlynn and I called to see Mr. Dever, a merchant, to have his reference for the letting the school-house Cor. Varick and Canal Sts. Mr. Chamberlain, the agent, said that though he had power to do as he chose, he preferred submitting this business to the board, as it was to be devoted to the purpose of a Catholic Church. Very probably he

wanted Dr. McGlynn to bribe him : but the Dr. was too honest to suspect this. Mr. Dever is a good and intelligent man : he assists Bishop Loughlin to find church property in Brooklyn. He resides at Sand's point, where he invited us. Peter Burtsell, my uncle, was a great friend of his. In the afternoon we went to Jones' Wood to enjoy the excursion of the Germans celebrating their 9th saengerfest. As a body they are a torpid race : but their love of music indicates a greater refinement than in the American or Irish lower classes. I married a Mr. Hamel to a Sarah Kelly in 4th St. near Ave. D. The fee given was $20 : I met there old Mr. Hamel, an eccentric man who gave me great account of the penances imposed by the priests in Ireland for drinking on Sunday or for dancing : sometimes a seven miles, or even a 60 miles' pilgrimage. At one time he went through three days penance for dancing, at a station where he had to pray the whole day. He spoke of Josephus, and the adulterations of his work : of the Haydock edition of the Bible, from which he quoted various events, ex.gr. David's dancing before the ark to prove that now-a-days we have not the true simple faith. I met three sons of his there and a brother and sister to the spouse. Mr. McCready slept at our house. The Maynooth authorities after he had studied with them 4 years of Theology, declined ordaining him : giving a great eulogy of his attainments, but objecting to his reserve and taciturnity, and a peculiarity in the selection of his companions. Dr. McCaffrey of Mt. St. Mary's says that his abilities are remarkable, his conduct excellent but that one year's acquaintance would not justify a positive recommendation for orders. The Abp. declined receiving him, as he had already when in Albany burned his fingers in accepting a similar case : which Dr. McGlynn believes to have been that of a Fr. Sweeny, of All Hallows, who could get only a recommendation of one professor who

July 111

thought that he could manage to get along as a priest, but he took to drinking : and was not smart. Mr. McCready is good, and knows his Theology : but has not the power of displaying it before others. He is very reserved in his manners. But does this justify exclusion from orders?

Thurs., 20th   I took a walk in the morning with Dr. McSweeny to see the improvements of St. Stephen's : Behind the altar there is erected a wooden screen : the work is rapidly advancing behind. Dr. Cummings is given up by Dr. Carnochem : another doctor gives him two months' of life. He is now in the country. We in the afternoon went to the first landing of Staten Island, and from the hill enjoyed the view of the bay. We criticised an article on Rossini in the Chicago Monthly probably written by Dr. McGovern : who must have translated, and that poorly, from the Italian. He never deserved the doctorship : having always been a self-asserting booby. Bishop Duggan refused to accept him, if he did not get the doctor's cap. So says Dr. McGov. I attended the singing class : at which the children are very attentive, in view too of the pictures that I promised to all who should be punctual at the rehearsals.

Fri., 21st   I heard Mr. Derenberg's second confession. He was never baptised. I announced to him that on St. Ann's day I should baptise him : without any public exhibition. In the afternoon I visited the Burtsells of 4th Ave. The Dr. was still going on his foolish way. He avoids me, because I spoke to him very plainly. I visited my mother in the evening, who had visited P. J. Morrogh who had the typhus-fever. I found there too Dr. Corcoran of Charleston, whose society has knocked Dr. Morrogh off his balance again : Dr. Corcoran received me in his underclothes : and said that chills and fever were the cause of his leaving Charleston. He told me twice that he had told his congregation, that they could not pray for

July 112

Abe Lincoln's soul : because he had ignored the church in life, and the church consequently ignored him in life and in death. He would open his Church on the day of humiliation appointed by Pres. Johnson, the acting-president of the United States : and he encouraged all to come and pray for forgiveness of the country's manifold sins, which had brought God's punishment on it. His discourse was misconstrued into his saying that Lincoln was damned : and that he could not open his church on the appointed day. The provost-marshal though a Yankee from N. Hampshire, knew that Dr. Corcoran was more of a gentleman : though he were a rebel, he would not abuse his clerical office to disseminate his views, though he spoke them freely to his friends. The provost-marshal would take no action in the matter. He said he came to see Dr. Cummings, Fr. Mullady & Dr. Morrogh : he would have nothing to do with Black republicans though I reminded him that we could be at dinner without having the nigger to dine with us. Mr. Lovejoy dined with me and had practised the subdeacon's ceremonies with me.

Sat., 22nd   Dr. McGlynn called in the afternoon. Chamberlain the Trinity-school agent said that the Trinity-board could not entertain his proposition of using the school for a Catholic Church. He determined to leave his future destination entirely in the Abp.'s hands, without proposing any further prosecution of his scheme : though he will continue it secretly. He will throw the burden of providing for him on the Abp. : the hospital will probably be broken up in a month, the Central Park Commissioners using all their influence to gain this object. Henceforward his workings should be kept secret : they were spoken of throughout the whole town. This prevented his being sent as pastor to St. James' : so it seems in all probability : for Fr. Preston had proposed his name for it : and

July 113

parishioners had asked for him. He had been there four years ago as assistant-pastor. This was given as a reason for his not being sent there : that he had something else on hand. Fr. Jas. O'Connor advised him not to go to the Seminary because as a Roman, he would be set upon by the Belgians and by Tandy or made accountable for the defects of the place. He determined if this place were offered to him as it had been offered before, to state his reasons why his presence would perhaps injure the place, but if told to go, he would not refuse to go there. Fr. Lancake came to hear confessions. At supper I criticised the Jesuits' fashion of changing their men so constantly : it lessened their influence with the people, because the people could not keep up with yearly changes. This had destroyed all parochial spirit in St. Ann's till Fr. Preston was sent here : who was to be a fixture here. His energy brought about unity in the parish. And he prevented my removal to the Cathedral on this ground. Fr. Lancake had told me of many changes that were to take place in 16th St. Some were to go to France for the tertiaryship : others were changed for health. The change of one man involved often the change of a dozen. I take a greater interest in the penitents that I know :

Sun., 23rd   Sunday. At Low-mass I preached on the Sacrifice of the Mass showing why it is the greatest act of our religion : and therefore the Church obliges us to hear mass once a week. Daily hearing of Mass is the best means of drawing God's blessings on us. I exhorted them to hear Mass on St. Ann's day. Fr. Lancake at 9 o'clock : spoke to them on St. Ignatius' system of examination of conscience. At $10\frac{1}{2}$ I preached a miserable sermon on the Gospel. I attempted to make a splurge and completely failed. The sermon was not practical : nor clear in the ideas which it contained. I had prepared it but not sufficiently. It humbled me. In

July

the evening I spoke to the Sodality of men what is contained in Bressani's Instructions on the necessity and conditions of prayer. I was present at St. Vincent de Paul quarterly meeting in St. Patrick's schoolhouse. A report was read of all the city conferences. Many members were absent being at the laying of the corner-stone of the Protectory for Destitute Children : Where there were present between 10 000 and 15 000 persons. Fr. Maguire read the prayer very poorly : his pronunciation is bad : though on this point he is very pretentious. He adressed to the conference a few words congratulatory of the various reports : but being ashamed of St. Patrick's which was below the others. Mr. Jonin the secretary welcomed the new members to the society in appropriate words but in a stammering manner : saying that they entered a society where no honours or wealth were to be found : where the title of practical Christian was the best passport to their Society : where they expended themselves for the poor. Mr. McNally was vice president. I afterwards visited Lawyer Morrogh's where I met the McLaughlins and my mother. I stayed but a short time. My mother told me that Dr. W. P. Morrogh had fell over the balustrade at the rosary-meeting : and was held down by three females, till Fr. C. Farrell carried him upstairs. This is all the result of Dr. Corcoran's visit. Four bottles of whiskey have been used in $2\frac{1}{2}$ days since his arrival. I was called out of bed at 1 o'clock A.M. to attend Mrs. Daniels who was dying. Fr. Lancake told me that Fr. Aubier who started for France yesterday intends to impress on some French young Jesuits preparing for missions among infidels the importance of taking in hand the blacks of the United States.

Mon., 24th   I went in the morning to see Dr. Morrogh : to whom I adressed some straightforward words, reminding him that not content with losing his own soul, he was by the scandal endangering the salvation of

many of his flock. Mr. Terry spoke to me as if there were no chance of
the doctor's ever leaving off liquor. He complained that Fr. Profillet
did not take any interest in the doctor's case : and that to Fr. C. Farrell,
the doctor would reply : medice, cura teipsum. I had Dr. Manahan to dine
with me. He gave me an account of a new work that he has undertaken of
giving a summary of all the controversies held in the United States. He
has great trouble in finding out all : and has discovered many of which
he had no knowledge before. He will give the summary in form of dialogue
between the Catholic and his opponent, leaving out all scurrility, and
rectifying quotations. He seeks the controversy of a Mr. Fay, about 1802 :
and also Kohlman's about 1816, and Thayer's about 1833. He finds it difficult to get copies. Edmund Burke about 1792, Archbishop of Halifax wrote
a long book like a railroad track without paragraphs or chapters. We spoke
on Dr. Forbes, whom he thought shallow, but good : only having stifled
his faith, through personal spite : this however was like a little branch
falling off a tree, gathering other branches, and other material, till it
became a great snag big enough to sink a large steamer. He thought Abp.
Hughes a tyrant, but with feeling. He loved B. Dubois who had petted him
when a curly-headed boy. He thought Abp. McCloskey feminine in his tastes,
not able to cope with other men, preferring therefore ladies' society. He
went to see Dr. Morrogh whom he pronounced sick as to require immediate
change of place for a week to restore him. He was very anxious to see Dr.
Corcoran who had been a pet of his in Propaganda. Dr. Manahan is 51 years
old : is now stopping at McClellan's in Sing-Sing : who, he says, has a
magnificent library, worth $20000, buying all the choice books of the
European markets. He reads a great deal : but writes nothing : though he
once attempted to translate St. Cyprian's De Unitate Ecclesiae. Dr.

July

Manahan slept at our house : he has left off excessive drink, but still takes his wine without stinting himself much. He dispenses with stronger liquor. I sent invitations to Drs McGlynn, McSweeny, Freel and Gardiner : to Frs. Nilan & Fitzpatrick, to Drs. Corcoran & Morrogh to dine with me on next Wednesday, the feast of St. Ann. I was at the singing class.

Tues., 25th   Dr. Manahan entertained me for an hour, speaking about a great variety of subjects. I sang H. Mass for a Mrs. Daniels whom I eulogised as good in life and good in death. I visited the McLaughlins, to see when I would find them at the Richmonds in Staten Island. I went to see Dr. McSweeny, with whom I took a walk : and spoke on the necessity of inculcating in our seminaries more independent energy, that each priest might do good without throwing the whole burden on the bishop. The priests must be pushing to build more churches. I received a letter from Fr. Preston, dated July 7 from Rome : he suffered from the heat, had seen the Holy Father, was busy reviewing Rome, was pleased with his visit to Propaganda, had met many who expressed great interest in me, gave the news that the bulls were sent to Fr. Conroy for Albany and to Fr. Laviale for Louisville; said Mr. Daschauer was well. Fr. Preston wished to be remembered to the Sodalities. I assisted at the Conference of St. Vincent de Paul, where a motion was made to adopt a grocery store, for which the members would give the poor tickets : a temperance-grocery is preferred.

Wed., 26th   Feast of St. Ann. I baptised Mr. Derenberg. He was a Jew, converted to Methodism, baptised by the Methodists with a number of others, who were all sprinkled together, whilst the words prescribed were being pronounced. Miss Doran & another lady were present. At 1 o'clock we had a dinner, at which were present Drs. Corcoran, Manahan, McGlynn, Frs. Nilan, C. Farrell, McGean, St. John, (who by the by still keeps this

July   117

name : he was exiled from the North during the war, and then succeeded
Fr. Bannon in the chaplaincy of a Missouri regiment : Fr. Bannon was sent
to Ireland as C.S.A. agent to dissuade the Irish from coming to the United
States and also from enlisting in our army). We had soup, lamb, broiled
chicken, pudding, pies, bananas, almonds, raisins, bourbon, cherry, claret,
champagne etc. There was no lively conversation till after dinner. Dr.
Corcoran is not talkative, though Dr. Manahan says that he is the smartest
man in America, and has quite a reputation in the South. He has a monomaniac antipathy to the Yankees : he complained bitterly of the burning of
Dr. England's grand library in Charleston. He has an intellectual forehead : but very fat chops. Fr. McGean is very loaferish : affects but has
no wit : is very awkward in gait : he brought up a question about selling
blessed medals for their own intrinsic value, affirming this to be lawful.
Drs Manahan & McSweeny (who had come after dinner) opposed him : Dr. McGlynn
& I agreed with him. Also Dr. McGlynn maintained that a court of law could
make the Jesuits pay a scholastic, wages for his teaching : even though the
scholastic had made a written agreement not to ask wages. I controverted
this position : for the scholastic could not prove coercion of any kind.
Dr. Manahan related that Abp. Hughes once said to some of his priests; who
were discussing the necessity of Canon Law in this country : that he would
teach them Monaghan canon-law : he would send them back to the bogs whence
they came. He told Dr. McGlynn that in Propaganda we were taught too much
of our rights and not enough of our duties : which was bad for there was
no canon law in this country. Fr. Orsenigo was present at dinner : he had
received $3000 from St. Stephen's. Dr. Cummings was quite peevish over
the matter : and had written to the Abp. to prevent Fr. Orsenigo from collecting. The Abp. told Fr. Orsenigo that he was pleased to see the Congre-

July

gation taking notice of the Assistant's services. With Fr. C. Farrell I afterwards visited Fr. Thos. Farrell. Fr. C. Farrell consulted with me as to what's to be done about W. P. M. who left at 5 o'c. A.M. on Tuesday, by recommendation of Dr. Manahan, and no one knows where he is gone. Drink is ruining him. I had altar class.

Thurs., 27th   Omitted by the Editor.

Fri., 28th   Mrs. Burtsell visited me informing that nought had been heard of W. P. M. I met Fr. Everett at a sick-call : a drunken woman threw herself from a two story window in delirium. He refused to absolve her or give her Extreme Unction : to frighten the drunken sots that were present I persuaded him to absolve her. Dr. McGlynn told me that Chamberlain, the Trinity School agent said expressly that the Corporation refused to let the school for a Catholic Church : and would not let it for a Catholic school. He told this to the Archbishop whom he left under the impression that he did not intend looking for a place for a church any more : in that neighbourhood. It was surmised however that the Leight St. church would soon have to sell out : a sensational preacher, Bushman, had contrived to keep the congregation together for the last two years. The Astor lease of 600 lots for $600 per year for 90 years, will end next year : this may give a chance of buying some property there. There are several claims against Trinity, which are bought out for a time by Trinity. To one family it paid $30 000 : and the claim can be re-entered at any period. Dr. McGlynn is going next week to Cape May to meet Fr. Jas. O'Connor : with whom he is well pleased. I lent him $95. I refused Mr. Lovejoy to lose time in the morning in teaching him ceremonies : I am engaged then in more important matter. He is a great hanger-on : and will never take a plain hint that his too frequent presence is not desired.

July

Sat., 29th   Omitted by the Editor.

Sun., 30th   Sunday. I celebrated 9 and 10½ o'c. masses in honour of St. Ann. Fr. Lancake said the Mass of the Sunday. I submitted the question to the priests that dined with me on Wednesday : and they could see no objection to celebrating the patron's feast with an octave, though this custom has not prevailed in this country. Fr. Lancake preached on St. Ann : The most beautiful creature the B. V. had not yet appeared, though each woman of Israel yearned for connection with the world's Savior : 1. Ann had been married 20 years : was sterile : but was reproached, as for a curse of God. She was resigned : Whom God doth love, he chasteneth. Witness the martyrs, all the heroes and heroines of our faith. Witness even Christ himself, who sanctified our tears by his own tears. Witness the B. Virgin herself. Thus St. Ann is our model for bearing adversity sent by God. 2. At last God favoured her : he who maketh the barren to rejoice with children : He gave her one child worth more than many. She, St. Ann, offered this child to God by vow. Parents should learn from St. Ann that they have received their children not merely to educate them for this world, but for heaven principally : I sang solemn H. Mass, Fr. C. Farrell assisting as deacon, he having volunteered because once assistant at St. Ann's, and Mr. Lovejoy assisting as subdeacon, for the 1st time. We had but an ordinary dinner. We discussed the propriety of priests' going to theatres, that they might improve in elocution. Fr. C. Farrell implied that he had seen Forrest, E. Booth, Matilda Heron etc. Fr. Lancake would have been anxious to go : but community life prevented him. At High Mass a Miss took Miss Huntley's place. Haydn's music with Mosart No. 12's Credo was given by the choir : Mr. Harrison loves the old authors. Being a 5th Sunday there was no sodality meeting. I visited the McLaughlins :

July

and with my mother went to the Morroghs of 26th St. : where Mrs. Burtsell endorsed monies from Ireland, where one or two houses still belong to the Morroghs of this country : though here the grand-children are so numerous as to make a very little come to each of them.

<u>Mon., 31st</u>   Dr. Reuben Parsons, who arrived last Wednesday from Rome dined with Dr. McSweeny and me. He is a very fussy, self-asserting, pigmey doctor : quite glad to hear that I was loyal, quite careful of his health, quite ready to prefer his own opinion to anyone else's, opposed to the Amer. College of Rome where he was educated, because he did not like Fr. W. McCloskey, though by us determined to uphold if he found it slighted in America, ready even to lecture for it. He was the 2nd prefect of the American college when I was there, and being over Theologians, whilst he was in Philosophy, made himself very disagreeable to every one, by his overbearing manner. He had been two years in Propaganda : against which he always spoke, when Fr. W. McCloskey opposed it : he was Dr. McCloskey's right-hand man for two years, was then deposed, and turned against Fr. W. McCloskey and the American college. Whilst in Rome he corresponded with the Metropolitan Record : but was made desist by order of Abp. Hughes. He is now residing with his mother, who is separated from his father, because he was too stingy, and she too extravagant. He told us of his sister at the Convent of Mercy, whose holiness and innocence were made at once known to him by her conversation! Francioni told me that my last letter had pleased him, and that he would answer it soon. It was about the wants of our diocese. Dr. McSweeny and I went to the Central park in the afternoon : we had been greatly amused by Dr. Parsons self-assertion. I attended the singing-class.

August

Tues., 1st I visited Fr. P. Smith, who arrived on last Wednesday, from the American college in Rome. He spoke against The American College : called it a failure. I warned him that in a short time he would consider it a comparative success, when he had looked around here. He implied that Fr. Cassidy of the American college was the author of the 1st article that appeared in the Herald against Fr. W. McCloskey : the author of the defense was Fr. Ambrose O'Neil. Fr. R. Seton called to see me. He lives in East-Chester : He was once in the Propaganda, in the Amer. college and afterwards in the Academia della Religione : would now like a country-parish, where there would be a fishing-lake. He is very eccentric : he protested against the custom of having more than two candles at the Low Mass of a priest, which he had found up in West Chester : and congratulated us Romans on our superior knowledge! In the afternoon Dr. McSweeny and I took a bath at Coney Island. The Dr. did not like the idea of bathing in public even with the full-bathing dress. I attended the St. Vincent de Paul conference.

Wed., 2nd Omitted by the Editor.

Thurs., 3rd Omitted by the Editor.

Fri., 4th Dr. Corcoran, and a German New Yorker just returned from Germany where he was educated, by name   and on his way to Charleston diocese, paid me a short visit. B. Lynch had wished B. Wood alone to sue for his pardon : but others wished to use their influence in his behalf, and too many intercessors here on earth do more damage, though, as Dr. Corcoran said, in heaven, the more the better. Dr. Corcoran was stopping at the Donnellys in Manhattenville, where it was very cool : though he was attacked by chills and fever : for which that part of the town is quite well known. I saw Mrs. Burtsell my mother; who showed me powders with which to make soda-water.

August

Sat., 5th   Mr. Berryan came to bid me farewell before going to Europe. He had been to East Hampton on Long Island : he spoke highly of Capt. Ryan & Mrs. Ryan and her sister Miss Northrup, as very pleasant associates : He praised Edward McCloskey as superior to his three brother priests George, John, & William, though he be but a lay brother. Fr. Lancake agreed with me that this country establishes that government is for the good of the people, whilst in Europe, it is for the advantage of authority and that the only logical way of deriving authority to the government is through the people, which has the right of limiting it. In France some catechims to the question : How many Gods are there? answered : one God and one king. Dr. McGlynn returned from Cape May : where he was disgusted with the attentions paid to ladies by men, when both in the water. He thought that he could do no good by mixing with the people, he only lowered himself in their estimation : he was then no longer the priest, but a gentleman not up to the fashion. He met a suspended priest, McGill, by name : whom Fr. O'Connor did not accept in the Pittsburgh Seminary : who used blackberry wine for mass : who was begging for money : and was too attentive to the bar-rooms and to the ladies.

Sun., 6th   Omitted by the Editor.

Mon., 7th   I started with Dr. McSweeny on a few days' excursion. We took the Albany boat, Dan Drew, had a pleasant sail, dined on board for $3,50 : in Albany visited Fr. Ambrose O'Neil with whom we took tea. He is very selfish, and light : cutting up E. McG. and too familiar with Anna : whom we met at walk with Peter Burtsell, who is stopping with the Cassidys his relatives : his mother is a Cassidy. On the cars Fr. A. O'Neil introduced to us a Fr. McGuin, of St. Patrick's, Albany : who was mellow : has a parish of butchers principally, has 500 parishioners : intends

August

building a church. We were on our way to Saratoga : paid $145. In
Saratoga we found no place in the Clarendon Hotel, or in the Crescent House
where Dr. Hamilton eyed us suspiciously, and at last were given a room
in a cottage attached to the Union Hotel, with two beds.

Tues., 8th   Early we drank 5 glasses of Congress water : walked in
the woods : went to see the races, which were very exciting. A man named
Gilpatrick won all the races : with different horses. I bet that the
negro would not be last : I lost twice. In the afternoon we took a long
walk. The negroes at meals seemed to serve worse when paid : and a new
one took charge of us at each meal in order to be paid. A chinese juggler
swallowed a sword and created paper in his belly.

Wed., 9th   Omitted by the Editor.
Thurs., 10th   Omitted by the Editor.
Fri., 11th   Omitted by the Editor.
Sat., 12th   I called at Dr. Morrogh's and found him far gone : but
gave him a good talk. Dr. McGlynn called upon me : and told me of a visit
to him of Dr. Norris & Dr. McMullen, whom he designated as rough, uncouth
customers. Fr. Lancake in the evening agreed that republican institutions
ennobled the people : 2. improved the Europeans that came to this country.
3. universal suffrage will and must be tried over all Europe. 4. it will
work well. Dr. McGlynn and Mr. McCready & E. Preston took tea with us.
Mr. McCready had disobeyed Dr. McCaffrey in not going to Mt. St. Mary's
for his week of prefectship.

Sun., 13th   Sunday. Fr. Lancake at 7 o'c. spoke about the delusive
piety of wearing scapulars etc. without avoiding sin. 2. of receiving the
sacraments without amendment. At 9 o'c. I spoke on the feast of the
Assumption as a day of rejoicing to us : as we see how God rewards a good

August   124

life in proportion to the good works performed. The B. Virgin is a model of a good life and consequently of a happy death. At 10 o'c. I preached Musso's discourse for the 10th Sunday after Pentecost on good works. After Benediction, I spoke to the Altar Society on the way of attending mass, as expounded by Bressani. E. Preston announced to me his intention of becoming a Catholic. Once he had looked on Fr. Preston's becoming a Catholic as the nearest step to Hell : he met W. Preston's wife a Catholic and Bishop Bayley : liked them, and was no longer prejudiced against Catholics. He once loved Calvinism : but found it too cruel. Henceforth he was always hesitating : he has not gone to church for several months in consequence of these doubts. His minister Dr. Clarke told him to search for the truth and hold it whenever found. He says hundreds of young men in Hartford are in the same state of perplexity : They want a church which will tell them : this you are to believe, and this no. He promises to come down next week to make his confession : this is the principal difficulty in his way. He was anxious to know whether he could go to Protestant service, that his people might not know that he had become a Catholic. I said no! A Mr. Wiley a great friend of his was present during much of our conversation : and was evidently unsettled in his religious opinions. He, Edward expects, will become Catholic too. Edward borrowed $10 from me : he had spent his money in treating Mr. Wiley! In the evening I went with my mother to the Morroghs of 26th St. where the Lawyer asked why a little water was placed in the wine to be consecrated. I explained the tradition about Christ's doing so : and also the symbol of the blood and water flowing from Xt's side.

Mon., 14th   Dr. McGlynn dined with me : we walked as far as 50th St. We talked over Dr. Cummings' likelihood to die soon. Dr. Goulet who attends

August

him says he may go off at any moment, or may linger for 3 months. He engages to make the death easier by taking away much of the bad matter gathered by the dropsy. The Dr.'s kidneys are out of order : the urinary matter pollutes the blood : and might cause craziness : does prevent breathing freely. The Dr. is prepared manfully to go before God. He expressed a desire to have Dr. McGlynn succeed him, as he had the right stuff in him : though for a time he began to believe that he was too censorious : so people called him. He may ask the A.bishop for this : but the Abp. will hardly give such a good position to one who bearded him. Fr. Starrs will call him too young : not having aught else against him. I attended the singing-class : and had to scold a few girls, for going on a picnic with boys without any grown-up person with them.

Tues., 15th   I said 7 o'c. and sang 9 o'c. mass : at this one I preached Bordoni's sermon on the joys and sorrows of the Virgin : to-day being the feast of the Assumption. Lawyer Morrogh breakfasted with me having received communion at 9 o'c. mass. Mrs. Morrogh was with him. My Mother came to consult me about getting Dr. Thos. Burtsell to cut a fistula in Bernard Kelly's back : we both agreed that it would be safer not, as the Dr. is now very tremulous in operations, from drink. W. P. M. yesterday drank 3 pints of wine! Dr. Keogh called on me to-day : announcing that on Fr. O'Connor's (ex-bishop of Pittsburgh) advice he had left Pittsburgh diocese and now belonged to Philadelphia. Fr. O'Connor said that now Dr. Keogh should let himself be ruled by the advice of his friends. Dr. Keogh says that all human motives, family ties etc. would attach him to Pittsburgh. He disliked leaving his diocese : but was forced to it by the ill-treatment of B. Domenec : who accused him of doing nothing, whilst rheumatism so prostrated him as to make it doubtful whether he would live long. The Bp.

August   126

was anxious to give him an excat stating him to be inefficient : the council laughed him out of it : He would only give the excat when he knew to what diocese Dr. Keogh would go. Dr. Keogh spoke of Fr. Jas. O'Connor with whom he pulled very well for 6 years in Pittsburgh Seminary. They are now again together at the Philadelphia seminary, of which Fr. Jas. O'Connor will be president, Drs. Keogh & Balph, and probably Dr. Corcoran will be professors. Bp. Wood remarked that he would soon have all Propda in his seminary. These propagandists can make this seminary the best in the country, they are all smart. Dr. Corcoran, so says Dr. Keogh, is the most learned man in the country : even in English literature. Dr. Balph is very smart : too easy to rule a class : too bashful to walk in town in daylight : a very fine preacher. Fr. Jas. O'Connor is a very good rector, but never popular : because his outward cast is of iron : appears too stern to students : was enchanted with Dr. McGlynn of whom he speaks as of a man of God, who is to push on to good, Abp. McCloskey. Dr. Keogh is whole-souled : has a very good memory : a fine mind : held a public disputation before the pope : In universa Theologia : and one in philosophy, & another in Ecclesiastical History : has a great nack at exciting students to study : pretending to be dissatisfied with their advancement. We went to Dr. Morrogh's but found him out. I attended the conference of St. Vincent de Paul, inculcating the necessity of commencing the census of the parish and also giving them ideas which they are to impress on the people in favour of the sisters' schools in preference to the public schools. 1. the sisters are more interested to promote both the temporal and spiritual welfare of the children than the public school teachers. 2. I saw the progress, by my system of giving them compositions to write, from which I can judge of their proficiency in Xtian doctrine, logic and English syntax. Dr.

August

McMullen of Chicago called to see me. He is a stern, self asserting man, very patronising, thinks that by the Monthly which he has lately commenced to edit, he is going to fill up the gap of Catholic literature in this country. Dr. Keogh told him that the Monthly was a failure : that Chicago was not the place whence it should originate; that not a single good article had yet appeared in it. Dr. McMullen gives out as a new idea, whatever appears new to himself.

Wed., 16th   Dr. Keogh and a Mr. Barr surveyor general of Pennsylvania dined with me. The conversation turned on the influence of New York on the whole country : of which New Yorkers have but a slight conception. The Catholics ought to have a newspaper gotten up by stockholders, who would elect the editor, and take the lead of all moral questions in the country. New York rules the country : and New York could be very easily ruled by the Catholic clergy : which contains men of the most solid learning. The priests are too much engaged at sick-calls to be able to get a proper idea of the country's needs. We visited Dr. Morrogh, who showed us the fine church and school of the parish. Dr. Keogh and I called on Dr. Cummings and found him out. Dr. McGlynn called in to see me : and we talked away on the needs of the Church in this country till 12 o'c.

Thurs., 17th   Dr. Keogh started for Philadelphia where he is expected to attend examinations for admissions to the Seminary. Abp. Spalding, Drs. Corcoran & Foley were on the ferryboat for the same train. The Abp. makes a great fuss about Props. He was popular on first going to Baltimore : he was soon found not to be refined enough for the society he met there. He does not find himself as much at home as at Louisville. He was a hard student, fond of advancement, ready at all times to write. He was an alumnus of the Propaganda. Dr. Foley was of the Roman Seminary : They were

August   128

at Sharon Springs. Dr. Keogh expected to be bored by the Abp.'s oft-
repeated jokes about old Kentucky. We dined at Fr. Thos. Farrell's where
we met Dr. Parsons & Fr. McCarthy and Burns, who in his 3rd year of
Theology returned for sickness from the American college of Rome. The
talk was as usual on the wants of our diocese : especially with regard to
the next generation. I met a woman who found ten children being taken out
west who clung to her, when asked if they were Catholics. She had stolen
two children from No. 1 Bond St. and placed them in the orphan asylums.
She had been two years at the Juvenile Asylum, where she had seen young
children dragged from their mothers' arms : to be cared for by the Civil
authorities, which declared the parents unable to feed them. In the
Juvenile asylum a priest cannot speak on confession : nor is allowed to
attend the dying. On Randall's island, the children are forced to go to
Protestant service & are allowed to go to mass. Protestants have six or
seven institutions for poor children. There were in the Juvenile asylum,
in 10 or 12 years, 10,000 children, of whom 5000 had Irish parents and
more than that had had Catholic instructions previous to their coming to
the Asylum. Jas. B. Nicholson thought we should be slow at asking our
rights from the city. In the evening I attended the singing class.

Fri., 18th   Omitted by the Editor.

Sat., 19th   Dr. McGlynn moved his books and clothing to our school-
house : as the Central-Park Hospital will be broken up in a few days. Fr.
Daubresse heard confessions to-day : Fr. Lancake being in retreat. At tea
I laughed at his idea of placing the assistants with their mothers & sisters
etc. : he thought it good, lest the young clergy should be make lukewarm
by the older clergy : learning to drink, or be careless of the sick.

Sun., 20th   Sunday. At 7 o'c. I spoke on the Assumption : taking

August

my ideas from the 2nd point of Hondry's Synopsis on this festival. At
9 o'c. Fr. Daubresse read the gospel : and commented on the words : 'But
he charged them that they should tell no man' of the cure performed on the
deaf and dumb, arguing that from Xt's example we should learn to be humble : and to be complacent of our good qualities 1st because they are not
ours, but God's who gave them : 2nd because we have reason to fear the
account of the stewardship of them, that we shall have to give to God.
3d because even the good that we perform, is mingled with evil. Wherefore
then have we to be vain. At 10 o'c. he took from the gospel as his text
the words "He hath done all things well." and thence proved that Christ's
way of curing the deaf and dumb man was well done, publicly, evidently to
prove his divinity. Miracles continue to be performed in every century
of the church. Because man's mind is proud, he refuses to pay homage to
proof even when it is made clear to him by plain miracles : man's mind too
is corrupt, & does not wish to know truths which will demand of him self-restraint. Christ by his miracles proved his right to teach. He did all
things well : and therefore his establishment of his church was well done :
he proves the authority of his church by new miracles. We are to accept
of the church's commands too. If Christ did all things well, his command
of humility, and of taking up the cross must be accepted by us. And we
are also to fulfil the precepts of his Church. Fr. Daubresse pronounces
English miserably, speaks poorly : and does not show great logical power.
Yet he is considered the most learned that the Jesuits have in this
neighbourhood. In conversation with him, I maintained that the church did
not take the lead in social reforms : that the bishops and clergy did not
seek the social improvement of the people as ardently as they ought. In
France I said, that the priests were once as wanting in respect to the

August   130

Episcopal authority as the bishops were to the pope. He thought that the Church always lead in the reform-movements : and that now priests, & bishops of France were ultramontane. Fr. Daubresse speaks frequently of his sure nothingness and the poorness of his preaching! He thinks that the secular clergy is exposed to great dangers, which ruin a great number of them. He told Bernard Kelly that he could not save his soul if he did not become a Jesuit. To the Sodality after Benediction I preached on the Assumption taking my ideas from the 4th and following points of Hondry's Synopsis on this subject. The children sang very well both at High Mass and Benediction. In the evening I visited Dr. Morrogh's : whence Fr. Charles Frobilles had been withdrawn, without notice having been given Dr. Morrogh, nor was any one sent in his place. Mrs. Burtsell and I went to the Morroghs of 26th St. : whence Charline Philpses was in the parlor. She and I agree very well on all social questions. We spoke of the Ketchmns' failure : of Hiram Ketchmn's tirade against Catholics : of his abolitionism. I said that we must educate the negro as well as free him. It is better to have immediate emancipation, that their education may come at once, lest after 50 years we should have to commence this same work. Had our forefathers freed the comparatively few slaves that they had, they would have saved us the 4 years' war, and the negroes would have advanced in knowledge & morals. We owe all the expenses that we shall have to undergo, as amends for defrauding them of their wages for so long. We find the effects of slavery in the Irish, who were oppressed, and had no means of education. Lawyer Morrogh told us how they used to occupy with their horses the hovels of the lower classes : who felt honoured by the distinction, and proud of their hovels being torn asunder to liberate these horses. What degradation! How could the people be noble that was subjected to such indignities! Ann

August

Burtsell had given my mother, Dr. Thos. Burtsell's impression of the way in which he was treated by his family : as if the Cassidys were exciting Mrs. Mary Thos. Burtsell to have the Dr. placed in a lunatic asylum that she might have the control of the money. She refused to cohabit with the Dr. : because he was too disgusting.

<u>Mon., 21st</u>   Dr. McSweeny gave me a full account of his stay at Niagara, where he found Fr. Cannon pleasant and philosophising on 'safe men' : but not a good guide to the Falls : of his trip down the St. Laurence, where the Indian pilot led the steamboat so skilfully over the rapids : of Montreal where the Sulpicians were extremely hospitable, almost offended at his not staying with them : of Fr. Conroy of Albany whom he found reserved, but carping at R. Doctors : of Fr. O'Neil, whom he thought not to have had a calling to the priesthood. Dr. McGlynn slept at our house, having to-day bid farewell to the hospital : which is already emptied of the patients. With Drs. Shroder and Teats, he wishes to retain acquaintance, both being gentlemanly and large hearted. The Dr. finds his stay for three years at the hospital as a gap in his life, in which there is nought of good to be found. He begins his career anew : as if just leaving college.

<u>Tues., 22nd</u>   Dr. McGlynn told the Abp. that he was now without any duty : and requested a permanent appointment, not a temporary one as the Abp. was inclined to give him, with the excuse of letting him build a church on the west side of the city. The Dr. started off to Long Branch to meet Dr. Keogh. I assisted as subdeacon at the Imm. Conception at a requiem H. Mass : and visited the Burtsells of 4th Ave. where I heard of new outrages committed by the Dr. against his wife and sister. I passed the afternoon reading Bulwer's Disowned. Fr. Everett married a couple   , the

August   132

banns having been published in St. Ann's, though I had recalled my assent previously given. I attended the meeting of the conference of St. Vincent de Paul where I again inculcated the necessity of having the census of the Catholics of the parish. The one of last year would present the Catholic population within the parish district at not more than 200 or 300 which is absurd : though the greater part of the congregation comes from other parishes.

Wed., 23rd   Omitted by the Editor.

Thurs., 24th   Omitted by the Editor.

Fri., 25th   Omitted by the Editor.

Sat., 26th   In the evening I went with Dr. Lawrence McCauley of Baltimore to visit the Manhattanville convent of the Sacred Heart. The vice-superior showed us the beautiful chapel : in which the sisters were at prayer. Every thing was very neat and orderly : good taste is the essence of every thing about the convent. The chapel will easily hold 300 persons : a fine organ gallery gives sufficient room to a large choir. There is also a small chapel of the 'Mater Admirabilis' in which a copy of the picture at 'Trinita dei Monti' of Rome is found. Another sister showed us the large study room used as exhibition-hall : in which a great defect is that the windows are too high from the floor to admit sufficient ventilation. The dormitory is very good : the girls all have white curtains around their beds : there is plenty of air in it. The other is not as well ventilated. There are many bath-rooms. The Sisters prepared refreshments for us. We then visited the Christian Brothers' establishment : in which the three dormitories are very crowded, having a row of beds in the middle of not very wide halls. The classes are separated by glass-partitions : as if to allow one brother be aware of the conduct of the other with regard

August 133

to the charge of the boys. The have a fine open yard with ball-alleys for play-time. The boys are allowed frequent boating and swimming. Brother Patrick the superior led us through the building : he is very intelligent. In neither place do they seem to have much fever and ague which proverbially belong to Manhattanville. Dr. McCauley is intelligent & deferential to authority. He thought much of Abp. Spalding : who, he says, is unassuming, but learned and truly pious, as he proved in a retreat which he gave to the priests of the Archdiocese. He obliges all his clergy secular and regular to attend the Theological conferences : these take the place of the examinations to which he has the right of subjecting all those who have faculties in his diocese. He had his Cathedral renewed : and his house enlarged. Dr. McCauley had been brought to death's door by bleeding in the throat : had to give up his parish : is now with Dr. J. Foley. The Abp. has required 5 new parishes to be erected in Baltimore. The Passionists have Dr. McCauley's late parish, 5 miles from the city, in a very fashionable quarter : for which they are not fit, because not clean : Americans do not see any connexion between holiness and filth. Dr. McCauley is naturally very neat and exactive of cleanliness. He was pleased with our house : the finest priests' house he had seen. Fr. Langcake heard confessions this afternoon. He was shocked at my thinking that Rome was too centralising in her policy : he could not conceal a shudder at what he conceived my Schismatical tendencies. Yet by arguing coolly with him, I made his astonishment decrease. He is to be teacher of classics during the ensuing year.

Sun., 27th   I spoke at 9 o'c. on the necessity of the children of the parish coming to the parish day-school 1. because we combined the advantages of secular and spiritual instruction. 2. because our teachers were

August   134

more earnest in teaching, because this was their duty to God as well as to the children. 3. because our children are taught the obligation of studying. Parents cannot save their souls, if careless of their children. Parents should not be so selfish as to refuse to pay the price of books, to send their children to a better school. At 10 o'c. I repeated these remarks and preached Musso's sermon for the 12th Sunday after Pentecost. In the afternoon to the men's sodality I explained the necessity and way to make meditation every day : and answered the objections : on which I took the instructions in Bressani's 'Doctrina Cristiana' : which, by the way, I do not like because too diffuse, without any life or energy. Fr. Langcake spoke at 7 o'c. In the evening I went to Dr. Morrogh's : where Fr. Maguire of Transfiguration was sent. He is a good, quiet man, quite polite in his manners : Fr. Trainor did not treat him well : having in his house many relatives who never went to bed at a proper hour : and he had to attend all the sick-calls without getting his rightful share of the perquisites. Fr. Trainor seems satisfied with the assistance of Fr. Daly, a low black-guard : to whom no one will go to confession : who speaks immodestly even in the presence of females : because forsooth he gets no salary, nor any share of the perquisites! The average of confessions since the jubilee at Transfiguration church was 25 on Saturdays! My mother and I went to visit the Morroghs of 26th St. : where I argued that spiritism is wrong, because God would not send the good spirits to systematically satisfy human curiosity : therefore if there is communication with any spirit, it is with the evil one : who tells some truths to gain confidence in the lies that he will afterwards tell. I thought that the imagination evoked the spirits, or rather created them. We spoke against Irish superstitions : which are widespread about fairies, and ghosts. A letter from Aunt Jane Susarello

August

(formerly Morrogh) of Turin announced that Pierina Romano (formerly Avezzana) of Naples had a son and heir.

<u>Mon., 28th</u>   Drs. Keogh and McGlynn returned from Long Branch. With Dr. Keogh I went to see Dr. Cummings who was in very good humour though in great danger of death. He jocosely said that he once tried to convert a bishop, but he had lost faith in the possibility of such an event. This he remarked, in allusion to Dr. Keogh's rupture with his bishop, and to our discussion with the Abp. He had heard Dr. McGlynn described as censorious. He asked to see Fr. Thos. Farrell who is his spiritual director; he had received Communion frequently. In the evening we entered on a spiritual retreat under the guidance of Fr. Driscoll, S.J. at Fordham, 25 other priests and I. The introduction was given at 8 o'c.

<u>Tues., 29th</u>   I found Fr. Driscoll's system very dry. He made the meditation with frequent pauses to allow us to reflect on what he had said. This I found tedious : because one cannot easily reason with another's logic or according to another's taste. He also assisted us in the review of the meditation. The priests were edifying in their adherence to rule and especially to silence : a thing not customary in the retreats of N. Y. diocese : and difficult, considering that we thus meet many whom we had not seen for several months. The fare was in French style. The room small : the bed hard.

<u>Wed., 30th</u>   Fr. Driscoll's system appeared more reasonable : I could follow his discourses. He abstained from all semblance of authoritative dictation : & showed excessive abstinence from positive allusions to the defects of our clergy. The position of St. Ignatius' seminary is well adapted for a retreat : plenty of fresh air was a good accompaniment. The scenery is very fine : the surrounding country quite hill and well culti-

August   136

vated : a large field for walking about, with sufficient shade, gave us ample opportunity of exercise.

Thurs., 31st   Dr. McSweeny was called away by the news of his father's sudden illness, which resulted in death before the Dr. reached home. Fr. Con. O'Callaghan also had to leave to attend the funeral of his mother, who died suddenly yesterday. R. I. P. Fr. Driscoll has not a smart mind : nor is he very practical. He follows, almost only reads, the Exercises of St. Ignatius. He does not give food, nor leave time for private meditation.

September

Fri., 1st   I made my confession to Fr. Schemmel, S.J., who spoke poor English. Four confessors were given among the Jesuits : none of whom I knew, or liked from their appearance. Fr. Clowry was the only secular priest appointed as confessor. Fr. Driscoll asked pardon for any pain given us at a previous discourse : but which no one had noticed.

Sat., 2nd   The Abp. who had made the retreat with us gave us Communion. All the priests at the conclusion of the retreat were in good humour. I have written on a separate paper a sketch of the various discourses given : which I therefore do not repeat here. Dr. McGlynn and I went to condole with Dr. McSweeny : he was at home : Fr. McGean told us that he bore the affliction very heavily : though still attending to the parochial duties. Fr. McGean spoke of his cousin Fr. Hughes as one to become very popular with the people : Fr. McGean in Fr. Hughes' company became a child at once. Fr. Hughes could pleasantly boss the people out of their beds, in the country. He has just been ordained : at the Highlands, a set of vestments, a chalice and plot of ground were given him for a Catholic Church : Protestants were the principal contributors. We spoke also of the denunciation of 'amicizie particolari' in French and Italian colleges, as teaching youngsters sins of

September   137

which the knew nothing : and abhorrent especially to American ears.
Card. Barnabo once suggested that they might easily destroy the boys'
chastity. In Montreal once, the denunciations were so vehement as to provoke a remonstrance from the Americans. One Irish Canadian, in my time,
was expelled for writing love-letters to a French boy. Fr. Langcake came
to hear confessions. We talked on the way in which he makes himself popular with the boys by apparent severity in serious matters and then a
lively interest in their sports. Thus he gained Peter Burtsell to like
him greatly. He knew Mrs. Morrogh and many of my relatives.

<u>Sun., 3rd</u>   Sunday. Dr. McGlynn saying 7 o'c. mass : remarked that
we must satisfy the children's craving for learning, coupling it with the
religious training that religious bound by the vows of poverty, chastity,
and obedience will be likely to give to the children. At 9 o'c I inculcated the necessity of sending the children to Catholic schools : and also
exhorted young, good and active men to take charge of the boys of the
Sunday-school : the more the better lest any boy should pass unnoticed in
the short time allotted for their religious instruction. This is the
noblest act that can be performed : training the young minds to religion.
At 10 o'c. Dr. McGlynn preached on the B. Eucharist : stating 1. that it
contains all that God can give : it is the wisist, the richest, the greatest
gift of God. Yet it surpasses all epithets that we can apply to it. We
must forget ourselves, in thinking of this immense act of God's love. 2.
Taking for his text the 48 to 53 verse of John VI : he showed several
classes that knew of this mystery. The obstinate Jews who cared nought
for Christ asked : who is this that he can give us his flesh to eat? Many
disciples who had followed him till now but found this speech to be too
hard? Who can hear it? But each one of us replies to Christ's saying

to the twelve : Do you also wish to go? O'Lord : to whom shall we go? thou hast the words of life. 3. And Christ considers this Eucharist as necessary to us as food is to the body : without which we cannot retain the life of the soul : as the inchoate union that will last forever : for through it, we have the pledge of the resurrection at the last day. 4. The holy fathers have used very emphatic words of this Sacrament : one says: Our souls must be fattened with the body and blood of Christ. 5. We need not envy the Jews who saw Christ and loved him. They must envy us that we have him so close to us; 6. We must visit Him in his temples. We have Him really present. For this reason, our temples are adorned with the most precious objects, with the noblest productions of art : we have lighted before Him tapers and lamps blazing to symbolise our living faith and ardent love of God. But we must give him what is more pleasing than such symbols : our devotion. We reasonably build magnificent temples, which we call his house : but the temple that he most desires is our soul. Fr. McColgan of St. Peter's, Baltimore, dined with us. He is building a church & came here to procure Mr. O'Connor of 11th St. our parishioner as architect. He divided his lot of 120 feet deep by 66 front, into parcels of 1 ft front, for which about $65 were the sufficient pay, and thus engaged the principal men to buy a foot each. It is to be built in the Byzantine style, though not as flashy as the 3d St. German church. He is not a smart priest, but an earnest one : much respected in Baltimore. Our conversation fell on the necessity of schools particularly for boys who have a vocation to the priesthood : they are corrupted by contact with boys destined to business, though under the guidance of religious. We spoke also of the good faith of Protestants : in which Fr. McColgan placed little trust. Mixed marriages he thought to be productive of evil, because the parents' authority led

September 139

astray the children, who became indifferent not knowing which religion to chose. This could be remedied, if the priests could visit the families. He spoke of two cases of conversions of persons who had never heard of Catholicity. Fr. Langcake became a Catholic without knowing anything of Catholic service, from reading Walter Scott's novels which he deemed unfair to the Catholic Church. Our boys' Sunday school could not open as I had announced for want of the keys, the janitor not being found anywhere. In the evening Dr. McGlynn and I went to see Dr. Cummings : where we met a Mr. Darcy, a Mr. Quintard, head of the Iron works and his brother-in-law Mr. Gorman : as well as Mrs. McDowall, Mr. & Mrs. Gerdes, and Mr. Jas. Morrogh. The Dr. was in very good humour. His church is fast progressing toward completion. The cost of the addition will be $75,000 : of which he engaged to collect $25,000 before commencing : to borrow $25 000 from the Irish emigrants' bank : and collect $25 000 after it's completion by lectures, concerts, fairs etc. Mr. Augero is to fresco the whole church : he thinks that it will be good to fresco it whilst the plaster is still fresh : thus the paint will penetrate to the wall and not be a mere coating. $32 000 were collected before beginning. The Dr. has dropsy, gout, liver complaint & rheumatism but has somewhat improved of late, without chance of getting well. We called at Mr. Morrogh's in 26th St. Dr. McGlynn argued strongly in favour of an Irish rebellion on account of the tyranny of the English : arguing that tenant-right should be forced upon the landholders, whose possessions are robberies from the Irish people : and deserve a legislative compulsion to force them to use the land for the benefit of the people, instead of preferring cattle to the people. Though Mr. Morrogh told a tale of Irish misery as witnessed by himself of children squabbling with little pigs for the most comfortable part of the sow as

September 140

their pillow for the night, yet maintained that this was the effect of circumstances for which exceptional legislature could not in justice be required : the British laws being the same all over the empire, gave as much freedom to the Irish as to the English. Mr. Morrogh belongs to the Irish aristocracy, was educated at Stonyhurst, England, and at St. Omer, France.

<u>Mon., 4th</u>   In the afternoon we left our card for Dr. W. McCloskey of the American college Rome : we met Dr. Brownson who took tea with us. He is writing a work on this Republic's Constitution and Destiny : treating of general government in a Catholic sense : and giving new ideas about it's love of republicanism, to be published by O'Shea, a Catholic : to force Protestants to take books from the Catholic publishers : without which they would be behind the age. His health is good : better than when he edited the Review, because not obliged to work much for a determined space of time. He thinks that he has derived his style from French books : his language often considered Saxon, is but the application of the Latin etymology to English : ex. gr. he translates the word = attendo, by = bend to.

<u>Tues., 5th</u>   In the morning I visited the Dorans, about Mr. Derenberg. Miss Doran had requested her father to dismiss Mr. Derenberg who had annoyed her by his constant adresses : he was accused of having a wife living. I fear that he will give up his Catholicity which probably he put on for her sake and her property's sake. She is a fashionable dress maker, and has a boarding-house. The old people are warm blooded Irish. In the afternoon we strolled to the Central Park. I attended the conference of St. Vincent de Paul.

<u>Wed., 6th</u>   In the morning I had a long travel after the several officers of the 2nd regiment : who have declined letting us occupy their

September

armory. I only found Major DeConrey who promised to use his influence to have this order rescinded. In the afternoon I attended the convention of delegates from the councils and conferences of St. Vincent de Paul : 53 were represented at the call of the roll : others came in afterwards. It was settled by Fr. Starrs, that the spiritual director should be informed if any member did not attend to the paschal duty : & he should have the member leave the society. It was debated whether a large conference, of over 60 members was too unwieldy to do good. Mr. Chanler of Philadelphia said that a large one brought much confusion, especially where politicians, quack doctors, lawyers sought the society's influence outside the conferences. Mr. Barnum had an elephant to plough ten times as much as one yolk of oxen : who unfortunately ate more than 100 yolk of oxen. So these politicians etc for the good they did the society, required it's great influence for themselves. Mr. Ternam of Brooklyn desired an address to be made to the priests, requesting them to preside at their meetings. This question was debated for two hours. 11 other points were to be discussed in the afternoon! A Mr. Kelly of Chicago repeated several times the panegyric of Very Rev. Mr. Dunn of that city. The Abp. Frs. Starrs, McNierney, Quin &   were present. I reorganised both the altar and literary classes.

Thurs., 7th   I saw Lieut. Col. Roberts who promises to have the armory shortly returned to us. He is a very fine, gentlemanly person : and has, I understand, great influence in the regiment : he had allowed the Fenians to drill in the Hall. The Sanitary commission had destroyed it. Capt. Rey, a bigoted man, opposes our having a S. S. there : Col. Reid is a protestant : but not bigoted. In the afternoon I attended the meeting of the delegates of the conference of St. Vincent de Paul : over which Bishop

September

Bayley presided. It was settled that the notoriously negligent member should be excluded from the conferences : but that a case of neglect of Easter duty should be made known to the spiritual director, who should act on this knowledge. A proposition for establishing a kind of Tract Society was held back by Fr. Starrs for the deliberation of the general council of New York : & therefore will not be acted upon. Mr. Coddington stated that 30,000 copies of dime novels were edited monthly : we require something to counteract these bad books, ex. gr. tracts etc. The children at Sunday Schools where there is a conference in the U. S. are about 12,000 : members of the conferences who help are 270. Mr. Chanler said that a boy is not like a ship always to be guided by the stern : but the news-boys, shoe-blacks etc. must have members of the conferences interested in them : to seek places for them. The news-boys frequently literally hook the papers from under doors to sell and like the London broomseller sells them at 6 cents because he stole the whole broom : a companion sold them at 8 cts. because he only sold the material, and made the broom. The Protestant aid-societies send their children where there are no Catholics, and are cautious that no Irishman speak to them. Some conferences denounced picnics, as pernicious to morals. Subscriptions lists were applauded for the raising of funds. Many conferences number the Catholics of their parishes : to see to what school the children go : and know to how many their aid may extend. In the evening at Dodworth Hall, a social gathering of the members took place. I was introduced to Mr. Chanler who had been a congressman and U. S. minister at Naples : he thought King Bomba a great man, but unwise in refusing railroads etc to his Kingdom. They would never otherwise have asked a constitution or expelled his son. I met a Mr. Churchill of Fordham, a convert, who had been kept back from the church by Dr. Forbes' defection.

September 143

I met Bishop Duggan, who was called 'Elegant extracts' because not deep but read in the poets etc : from whom the boys of the Amer. college stole oils & soaps. I met Dr. W. McCloskey of the Amer. College Rome, grown quite fat, and Bishop Loughlin. The Abp. & Bish. Bayley were there. I met also Fr. Doane of Newark of Roman Seminary cracked in voice and in manners.

Fri., 8th   I commenced a series of lectures to the girls of the sisters' school on the Ten commandments. Mr. Roberts lent us the Fenian Hall in 814 Broadway on the 4th story : all strangers had been excluded from the 7th St. Armory. I heard confessions in the evening.

Sat., 9th   Dr. McGlynn and I visited Fr. Thos. Farrell : where we met Dr. Cassidy of the Amer. College Rome : quite young nor of deep thought. Fr. Langcake heard confessions.

Sun., 10th   Bishop Wood of Philadelphia said mass and dined with us : as Fr. McConomy also. The bishop was a Propagandist and spoke principally of the college. Fr. Langcake preached at $10\frac{1}{2}$ o'c. on the B. V. 1. how we should be sorry over the birth of children rather than rejoice : because physically they are a mass of flesh, mentally they are without the use of reason, like brutes, morally in sin and worse than brutes. 2. how the B. V.'s birth gives joy because perfect in body, in mind and holiness. 3. Her holiness must have been great : because she made good use of the capital given her by God : each grace is doubled by each correspondence : as in geometrical proportion : as an inventor of the chess board asked the king of Portugal in reward for his invention, one barley corn doubled in geometrical progression by the 64 squares : the barley could not be held by all the navies of the world. If a man had one dollar and always doubled it in geometrical proportion for 64 days : his wealth would not be held in the ships of the world. Commencing with a five dollar gold-piece doubled

September   144

similarly 64 times, the bullion would be equal to several globes as large as the earth. From these imagine likewise the progress of the Virgin's holiness during the 9 months in her mother's womb : since she was conceived without sin, and with a holiness equal to that of the Cherubs, Seraphs, angels etc combined. We can rejoice, because the Virgin's holiness teaches us to progress in holiness : and because it makes her aid powerful to us. About 120 boys were in the Sunday-school : I gave pictures to all. I visited also the girls' Sunday school : sang Vespers and spoke to the altar society on the ceremonies of the Mass from Bishop England's explanation. I visited the McLaughlins.

Mon., 11th   Dr. McSweeny visited me : we took a walk in the morning and went to Staten Island in the afternoon. He stated how Moriarity had incurred the Abp.'s displeasure by asking Fr. Healy, if the Abp. went to Boston to have a coadjutor appointed : and declared he would not ordain him priest, if he had not made him subdeacon : and at the request of Fr. O'Sullivan his uncle, allows him to go to Albany, if Fr. Conroy accepts him. Fr. O'Toole had been reprehended for preaching on Temperance to Prot. societies and had continued. Fr. Starrs desires Dr. McSweeny to discontinue instructions to the children : because his successor might not wish to do it. Dr. McSweeny's father had resigned himself to death at once : and received all the sacraments. The Dr. did not see him during his last illness of 11 hours. R. I. P. Dr. McGlynn went to New Rochelle. Mr. McSweeny some 20 years ago came to this country with £10 : of which he immediately spent £5 for Patrick's schooling in Philadelphia. He died having given an excellent education to 5 boys and three girls.

Tues., 12th   Dr. Manahan called to see me : he is hunting after books of Catholic controversies held in the U. States. He will call his new work

September

'The American Catholic Museum'. I visited my mother : and saw Fr. Maguire, who has less to do than at St. Peter's. I attended the conference of St. Vincent de Paul, to which I spoke strongly about the attendance to the instruction of the children in Catechism.

Wed., 13th   Dr. Manahan dined with me. He promises to prove that the books of the new Testament were not known to unbelievers in the primitive church, according to the 'disciplina arcani'. Certainly the passages about the Eucharist etc were not in their hands. Bryan of 5th Ave. has lately established a bank, by which he expects to gain or lose a milion.

Thurs., 14th   To-day the Theological Society voted itself out of existence, appointing a committee to ask the Abp.'s approval of a new society. The Theological Society was not acceptable to many of the clergy 1st because no member had a voice in the election of officers. 2nd because they were not asked to frame the constitution. 3d because they imagined it to be a clique of Romans and abolitionists. 4th because the principal author Dr. Brann was of Jersey diocese. The motion met with great opposition from Drs. Brann and Gardiner : but was approved by all the others. Fr. Thos. Farrell, Drs. McGlynn, McSweeny, Brann, Gardiner, and I are the committee. Fr. McCarthy invited Frs. Moran, Thos. Farrell, McLaughlin, Cooney, Dr. McGlynn and me to dine with him.

Fri., 15th   Dr. McGlynn persuaded Fr. Thos. Farrell to go to the Abp. to speak about the Theological Society, and the committee that is to wait upon him : that in case he should decline approving the Society, we may be spared the trouble of calling upon him. I spoke to the girls' school on the commandments in general. Fr. Cooney of the Order of the Holy Cross took tea with us. He had been a chaplain of an Indiana-Irish brigade four years. In an army of 160000, there were four chaplains : at least one sixth

September 146

being Catholics of the 16000 men. Four of the order of Holy Cross were chaplains in U. S. armies, Frs. Dillon, Gillen, Cooney etc. The Protestants thought the Catholic chaplains the only workers, and remarked the good conduct of Catholic soldiers after confession. Fr. Cooney is to be editor of the Ave Maria. Dr. McGlynn is a life-subscriber : I subscribed for two years : to encourage this beginning of a Tract Society. Fr. Cooney told us how Fr. Smarius S. J. rendered himself obnoxious to Protestants by ridiculing them. In their college at Fond du Lac 12 Protestant students rebelled against being present at his discourses. Fr. Sorin is superior of the Order of the Holy Cross in this country. It is for the teaching of the poorer class : and is in this country composed of Irish.

Sat., 16th   Fr. Langcake came to hear confessions.

Sun., 17th   I spoke at 7 o'c. mass on the Sorrows of the B. V. Dr. McGlynn said 9 o'c. mass. Fr. Langcake sang High Mass. I preached on death : the best ideas were taken from Musso's sermon for the 15th Sunday after Pentecost. Miss Aiosto sang as soprano : but is a mezzo-soprano. I pay her at the rate of $400 a year. To the boys I spoke on the commandments in general. I distributed pictures to all the girls present. I preached on the Sorrows of the B. V. to the Sodality from Hondry's synopsis on this subject. I visited the Morroghs of 26th St. : where a presbyterian was led into business against his will by Mr. Morrogh. We spoke about the destination of the poor of New York : and commented on a letter written by Cathy Avezzana about property of Gen Avezzana's, held in Mr. Morrogh's name for convenience' sake : of which John Avezzana receive the rent, without paying the taxes, and allowing all the risk to be against Mr. Morrogh who profits nothing by the nominal ownership.

Mon., 18th   With Dr. McSweeny I took a walk on 5th Ave. : in the

September

afternoon we visited Fr. Thos. Farrell, where Dr. Parsons gave me an account of a rupture between him and Bish. Conroy because he said that 24/25 of Italians were opposed to the temporal power of the pope : and because he distinguished the human element from the divine element in the authority of the church, saying that the English in Rome induced the pope to sympathise with the South, and oppose Fenianism in Ireland : and that he was mistaken under both respects. I visited the Burtsells of 4th Ave. where after a long talk with the Dr. I gave him up as incorrigible in his drinking habits except through special grace to be obtained by prayer. Miss Fanny Cassidy got a free pass for me on the N.Y. Central R. R. from Mr. P. Cagers her brother in law.

Tues. 19th   In the morning Dr. McSweeny and I took a stroll to Central Park where we discussed the last distribution of prizes in the Propaganda : in which we considered none who received the doctorate to deserve it but A. Ko, a Chinese. Buckeridge received the gold medal. Ed. McSweeny took the premium for Moral Theology : and proxime accessit for his other three classes. In the afternoon I went to New Rochelle to give Dr. McGlynn (who is taking Fr. Thos. McLaughlin's place) a letter from Dr. Cummings demanding an interview : in which he told him that he asked the Abp. to send Dr. McGlynn to St. Stephen's. Dr. McGlynn consented, not acknowledging as a favour, nor courting the place, to assist Dr. Cummings.

Wed., 20th   I went to New Rochelle with Dr. McGlynn : had a grand drive to opposite City Island : and a fine swim from Mr. Lacy's grounds. In the afternoon I attended at the altar and literary classes.

Thurs., 21st   Dr. McGlynn dined with me : and we went to Fr. Thos Farrell's where we met a party that had presented to Dr. O. Brownson an annuity of $1000 : for which were paid $7000 collected from priests and

September   148

other prominent Catholics. The Dr. spoke a great deal about his new work
to be published within a month. Frs. Malone, McCarthy, Farrell pay an
excessive deference to the Dr., who puts on always the airs of a professor
before his school-boys. The Dr. wishes to publish a book through a Catholic publisher O'Shea : that Americans will have to read, to be up to the
age. His review decreased in circulation when he withdrew the Theological
part from it. O'Shea is the best Catholic publisher. Fr. Starrs called
at our house to see Dr. McGlynn a few minutes after he had started for New
Rochelle. I induced Fr. Starrs to admit that 500 priests would find enough
to do in New York city : that churches are wanted on both the Eastern and
Western sides of the city : admissions not very great in themselves but
extraordinary as being received by Fr. Starrs. I sent a note to Dr. McGlynn.
I visited Dr. Fr. Sinclair : just arrived from Rome for Buffalo diocese : he
is a propagandist and a German. He told me that Fr. Jurzick of Copenhagen
was in Christiania. Dr. Sinclair is a good priest but not of great calibre
of mind. He stayed at the church of the Holy Redeemer. I visited the
Burkes at 19 E. 11th St.

Fri., 22nd   Fr. Ambrose O'Neil visited me : spoke highly of Fr.
Conroy's social disposition, fearing that henceforth he would become gruff,
that he might not be too familiar with his priests, when he is consecrated
bishop. Fr. O'Neil is anxious not to be sent to the country lest lonesomeness should induce him to drink! Dr. McGlynn called here : whence he went
to Fr. Starrs who told him that the Abp. wished to appoint him as first
assistant to Dr. Cummings', "because the Dr. was still living " (sic) Dr.
McGlynn requested to have a note defining his future position at St.
Stephen's and not before Fr. Quin was appointed elsewhere. Mr. Fairbrother
reported his visit to the Abp., in which he told how Fr. Hecker had said

September

that his document was not of any avail to a priest, but that it's subject was of vital importance. The Abp. promised to give it his consideration : was pleasant in his manner : and Fairbrother told him that he would not end here, unless action were taken on the subject. The Abp. remarked that Fairbrother was not a man to drop such a subject easily.

Sat., 23rd   Dr. McGlynn called : we went to Fr. Thos. Farrell who gave us an account of his interview with the Abp. about the Committee of the Theological Society. The Abp. blamed gently Dr. Brann for his love of notoriety : and said that he would like a conference to which the clergy of his diocese might be called : he would not ask the clergy of other dioceses. Fr. Langcake heard confessions : We talked of the Jansenist spirit of the old Irish clergy, and of the Sulpicians which prompt them to refuse absolution without good cause.

Sun., 24th   Fr. Lancake said 7 o'c. mass and preached at $10\frac{1}{2}$ o'c. on the Gospel about 'Pride'. 1. The Angels and our first parents were condemned for pride. Pride is the beginning of all evil. 2. God incarnate gives us an example of humility in his birth of a poor woman in a stable, in his whole life, in his passion and death. 3. He inculcated humility by word and example when he washed the feet of his disciples at the last supper. 4. He teaches humility in to-day's gospel (of the 16th Sunday after Pentecost). 5. We are all infected with the spiritual cholera = pride, in a greater or less degree. 6. We must imitate St. Austin who prayed to God : Noverim te, ut amem te : Noverim me, ut conternuam me: and St. Teresa who prayed to God not to allow her to live if she were not despised. 7. This is the greatest perfection that we can reach : because thus we shall be like unto our divine Saviour. He commended the collection for the Seminary : because we had not one tenth enough of priests, even though we sought to

September   150

multiply ourselves by extraordinary exertions. I recommended at 9 o'c. : parents to give their children to the ministry and the congregation to give money for their support. In the afternoon to the boys I spoke on the 1st Commandment : to the girls on the commandments in general recommending to both Sunday-schools the custom of writing an abridgement of the instructions with the promise of rewards for the best compositions. I spoke to the men's sodality on the 'Our Father' taking my ideas from Ferreri's catechetical instructions. Fr. Monahan of New Orleans dined with us. We spoke plainly in favour of the Fenians : but Fr. Langcake's love of his country's government was excited by the oppression by the English of the poor Irish. He thought that the majority of the evils of Ireland were caused by the Irish themselves. He would not deny (nor affirm) the justice of Irish rebellion against England (of which he is a native) : but he did not deem it ripe, nor promising the slightest success. I visited the Morroghs of 26th St. : the McLaughlins and my mother were there. We discussed the right the church had of placing impediments invalidating marriages. I heard that little Fanny Avezzana had died in Turin of typhoid fever on the 29th August : eleven years old.

Mon., 25th   I heard the confessions of five Dominican nuns, whom Fr. Monahan has brought from a Dublin convent to take care of the deaf & dumb of New Orleans. They breakfasted with me : and showed intelligence. They admired our pictures, and our church : and spoke very well, though their accent was rather peculiarly Irish. Dr. McSweeny called in the afternoon : we walked together as far as St. Teresa's. I saw Frs. Boyce and Ferrall. The latter I impressed fully with the necessity of many more priests and churches in New York : 500 priests would have enough to do. Fr. Boyce had printed pictures of his church and maps of the parish as premiums at

September 151

Sunday school : he has also established an academy under the Christian brothers with $12, $8 and $6 a quarter : it with the church forms a nice picture. Br. Ambrose presides over the school. At the Singing class I found a division between the boys : I sought to laugh them into a reconciliation and failed. Mr. O'Keefe bound for Rome thinks more of hair-oil, than of Theology.

Tues., 26th   The committee of the Theological Society, Fr. Thos. Farrell, Drs. McGlynn, McSweeny, Brann and I (Dr. Gardiner did not come) presented ourselves to the Abp. to ask him to call a meeting of priests to form a new academical Society, the former having failed. He said 1st a bishop does not wish to oblige the clergy to form an academical society. 2nd. he would encourage such a society if it did not publish it's debates and essays. 3rd. he did not think we had the men to form an academical society, whose position would be acknowledged above others in the community. 4th. he could not ask priests from other dioceses : and scouted the idea that he could patronise the men of learning of the country. 5th. he had the intention of calling an informal synod of the clergy, at which he might start the 'moral conferences'. Dr. McGlynn told him 1st. we found all the defects in the Theological Society that had been pointed to by the Abp. 2. we came anxious to break up the old Society and expected the Abp.'s negative. 3d. we accepted the 'conference' as adequate to our wishes. Dr. Brann sought to insist upon the utility of a Theological Society : The Abp. slightly ruffled insisted that our failure was not a presage of future success. = all this trouble was gone to, to rid the Society of Dr. Brann. He did not dine with the rest of the committee for which I had dinner prepared. I attended the conference of St. Vincent de Paul.

Wed., 27th   I was called to New Rochelle to attend two sick-calls on

September   152

David's Island instead of Dr. McGlynn who has been taking Fr. McLaughlin's place. A dying Catholic acted rather obstreperously : was not very anxious to receive the Sacraments. I was not treated with excessive courtesy by the Dr. on duty. I attended the altar class. The literary-class was greatly decreased by two French boys Tessier and Festa retiring for fear of being whipped by the other large boys. I attended the Fenian lecture by Lieut. Col. Roberts of the 2nd N.Y. Vols. in the Union Hall of Cooper Institute : which was filled. I entered as he was saying that the Fenians did not want the pope's interference to help their cause. If some clergymen denounced them, they did it on their private responsibility. A priest had told him that for one that denounced them, a hundred priests sympathised with them & No bishop could condemn them or prevent them from approaching the Sacraments till Fenianism was proved to be a sin : and certainly it was not a sin to organise men militarily to provide for the event of a war with England (this was against Abp. Kenrick's, of St. Louis, assertion) because our U. S. militia is such an organisation. He knew that Te Deums would be sung in Rome as well as in Dublin for the Fenians' success. He was immensely applauded for these expressions, in which he was quoting my authority : for I had suggested these thoughts to him a few days before : as also that in New York Fenians could always be admitted to the Sacraments. He hoped that the U. S. would use British neutrality against England : and laughed to scorn the fright of the English at Fenianism.

<u>Thurs., 28th</u>   Fr. Mognahan took breakfast with Dr. McGlynn and me. In the afternoon I visited Mr. Tiers : who is still sick of the palsy. I went to see Dr. Parsons at St. Joseph's : and on my return home found that Dr. McGlynn had given up his temporary care of New Rochelle. I visited the singing class: in which the boys are still divided into two parties.

September

Fri., 29th   Dr. McGlynn and I went to Dr. Cummings' where we found Fr. Barrett just returned from Rome after a 9 years' stay. Dr. Cummings was in good humour and apparently better in health. I brought Fr. Barrett to stay with me. Mr. Graves was brought to me by Dr. McSweeny to get lodgings. He is a convert, was in the Propaganda for $4\frac{1}{2}$ years : now returns in his 3d year of Theology, to take care of his mother & expects to be ordained a few weeks after his arrival at home. He let his mustachio grow during the voyage. I gave the instruction to the girls of day-school on 2nd part of 1st commandment : and heard confessions in the evening.

Sat., 30th   Drs. McSweeny and Freel came to visit the two from Rome. Fr. Langcake heard confessions. Dr. Freel dined with us.

October

Sun., 1st   At 7 o'c. I spoke about the seminary collection : as well as about the rosary. At 9 o'c. Dr. McGlynn spoke about the collection, encouraging it in a few words, taking for his text : "The harvest is abundant but the workmen are few." At $10\frac{1}{2}$ o'c. Fr. Lancake sang H. Mass. I preached on the Rosary : especially on it's connexion with the mystery of the Incarnation. I spoke also about the collection stating that we have not one tenth of priests requisite for the diocese : The seminarians make a sacrifice of themselves : and we have to support them since their ministrations when ordained will be for our benefit, and those over whom we have a charge. Dr. McGlynn and Fr. Barrett were at St. Stephen's. I took Mr. Graves to see our Sunday-schools. He was delighted. Both he and Fr. Barrett remarked the extreme neatness of every thing about our church. I preached at the boys' S. S. on the 2nd part of the 1st commandment : to the girls on the 1st part. To the Rosary Society I preached on the Rosary : Fr. Barrett sang Vespers.

October   154

Mon., 2nd   We, all four, attended the Month's mind for Dr. McSweeny's
father in St. Teresa's. Dr. McGlynn took Fr. Barrett and Mr. Graves to see
Fr. Killeen at Red Bank. At Dr. McSweeny's house I defended the Fenians a-
gainst Fr. Boyce : I maintained that Revolution in Ireland was lawful : and
2. that no bishop had a right to denounce it, as a bishop and 3d that he
could not make Fenianism, a reserved case, till he proved it a sin. 4th
that the bishop's prohibition of Fenianism would not make it unlawful, till
he had good reasons for his prohibition : 5th that he might deny jurisdiction entirely over those who were Fenians. 6th that Abp. Kenrick was illogical in saying that Fenians were inadmissible to the Sacraments because he
considered them an immoral society, or a secret society. 7th that his public statement of what he had stated in private through a newspaper did not
in any way bind his priests : 8th that it did not withdraw any jurisdiction.
9th nor force the priests to exact a withdrawal from Fenianism, 10th that
this letter has intrinsic marks of his being in a passion at the time he
wrote against the Fenians who had published that a funeral service would
take place in a church, without having consulted the priest. Mr. Moriarty
dined with me. The Abp. had given him permission to leave the diocese :
and even showed him that it was good, for body and soul that he should leave
it : for the body, because he would be in the country : for the soul, because
a large city's temptations were too great for him : but the Abp. exacted
that his uncle Fr. O'Sullivan of Hudson and the Albany diocese should pay
what had been expended on his education by New York. Fr. Starrs told Mr.
Moriarty that New York was very well supplied with priests. Mr. Moriarty
is talented : being handsome, would soon be sought after by the young ladies.
He gave offence to the Abp. by publishing that he went to Boston to get a
coadjutor for Bish. Fitzpatrick. He regrets having consented that his uncle

October 155

should apply for his removal from N. York : he thought that the Abp. would never consent. Mrs. Burtsell and McLaughlin visited me : with letters from the Avezzanas of Italy. I felt very sick in the evening and went to bed at 7½ o'c.

Tues., 3rd   Mrs. Hargons visited me with her eldest daughter. Mr. Fairbrother told me that on last Thursday having called on the Abp. to ask an extension of the jubilee for the soldiers : he was told that this was business of the pope and bishops and that the soldiers had been made fully aware of the publication of the jubilee. The Abp. was very angry and would not hold further discourse with Mr. Fairbrother. Dr. McSweeny and I walked to see the stone-cutters blocking out the marble for the new Cathedral on 4th Ave. & 50th St. We agreed that Mr. Graves is a fool. Dr. McGlynn, Fr. Barrett and Mr. Graves returned from Red Bank : where they had gone boating with Fr. Killeen. The Abp., as Dr. McSweeny tells me, called Lieut. Col. Roberts to an account for having praised his prudence in not condemning the Fenians : the Abp.'s private judgement is that Fenians cannot be absolved.

Wed., 4th   Fr. Preston arrived home to-day after exactly four months' absence, on his trip to and through Europe. He says that he has an immense amount of provisions in his mind, which he has not yet been able to digest : viz : he requires time to reflect on all that he has seen. He was very favourably impressed with Rome : in which he stayed but ten days! The pope's affability pleased him : and Card. Barnabo's off-hand style. I took Fr. Barrett and Mr. Graves to see Dr. Freel. Mr. Graves said that he learned more about Propda since his arrival in N. York than during his five years stay there. We talk very placidly of it's defects. 'Amicizia particolare' is the besetting evil of superiors and students. Among these a certain Egyptian   , and a Chinese   were excessive in making

October   156

love to Fr.   of Dublin. We met Bishop Loughlin; who is very shallow in mind. I had the altar-class in the evening. The official letter came to Dr. McGlynn.

Thurs., 5th   I heard the confessions of the girls of the 42nd St. Industrial School and with Fr. Nilan took a drive to Macombe's dam. Fr. Nilan shows himself quite intelligent on the Fenian and Negro question, and also about Roman Institutions. I visited with him the Select school of fine classes, and the Industrial school of five departments of sewing or embroidering. The building is very airy. Sr. Helena is superior of the Sisters of Charity who have charge of both institutions. The classes are separated by glass partitions. In the afternoon we met Dr. McSweeny and Fr. Barrett out walking together. Fr. Barrett's brother came to meet him, & is of no more brilliancy than the priest : who is a weak brother of no great talent, and not having been very studious.

Fri., 6th   Dr. McGlynn and I visited Dr. Cummings, who passed a poor night but was in admirable humour, telling very amusing anecdotes of Graziosi. We met Fr. Gamboville there too : who is a good man. I gave instructions to the day school children on the 2nd commandment : and heard confessions in the evening. Dr. McGlynn and I visited Fr. Thos. Farrell who had been confined to bed by a severe cold, caught whilst preaching in Providence at the consecration of an altar in Fr. Kelly's church.

Sat., 7th   Mr. Graves managed to get off to-day. I visited Fr. Nilan and arranged to take a trip to Canada with him. Mr. Edw. Preston came to stay with us for a few days : he is a Catholic with regard to belief but is afraid of confession.

Sun., 8th   I said 9 o'c. mass and sang $10\frac{1}{2}$ o'c. : Fr. Preston preached on confession, illustrated by the gospel of the day (18th Sunday

October

after Pentecost). He, beforehand, expressed his joy at his return to his own home. He had prayed in every temple in which he knelt for this congregation. Their prayers had obtained for him a pleasant trip not marred by a single accident. He had obtained in return for them the papal benediction with a plenary indulgence : which he would confer on the following Sunday. At dinner Mr. Daschauer and Mr. Harrison were with us : I preached to the boys and girls on the 2nd part of the 1st commandment. At supper Mr. G. Preston, E. Preston and Miss Burges were with us. She is a nice, pleasant young lady. In the evening I went with my mother to the Morroghs of 26th St. : where we discussed the right of the Irish poor of having laws made to protect them from the cruelty of the landlords : who refuse to lease the ground for more than a year at a time, and soon eject the tenant that has improved the land.

Mon., 9th   Mr. George Preston was married to Miss Burges before 8 o'c. mass : which was 'pro sponso et sponsa' by Fr. Preston. I assisted as subdeacon at the requiem High Mass for Roger McSweeny, Dr. McSweeny his brother acting as celebrant, Dr. McGlynn as deacon. We went to Calvary Cemetery : and afterwards dined at S. Malone's : where Frs. McCarthy, T. McLoughlin, Drs. McSweeny, McGlynn and Rev. Mr. Moriarty were also.

Tues., 10th   I visited Miss Jones from Pittsburgh, introduced to me by Fr. Jas. O'Connor of Philadelphia, who is now staying at Mrs. Macaulay's School at 253 Madison Ave. Cor. 40th St. She is a nice girl : Fr. O'Connor expects me to arrange frequently to hear her confession. She is obliged to go with the other Catholic girls to the French church. She is sent to Mrs. Macaulay's because it is a very fashionable school : and, as Fr. O'Connor says, we must deal kindly with people's whims : for she would have a better education in a Catholic convent. Dr. McGlynn left us to take up his quarters

October   158

at St. Stephen's.

Wed., 11th   A Mr. Cronin called on me to give me lessons in elocution. I took two in one day. The principle he teaches is to speak without using the lungs, but merely the mouth, on rotundo. I paid $10 for his trouble. In the evening I visited the McKnights, who forced me to take tea with them. I attended the altar-class : and afterwards visited Dr. Morrogh, and my mother.

Thurs., 12th   In the afternoon we had the 1st exhibition of the parochial day-school, which was excellent. The premiums were very handsome. Fr. Preston spoke on the utility of secular learning, which is always cherished in the Catholic Church : but it must be based on religion to enoble the individual and the State. The State has ignored this : the Church is anxious to provide a remedy for the defect of the State : which only promotes secular knowledge. In the evening I visited Dr. McGlynn, installed at St. Stephen's, who had three marriages and one baptism to attend to whilst I was there.

Fri., 13th   Fr. Nilan called to see me and state that he would not find it possible to start on Monday, because Fr. McCarthy will be in Albany. We heard confessions all the afternoon and evening.

Sat., 14th   I invited Fr. McGean to preach for me on Sunday two weeks. He made a show of resistance : but is bursting with pleasure at a Roman doctor inviting him to preach. We had a great number of confessions to-day, in preparation for the papal Benediction to be given to-morrow.

Sun., 15th   Sunday. I preached Musso's sermon for the 19th Sunday after Pentecost. We had solemn High Mass, Fr. Preston celebrating, I acting as deacon, and Mr Regnand S. J. as subdeacon. After Mass, Fr. Preston, in cope, gave the papal Benediction having first said that the pope being vicar

October 159

of Christ had delegated him to give this blessing. 2. that though the pope was persecuted he was full of confidence in God. 3. that the gates of hell should not even now prevail against the Church founded on the rock, though he might suffer temporarily. We used the splendid vestments brought home by Fr. Preston from Lyons : all apparently of massive gold, in very good taste, though in French form. He paid $1200,00 in gold = $1700,00 in greenbacks for two full sets including cope of gold, and of purple; a red chasuble, several benediction veils, and two plain, white and purple, chasubles: a saving, he thinks, of at least $2000! I spoke to the boys and girls on the 1st part of the 2nd commandment : and in the evening visited the Morroghs of 26th st. where were also my mother, the McLaughlins, Mr. Belcher, Charline Wheelock, and Mr. Cray, and his daughter Miss Cray, cousin of Charline, the two last from Boston.

Mon., 16th   In the morning Dr. McSweeny and I visited Fr. Killeen of Red Bank, N.J. who took us out rabbit-hunting : it turned out to be merely hunting without catching. We played at cards in the evening for 3 hours. He has built a nice country house for himself : and says that he is more satisfied with this country life than with city life. We talked about Dr. Brann, who told his bishop that if he were removed from Jersey city he would demand his excat.

Tues., 17th   I returned home early to assist at Charline Wheelock's marriage with Mr. Belcher. On the cars from Red Bank I met Mrs. McCormick, who spoke about her daughter Lizzie, married lately to Mr. Donnelly, who failed two weeks after his marriage. They live in Montreal. I stopped to see John Avezzana, Vice-Consul of Italy : who now lives in 57th St. near 1st Ave. The Marriage was performed by Dr. Irving in the Episcopal Church Cor. 30th St. & Lexington Ave. The English ceremonial is very fine : Dr.

October 160

Irving was rather theatrical in his declaring them man & wife. A very fine lunch was prepared in 26th St. cottage : I was introduced to Dr. Irving, a middle aged man, not very bright, yet very gentlemanly, who after a few words with the married couple, retired because of a nervous headache. I presented a fine cameo of the Savior to Charline. Miss Cray sought to sit near a single gentleman, next to whom the bride once sat, with the hope that the proverb should become true, that he would be her husband. The Masons, & Mrs. Gen. Allen, and a Miss Belcher were there besides the Richmonds, McLaughlins, Morroghs of Yorkville, Dr. Morrogh and my mother and the Avezzanas. I went to Shady Dell with the Richmonds : with whom I had a very pleasant chat.

<u>Wed., 18th</u>   Dr. and Mrs. Richmond took me to see the lighthouse near their country-house from which we had a fine sight of Raritan bay : and South Amboy. I returned home in the afternoon and attended the altar class.

<u>Thurs., 19th</u>   With Dr. McSweeny I visited Fr. McCarthy and Fr. Nilan : and met with them Fr. Tom Quin of Rhode Island. We heard that at Albany, the bishops spoke about Mt. St. Mary's as almost the only place where one can get a decent education because B. Conroy was a Mt. St. Mary's student. In the afternoon Dr. McGlynn called to see me with a Mr. Murphy from Chicago bound for the Propda Rome : we visited the American institute fair but went through it so rapidly that it has hardly left any impression on my mind. I noticed the plan of pneumatic railway as also the cow-milking-apparatus. I had my profile cut out by a clever old man in ? minutes, and very well. The premiums were being given out. In the evening I went to the orphan's festival where the company from New Bowery Theatre played 'the serious family' in which a serious family is taught how to enjoy a ball. The Bryants gave us a specimen of their minstrelsy. Mr. & Miss Geary played and sang

October   161

for us. 'The jealous philosopher' was the last peice : in which the philosopher gets jealous of a girl, dressed in man's clothes, who pays addresses to his wife : and is then ashamed of his jealousy. I went out after the Bryants' part. The house was packed.

Fri., 20th   I commenced giving the girls the instruction in the morning and found it much more agreeable than after dinner as I did formerly. I went to a German priest of 3rd St. Church for confession. I visited Dr. McGlynn and supped with him and Fr. Gamboville, who gave me very strong coffee that produced a very troublesome diarrhoea.

Sat., 21st   We heard confessions as usual. I visited Fr. Nilan to inform him that the Albany day-boats don't run any more. Fr. Tom Quin gave us letters for two priests in Quebec.

Sun., 22nd   I sang High Mass. Fr. Preston preached on the necessity of faith, taking for his text the day's gospel (this being the 20th Sunday after Pentecost) and gave hard raps to the spirit of the age which ignores faith, and especially to Episcopalianism seeking to gain Christian Unity, rejecting the centre of unity appointed by Christ, and which lately (in the conference at Philadelphia) expressed the hope of obtaining converts among the Italian Clergy and laity, among whom many sought a reformation like the English one. Fr. Preston said some clergymen might desire to get married : some laymen were infidels : but neither would think of Protestant Episcopalianism. I spoke on the 2nd commandment about vows to the boys' and girls' Sunday school. In the evening I visited the Morroghs of 26th St. : where were the McLaughlins and my mother.

Mon., 23rd   To-day Fr. Nilan and I started by the 7;30 Hudson R. R. on a two weeks' tour. The foliage along the Hudson was magnificent : We admired the many various hues given to the leaves by autumn. We dined at

October 162

Fr. A. O'Neil where we found Dr. Conroy and Fr. Burke. Fr. Nilan and I undertook the defence of the Fenians very strongly against the Bishop, who expressed great surprise at my sympathising with their cause. I think we prevented him from a public condemnation of them. He invited us to sleep up at the Cathedral house where we could have more quiet rooms than at St. Joseph's. We laughed at Bish. McFarland, who backed out of a condemnation of the Fenians, because they absented themselves from his Church on a grand collection day : and then said that he had no objection to a Fenian excursion for Fenian purposes : and that if he thought that the Irish had any chance of liberation from England he would assist them, aye even go in person. I know that Dr. Conroy prevented Fr. O'Hara of Syracuse from lecturing for the Fenians : and is thinking of calling Fr. to an account for so doing. In the evening we visited Troy Seminary : where Fr. Healy entertained us a while. He spoke of the Seminary library which has few good Theologians, though about 4000 vols. He is a poor professor, not having the facility of communicating his ideas to others. He brought us to see Fr. Tandy, the procurator, who put on airs of superiority over those who were his companions in college, has a very small mind, is quite pompous : who gave us tea in his own room. He had been a companion of Fr. Nilan's in St. John's, Fordham. We saw also Fr. Vandenheude, the president, who spoke in bad English, and told us that the people here are too civilised : and more Xtianity is needed to keep them backwards in civilization. He never was made to rule Americans : though he and his Belgian associates are good and learned men! We had a less idea of Troy Seminary on leaving than on entering it. No ruling spirit is there. In Albany we had a long talk with Fr. Walworth before going to bed : we talked of the inspiration of the Bible, merely giving to Moses' historical books the credit due to any historical work,

October   163

and requiring inspiration in matters of faith & morals.

<u>Tues., 24th</u>   We said Mass in the Albany Cathedral : where the altar-stones are raised above the altar most awkwardly. At breakfast were the Bishop, Fr. Walworth, Fr. Ludder and Fr. Wadhams; who started for Europe an hour afterwards. Fr. Nilan & I visited Mrs. W. Preston who spoke rapturously about Dr. Conroy's consecration : Mrs. Cayzer, who spoke on the same topic : Mrs. W. Cassidy who asked me about the Burtsells of 4th Ave. N.Y., and Miss Fan. Cassidy, who too was anxious about her sister Mrs. Dr. Thos. Burtsell. I gave them the message that they intrusted to me, viz : to say that every thing was getting along quite smoothly. At Fr. O'Neils we met Fr. Cull, who is a disgusting fellow, Fr.   , who is at Greenbush, and respectable-looking, & Fr. Daly of Utica who invited us to stop at Utica till he got there. Accordingly we left by 1 P. M. New York Central on which Miss Fannie Cassidy had procured from P. Cayzer a free-ticket for me and as many friends as I could put names on the ticket. We stopped at Utica where Fr. McDonald received us quite hospitably and made us take dinner. We met there a Fr. Phillips, a Maymooth man. We entered on the Fenian question and found that Irishmen denounce their own countrymen more than any one else. Fr. MacDonald sympathised with the Fenians. Fr. Daly's old father stupidly bored us for 3 hours with running down his countrymen. Fr. Daly came in at about 10.30. In the mean time Fr. Pat. Smith took us to visit Mrs. Kearney, where we met Alice Kearney who both entertained us for an hour with light talk. They had been anxious to see a live Roman doctor. They want a new church : and promise liberal sums for this purpose : their present church is the Symbol of poverty. Fr. Pat Smith is in raptures with the Utica Society : and has several engagements per evening. He has been here for two weeks, during Fr. Daly's being at

October

Saratoga in his place. We visited the O'Neils. The father delights in speaking very loud to one's ears : the Mother is an intelligent woman, and the brother is quite manly. Fr. O'Neil asked us to visit them : I believe that they are not very popular in Utica. Fr. Daly kept us up till 12 o'c. and accused me of putting on airs, because I didn't drink : he knew our family as an old Knickerbocker family.

<u>Wed., 25th</u> In the morning Fr. Daly drove 4 priests and a seminarian, a Mr. to see the Trenton falls, but about half-way we broke down, the horses running away, and pretty nearly smashing carriage and us to piece against an embankment. Fr. Daly was half-tight. Fr. Nilan rode back : I walked 7 miles to Utica. We noticed Fr. MacDonald riding with a Miss Hogan, quite a young lady, because she was a Fr. Hogan's sister!! We started for Syracuse, where we stayed at the St. Charles hotel having good rooms, and beds but poor fare. We called to see Fr. O'Hara, but he was absent : and Mr. Andrew Lynch in Salina, who also was absent : though at his place a Miss Van Loom entertained us pleasantly giving her experience at Manhattanville and in California, and an account of the theatrical exhibitions of the Syracuse families.

<u>Thurs., 26th</u> Mr. Andrew Lynch showed us the salt works, in which the process is simple. Some spread the salt-water in large wooden vessels, till the sun makes the water evaporate : and the salt remains. Others use artificial heat for the same object. We saw the springs and baths of Syracuse Excelsior waters, like sea-water. We called at Fr. O'Hara's : he was absent but we saw his brother, a gawkish youth, and we called at Fr. McMenomy's too : he was absent. His church and house and school-house are very good. He and Fr. O'Hara peck at each other on Sundays. Mr. Andrew Lynch treated us to a dinner at a restaurant's, disappointed that we did

October

not wait for tea-time. We started in the afternoon for Niagara : which we reached at 10 o'c. P. M. : Fr. O'Connor met us at the depot.

<u>Fri., 27th</u>   It rained : but we visited the Falls : we talked all day of Propda, Rome, and Bish. Timon's doings. Fr. O'Connor has built an extension to his church : is always active at some good work.

<u>Sat., 28th</u>   We went to Buffalo : had a discussion about the Fenians with Dr. Barker, a Propagandist : Fr. Nilan & Dr. Barker had a tilting match as to the respective merits of Propda and the American college of Rome at the dinner-table, before four seminarians who live at the bishop's house and are taught by Dr. Barker. We visited the Jesuits' to see Fr. Durthaller, who was absent : Fr. Vetter, a sleak individual, received us coldly. A fine church of theirs is nearly completed, & will cost $60,000.00 : a great sum for Buffalo.

<u>Sun., 29th</u>   Fr. Nilan preached at High Mass on the gospel : the sermon was short, and devoid of practical lessons & not animated. Fr. Cannon sang Mass. In the evening I lectured on the Mass = a Sacrifice = very few were present on account of the careless advertisement that Fr. Cannon gave of it : The Entrance fee was 25 cts. During the day Fr. Nilan & I took the boat to the Canadian side : had a splendid view of the falls : saw the museum & rode to the Suspension Bridge.

<u>Mon., 30th</u>   We took the cars for Lewiston : and went by the British boat over Lake Ontario to Toronto : where we stayed at the Queen's hotel, arriving too late for the boat that went to the rapids. We walked about Toronto which pleased us, though very quiet. We went to the bishop's : where Fr. Jancot, the rector, entertained us very pleasantly, we spoke to him in favour of the Fenians. We met also there Frs. Lee, and Laurent attached to the church as also Fr. Methot of Quebec. The bishop kept us

October

a long time talking about the wants of the missions in the United States. All seemed to wish Canada annexed to the States.

<u>Tues., 31st</u>   We had a dreary ride in the cars, the whole day to get to Montreal : where we stayed at the St. James' hotel. The country along the road was desolate : the towns & villages poor.

November

<u>Wed., 1st</u>   We went to High-Mass at Notre Dame : the parish church : where we were much edified by the demeanour of the congregation. The church is large, but not clean, nor artistic : it makes no great impression on one who saw the European churches. In my childhood I thought it stupendously large. There are in it two tiers of galleries. The ceremonies were in full Roman style : the present bishop Bouget being anxious to have even peoples' nails cut in Roman fashion if there be any particular fashion for such business! We heard a French sermon : on All Saints : in which was determined 1. who are the saints 2. what is their state, 3. what we have to do to reach their happiness. 1. The saints are men and women : the rich who used their wealth well, the poor who sanctified their souls in the midst of tribulation etc. 2. The saints see God, and in him find complete happiness. Their intelligence is perfected, because they see the Essential truth. Their will is satisfied by the Infinite goodness and beauty of God. 3. We must mortify our passions & use this world well to gain heaven. We afterwards went to St. Patrick's : which is a beautiful church where the priests invited us to dine next day. Fr. Brown is rector : Fr. Dupin is one of the assistants; I knew both of them in Montreal college, 12 years ago. At the seminaire I met Fr. Leclair, who gladly received me. Fr. Perrault too my old confessor was very hospitable. I met Fr. Billon, Palatin,   , whom I knew in the college. We dined after the Sulpicians.

November   167

The fare was good and abundant. I bought some flannel shirts which cost
as much as in New York. We could not get good gloves : in fact everything sold in Montreal is too rough, made for working people or too thick,
made for the severest cold weather. We strolled about the city, especially
admiring the fine wharves. We settled accounts with the hotel = $4,00 (in
greenbacks) and went to the 'Seminaire' : whence we could not go out after
7 o'c. The room given us had two beds, a few chairs, wooden floor and no
fire. In the afternoon we visited the Jesuits : who have a fine college
and are building a very large church designed by Keiley, pushed forward by
Bishop Bouget who wants an excuse to have the Sulpicians deprived of the
parochial control of the whole city : for in Rome he will adduce the necessity of the Jesuits' having parochial rights to support their church. Fr.
Lefebere hinted to me that the Jesuits' college does not produce good
boys. We thought the Jesuit fathers too cold and formal : Mr. Finnegan, a
scholastic of New York and Mr. Raiscot whom I knew in college treated us
quite warmly.

Thurs., 2nd   We awoke at 9 o'c. and were ashamed to attempt to say
Mass at such a late hour. We took a cab for the 'Grand Seminaire' at the
mountain : where we assisted at the requiem High Mass in the Seminary chapel : which is very fine and chaste. The Seminarians number about 90 : the
college about 100. Both were edifying in their deportment : and they all
sang magnificently. We saw Fr. Lefebre, my old teacher of Syntax, a whole-
souled, earnest minded man, who though severe was always loved, because he
showed a real interest in those under his care. He received me with open
arms. 1 saw also Frs. Dequerre and Parent who were in the college as students with me. Fr. Lefebre showed me the 'cabier d'honneur' of his class
in which I found several compositions of my own : one of which surprised,

November   168

as really good in French. The building was made for a Seminary and therefore the rooms are too small for class-rooms for the college. There is but a wooden partition between the college and the seminary. In the seminary I met Frs. Larue and De la vique : whom I knew of old. We dined with the Seminarians in a quite crowded refectory; the reading was about the Sulpicians' history : the reader was disgusting. In recreation, the custom was to walk in fours & fives. We visited the Hotel Dieu : through which Fr. Marcellin whom I knew in the college, led us. The hospital is very neat : and gratuitous. The Nuns of St. Joseph have care of it. The chapel is in very fine taste & has a nice cupola. We sought after Fr. Nercam at the Congregationalist Sisters' : where he showed great gladness to see me. He was rector of the college, when I was there. He once in a letter characterised me as "toujours bon, et toujours dissipe". We attended a sick-call with Fr. Leclair : and missed the afternoon train for New York. I paid the cab-driver $5,00 (in gold) for the day's work. He said, he averaged $2,00 a day.

Fri., 3rd   We said mass in the morning and left Montreal by 8.30 train. Our impressions about the Sulpicians were very favourable : they are good and pious men : but there is no artifice or show of shrewdness in their dealings with others : they are open-hearted and lively, and trustful even with strangers. Fr. Nilan and I were exceedingly pleased with them : and contrasted them with the stiff, suspicious, and sleak dealings of the Jesuits. The Montreal Sulpicians, so Fr. Perrault told me, were anxious to have the Troy Seminary : but the Baltimore Sulpicians feared that their own house would fail, and got the Parisian Sulpicians to prevent the Montreal folks from taking it. Fr. Vandeheude spoke lately to Fr. Larue, encouraging the coming of the Sulpicians. Our U. S. boys find

November   169

the Sulpicians too severe : and not taking cognizance of our American independence of manner : which they consider to be pride. We admired the long bridge over the St. Lawrence : and the beautiful country of Vermont & arrived in Albany by the Rutlend R. R. at about 9 o'c. where went to Ambrose O'Neil who undertook the defence of Fr. Daly against our attacks. Hearing that Mrs. Thos. Burtsell was in Albany, I went to see her. I saw in her stead, William Cassidy, who told me that the Dr., having behaved boisterously one night, had been put in the Tombs : and then it was now a question whether he should be sent to Litchfield, Ct, or to Mount Hope for insanity. He had ill treated his wife, & Mrs. Paddon, into whose house he broke to get at his wife. I disapproved his being put in the Tombs : but said that it is useless to cry over spilt milk. I objected to Litchfield as not trustworthy : and said that he could never be sent to Mount Hope, for he was not insane.

Sat., 4th   I saw Mrs. Thos. Burtsell : who expressed great anxiety to return home soon. I returned to New York by the Hudson R. R. having missed the Albany train in which Fr. Nilan returned. I had said mass at St. Joseph's for the Burtsell family. I was favourably impressed with the inside of St. Joseph's : the outside is too irregular in the plan. I heard confessions as soon as I reached home.

Sun., 5th   I sang High Mass. Fr. Preston preached on the glory of the Saints in heaven. I went to both Sunday Schools but spoke in neither. In the evening I went to the Morroghs of 26th St. Mr. Daschauer dined with us. I got more details about Dr. Burtsell from my mother.

Mon., 6th   I visited Miss Anastasia Burtsell : who had concurred with the Cassidys, in having Dr. Thos. Burtsell arrested. He was in the Tombs a week, without clean apparel. Ambrose Cassidy had once been bailed

November   170

by Dr. Tom : Yet A. Cassidy brought Peter Burtsell the morning after the arrest to have his father convicted and sent to the Tombs. I saw Dr. Tom : who spoke about indifferent subjects whilst strangers were present, but was glad at my condoling with him afterwards. In the morning I had taken a walk with Dr. McSweeny, who told me that Fr. Maguire had publicly denounced the Fenian leaders as thieves, and bound to restore the money received for Irish bonds. I went to Mr. Fairbrother's funeral with Dr. McGlynn and Fr. Gallagher from Raphoe Ireland. Mr. Fairbrother was buried in Calvary, not having enough to pay for his grave. I said mass for him in the morning. R. I. P.

Tues., 7th   In the afternoon I visited the Decoppets and Miss Ann Burtsell who were very bitter about the treatment used with Dr. Thos. Burtsell. The Gallaghers seemed anxious to keep out of the trouble, & maintained silence when the subject was broached.

Wed., 8th   I went to Dr. Morrogh's to dine and found that they had changed their dining hour. I met Fr. Hughes (once known as snothy-nose Jimmy) whom I found to be more refined than I expected. Dr. McGlynn tells me that he has done great good in Hartford. He was obliged to pay tax on his perquisites, masses, salary, and even on a $2000 donation from the people on his departure for Europe. I paid my revenue tax of $10,20 : I counted my salary, and masses = $800,00; and 20 cts fine for requiring the notice. I saw Miss Anastasia Burtsell who showed me the Dr.'s bills for groceries, refreshments etc. I held the altar-class this evening.

Thurs., 9th   I visited Dr. Thos. Burtsell : with whom I found Miss Ann Burtsell and Mrs. & Lizzie Decoppet. I proposed to Tom to rent his present house for $600 and with this money go a-travelling, of course with the consent of his wife. I visited Dr. McGlynn, with whom & Fr. Gallagher

November   171

I went to Brooklyn to see Dr. Freel; but he was out. We were impressed with the want of dignity of Bp. Loughlin.

<u>Fri., 10th</u>   Fr. Killeen visited me this morning and invited me to his place on Monday next. I gave instruction to the girls' school on 'Blasphemy and Cursing'. & heard their confessions in the morning. In the afternoon I went to Fr. Schauer of 3d St. (Redemptorists') to confession, and then visited Miss Anastasia Burtsell who promised to give $500,00 for Tom's trip.

<u>Sat., 11th</u>   I took a rambling walk in the morning and wrote out a sermon on Purgatory.

<u>Sun., 12th</u>   I preached at 7 o'c. & at High Mass on Purgatory : and to the boys' on 'Blasphemy & Cursing' not having time to speak to the girls : sang Vespers. In the evening at Dr. Cheever's church I heard Chaplain French and Gen. Fisk speak on the freedmen's condition. Chaplain French spoke about Georgia & Alabama where he said the negroes are clamouring for bread, clothes and coffins. The physicians of Milledgeville, Georgia, have combined not to assist the negroes unless prepaid, viz : not at all. Mr. French says that 30 000 freedmen will die before March : & 50000 if the North does not assist them. Gen. Fisk gave a better account of Tennesee : but described the whites' feeling against the negroes as bitter in Kentucky.

<u>Mon., 13th</u>   Drs. McGlynn & McSweeny and I visited Fr. Killeen at Red Bank : and had a row in his boat : and played cards in the evening : and mercilessly cut up Dr. Brann.

<u>Tues., 14th</u>   We exercised ourselves at various feets of gymnathics in which Fr. Killeen is 'facile princeps'. On our return to New York Dr. McGlynn and I visited St. George's church which was burning. It was a

November   172

splendid building. With Fr. Preston we talked on the wants of the diocese
and against the supine laziness of the Authorities. Fr. Moriarity with
Fr.   of Boston called to invite us to a little Soiree at his house
in honour of his ordination which took place on last Saturday. Bp. Conroy
of Albany imposed hands on him. Abp. McCloskey refused receiving Fr. Gallagher
suspecting that he had had some discussion with his bishop McGettigan who
is a friend of Abp. McCloskey's and was snappish telling him that he could
say mass only on last Sunday. Dr. McGlynn says that Fr. Gallagher is a
good, and smart priest : educated in Holland and Belgium. Fr. Menelli an
Italian priest who was tight once or twice, and collecting intentions which
he had no intention of fulfilling, has not yet been ordered to omit Mass :
though Dr. Cummings having dismissed him from St. Stephen's informed the
Abp. of these facts through Dr. McGlynn.

Wed., 15th   I took lunch at Dr. Morrogh's. We had a grand dinner
at 5 o'c. in honour of Mrs. Hassard's birth-day : the guests were Mr. &
Mrs. Dashauer, Mrs. Livingston (a Protestant sister of Mrs. Hassard), Mr.
John Hassard, sub-editor of the Chicago Republican, Mr. & Mrs. Cornell of
Yonkers, a nice couple. She was placed in a convent for 6 months after
marriage : till she was a confirmed Catholic. I had the altar-class : and
about eight of the larger boys of the parish came to request me to reestablish
the literary Society.

Thurs., 16th   I heard Mr. Tiers' confession. He, through nervousness,
constantly sends for either Fr. Preston or myself, without any reason. It
will turn out to be the story of = wolf! wolf! I visited Dr. Thos. Burtsell,
who shows no sorrow for his past ways, and is indignant at the way in which
he was treated : he is pushed to this by his sisters (at least, I imagine
so) Miss Ann Burtsell, & Mrs. Decoppet, whom I found there. They took me

November

to task for pronouncing grievous as grievious, and calling Adam and Eve our forefathers. This mortification will be a new motive for my paying more attention to the study of the English language. I visited Miss Anastasia Burtsell, who is afraid to speak even of living with her brother Dr. Tom : Peter is not a generous boy : he has grown very selfish : and I am afraid that contact with the sensual Ambrose and infidel William Cassidy will make him become bad and lose his faith : especially as his temporal interests (and he understands this well) prompt him to lean upon the Cassidys, who being all powerful in political circles will be able to cut out a good temporal career for him, to which his talents will enable him to reach. In the afternoon I visited Fr. McCarthy the fattest priest in the diocese, who is good-hearted, talented, very pleasant in conversation. He expressed great surprise at our rejecting our old organ, which he heard at St. Gabriel's, and thought very good. He was disappointed at the discourse and delivery of Bishop Lynch on that occasion.

Fri., 17th   I gave the instructions to the girls in the morning on the 3rd commandment. In the afternoon I obtained for Mrs. Burtsell from Wheeler & Wilson, a sewing-machine whose cost was $85, for $60 : this being a clergyman's privilege. I went to confession to Fr. Schauer the Redemptorist and visited the Redemptorists' church which is very fine, and then took lunch at Dr. Morrogh's. I visited Miss Jones, at Miss Macaulay's school : She is quite happy, & contented with her companions, who however are curious about scapulars etc and repeating the 'our father' many times. She found some difficulty in going to church on the holidays of obligation, and cannot go to confession as often as before & is dissatisfied with the French church, where her seat is uncomfortable and she is scandalised by French carelessness in getting late.

November   174

Sat., 18th   I put $150.00 in The Bank for Savings in Bleecher St.
We have Mrs. Hassard at all our meals now. Before she did not come down :
thinking that I was opposed to it : as she is to go away in a few days, I
am not displeased. She and I were rather distant, while Fr. Preston was
in Europe : as she came to our house never acknowledging my presence in any
way.

Sun., 19th   Sunday. We published that the concert at the opening
of the new organ will take place on the 17th December. Fr. Preston preached
at High Mass on the gospel applying the parable of the mustard seed to the
Church's beginning and growth : and ridiculed Protestant missions as means
of giving the missionaries & wives & children comfortable homes : the
missionaries remain on the outskirts of heathendom, printing bibles; one
of them had three converts of whom one fluctuated according to the raising
or depreciating of his salary : another had two converts and writes for
more money to attack the Man of Sin, who has 80,000 in the interior of the
same Chinese province (Marshall's comparison between Protestant & Catholic
Missions). I spoke to the boys' and girls' Sunday School on the 3rd commandment.
Mr. Dachauer dined with us. In the evening I went to hear Dr. Moriarity
of Philadelphia, lecture on the relations between Science & Revelation &
could understand nothing absolutely of what he said. He speaks very loud, is
monotonous, and does not articulate distinctly. I met Fr. Nilan & Dr. Freel:
the three of us went to the Zebra Church and heard Dr. Bellows tell us to
trace the streams of our passions and interests & end with the 'Our father'.
After service there was a fine tenor solo : the organ is very good. The
church inside is bear : but very well filled. Fr. Nilan & I went to the
Morroghs of 26th St. where were my mother and Mrs. McLaughlin. They noticed
Fr. Nilan's resemblance to his uncle Fr. Ryan. We had a grand discussion

November

about the Fenians.

Mon., 20th   At dinner Miss Denning was present besides the Hassards, and Fr. Duranquet, who is very uncouth in his looks, though a hard-working Jesuit, employed at the Island : making lately 20 converts a month among the prisoners. I cannot enjoy the conversation with the Hassards & Co. The fault is greatly mine, caused by my bashfulness : & I am too serious for light talk. In the evening I took J. Burke to see the where some fine statues where exhibited, as also Somerset House in London and an apartment of Windsor Castle, which is very rich : and views of the Vatican and Coliseum and a few other buildings. I felt nervous at the exhibition of the statuary for J. Burke's sake, because many of the statues were nude.

Tues., 21st   The rain obliged me to stay home the whole day. I went to see Edwin Forrest play Othello. I studied his manner attentively : he is not natural, exceedingly noisy : but certainly his mind is great, he expressed Othello's jealousy with great power. Miss Jane Percy acted as Desdemona and did her part well : McCullough acted as Iago & very well.

Wed., 22nd   Fr. Nilan called to see me. We talked about Dr. Brann's rupture with Fr. Lenez : whom he spoke of in a sermon 'as an odd Frenchman, who did some good and soon vanished' : Fr. Hennessy wrote against Dr. Brann in the N.Y. Tablet, for having slighted Fr. Lenez : not mentioning him, as one who built a church in Jersey, whilst the Dr. was enumerating the founders of Catholic Churches in Jersey & neighbouring counties. I walked with Fr. Nilan to Grand St. talking against the Jesuitical idea of humility, which is to despise oneself, as incapable of good : never teaching to use God's gifts to us for His glory. This is their practical idea of humility. In the evening I met the altar and literary classes. A Mr. Humphry

November

(brother-in law) to Miss Denning, dined with us & is clever.

<u>Thurs., 23rd</u>   The rain continued the whole day. Mrs. Hassard & Son Miss Denning and Fr. Preston started off for Chicago where the Hassards are to take up their constant residence. I suppose they took Fr. Preston to sweep the place for them! Mrs. Livingston supped with us. I went to see Edwin Forrest play Virginius. He represented the character very well : his exhibition of alternate passion and calmness at hearing of Virginia's (Miss Agnes Perry, who is a superb actress) mishap was excellent : as also his madness after killing Virginia was admirably rendered. Mr. McCullough played as Icilius, and his acting was good : Collier acting as Appius Claudius did poorly. Shakespeare's had an immense mind : a never-ending knowledge of human nature!

<u>Fri., 24th</u>   Dr. McSweeny called to see me : we had a walk together. We were nigh coming to a breakout on account of his considering the Fenian leaders to be rogues : and his own countrymen to be incapable of self-government. Abp. McCloskey proves the leaders not to be good because they don't go to confession : and with the same breath says that he would not give them absolution! He approved of Fr. Maguire's assertion that they were bound to make restitution for selling Irish bonds! and asserted that the priest who bought the Irish bonds would commit sin, by thus encouraging the poor to buy them!!! Fr. Maguire was frightened at hearing that a Fenian had threatened (to Dr. McSweeny, through fun) to horsewhip him : The Abp. thought seriously that the Fenian was capable of undertaking it!!! At Eugene Kelly's I met a Eugene Plunkett, clerk who very impertinently told me that I ought to correct and reform St. Ann's choir (though he didn't know whether it needed reform, but the generality of Catholic choirs need it, ergo etc). Plunkett said that Remi our basso called tom foolery what

November   177

was going on at the altar at Mass & the installation of Abp. McCloskey. I confessed to Fr. Shauer the Redemptorist. In the morning I heard the girls' confessions and gave the usual instructions on the 3rd commandment.

Sat., 25th   I took a walk to 40th St. in the morning, alone. Fr. Tissand S. J. came to hear confessions. He is a most uninteresting man, dirty, unpolished, small-minded. He is the treasurer of the college at Fordham & says that the new college is in the process of building : one wing will be built for the present.

Sun., 26th   Fr. Tissand sang H. Mass. I read at 7 o'c and $10\frac{1}{2}$ o'c a letter from the Abp. requiring a collection in the city-churches for the American college at Rome, and I encouraged very strongly. 1. because this college gives immense facilities for clerical training, 2. because The Theological and Moral Philosophical studies are pursued better in Rome than elsewhere, forming the principal item of Roman education. 3. because they have traditions of centuries as a guide, whilst in this country, we are but learning experience. 4. because the American students come in contact with the great Catholic minds of the world in Rome, which is frequented by the Greatest Scholars. 5. because coming in contact with Propagandists, composed of some 80 nationalities, they learn more of the characters of the different peoples than elsewhere. I preached afterwards on the Gospel of the day : viz : last Sunday after Pentecost. I spoke in both Sunday schools on the 3rd commandment : as well as to the Sodality of Men after Vespers, showing them how to sanctify the Sunday, which is a Social homage to God, being a day set apart by the Church Society for the service to God (not merely an individual service to God) and therefore does the church require assistance at the sacrifice of the Mass, a Sacrifice being a public and social act; and also requiring parents to instruct their children, pastors

November 178

to instruct their flocks, and charitable men and women to teach children their catechism, all these being appurtenances of the social life, in which one seeks to assist the weakness of another : for this was society formed by God, that each one might assist his neighbour : for the defects of one make us need the help of another who has the quality of which we may be defective. This establishes the dependence of the various members of society as there is dependence among the members of the body. Hence I deduced that the men of our parish were obliged to assist at the Sunday School, which would easily become the best in the city : the class of boys is excellent, and of that middle-class which rules in American Society. At dinner I had a discussion with Fr. Tissand on the middle ages : he thought they were far better for faith and morality than the present age. I maintained that the faith now was more enlightened : the immorality less gross than then. The Middle-Ages cared for the nobles and the clergy and ignored the people : which has no history in that period. Now the people is the object of History because active in it's own government. I preferred the faith of the Theologian to that of the ignorant Irishman, whose faith however prompts him already to do so much good : he would do much more if he had a more reasoning faith : because he has the grace of God that will prompt him to use his greater knowledge for good. Mr. Dachauer agreed entirely with me. In the evening I attended a discourse of Rev. Dr. Dix, rector of Trinity Church, in Calvary Church about the house of St. Barnabas : in which are received women who have no shelter at night : and meals are given to men, women and children who have no reliance for support. This relieves especially poor persons, convalescent enough to be dismissed from the public hospitals, not strong enough to work : poor widows who can leave their children there during the day, whilst they are at work : strangers who have no means to board

November

elsewhere. This house was established in July : 30 persons were boarded in that month, 66 in November : 900 meals were given in July, 3200 in November. The inmates receive moral instructions by day. Contributions in money, food and clothing are requested : all are invited to visit the institution. Dr. Dix is a good man & speaks plainly : but has a fixed intonation which displeases. His explanation of these simple facts would have been more effective, if not read. He made a few caustic remarks about this city being called Christian, whilst there is more vice in it than was ever known in Sidon, Tyre, Sodom or Gomorrha. The thought of 'city missions' in New York should thrill every Christian heart : and make good people more generous in contributing for the relief of the poor, for the reclamation of the depraved. The 'city-mission Society' exists for 30 years : It's first object was to bring Episcopal doctrines before the working-classes, and take from Episcopalianism the stigma of being Aristocratic, by opening free-churches for the working-classes. Now it has a new object to bring these doctrines home to the poorest classes : by relieving their temporal distress and through this, reaching their hearts. A sisterhood of good matrons has charge of this institution, which is at 206 Mulberry St. Tickets are sold entitling the poor-bearer to one meal : 10 are sold for 1$: they can be given to beggars rather than money : which they may abuse. Thus the institution can be supported. Calvary Church is very neat : and it's inside plan is very pleasing : though cold, for want of painting. The Music was plain-chant. I like the Episcopal service : and regret that the Catholic Service, which would be far more telling, loses not a little of it's force by the accompaniment of a foreign tongue. The Episcopal prayerbook with truth says that this is repugnant to the custom of the primitive Church : Though rebellion and schism are far worse than any disadvantage

November 180

rising from obedience to the present law of the church, requiring the liturgy to be recited in Latin. I hope this law will be changed. I was amused at Mr. Dachauer asking me to translate a piece from French into Italian. French cannot be sung in Church because understood by many. Italian can be sung because not understood : a fine requisite to do good, that the singing should not be at all understood! Our Jesuits and religious bodies, not being English speaking, would never think of a movement to remove this objection from our service : unfortunately they exercise great influence in the Church here. Religious bodies are cramped by puny traditions, originating from some small mind : a master mind is required to emancipate them. Frenchmen especially seem to be small minded : on one side accepting the most foolish infidelity, on the other the queerest notions of homage to God. Here we have accepted almost all our religious notions and customs from Frenchmen. I was disgusted with the vulgar way in which Fr. Tissand said Mass! In the evening I went to the Morroghs of 26th St : where we studied the geneologies and affinities of our several families, the Morroghs, the Avezzanas, Burtsells, Plowdens, O'Connells and O'Donohues.

Mon., 27th   Dr. Brann dined with me. He has been removed from the Immac. Conception to St. Peter's because he quarrelled with Fr. Lenez and de Concilio. Hennessy has been made pastor of Elizabethport. Dr. Brann thinks that the principal pewholders of the Immac. Conception will go to St. Peter's : Fr. Kelly it's pastor is now old : Dr. Brann told the congregation that he would never leave Jersey City with his consent. He has a philosophy class of 36 students! He tells me that his sister, the nun, was followed from St. Louis by a Col. Alexander who fell in love with her for her beauty and musical talents : She was also a good linguist, in fact the smartest woman ever known by Dr. Brann, whose portrait she held along

November   181

with the crucifix on her death-bed. Dr. Gardiner in his obituary of her said that she partook largely of the family heritage of intelligence : and that her sorrowful mother hanging over her bier reminded him of the 'Stabat Mater Dolorosa Juxta crucem'. Dr. Brann in some things is a simpleton : in others a knave : always a liar! Mrs. Burtsell told me that Dr. Morrogh has again taken too much. In the evening I went to see Edwin Forrest play Hamlet : Here I could make a fair comparison between him and Edwin Booth : the latter is a far more refined, more intelligent, and interesting actor. Forrest is too uproarious and not sufficiently deliberate. Miss Agnes Perry acted as Ophelia, excellently but did not sing at all. All the other actors were third rate ones : viz: Collier, Nunan, etc and Mrs. Ralton etc.

<u>Tues., 28th</u>   Fr. Orsenigo came to hear the confessions of Frank A. Otis and Miss Almira Smith. Dr. Parsons dined with me : and gave me his impressions of two Franciscan monasteries (Conventual reformed) where he resided on account of sickness. He found the monks lazy, ignorant, inobservant of their rule, very familiar with the people and with females, when the men were away, joking with young men about young ladies, talking about impurities, using very immodest expressions. It will be a great blessing when the monks and priests of Italy are lessened by at least two thirds! Dr. McGlynn and I took a walk to Central Park, where we met his neices, the Olivers and one nephew : all very intelligent youngsters. Dr. told me of the Abp.'s consenting with difficulty to have the churches incorporated by the new law requiring the Abp., Vicar Gen., pastor and two laymen as a corporation to hold each church : because a heavy tax was imposed on the transfer of property : which Fr. T. Farrell persuaded him to go to Washington to have abolished. Mr. Glover had already been refused this from Washington. Fr. Orsenigo supped with me : I married a Protestant to

November

a Catholic with full ceremonies through forgetfulness!

<u>Wed., 29th</u>   Frank A. Otis and Miss Almira Smith would only hear Fr. Orsenigo's mass and receive communion from him, though I was saying mass at the High-Altar whilst they were in the church. Fr. Orsenigo thinks that there are too many monks and priests in Italy, who being in idleness, easily use their active minds in doing wrong. I agreed with him. He thinks also that many Italian priests are too subservient to rich families : to which under the name of chaplain, they act as 'honourable' servants : frequently too fawning. I agreed with him. Frs. Nilan and Healy called to see me for a few minutes. Fr. Healy tells me that Fr. Hughes his co-assistant at St. Peter's has been sent to Rondout, to give place to a Fr. Ryan who fought with Fr. Briady of that place. Fr. Hughes was becoming too popular at St. Peter's to retain Fr. Quin the pastor's good graces. Fr. Healy would be anxious to build a church near the Battery! where he says he could get a plentiful congregation! Fr. Nilan dined with me. Mr. Otis asked me to ask Fr. Orsenigo to say Mass for the wedding, in case Fr. Preston had not returned by to-morrow. He, Mr. Otis, had ordered Mr. Fox our sexton to reserve the middle-aisle for his friends, and also to keep the 'Biddies' out of the church during the Wedding!!! I countermanded this latter order : and as to the reserving of the pews, I made it emanate from me! Fr. Nilan and I walked to 42nd St. : and arranged to have our pro-Fenian pamphlet ready for January 1st 1867, giving the philosophico-theological opinion of two priests on Fenianism. I met Frs McCarthy, the pastor of Holy Cross, and T. Quin of Rhode Island who is in bad odour both of his bishop and of sanctity : though the two do not always go together! On our return homewards Fr. Nilan and I arranged to visit the various public institutions of New York City, and commenced by visiting the headquarters

November

of Fenianism in Union Square on 17th St. Mr. Kilian was surprised almost suspicious to find two priests visit the house : but kindly led us through the several apartments, telling us that the Irish bonds were being stamped and would be published within four days. He introduced us to Mr. O'Mahony the head-center. They both expressed the expectation of a war of the United States with Great Britain : Mr. Kilian thought that the Fenian Brotherhood could create such complications as to force this country to fight against Great Britain. He then remarked that the Clergy had unfortunately opposed the Fenian Movement : and thus threw a slur on Fenians, to whom the Clergy attributed dishonourable motives, and prevented others from joining the Association. We gave them then our ideas 1st that the Irish must rely on themselves. 2nd. that the clergy does not oppose them 3d. that individual bishops and priests might speak of them, on their own individual responsibility, but not in their clerical responsibility. 4. that many favoured them as strongly as other clergymen opposed them. 5. that the Fenians had a right to declaim against any clergyman, who denounced them from the Church. 6th. that the Clergy has no right to dictate politics to Irishmen. 7th. that no priest could deny absolution to a Fenian because a Fenian, 8th. that Abp. Kenrick's letter had no Ecclesiastical importance, because written to a secular paper and not to the clergy or the faithful. 9th. that the Fenians must learn to distinguish between the clerical character and the political opinions of priests. 10th that Fenianism is not condemned by the Church, because not a secret Society, by which in the technical language of the Church is meant 'a Society whose members are bound by oath or pledge to the overthrowal of religion or government' : of course the government and religion must be legittimate, that their overthrowal may be a crime in the eyes of the Catholic Church. A Society, even with

November

secret aim for the overthrowal of Episcopalianism, is not wrong : so also for the overthrowal of the British government in Ireland, which was never legittimate or if ever so, forfeits it's rights whilst perpetuating wilfully grievous and national evils in Ireland. 11th. that Fenians have a right to determine the policy of this government towards England, by lawful means. I was amused at Mr. O'Mahony, saying that he would never directly oppose a clergyman, because there was no luck in it; he would not go out of his way to avoid another gentleman's insult, but he would avoid the occasion of being insulted by a priest. Mr. Kilian, asked : if he an American citizen would have his Irish politics dictated to him by a Dr. Cullen? Mr. O'Mahony is slow in speech, as if weighing every word : and put on a searching eye, to fathom the sentiments of him who speaks to him. Mr. Kilian is free in speech & communicative, and honest in purpose. We came away quite satisfied with our interview. They keep the Irish flag flowing under the American flag, as they explained, in deference to the American people : and because they are American citizens! Fr. Nilan supped with me. I attended the altar class and literary Society : and castigated Fr. Orsenigo for his having asked, at least indirectly, to say the mass for the Otis & Smith marriage for Otis repeated to me words that I had spoken to Fr. Orsenigo.

Thurs., 30th   The Archbishop arrived at 10½ o'c. and hearing that Fr. Preston was not home said that 'had he known of his absence, he would not come to St. Ann's : it doesn't look well.' I answered that Fr. Preston had sent a telegraphic despatch to me yesterday, stating he could not return before Friday. I had intended absenting myself from the wedding : which the Abp. on going to the sanctuary noticed and remarked : 'You are to be present, are you not?' The reason of my absence would have been to make Mr. Otis feel the indelicacy of his conduct : rather than give further annoy-

November

ance to the Abp. I assisted at the marriage. The Abp. told the people that marriage was now not only a contract but a sacrament : he told Mr. Otis that a loving father gave to his care a loved daughter : and he told Miss Almira Smith that she was to have a protector, whose name had not borne reproach. The Church was crowded : and very many Protestants were present, quite noisy before, but quiet during the service. Fr. Orsenigo said the mass : the Abp. gave the Nuptial Blessing after the 'Pater Noster' and recited the prayer 'Deus Abraham etc' after the 'Ite Missa est' and gave the 'Benediction' : both new ceremonies as far as I can learn : as well as the admittance of the bride and bridgroom to the steps of the altar. At the Abp.'s solicitation I went with Frs. Orsenigo and Fransioli to pay our congratulations to the married couple at their residence 14th St. and University place. The reception was quite grand : though I knew few there. The presents made to the bride were very rich especially of silver and gold table apparatus. The lunch-table was very neat and well provided : though purposely I eat nothing. After dinner at home, I visited the Tombs with Fr. T. Quin of Rhode Island who is acquainted with all the officials. We remarked especially the 'Bummers' hall! : where night-disturbers are confined : and also we saw many cells in which murderers are kept, among others, Friary; and the forger Ketchum, quite young, intelligent and remarkable in countenance who was talking with his sister:and Jenkins quite old, and intelligent in looks, who was reading. We saw several awaiting for sentence of confinement, but not outwardly respectable persons : and several drunken women brought in. The prisoners look out by a small window. Fr. Nilan & Dr. McSweeny visited me in the afternoon : we took a walk meeting Dr. Parsons : and Dr. McSweeny and I visited Dr. McGlynn, who supped at our house : and Dr. McGlynn and I attended a childrens' party at a

November 186

Mr. Daly's in 3rd Ave. near 28th St. where I met Mr. & Mrs. DeLacy with their son & daughter; Mrs. Kelly and her children John & William Kelly and others. We had quite pleasant music, dancing and lunch.

December

Fri., 1st   I heard the confessions of the girls and gave instructions to the girls' school : in the afternoon visited Miss Anastasia Burtsell, who tries to stick to the 4th Ave. house, by her claims of board paid in advance. She thinks that Tom & Mary cannot live safely together. So does William Cassidy who was in town this week. Tom sent word that Anastasia must leave before he returns home. She asked me not to desert her. William Cassidy thought that the World, of which he is a co-editor, would have to give up since the victory of the Republican party : but unofficial business pouring in, will sustain it.

Sat., 2nd   Fr. Preston returned home to-day : he thought Chicago next to New York in activity : found Bishop Duggan quite gentlemanly, and saw a good set of priests : remembered especially Fr. Roles : whom he imagines to be a good preacher : Dr. McMullen, Dr. Butler sr whom he liked, Dr. Butler jr & Dr. McGovern : found St. Mary's, the bishop's, quite neat with no pretension to good music : and at Fr. Roles' good music. He went to the opera (Gran's) with the Hassards and was disgusted with the singing, not liking tenor, soprano, or basso or contralto : & was only pleased with Zazzaniga's acting. Mrs. Hassard was not pleased with the house : but could find no better. The streets are plank roads : and great dust is the consequence : are now commencing to pave. I bought merino drawers at Stuarts for $4,25 a pair : and spectacles at : Ybackers $2,00 and $6,00 a pair.

Sun., 3rd   I sang High Mass : and spoke at 9 o'c. on the American

December

college in Rome. Fr. Preston preached on the particular judgement : where our accusers will be the judge, the devil, our guardian angel, and ourselves. The judgement takes place, whilst the friends are near the dead body. The way to escape the evil sentence, is to accuse oneself to the priest in the confession. He said he had before him persons whom he knew would be eternally damned if they were to die presently : they had let Easter after Easter pass by without going to confession! I spoke on the 4th commandment to the boys and girls' Sunday Schools. Fr. Preston and I, at meals, talked of our fine set of bishops. He ventures to prophecy that Frs. Quin and Starrs will be bishops yet! I would be astonished, he said, if I knew the names sent on for Albany. I suspect they were Frs. Conroy, Starrs & McNierny. He expects Fr. Williams will be bishop of Boston. I heard a part of Abp. McCloskey's lecture at St. Vincent de Paul's : which was packed. Some French ladies were indignant at the Irish being there : 'for it was a French Church'. The lecture had as it's text : 'I have given thee as an inheritance the nations of the earth : and to thy rule the utmost boundaries of the earth'. What I heard was but a school-boy declamation : Monarchs had sought universal conquest : to One alone was it given. Some had ruled many nations : but to one was decreed the boundaries of the earth as the only limit to his empire. It commenced by small beginnings, 12 poor fishermen : and among it's first adherents were few nobles, as St. Paul says : it has increased from century to century, by blood not of others who were conquered, but of it's own members shed in testimony of it's truth, as in Jerusalem, so in Rome, so in Ephesus, so in Lyons, so in Smyrna. The development has been slow : and increasing with time. At the present age Apostolic missionaries preach the subjection to Christ among heathen nations. We too are to assist the spread of the gospel among heathens. He then commenced the history of the 'Society of the Propagation of the faith' which rose after the horrors of the French revolution. I left here. The beauty of the question is that in fact, the money contributed in these United States is not generally sent for the spread of the gospel among the heathens : but the bishop is authorised to keep it for his own diocese, which is considered a missionary country. This is fair : but the talk about missions to the heathen is deceitful, and leaves a contrary impression. Buffalo diocese certainly keeps the money. I suspect Fr. Lapont keeps the money for his own church. The Sisters of Charity everywhere establish the association, and send the money to him!!! because he has the Church of St. Vincent de Paul, their founder : and has the enterprise to stimulate their zeal!!! I went to the Morroghs at 26th St. : where Mrs. Morrogh is sick. With Mr. Morrogh, my mother and I discussed a letter from Mrs. Collins of Limerick, giving an account of their old friends. We discussed also my aunt Eliza Burtsell's will who left her property so that her brothers and sisters should have it during their life, her brother John's children should have it if they survived her brother and sisters, but it would revert to those if her brother John's children (my brother and I) should die beforehand. This is the interpretation that Mr. Morrogh gives to the will. The codicil annexed to the will is of no account because not attested. The codicil explains her mind : which Mr. Morrogh considers not clearly laid down in the will, but sufficiently so, to prevent the claims of my brother John's children on the property : because no mention is made of our heirs. Also it seems that though the property is given to her brothers and sisters in trust for us : yet because they are allowed to speculate with it they would not be responsible to us for it, if it were lost by their speculations. This is hard to believe! The strong-minded woman consulted no lawyer in making her will! In all

December

probability the Burtsells would owe us a great deal of money : if my father had used a lawyer against them. He had borrowed $25,000 from them, which he lost. To pay them he made over all his property. Charles O'Connor was their lawyer. My father declined taking a lawyer against them : and accepted of Charles O'Connor's terms. Had he used a lawyer, the terms would have been less sweeping : for instance : it might have been settled to give them the property till they made back their money with it's interest : but by this time they have made largely by their depriving my father of all his property! The house now is said to be worth $120 000. It stands at corner Wall St. and Broad St. opposite the Exchange. My father held a large Stationery there. My mother gave birth to me when my father announced that he must give over the store : my aunt Anastasia tells me that he would have had to do this even before his marriage : that for three years, the house had been no longer his. I doubt this! Dr. McGlynn called on me on his way to Staten Island where he was to give a lecture at Fr. Lewis' church : Dr. Brann had not given the promised discourse at St. Stephen's on the American college, prevented by his installment at St. Peter's Jersey City. Dr. Cummings & family are very rude, and indelicate. Mrs. McDowall orders two loaves of French bread & will not allow more to be bought & had two cups for the 2 priests and all strangers to drink coffee! Dr. Cummings gives $5,00 for a marriage though he may receive $50,00!

<u>Mon., 4th</u>   I went to see Dr. Thos. Burtsell at the Hospital : he was out walking. I visited my mother : and had to give a severe scolding to W. P. M. for being tipsy. In Dr. Fox's company, he is always under the influence of liquor. Dr. Fox was a protege of W. P. M. in Fordham and R. American Seminaries : I know he was sent the last because afflicted with an improper disease contracted in Paris! on his way to the American college

December

in Rome! to become a priest! He is now a medical doctor!

Tues., 5th   Dr. McSweeny and I took a walk to the Central Park during which we spoke lightly of the Abp.'s manner of preaching and the absurd practise of obediences in Propaganda ex. gr. Lazzaro Lazzarovich, prefect, made his camerata turn over a dying horse to relieve the animal! In the afternoon I visited the Decoppets, Ann Burtsell and Gallaghers at 111, W. 32nd St. I found Dr. Tom there : whose sore eyes obliged him to return to the hospital one hour after dark! They are, I believe, annoyed because I speak favourably of Tom's wife. A Miss Murphy being present prevented us from speaking about Dr. Tom's position. I went to the opera to see 'Martha' played. Miss Kellogg as Martha sang well and played better. She is ugly on account of her large mouth. Miss Phillips is much like a Jew in countenance, but sings well and plays well as contralto, as Betsy. Mr. Itire is a good player : but has not great life in his singing. Mr. Antonucci, as basso, did not please me. The chorus was composed of about 40 singers. I took a seat in the parquette (price $2 00).

Wed., 6th   I visited Fr. McCarthy (Fr. Nilan was out). We talked over the elections of yesterday for mayor and Counsellor : both thought well of Hoffman and O'Gorman. I visited Miss Jones at Miss Macaulay's school : where there are about 70 boarders, who have from to-day a 4 days' vacation for Thanksgiving day. I arranged with Miss Jones that she should go to confession and communion on Friday, the feast of the Immaculate Conception. I took my first lesson at horse-back-riding at Dickel's riding-school Cor. 5th Ave. & 39th St. I bought 20 tickets for $30, had for 1st teacher an Austrian, who knew only German. I told Mr. Dickels that I should have to learn German to learn how to ride. I shall have to go between 4 & 5 o'c. to get instructions from an English-speaking teacher. I went from

December

1 to 2 o'c. I trotted a great deal : which made my bones ache a great deal. At dinner we had Mr. O'Connor and Mr. Dachauer. I had lately written a note to Mr. O'Connor telling him never to read my letters to the Chancellor : and never to attempt to give a dispensation from an impediment or from the banns : as being a layman he was incapable of Ecclesiastical power ex. gr. to dispense in any law of the Church. We were quite pleasant together, this notwithstanding. Mr. Dachauer gave me a French Oratoria to translate into Italian : because singers more easily pronounce Italian! Fr. Nilan and I took a walk to 42nd St. and back again. He had heard confessions at St. Columba's where he found the two priests Frs. McAleer and O'Hare violent secessionists, proslavery men and anti-Fenians : neither showing much calmness in arguing against him. I attended both the altar and literary classes : and found the latter not well attended.

Thurs., 7th   I said Mass at 9 o'c. Snow and rain prevented many from being present at the Mass, which was in Thanksgiving for the blessings bestowed upon our country : this day having been so appointed by the Civil Authorities, the Abp. gave a verbal message to some of the city-pastors to have a late Mass, High or Low, as they pleased for the celebration of 'Thanksgiving Day'. Dr. McGlynn called and told me that he had come to an explanation with Dr. Cummings declining his unfriendly criticisms and his complaint-seeking humour : and among other reforms, Fr. Gamboville is for the future to take care of the house-keeping, superseding Mrs. McDowale who, though before favourable, will henceforth be inimical to Dr. McGlynn. The Dr. told me also how he visited a poor child, Catherine Morissey, in the 'home for the friendless' in Madison Ave. by request of a poor woman, but in spite of the matrons of the house, two of whom treated him rather roughly, because of his popish mummeries, (for reciting the prayers in Latin) and taunting Catholics with not taking care of their children. She would not leave the child's bed-side, that he might hear the child's confession : He gave absolution : and extreme Unction 'per breviorem' because a man threatened violence. He acted quite calmly, appealing to the humane and Christian feelings to no effect. He had forced the door to the child's dormitory : and there got the child to say that she wanted his services. He thinks of bringing the case before courts of justice : and showing those persons not to be good custodians of the child. I heard the confessions of the Sodality-girls to whom Fr. Preston has been giving a three days' retreat in preparation for the feast of the Immac. Conception.

<u>Fri., 8th</u> Fr. Preston said 8 o'c. Mass for the Sodality, to receive new members etc. preaching before Mass. I sang Requiem H. Mass for the sister-in-law of Mr. Kelly, our S. S. superintendent, without 'Dies Irae' because Mr. Dachauer could not accompany with the Melodean difficult music. I assisted at the Solemn H. Mass at the Church of the Immac. Conception where Dr. Brann preached. I heard half the discourse : in which he asserted that we should receive definition of the Church about the Immac. Conception : as we obey civil laws : though the Church defines a fact decreed by the Almighty from eternity : and that the fact of Mary being Mother of God prevents her from contracting original sin (which we call mortal, because making the soul an enemy of God) : also because emnity was to be between this woman and the serpent (the devil) but she would have been a friend of the devil if ever in original sin : Thus the church in this century of materialism, defines many doctrines sought to be overthrown 1st her authority 2. the Incarnation. 3. Her love of moral worth in creatures 4. and holds up as our model the humble virgin who is queen of heaven, purgatory, and earth : whence voices to-day meet in praising her : and in

December

this church, if he had another sense, he could see Angels gathering to pay honours to the Immaculate Virgin, protectrix of that parish and also of the whole United States. Dr. Brann's manner is too fussy to please me : his language was good but by no means elegant : He has improved since I heard him last. He did not wait for dinner : I did. I confessed in the afternoon to Fr. Shauer : whom I desert, because of his bad English and his bashfulness to speak piously to me. I heard confessions in the evening.

Sat., 9th   Dr. McSweeny and I walked to 50th St. : discussing the late Fenian split : in which 10 Senators have deposed O'Mahony from the presidency of the Brotherhood. I thought that constitionally O'Mahony was right, though I sympathise with the Senate : but thought the division but temporary. Dr. McSweeny gloated over his foresight that the Fenians would come to nought!

Sun., 10th   Sunday. I sang High Mass : having said, and preached at, the 9 o'c. mass. I talked on the Immac. Conception : showing the doctrine of the Church it's reasonableness because Mary should not be less than Eve, and because Mary the Mother of God should never be the enemy of God or the friend of the devil : and the Church in our age has but published the decree of the Almighty from eternity and the belief of all ages of Xtianity. Fr. Preston spoke on the same subject, with similar ideas, but very nice language. I visited but did not speak in, the boys and girls' S. Schools. I refused to a priest, Menelli by name, permission to say Mass : though Fr. Preston not knowing him had told him he might. This Menelli is an Italian about 50 years of age, who when attending at St. Stephen's, collected more intentions, than he intended to or could fulfil : had been under the influence of liquor, and once got a black eye probably in a drunken brawl; put the clock half an hour a-head to commence H. Mass sooner, because he

December

was hungry; received a 'Celebret' from the Abp. first 'per mensem' and then 'in transitu' subject to Dr. Cummings' pleasure : was discarded by Dr. Cummings, and the Abp. hearing of the above facts told Dr. McGlynn that he would send a letter to the Dr. withdrawing the 'Celebret' : which letter the Dr. should have conveyed to Menelli, but the Abp. did not write the letter : though Menelli heard of it from Dr. McGlynn. Menelli sent 'Reverendo Patri Pastori Ecclesiae Sctae Annae' this letter : 'Veni mane dicere missam, sed vicarius noluit, dicens me habere suspensionem ab Archiepiscopo : hoc falsum, et qui hoc dixit, dabit ei Deus mortem subitaneam. Rev'de pastor, da mihi pecuniam pro itinere, de qua dixi tibi heri : diverso mode coactus petere a protestantibus : intellige : hoc sufficit intelligenti paucae. Vale. Italo-praesbyter'. This is the letter almost word for word. I wish it, lest he should become a protestant, to expose him. Mr. Dachauer dined with us. I translated this for him. Mr. Remi also, our basso, dined with us. He is very humourous but not witty. He speaks French and Italian fluently : the conversation fell principally on music and concluded that Paris was the greatest place in the world for music in the operas, where no expense is spared to make amusements of all kinds complete. In the evening I went to Calvary Church to hear Dr. Vinton preach on 'St. John the Baptist' : who 1st is a child of prophecy, as the angel of the Lord to prepare the way for Him. 2nd. his life and preaching of penance made the best preparation for the coming of the Lord. 3rd. his qualities of self-denial, humility, and firmness made him fit to be the herald, the morning Star that announces the approach of the Sun of Justice. A fuller account of this sermon is written out by me : it will be the model of a sermon of mine on the same subject next Sunday. Dr. Vinton speaks well, calmly; his systematic division prevented him from growing warm over his subject.

December   195

The church was 2 thirds full : the music was fine : and I am delighted
with the English services and singing. I went to the Morroghs of 26th St :
where I met my mother and my cousin Mrs. McLaughlin. We discussed the
dissolution of Fenianism : for which there are brighter prospects a-head
that come from the conflict of ideas, showing the necessity of more perfect
government.

<u>Mon., 11th</u>   By the $9\frac{1}{2}$ o'c. tr. Drs. McGlynn, McSweeny and I went
to New Rochelle to hear confessions during the jubilee. Dr. McGlynn told
me that Catherine Morrissey had been ejected from 'the home for the friendless' though one lung was wholly consumed. Mr. Shucker had gone there to
see the institute : He learned that of 1250 children, the immense majority
were children of foreigners, among whom were no Catholics now, and the
Catholics were generally loyal to their faith : and therefore as few of
them were admitted as possible : the institution has several industrial
schools attached, where the children are almost self-supporting, being
paid for their work in tickets exchangeable for clothing : receive Evangelical instructions, read the Bible : the principals are Evangelical.
Mr. Shucker was private secretary to Chase, when minister of the finance :
he wrote a letter to Chase, saying that he appreciated Mr. Chase's intentions in being present at Cleveland Christian Commission meeting for
evangelising the masses, but thought that Mr. Chase would find all other
organisations but the Catholic church to fail in this object. Mr. Chase
replied that though he admired the Catholic Church for it's unity, harmony
and subordination, he thought that there is in it a tendency to despotism
and excessive centralisation! Mr. Chase showed shrewdness here. Mr.
Shucker excites Dr. McGlynn to commence some institute : he will collect
some $5000 from his Protestant friends! Mr. Shucker was told that Catherine

December   196

Morrissey was sent to the Alms House : she was turned into the public street two days after his visit on Thanksgiving day. They took him for a Jesuit so he says. Miss Raymond's account of Dr. McGlynn's visit makes the Dr. out a hardened papist. At New Rochelle we visited Mr. Isling's villa : where two Catholic employees received us hospitably. We visited the flower hot house : white flowers are always in demand, and receive a high price. New Rochelle is rather bleak on account of the snow and rain. We discussed warmly the prospects of Fenianism : Fr. McLoughlin and Dr. McSweeny making light of it. We heard confessions for $2\frac{1}{2}$ hours. Dr. McGlynn returned to the city.

<u>Tues., 12th</u>   Fr. McLoughlin and I visited David's Island where he had two sick-calls. The patients now are about 150. I met the chaplain Lowry, a neat dandy. The wards are good. We had rough water and rain. I came home by the $4\frac{1}{2}$ o'c. train. In the evening I went to see the 'Africaine' at the Academy of Music. Miss Carozzi Zucchi played magnificently and sang well, as Selika : Miss Ortolani acted well as Inez. Mazzoleni acted and sang quite well as Vasco di Gama. I was surprised that to Bellini was assigned the secondary part of Nelusko. Antonucci sang and played Don Pedro : whilst Rorini sang as the Brahmin priest. The music seemed to me of a new kind entirely : The stage scenery was not very good.

<u>Wed., 13th</u>   I took a walk to see Fr. Nilan, with whom I found Fr. Healy, of St. Peter's, a mind of very little compass. We visited the schools, both select and industrial, attached to Holy Cross Church. The class-rooms are quite large : the children appear healthy : no sick were in the infirmary. Sister Helena showed us the building, expressing herself pleased that the clergy took an interest in their institutions. At dinner we discussed the Fenian question : Frs. McCarthy and Healy not placing

December

trust in the Fenians. We thought that the present troubles would result in a more consolidated and better regulated government of the Fenians. Fr. Nilan positively asserted that Stephens, the Irish Head Center, was arrested and released by a Fenian who was a magistrate in Ireland. Fr. Nilan too asserted that Mantle Marble had threatened the Abp. that if he did not withdraw a petition to the Common Council for the sisters' having possession of a certain hospital, I believe in 60th St., an anti-Catholic riot would arise : This cowed the Abp. into withdrawing the petition. I attended the literary and altar classes.

Thurs., 14th   Dr. McSweeny and I took a walk to 60th St. In the afternoon I took a lesson of riding at Dickel's. In the evening I went to hear O'Gorman's lecture 'On Christmas' for the benefit of the Sisters of the Good Shepherd. The house was packed. O'Gorman is a magnificent speaker : his style is quite poetical : he is calm and dignified whilst speaking : his audience is kept perfectly enraptured with what he is saying. I shall endeavour to write elsewhere an abridgement of his lecture. Fr. Nilan and I went afterwards to the Academy of Music to hear the concert in Wallace's memory. We heard Miss Kellogg sing magnificently : and Mr. Campbell also sang a solo grandly. They had a magnificent chorus for the 'Ave Maria' and the finale of the 2nd act of Lurline. All the pieces sung were Wallace's : a fine audience was in attendance. Wallace leaves a wife and children who are to receive the proceeds of the concert : after a monument is raised to his memory. Thus a musician is assisted after his death and not before!

Fri., 15th   I heard the confessions of our own children, gave the usual instruction to the girls school; and heard the confessions of the children of Holy Cross parish. I met Fr. Nilan's brother : who knew my

December   198

brother John, and considers him quite a smart young man. I met there
Fr. Joe Woods. I took a riding-lesson at Dickel's and fell without hurt.
I visited my mother and scolded W. P. M. for drinking. He had been with
Bishop Rosecrans, who had four seminarians with him to be sent to Rome.
I heard confessions in the evening.

Sat., 16th   I left my card for Bishop Rosecranz at French's Hotel
in Chatham St. I surprised Fr. Preston by saying that I did not respect
Pius IX's theological opinions : as he did not make a thorough theological
course, through infirmity.

Sun., 17th   I preached at High Mass a greatly modified discourse
of Dr. Vinton's preached last Sunday at Calvary Church. At 9 o'c. I
exhorted the people to prepare for Xmas by a good confession. At High
Mass sung by Fr. Preston, the new organ was used. I gave instructions
to both Sunday Schools. In the evening we had a grand concert under the
direction of Mr. Dachauer the organist, on occasion of the opening of the
new organ. Mr. Dachauer, & Mr. Dessane of St. Francis Xavier's, and Mr.
Pecher of St. Peter's performed on the organ : but the organ, being only
about half-completed, could not be used to their satisfaction. A grand
chorus from Gounod commenced the singing-programme : it followed by an
English piece 'Show me thy ways, O Lord', by our soprano, Miss A. Wells,
who sings beautifully and a Tantum Ergo sung by our basso L. Remi, whose
voice is very resounding : and then by a Duetto of Remi and Miss M.
Bodenhamer (who sang very poorly had a tremolo in her voice and was trem-
bling all over whilst singing) formed the first part of the concert. In
the 2nd part the celebrated chorus : 'Tuche la terra adora' of Meyerbeir's
Africaine was sung better than I heard it in the opera a few night's ago.
Miss O. Gomien's contralto piece was exquisitely rendered. A quartetto

December 199

followed, with accompaniment, in an 'O Salutaris.' Miss Bodenhamer sang 'Pace, Pace, O Dio' of Verdi tremblingly. (I modified the words adressed to Leonora as adressed to God.) Negri's 106th psalm, a grand chorus in 4 parts, ended the concert with great eclat. The Organ was ordered in May 1864 : but Erben is a slow worker. It is to cost $5,000,00 given to Erben, besides our old organ valued at $3,000,00. It has about 40 stops : has nearly 3000 pipes : and three banks of keys. It has been painted by a distinct contract : the paint will cost a good deal. Fr. Preston considers that music is essential to the church : and thinks that the most powerful (almost the only) motive for people to go to church on Sunday (-at least to Vespers) is good music. He goes in also for modernising Church music : as we ought to modernise everything else in the Church. The Abp., and two Jesuits, Frs. Starrs, McNierney, and Donnelly were present, as Dr. Anderson. We had a pleasant supper. The Abp. likes to relate anecdotes, and give forth 'bons mots'.

Mon., 18th   I went to St. Stephen's to see Dr. McGlynn; he was attending sick-calls. I saw Fr. Gamboville, from whom I learned that the brothers of the Holy Cross are under no rule, because their superior, Fr. Moreau, though a good man, and their founder, has no control over them. Thus Fr. Lafont was right to break with them. Now they are under Fr. Lorin in the United States : who is not as pious but a better administrator. Fr. Lafont finds it difficult to get good French lay-teachers in this country. Fr. Gamboville thinks that money spent for church-music should be spent in helping the poor! I thought that the fine music attracted those who would give high-pew-rents, which upheld a parish. He thought our people heard too many sermons! I showed him that four fifths of his congregation never received any instruction! I saw Dr. Cummings, who felt too cold to shake

December 200

hands, but yet told several good anecdotes! about the Sailor Kane, who was slewed by his brother etc. I took a riding-lesson at Dickel's and am gaining 'my seat' better. We had a dinner at 6 o'c. at which Mr. Dachauer, Alibert, Dessane, Remi, and Mrs. Dachauer, Misses Wells and Gomien were invited guests. I talked in French against Napoleonism, and in favour of Fenianism. The principal topic of conversation was music. Miss Wells is very handsome and intelligent. Miss Gomien is timid. Mr. Remi is a joker : Mr. Dessane is by no means brilliant. Mr. Alibert is pleasant, but of no great intelligence. Fr. Preston monopolised the ladies : which, I think, displeased the gentlemen.

Tues., 19th   I visited my mother. I took a riding-lesson. I went in the evening to see Edwin Forrest play Febro, the Broker of Bogota, a character that does not call him out at all. Mr. Wheatley played De Camerero, and acted as a cool, shrewd rogue would act. Mr. McCullough acted as Ramon, Febro eldest son, tolerably well : Becks, as Francisco, was wretched. Nunan as Viceroy made a tolerable appearance. Miss Agnes Perry did her part as   excellently.

Wed., 20th   I attempted to preach on Xmas alone : I find the system calculated to develop thought and bring out classic language. I bought gloves at Stuarts for $1,75. I took a riding-lesson, attended the altar and literary classes : in which latter the pieces were from Revolutionary War : by Scannell; Shakespeare's Anthony's speech over Caesar by J. Burke : and Byron's Battle of Watertoo by L. Tessier : all recited well, especially Tessier. I assisted afterwards at a concert & reading given by the 'Marion Division' of the Sons of Temperance : I heard Prof. Brown declaim the 'Charge of the light Brigade' quite well : the Dobson Brothers played on the banjo! Miss Reynolds, a girl of 9 years,

December

sang the song of the chimney-sweep magnificiently : she is a prodigy of a songster : singing the falsetto grandly. I heard Prof. Brown and his lady-pupil (Mrs Dougherty, formerly Miss Watson), speak from the 'School of Scandal'. Prof. Brown spoke poorly; she acted her part very well, better than I expected. The piano also was played nicely.

Thurs., 21st   I took a riding-lesson at Dickel's, where I found Fr. Preston riding his horse, which is very shy. In the evening I went to see Edwin Forrest play Daman, with Mr. McCullough as Pythias and Miss A. Perry as his betrothed : whilst Mrs. Farren acted as Damon's wife. Edwin Forrest is altogether too wild in any emotion : he has no delicacy of feeling : he cannot act any part that requires refinement of taste.

Fri., 22nd   I heard no children's confessions, because the Sister had not examined their conscience! I took a walk with Dr. McSweeny, during which he told me that the Abp. had refused his sanction to a Chaldean priest's begging for the Holy land, on the ground that he had no authorisation for his object. He had not said Mass in public : but in the convent lest his saying mass should be an advertisement for him. He has gone to Canada. The walk did not benefit the instruction I gave to the children of the day-school. I took a riding-lesson at Dickel's and heard confessions in the evening.

Sat., 23rd.   I called at the Redemptorists to go to confession : but they were engaged at dinner. We did not have a great crowd at confession : a thing surprising at Xmas : though we had more than we could hear.

Sun., 24th   I sang High-Mass and said 9 o'c. mass at which I spoke of Xmas. Mr Dachauer dined with us. It rained so, that the girls had no Sunday school : the boys were few. I did not give the usual instruction. With a severe headache I went to bed at 8 o'c.

December

Mon., 25th   Christmas. Fr. Preston said Midnight Mass, with a few friends present. I sang 5½ o'c. Mass, the children singing. I spoke on Xmas after the Communion : there were not many communions : the great number having received yesterday. I said 7 o'c. and 7½ o'c. mass : the latter had not been announced. Fr. Preston sang High-Mass; I acted as deacon and Mr. Macauley S. J. acting as subdeacon : I preached. The altars were nicely adorned with evergreens and natural flowers. Mrs. Livingston had the charge of this department : whilst Mr. Wood adorned the church with the evergreens. These cost 15 cts. a yard : 600 yards were used. The bouquets cost $6,00 each on the high altar : we bought six bouquets : others were sent in. Mrs. Livingston superintends the boys' dressing : and has improved their surplices by pink and blue ribbons or tassels. We had Benediction of the Blessed Sacrament after Mass. At dinner I spoke against the use of the Latin language at public service : I preferred in this respect the Episcopal Service. Fr. Preston asserted that Episcopalians found motive for admiring the Catholic Service : because being in Latin, greater reverence was shown to the Eucharistic Mystery. Mr. Macauley kept silence : but when asked to speak, thought it best to follow the judgement of the Church Superiors. I thought that the Superiors often required counsel : 50 years hence it might be considered greater wisdom to have the Mass in the vernacular that we had as good sense as our forefathers : that we had abandoned the spirit of the Church, which had established the epistle, prayers, and gospel as a preparation for the faithful to attend the Mass properly. Fr. Preston thought I was too free in speech : though he admitted the right to my opinion. I visited my mother, making her a present of $25,00. Mr. Macauley told me that Peter Burtsell was too often absent from School to profit much this year. I knew Mr. Macauley at 16th St. School fifteen

December

years ago.

<u>Tues., 26th</u>   My mother called to see me, and sew my shirts. I sent prayer-books to Mrs. McLaughlin's children and to Lizzie Decoppet. Dr. McGlynn called to see me : he gave me an account of Dr. Cummings' discourse which was in good taste and in a Christian spirit. They had a grand children's gathering to the number of 2500 to whom pictures, candies, & cakes were distributed : after they had been amused by singing, & speeches. This was a decoy to inaugurate a grand children's mission. I am booked to help to hear their confessions on Thursday. We walked to Holy Cross to engage Fr. Nilan for the same purpose. Dr. McGlynn had prompted the people to send in donations for the children of the parish : and had hinted at the necessity of St. Stephen's having an orphan asylum of it's own. I took a riding-lesson at Dickel's. I visited Peter Burtsell : Miss A. Burtsell was not at home. Mrs. Burtsell & children are well at Albany.

<u>Wed., 27th</u>   Fr. Killeen called to see me. We talked of old times in Rome : I told him that daily I was getting more disgused with the system of obedience required in Roman colleges : that it required a great elasticity to rebound from the pressure received there : that I had learned never to treat a boy harshly; because I was treated the most harshly when I endeavoured to be most virtuous : that I wondered how I never lost the wish for the priesthood when I was sorely tempted to leave the Propda and not take the oath. I took a riding-lesson at Dickel's. Dr. McGlynn and Fr. Killeen (again) called in after our dinner : we discussed the orphan-asylum-arrangements : and I told how I had not been answered by Mr. Nicholson, when I wrote expressing surprise that a former note had not been answered. Dr. McGlynn and I visited Dr. Parsons, who was administering affectionate glances to his little sister Emily, whilst we were with him : we booked Fr. O'Farrell

December 204

for confessions at St. Stephen's. At the Transfiguration we found Fr. Trainor laid up with constipation that had nigh brought him to the grave : we left word for Fr. Quin to come to hear confessions at St. Stephen's. We saw Fr. O'Callaghan at St. James who was indignant at Dr. Cummings because he, hearing that Fr. O'Callaghan was to be sent to St. Stephen's as assistant, had declared him to be unacceptable. We also booked Frs. Boyce and Ferrall for confessions at St. Stephen's. I had a merry-making reception for the altar and literary classes, giving cakes & fruit. E. Byrnes recited a piece from Tom Moore very well. J. McBride has no talent, though his father wishes him to be a priest.

<u>Thurs., 28th</u>   I heard confessions at St. Stephen's from $10\frac{1}{2}$ o'c. A.M. to 7 o'c. P.M. The children were not well prepared. The greater number though of 10, 12 & 15 years had not been to confession or communion. At dinner were Frs. Gamboville, Gallagher, Boyce, Beretta, O'Callaghan, Quin, Nilan and O'Farrell. I hurt Fr. Gamboville by asserting that half the French people did not know how to read or write. He had heard of my discussion with Mr. Alibert : and tacked on the question of French freedom. I laughed at the freedom refused the conference of St. Vincent de Paul to meet, whilst free-masonry was being approved. Fr. Gallagher thought that this country gave only freedom to do evil. viz : to shoot etc. I showed how European governments improved the higher classes, not caring for the people : whilst here the people is elevated. Dr. Manahan called in to see Dr. McGlynn : and was wrapped up in his new scheme of publishing 20 vols about New York's reminiscences, Catholic Controversies in the United States etc. etc. I heard Schuyler Colfax, speaker of the house of representatives give a lecture of his trip 'across the continent'. He spoke very rapidly but intelligibly. The greater part of the lecture described his journey

through Texas to Colorado, in which he told of one silver ledge, that being a mile and a quarter long already brought $60,000,000, of silver : though 20 of 100 companies had not been compensated for labour expended. He gave a grand description of the rocky mountains, with their cathedral-like and statue-formed heights. He told how U. S. Grant had been stationed at Vancouvers Island where the royal red and the loyal blue were seen harmoniously together : and how Phil Sheridan, a lieutenant in Oregon had told his men he was going to gain a captain's rank and is now major general, and is worthy of the two stars. He gave as an event most astonishing that he went down a hill in California 1600 feet steep with 35 turns in $9\frac{1}{2}$ minutes : and the driver complained that he and companions were not scared worth a cent because they cried-faster-in the descent. He told of a fall of 2600 ft : 16 times greater than Niagara Falls. He told how his journey to the west had been endangered by the Indians who massacred parties behind and before them : and were no longer the mild Indians of Fenimore Cooper's novels. He told of his impressions of the Mormons. Their Salt Lake City was the most beautiful he had ever seen with it's cottages and verandas. Salt lake's water will hold up a man unable to swim as a cork is kept afloat on other water : though fresh-water rivers flow into it. Polygamy was the bane of Society. In a discussion in Brigham Young's house, Brigham said that God had most tried him when requiring him to take many wives : and that he would be glad to get a new revelation to stop polygamy. Carrington, editor of the Mormon newspaper, said he would kill his own son, if it's necessity were revealed to him. Colfax heard a sermon from a junior elder : in which there was nothing unacceptable to the most orthodox Christian. Brigham Young described, in a sermon, God as having a body and passions as men have, and called imposters them who say he is a pure spirit.

December

Their theory is that women must bear with the misfortune of a husband's divided affections, to gain greater glory in heaven. What misery must not be created in a woman, who sees her husband give his affections to a girl of 17 summers? This feeling has obliged many of the 'Saints' to have many cottages in which the many wives are kept? What loneliness for the abandoned ones? What dissension among the children? What effects of favouritism? What horror to have a man married to his wife's sisters, neices, cousins etc.? Colfax said that this institution must soon bring the Mormons in conflict with the United States. He found the 'gentile families' deploring polygamy. The ladies were the recipients of the many wives' complaints of neglect : though they returned the visits of only the first wives. Salt lake city was in a ferment on account of Colfax's plain talk. It was rumoured that he had brought a command from President Johnson to Brigham Young to have a new revelation prohibiting polygamy. A remedy to this institution would be to give facilities to miners and Jews to immigrate to Utah : where, he said, the 'Saints' are Sinners and the Jews are gentiles. He would leave them the Mormon bible : but he would prevent them having revelations contrary to the natural law and the law of the United States. The Pacific R. R. was a grand scheme to develop the resources of our country : California was praying for it : it would consolidate our immense territory.

Fri., 29th   I went to Eugene Kelly's to get a bill of deposit of $100 for Fr. Adam : and took a riding-lesson at Dickel's where Fr. Preston was too. I was visited by Mrs. Decoppet and Liza. Mrs. Decoppet told me of two sharp letter lately written by Mrs. Thos. Burtsell to Dr. Tom raking up stories of four years' ago : a most untimely action as Dr. Tom was becoming more inclined to live well. I heard confessions in the evening.

December

Sat., 30th   I visited Dr. Thos. Burtsell at St. Vincent's Hospital whom I advised to return home, first having told Mr. Ambrose Cassidy and requested Miss Anastasia Burtsell to leave his house : he should then be calm in being bossed at home. He ought not to be unkind to Anastasia, who probably will leave her money to his children but would not do so if treated harshly by him. He could be stiff but not unchristian with the Cassidys who had not shown proper respect for him. He should consider all this advice as not given, if he intended to take liquor again. He had received two untimely letters from Mrs. Thos. Burtsell recalling his bad actions for four years.

Sun., 31st   I sang High-Mass : Fr. Preston preached on the 'events' of the past year which had been used for the profit or damage to each individual. I gave instructions to the boys' SS. and gave them and the girls laced pictures as New Year's presents : and asked the teachers to form a S. S. organisation to consentrate their abilities of doing good to the children. I heard Dr. Bellows' at the Zebra Church 'On Time' and visited the Morroghs.

1866

January

<u>Mon., 1st</u>   At 7 o'c. Mass taking for my text the words of Rev. XXIII 'The former things have passed away, behold I make all things new' I hoped the past had made a deep impression on our souls and had gained merits for us in the sight of God : but that the time itself was irrevocable: and whatever we had done, we should seek to commence the new year with new fervour in doing good. Fr. Preston sang 9 o'c. Mass : and wished the congregation a happy New Year. Together we called on the Archbishop. We met there of course Fr. McNierney, Mr. O'Reilly, and George Hecker and son came in whilst we were there. We spoke about Brownson's new book. The Abp. told us that Dollinger had denied Brownson's knowledge of the 'Fathers', though he pretends to the knowledge. Mr. O'Reilly preferred Healy's portrait to Elliot's, of the Abp. The Caggers have Eliot's. George Hecker has all the principal traits of character of Fr. Hecker, the Paulist. We went afterwards to the Decoppets, Gallaghers & Miss Ann Burtsell at 111 32nd St. where we met Mr. Ingolsby and his son-in-law Mr. O'Rourke : the former an old acquaintance of our family, the latter knew my brother, John, at Donnelly's Dry Goods' Store. I saw Dr. Thos. Burtsell & Mr. Decoppet downstairs. I had two sick-calls. I afterwards visited Miss Anastasia Burtsell & Peter Burtsell (who had called on me) where I met young Mr. Paddon. I visited the McLaughlins where I met two Germans : and my mother Mrs. D. Burtsell's where I saw Dr. W. P. Morrogh with Dr. Fox (M.D.) just recovered from Delirium Tremens.

January

Tues., 2nd   Omitted by the Editor.

Wed., 3rd   I assisted at the Pontifical Requiem High Mass for Abp. Hughes to-day being the anniversary of his death. Abp. McCloskey celebrated the Mass. There were but few clergymen present, none being invited, and few of the laity. The music was good : but without any special attraction. The singers are good artists but have not good voices. I took a horse ride at Dickel's where I met Fr. Preston. I attended the altar class : and afterwards presided over a new Sunday School organisation, which I have undertaken to better our Sunday School. Mr. Coddington is the most intelligent member. It is presently composed of sixteen members. The object is to debate on the means of exciting the emulation of the boys to learn their catechism. A fine is to be imposed of ten cents on any member who absents himself from the meeting on the first Tuesday of each month. Monthly dues, of which the amount is left to the individual's pleasure, are collected to be directed to further the Association's object. A Vice-President, Secretary, Treasurer and Librarian are the officers appointed : the last three by the Association, the first by the president. The Sunday School is to be divided into six sections : with three grades of teachers in each to give greater importance to the junior teachers in the eyes of the boys. Mr. Kelly was appointed vice-president : Mr. Griffin jr Secretary : Mr. Donnelly Treasurer : Mr. Melling, librarian.

Thurs., 4th   I went out to walk with Dr. McSweeny, who, as usual, entertained me with a tirade against Frs. Starrs and McNierney. Going afterwards to St. Stephen's, I found that Dr. Cummings had died early in the morning, not having confessed or communicated but being anointed when senseless. He was already laid out in his coffin : Mrs. Gerdes told me that he had died placidly. He then looked as he had looked ten years ago.

January 210

I dined with Fr. Gamboville, Gallagher and McLaughlin : and with Dr. McGlynn went to take a Russian bath in 27th St. : after which I heard confessions of the children of St. Stephen's parish for several hours : took tea with the same priests as were at dinner with the accession of Fr. Quin who said that he had had a design of requesting the Abp. to send me to Transfiguration to take care of the Italians. I told him that I preferred taking care of the English-speaking people. He thought of this means to get away from Transfiguration church. He said that now the Italian minister Bertinati and Fr. Panifolo the Franciscan had agreed to erect an Italian church, to be under the care of an Italian Franciscan.

<u>Fri., 5th</u>   Omitted by the Editor.

<u>Sat., 6th</u>   Omitted by the Editor.

<u>Sun., 7th</u>   Sunday. . . .I preached at 10½ o'c. on the Epiphany, the composition was my own : and I was afterwards told that many considered it the best sermon I had preached : I believe, because I was more practical than I had been heretofore. . . .

<u>Mon., 8th</u>   At 10½ o'c. Fr. Preston and I reached St. Stephen's to attend Dr. Cummings' funeral. A great number of priests were present : I particularly remarked Drs. Keogh, & O'Hara of Philadelphia, Drs. McSweeny, Freel, Morrogh, Frs. Jas. O'Connor of Philadelphia, Killeen, all Propagandists. Bishop Wood of Philadelphia a propagandist was present too. The church was magnificently decorated. The coffin was of metal of walnut-colour. A great quantity of natural flowers in wreaths & crowns and crosses were near it. The music was under Berge's direction. The Mendelsohn union, and the choirs of St. Stephen and St. Francis Xavier's were invited to sing Cherubim's Requiem Mass. I did not fancy the Dies Irae : Miss Clarke sang an 'Ave Maria' for the Offertory richly. Fr. Hecker preached the funeral discourse,

January

passing a eulogy on Dr. Cummings as a priest and a man (among my other papers will be found a synopsis of the discourse :) The Abp. gave the absolution after the sermon. Dr. McGlynn assisted by Fr. Gamboville as deacon and Fr. Gallagher as subdeacon celebrated the Mass. The church was immensely thronged : yet very cold. I did not hear a sob; a thing very rare at the funeral of a priest when Irish Catholics are present. Many distinguished laymen were present; and many of his congregation had kept a watch-guard of honour near his bier since he was placed in the church yesterday afternoon. A magnificent lunch was set out for the clergy and invited laity : composed of things beautiful to look at but not at all substantial. Bp. Wood seemed not to wish to let Fr. Jas. O'Connor or Dr. Keogh stay in New York. Dr. Keogh asked me to become New York correspondent to the Catholic Standard, which he has just commenced to edit in Philadelphia. I dined at Dr. Morrogh's with him, and Fr. Maguire and my mother. I afterwards visited Miss A. Burtsell. Peter Burtsell growing tired of school has received through Mr. Cassidy's influence a desk in the Surrogate's office with a salary of $100 a month. I had hoped that he would continue to study till he had graduated. The study of philosophy would have enabled him to learn law, for which he shows an inclination. The bait thrown out to him is too exciting to let him return to dry school-books. He thought himself called upon to do something for his family under the present circumstances. He is 16 years of age.

Tues., 9th   I took a horse-ride at Dickel's. During dinner Fr. McKenna of Brooklyn a Maynooth-man came to consult me as to the best way of raising a literary class : he had heard of mine's success. I took him to task about the Maynooth-oath which obliges it's alumni to uphold the right of Victoria and offspring to rule Ireland, and not to do anything

//January 212

for the overthrowal of the established Church. He first argued that an oath did not bind any more than one's duty extended : the duty of Irishmen was quite doubtful with regard to both the said objects : therefore the oath's binding was doubtful. I argued that it was a sin to take an oath without a design to fulfil it. He then argued that one who held the oath to be binding when they took it, might afterwards be persuaded of it's unbinding character. I thought that the majority of Maynooth-men ought to know what they were doing, when they took the oath. He then had to allow that he believed the oath to be righteously taken : and yet the Irish priests had still a right to overthrow the British government because illegittimate. I could not reconcile his contradictions! He opposed the Fenians: because the priests in Ireland opposed them. I told him they ought to assist an organisation which tended to promote the independence of Ireland. Dr. McSweeny and I took a walk to 42nd St. : gave me the usual tirade against Fr. Starrs, and included Fr. McGean, whom he and I agreed to be extremely small. In the evening I visited Mr. & Mrs. Navaro at 25 Washington Place : they are both very agreeable and intelligent. The boy came and kissed me good night-Hispanico more. I afterwards attended the conference of St. Vincent of Paul in which I took the members to task for neglecting the census.

<u>Wed., 10th</u>   I wrote the preamble to my essay on Fenianism. Dr. McSweeny and I talked over St. Stephen's parish : and the funeral of Dr. Cummings : and treating of the common opinion among priests that Romans form a clique, whilst they are most cliquish, Dr. McSweeny remarked that if for instance Dr. Morrogh were suspended, he would not hold out his hand to raise him : whilst other priests friendly among themselves would move every stone to assist their fallen friend. I took a ride at Dickel's. Dr. McGlynn supped with us. I hurried the drilling of the altar boys : and

January

adjourned the literary-class because there was no quorum at 8 o'c. till next week, in order to take a walk with the Doctor. We went to the upholsterer's who had decorated St. Stephen's, following Dr. McGlynn's design : also to the carpenter's, to see that both would be present at the church early to-morrow to make preparations for the photographer, Brady, who says that he had never seen a church even in Europe more tastefully draped, and was anxious to have a photograph of it in it's present condition. Dr. McGlynn designs having 100 large and 5000 small photographs taken as a memorial of Dr. Cummings. We then went to Dr. McGlynn's mother's where we found his brother Michael and his sister Mary and had quite a pleasant chat especially about Dr. Cummings' earlier days : the McGlynns had given him great assistance when he commenced St. Stephen's parish. In the afternoon I had visited the O'Reillys of whom I met one Mr. O'Reilly and his three unmarried sisters and one married viz : Mrs. Maitland and her son. The three unmarried sisters are advanced in years and yet light in their talk. They hinted that priests came to visit them to screw money from them. They talk about their grand relatives and many friends. I cannot bear their ways. I showed that a priest need not be a Jesuit to be good : the contrary of which proposition I saw the Jesuits had left impressed on Mrs. Maitland's mind, who thought that every secular priest was in great danger of damnation and was only anxious to become a bishop : both which propositions she said that the Jesuits had made her believe. She goes to the Jesuits'.

Thurs., 11th   I assisted at **Fr.** Mulledy's funeral. On my way I met Fr. McKenna of Brooklyn : whom I convinced of the necessity of more priests and churches in New York city. Fr. Curran sang the Requiem High Mass assisted by Fr. Joe Woods and   The office for the dead (one nocturn and lauds) was recited before Mass. A few words were spoken shabbily by Fr. Hassan of All Hallows. He said that "he had only known Fr. Mulledy for three months : but in that time he had found him a noble, just, honest man : even in his anger he was manly. His was the best panegyric, that he could make of him. In his youth he had been a rival of Perrone (a classmate of Passaglia's under Perrone). But the congregation of Yorkville could best speak his eulogy. The four sodalities founded by him to make all his congregation go monthly to confession, spoke his praise." About 30 priests were present : the body was taken to Fordham to be interred in the Jesuits' vault : because he had been re-admitted to the Jesuits' order on his deathbed : he had been expelled for drunkenness : afterwards on uncertain intervals he would go on a spree : He was for a long time chaplain at Ward's Island : and for two years acting pastor of St. Lawrence's Yorkville. As far as I knew him, he was of a very crabbed temper, (very unsympathetic.) Frs. Joe Woods, Malone, McCarthy, Dr. McSweeny and I strolled along Central Park to see the skating crowds : and we dined at Fr. McCarthy's, where Fr. Tom Quin and Fr. Nilan helped to make the company larger and gayer. We discussed the moral case whether on a fast-day of obligation in New York, which had not the same restriction in Brooklyn, a New Yorker could go to Brooklyn to eat meat. I affirmed : Dr. McSweeny and Fr. Nilan denied that a New Yorker could do so without committing sin. We discussed whether if celibacy were abolished, two thirds of the priests would marry : I was the only one who held the negative opinion. Afterwards Frs. McCarthy and Joe Woods imitated Italian opera singers so as to cause us to roar laughing. Frs. Tom Quin, McCarthy, and Woods also sang some fine songs. Dr. McSweeny, Fr. Nilan and I attended the Fenian meeting in Cooper Institute, to close the Fenian Congress held in favour of O'Mahony. Mr. Meany spoke well : as also Mr. Kelly of Indiana. We heard several speakers whose names I do not

January   215

recall, who were quite respectable in style and address. I heard ten speakers : and hence I derived a greater respect for the Fenian Brotherhood. The delegates presented quite an intelligent appearance. I disliked their denouncing Roberts & Co. as traitors, miscreants etc.

Fri., 12th   We heard the girls confessions in the morning. I gave the instruction on the 6th commandment to the girls recommending them not to write. I visited Dr. McGlynn who dined with us. He told us the objections the Abp. gave to a female messenger sent by Dr. Cummings three months ago to ask for Dr. McGlynn as an assistant. 1. Fr. Starrs had told the Abp. that Dr. Cummings would not like Dr. McGlynn. The female messenger replied that Fr. Starrs had known otherwise : for Dr. Cummings had asked for Dr. McGlynn, when Dr. Cummings went to Nassau a year ago. (Why did the Abp. tell this when now Dr. Cummings now asked for Dr. McGlynn). 2. Fr. Starrs told the Abp. : that the position of St. Stephen's required an Irishman, perhaps because Dr. Cummings was an American, & Fr. Gamboville a Frenchman. (A strange requisite in America, that a man should be Irish to be promoted : Dr. McGlynn's name too is not totally un-Irish). 3. Dr. McGlynn's health was not good, though Dr. McGlynn had told him (Abp.) frequently that it was good yet he (the Abp.) feared it was not good. 4. Dr. McGlynn was changeable : implying that he might like St. Stephen's for a short time but would become discontended and anxious for reformation. I felt too unwell to hear confessions in the evening.

Sat., 13th   Omitted by the Editor.

Sun., 14th   Sunday. Though unwell I said 9 o'c. and sang 10½ o'c. mass : I visited both Sunday Schools, assisted at Vespers and baptised. My mother and Miss A Burtsell visited me to overwhelm me with remedies which I declined. Fr. Preston spoke very strongly about the duties that parents

January 216

owe to children to teach them the faith, and ridiculed the poor ignorant parents who uneducated make themselves the judges of the respective merits of the public and the Catholic parochial schools. He took occasion for this from preaching on the childhood of Christ.

Mon., 15th   I with Fr. Nilan visited the public school in 47th St. bet 8 & 9th Aves. The principal is Mrs. McCloskey, who gathered several classes in the principal hall, where they went through several evolutions of callisthenics, which were quite interesting. We afterwards visited the Catholic Orphan Asylum, in 5th Ave.; Sister Borromeo showed us through the house. I remarked that all the boys look disconsolate, & lifeless : in one class a boy asked to sing began a hymn to The Blessed Virgin & was laughed at by the others. In another class all the boys with the sister-teacher fell on both knees at our entrance : Fr. Nilan examined some boys in Arithmetic : the choir and band played a Kyrie eleison for us. In the infirmary were two boys. The house looked very neat and clean : but is exposed to many drafts. I met at Fr. Nilan's his brother and a Mr. Connolly a contributor to the Metropolitan Record. After dinner at which Fr. McCarthy was present, Fr. O'Hare called : and we had several discussions about the U. S. Constitution. He considered the Supreme Court to be the highest Authority in the land. I held that it was judicially : but that Congress was above it as it's creator. Fr. Nilan and I went to see Edwin Booth play Hamlet at Winter Garden. He plays magnificently and is quite a model of speaking and acting.

Tues., 16th   Omitted by the Editor.

Wed., 17th   I took a ride at Dickel's. Dr. McSweeny called on me. I took lunch and dinner at Dr. McGlynn's with him, and had a long walk to the Central Park, admiring the skaters. The Doctor told me how the Abp.

January 217

had called on him on Saturday, and told him that he should hush the building of the church, for it was his (the Abp.'s) wish that Dr. McGlynn should remain at St. Stephen's. This was the announcement that Dr. McGlynn was to be pastor! for which Dr. McGlynn thanked him and asked his blessing for the position newly conferred upon him. No word of sympathy, or encouragement was given by the Abp. who had no feeling & no heart. Dr. McGlynn announced himself as pastor on the Sunday. This is a triumph of progress over old-fogyism, of virtue over cunning! I attended the altar-class : there was no meeting of the literary society, there being no quorum.

Thurs., 18th   Dr. Thos. Burtsell called to obtain my mediation in the family difficulties. At Mrs. Garrick's I met Fr. John Kelly of Amboy. I dined at Fr. Thos. Farrell's, where he had invited several priests to rejoice over Dr. McGlynn's appointment to St. Stephen's. Fr. Hecker came in and proposed a plan of forming a tract Society to spread Catholic influence and doctrines. In the evening I attend Bishop Simpson's lecture on 'New York-a field for missionary labour' delivered in St. Paul's M. E. Church. A collection was taken up to realise $17,000 to build a missionary church in Ave. A. near 11th St. A few parsons gave $1000, $500, and $100. Bishop Simpson is a fine speaker, and quite practical in his views. He praised the Catholic Church for having women-societies directed by church influence: which he thought affected the Protestants of America, more than the priesthood.

Fri., 19th   Omitted by the Editor.
Sat., 20th   Omitted by the Editor.
Sun., 21st   Omitted by the Editor.
Mon., 22nd   Fr. Nilan and I met on board the Jersey ferry-boat : We took the 8 o'c. train for Washington : found the road very monotonous and

January

and uninteresting : found no convenience for meals : and arrived in
Washington at 6 o'c, & put up at the Metropolitan Hotel, in which we got
two back-rooms, tolerably good. We went to see Maggie Mitchell play at
Grover's Theatre, in the role of Marie the pearl of Savoy. She acts
magnificently. Her change from joy to sorrow and from sorrow to joy is
well done. E. Lamb played very well : and the part of   , Marie's
friend was well acted by   The play was very moral. The specta-
tors were frequently moved to tears.

Tues., 23rd   We visited the Capitol : which is truly a splendid
building, of white marble. The dome is grand : Brumidi's painting sets
it off beautifully. The pictures are but second-rate that adorn the hall.
We attended both houses of Congress. The House of Representatives was
noisy, and rather disorderly. Speaker Colfax was at his place. The Chaplain
opened the house by a prayer for light from God. Some of the members paid
little attention to him. A resolution was proposed by Mr. Henderson to
give Texas as a colonising ground for the freed negroes : because Texas
by her rebellion was no longer a state but a territory. Then commenced a
serious debate on the proposed amendment to the constitution in relation
to the apportionment of Representatives and direct taxes. The principal
speakers that caught my attention was Stevens, not a good speaker, but a
determined obstinate man. Brooks pretended to wish to have Indians, Chinese
and women to vote : in order to defeat the bill. Mr. Blaine from Maine
was very earnest. In the Senate we heard Fessenden : quite a plain speaker
but an able debater. We heard Davis speak too : and Reverdy Johnson whose
teeth do not allow him to articulate well. The Senate was very decorous :
and yet the debate was quite spicy. We visited Mr. Richards, a shoe-dealer
under the Metropolitan Hotel to whom Fr. Nilan's brother introduced us.

January

He speaks contemptuously of the North. We visited Gen. Hardie to whom Fr. Preston gave me a letter of introduction. He is very intelligent : and gave us a long account of his difficulty with Fr. Walters in Mrs. Surratt's case : Fr. Walters had accused him of placing conditions on his spiritual attendance, whilst Fr. Walters' imprudent expression of disloyal sentiments made him an unsafe person to visit Mrs. Surratt. We again saw Maggie Mitchell but in a less pleasing play : as the little bare-foot. She played well : E. Lamb acted as her brother

Wed., 24th   Mr. Goodyear, M. C. for Schoharie, to whom I had a letter of introduction from Mr. Cassidy, asking him to introduce me to the president, said that this was almost impossible : as the president only had receptions on Tuesday evenings. He was disinclined, I think, to assist us because we were Catholic priests. Suspecting this, I showed by speaking of the pope as the only other ruler of a people elected, that I did not wish to hide the fact. We went to Gen. Hardie's office : where he gave us in charge to a Mr. Barry, quite a good and pleasant man : who took us to see the Smithsonian Institute, in which a fine museum of birds, fishes and shells etc. is the principal feature, besides a library of academical works. The colonies of Holland equal Spain & Portugal together in academical works. Great Britain has more than any other country. Italy is well represented. We visited the Patent Office : a magnificent marble building : in which are kept all the objects of which a patent has been given : the post office too is a fine large building. We saw the Treasury Office : in which 500 female clerks are employed. The place was pointed out to us where Burroughs was shot by Miss Harris. All these buildings are on a very grand scale : of white marble, having magnificent pillars to adorn their exterior. We saw the several apartments of the White House : and were told exactly where

January 220

Pres. Lincoln stood on reception nights : and where Pres. Johnson stands on the same occasion. The rooms are rather small but well decorated. Relic seekers had even cut the curtains. We afterwards went to the Navy-yard : passing through several of the work-shops, and saw the Monitor was explained to us in all it's parts by the officer on board. It has four large cannons, is generally eleven inches thick of iron above water : the machinery is quite simple : but very interesting to be seen. In the evening we called at Fr. Walter's : where we met Abp. Spalding, Frs. Boyle, McCarthy, and Wigott S. J. They were all very fine men. Fr. Walter's is quite active and intelligent, hasty but kind and outspoken : quite opposed to the negroes and to Yankees. Fr. Boyle is quite playful, always telling anecdotes of himself, intelligent : Fr. McCarthy is good but not of very thick metal. The Abp. spoke bitterly of fanatical Yankees. In manner the priests speak frankly with the Abp. : but show a childish way in speaking of 'being caught' by Abp. Kenrick in ex. gr. taking whiskey etc. Fr. Wigot is a poor fellow, hardly speaking English. We had seen him at the college nearby where he treated us very poorly. Frs. Walters, McCarthy, Nilan and I joined in a talk against the Jesuits. Fr. Walters found that the Sisters of the Visitation would only have the children of their school go to confession to Jesuits : They were Fr. Walter's parish children. Fr. Nilan and I went to Canterbury : where we saw ballet dances, and minstrels, and the female clerks of Washington.

Thurs., 25th   With Mr. Barry we went to Georgetown college : where Fr. Maguire the president took us around the building : a small museum, a library of 30 000 vols, experimental apparatus, and fine dormitories, with the fine prospect are the principal ornaments of this, otherwise not grand, place. We visited the academy of the Visitation nuns : accompanied by a very intelligent nun, who showed us the building. The chapel is neat. A girl played on

January   221

the harp for us. We visited the Washington observatory : where we admired
the four fine instruments which are there. One lately put up at a cost of
$10,000 is the finest in the world. We visited the O'Conor Don at Willard's
hotel. He is quite a fine young man, intelligent, but imbued with pro-
Southern ideas, which we tried to overturn. We dined with Gen. Hardie :
his wife was pleasant, but the general is the better of the two. We visited Mr. Chanler M. C. to whom J. McLaughlin had given me a letter of introduction. We argued on the right that the negroes should have perfect freedom by a change in the constitution : He thought that the South was free
to leave us, when we changed the old constitution. He is a very fine man.
We went to Fr. Walters' : where we again met Abp. Spalding and Fr. McCarthy :
with whom we had quite a pleasant talk. The Abp. was to have lectured on
the "Crescent and the Cross" but the lecture was postponed on account of
the bad walking which would have prevented many from being present.

Fri., 26th   We visited the City Hall, where we saw Marshall (formerly
Colonel) O'Byrne, to whom Fr. Nilan's brother introduced us. He pointed
out to us Col. Baker who was being tried for the false imprisonment of Mrs.
Dobb. Judge Fisher is a calm judge. Mr. Stanton, Baker's counsel does not
show sufficient skill : whilst Bradley is quite shrewd. He is Mrs. Dobb's
counsel. We saw also Judge Carter. We visited the Capitol : and mounting
the dome had a magnificent view of the country surrounding Washington. We
assisted again at both houses of Congress. In the Senate we heard Mr. Davis,
a tiresome speaker. In the house of Representatives we heard Mr. McKee from
Kentucky speak in favour of the Southern States not being allowed to send
disloyal representatives to Congress. Mr. Chanler took us to see the various
committee rooms, the Agricultural is well frescoed : as also the Naval and
Military rooms. He introduced us to Senator Morgan : who showed us the

January

Senate marble-room the president's room and the vice-president's all fine rooms. We saw also the heating machinery : and admired the fine marble walls of the lowest floor. We left Washington by the 4½ o'c. train and stayed at the Continental Hotel, in Philadelphia for the night.

Sat., 27th   We visited Dr. Keogh and Fr. Jas O'Connor. We saw the Philadelphia Cathedral : a magnificent building. Brumidi's frescoes are too large for the church. We reached New York at 4 o'c. I heard confessions.

Sun., 28th   Sunday. I sang High Mass : and visited both the Sunday Schools. In the evening I heard Dr. Washburn preach in Trinity Chapel (25th St.) for the benefit of St. Barnabas' home. He sought the cause of the poverty and vice in New York. He said it was the luxury of it's wealthy inhabitants : who fostered by their pleasures a similar spirit in the poorer classes, which were tempted to imitate their life without working, and their pleasures even through thieving and other sins. A larger synopsis will be found among my other papers. He has a fine voice and delivery, but excites no feeling. I visited the Morroghs of 26th St. : where I found my mother, Mrs. McLaughlin, and Mr. Deane just come from California. I defended the Fenians : Mr. Deane who is a Fenian was quite pleased to see a priest, as he said, ably defend them.

Mon., 29th   In the morning Dr. McSweeny and I visited Dr. McGlynn where we met Mrs. & Michael McGlynn. Michael told the story that a lady cried 'Sour-grapes' whilst Dr. Cummings was preaching on the burdens of Marriage-life. I visited the Garricks in the evening : the two girls jumped for joy, when I asked Mrs. Garrick to take a table at the fair.

Tues., 30th   Drs. McSweeny, McGlynn and I took a stroll to Centralpark. Dr. McGlynn was anxious to have Fr. McGean's character well defined

January

by Dr. McSweeny : because he is thinking of asking that Fr. McGean be made his assistant. . . .

Wed., 31st   Omitted by the Editor.

February

Thurs., 1st   Omitted by the Editor.

Fri., 2nd   Omitted by the Editor.

Sat., 3rd   With Dr. McSweeny I took a walk to 50th St. : where entering the Cathedral precincts we had a better idea of it's magnitude. I heard confessions in the afternoon.

Sun., 4th   Sunday. I preached on the way of sanctifying the Sundays and festivals, established by the Church. I explained the 9th Commandment to the boys' and girls' S. Schools. Dr. W. McCloskey called at our place : and told us that he was quite pleased with the $10000, had in our diocese for the Roman-American College! I went to hear Abp. McCloskey's lecture at St. Teresa's Church on Faith : and it's responsibilities. A synopsis of it is given in my first correspondence to the Catholic Standard. He commenced by acknowledging the privilege (?) he had for the first time of adressing St. Teresa's congregation. He would speak to them of faith, which is a gift of God by which we firmly assent to the truths which He has taught us. We cannot merit faith by any act of ours : and the greater part of those who were now adressed had not even to concur with an act of theirs to the grace of God : for by baptism they had received the habit of faith before they were capable of an intelligent act. Around us we behold a constant struggle for the acquisition of faith. Many are really earnest, & willing to sacrifice all for this pearl of pearls. Others know what is Truth : they have the historical evidences which convince their minds : but they have not faith, for this would bend their wills to accept the Truths which

February 224

they have sufficient reasons to know, but the acceptance of this knowledge would require too many sacrifices which they are unwilling to make. Faith embraces all the truths taught by God : we must seek a rule of faith which will keep them in their integrity. Two tests of faith are the ones acknowledged in our midst: which is the one appointed by Christ can ascertained by two remarks. The two rules of faith are the private interpretation of the Bible, or the authority of the Church. 1. The Church existed before the Bible. Many were converted before the Bible was written. A part of the new Testament was written, 8 & 10, years after Christ, another part at the close of the first century : and the whole was not gathered together till 150 years after Christ. In the mean time Christians believed all the truths taught by Christ : hundreds of thousands were martyred for them. How could the private interpretation of the bible be their rule of faith? They learned all from the Church. 2. The truth is but not contradictory : and the rule of faith, which is only concerning the truth, cannot be that which practically induces many contractions : but every one's private interpretation of the bible necessarily leads to contradictions & has practically done so : hence not it, but the authority of the Church which can command unity of faith is the true rule of faith. The responsibility of faith is great. We notice that Protestants attach the faults of Catholics to their faith : thus showing that Catholics are identified with their faith : whilst we do not attribute the crimes of Protestants to Protestantism. Hence Catholics are to practice their faith lest they should scandalise those out of the Church. The O'Conor Don called on me to be excused from an engagement, by which me was to dine with me on Tuesday. O'Gorman had invited the Abp. to meet him the same evening.

Mon., 5th   I wrote my first letter to the Catholic Standard of

February

Philadelphia, edited by Dr. Keogh : it was a shabby letter. I went, by invitation, to dine with Fr. McLoughlin and a party of friends in New Rochelle. We denounced the Jesuits; thought little of the Abp.'s logic last evening, and agreed with the Catholic priest who denounced a priest of Troy for refusing the rites of the Church to a dead Fenian, in to-days Daily News. I regret saying several things because Fr. Boyce was there : he is a toady, and an envious cur. He thinks that the Immac. Conception of the B. V. M. is not a dogma of faith! and that a child breaking silence in school commits a sin by wasting time! Frs. McCarthy, Malone, McGovern, Dr. Malone, Dr. McSweeny were there also. When I got home Dr. McGlynn called to see me, informing that Abp. Spalding had expressed himself disgusted with me, a young man, speaking (when I last met him in Washington) of nothing but politics, the negro etc. This is dishonest, because I avoided politics, except where he & Fr. Walters thrust them on me.

<u>Tues., 6th</u>   I went to hear the confessions of the Industrial School children in 42nd St. parish : and walked homewards with Fr. Nilan. I dined with him and Fr. McCarthy. In the evening I went to hear Abp. Spalding lecture on 'The Church the Civiliser of Nations'. He briefly reviewed the so-called civilisation of heathen nations : showing how the Roman and Greek so-called civilisations were too sensual to really ennoble man : the erection of grand buildings, and magnificent statues may show great refinement, but do no form true civilisation. It is a fact of history that Rome and Greece never thought of building an hospital, or an orphan asylum, which symbolise the care given to men, and the anxiety to better our fellow-creatures. It was fashionable, 100 years ago, to praise Chinese civilisation : This is ludicrous to those who know how devoid of all true moral influences the Chinese have been, since sknown to us : whilst they have been stationery

February   226

in their physical culture. They never perfected beyond the pocket-compass
that guided them by land : their junks have been stereotyped from century
to century : their first knowledge of astronomical instruments was conveyed to them by Jesuits missionaries. The heathen so-called civilisations
knew not what charity is, nor honesty, nor had any idea of chastity as
known to Christians. The Church of Christ brought into the world new ideas
of civilisation. Christ crucified sent to the world twelve poor men as his
messengers : yet the world accepted of their message and though Roman power
and Greek refinement opposed the new philosophy, it gained so many adherents that the two former disappeared from the face of the earth, and it
alone remained. The blood of martyrs had once been the seed of Christians.
Christianity ruled the Roman empire : but survived it, when the barbarians
destroyed it. The Church bent before the storm : but then rose majestic to
rule and tame these barbarians. It made them Christian. Ireland was the
first to become Christian : and it's prerogative was that no martyr's blood
was required to seed it's duration. The soil was so fertile : that it's
roots took such deep possession that 1000 years afterwards when a storm of
three centuries commenced and lasted without intermission, all else of
earthly goods were robbed of the Irish people, but this jewel remained in
their possession. Irish apostles helped to propagate the gospel over the
countries of Europe which had been overswept by the barbarians. The Franks
were converted by Remigius : the tribes that came to Germany by Boniface
assisted by the Irish Vigilins : and other many spread the light of Truth
from England to Italy : and from the North to the South : Augustine and his
forty monks converted England : Rupert Batavia, etc. a remarkable fact is
too that these apostles, almost without exception, asked authorisation from
or were directly sent by the bishop of Rome, successor to St. Peter, who by

February

our Lord was declared his special representative. Thus in the ages in which the Church had great rule : we see magnificent Cathedrals erected to God, universities established, in Paris, in Cambridge, Oxford, Saragossa, Naples, Florence Pavia, Rome etc. etc., parish schools near every parish-church, the rights of the people protected by the Church. Thus Card. Langton headed the Barons who at Rungmede required King John to sign Magna Charta, thus Catholic times inaugurated the right of 'Habeas Corpus' the right of trial by jury (which has lately degenerated into so many abuses). Thus in Catholic times the compass was discovered which led to the discovery of America : the printing press, the real rotation of the earth around the Sun etc. etc. Thus the Church, the true Church of Christ, has been the civiliser of the nations, that has given us what we boast of now-a-days as the perfection of the human race. Some think that the 'reformation' so-called brought in a great many new principles of civilisation : but rather it has done the contrary. In Protestant countries men give a thousand dollars for a shawl : but not for a church. A gate of a Cathedral of the Middle Ages is worth more than any church built in Protestant times. Now-a-days the principle is to give to oneself, not to God. The Irish are a grand exception for they still give their money with generosity to build churches to God's honour : they are worthy of the middle-ages : this is the highest compliment that can be paid them. The church was packed. A sumptous lunch of Martinez Maison Doree was served up at the house : during which Dr. McGlynn described the Abp. as a Basil speaking to the Xtians of the early ages. He was tickled. Fr. Foley acted foolishly in giving light talk about the ladies to us.

Wed., 7th   In the evening I went to dine with Abp. Spalding at Dr. McGlynn's. The O'Conor Don, Charles O'Conor, Jas T. Brady, Jas. B. Nicholson, McMasters, Walter McGee etc. etc. besides a number of priests

February 228

were present. Dr. McGlynn again called the Abp. a Basil speaking to the early Xtians : the Abp. thought the Dr. had kissed the Blarney stone : but called him a whole souled host. Charles O'Conor was toasted, and alluded to his anxiety to have Abp. Spalding appointed as Abp. of Baltimore when the Administration was opposed to him. James T. Brady professed great friendship for Dr. McGlynn : as long as he did not become immoral : and called himself a Catholic : and said that only the Catholic religion made men happy, as proved by the light-heartedness of Catholic priests, in contradistinction to the angularity, & crossness of protestant ministers.

<u>Thurs., 8th</u>   I acted as master of Ceremonies at Dr. Cummings' Month Mind, Fr. Tom Farrell acting as celebrant, Fr. Jos. Woods as deacon, Fr. McGean as subdeacon. Dr. McGlynn gave a magnificent eulogy of Dr. Cummings. He reviewed his earlier years, when the fond care of a mother watered his early yearnings for the priesthood as a means of promoting God's glory, and men's welfare : for she had him admitted when still almost a child to the college at Nyack, a preparatory institution for Ecclesiastical students; and willingly again parted with him, though her only boy, that he might go to Rome, to the college of Propaganda, that hus he might drink nearer to the source of the fresh waters of truth, and nestling more closely than is given to most of us, to the bosom of Holy Mother the Church, might be warmed with warmer love, purer charity for mankind. There for 14 years he disciplined himself for his labours of after years. In the spirit of prayer, and self-denial he prepared his soul for great things : for, as he afterwards wrote in a letter to Abp. Hughes, always the greatest passion of his life, was to labour for the conversion of his native land. And when after years of long preparation, he returned to the land of his birth, his zeal was unremitting, his courage dauntless though he was placed in a parish,

in which the burdens were so numerous as would have crushed one of less energy and elasticity : for besides the numerous night and day calls of the sick of the parish which then extended over a very great portion of the city, he had charge of Bellevue Hospital, in which hour by hour he had been accustomed to relieve of the burden of their sins the dying poor ones, who were gathered there from the whole city. Abp. Hughes felt that he could not allow this bright light to be kept long under the bushel : and when the people of the neighbourhood of 28th clamoured for a pastor, the Abp. said that he would give them the best of his priests. Here the new pastor built an humble chapel : in which the congregation soon swelled so as almost to burst the wall of the small edifice and he was forced to rear the present parish church of St. Stephen's, the finest and largest of the city. Here his eloquence, and his practical piety and magnificent instructions had formed a congregation intelligent, and truly zealous for God's glory, generous in giving it's earthly wealth for the good of souls! Dr. McGlynn recalled his personal relations with Dr. Cummings and touchingly spoke of God's providence that had destined him to anoint Dr. Cummings at his last hour, who had 12 years before given to him for the first time the bread of life : and how he had formerly breathed his childish griefs and sins to him who had earnestly requested a short time before his death to have him as his associate in being a father to the faithful of St. Stephen's parish. God seemed to have deprived them of this father : and to have torn him from them ruthlessly : but it was in order to purify their hearts and to glorify his servant : and bringing nearer to Himself this great labourer of His Vineyard, raise too their thoughts inseparately united to their deceased pastor, Fr. Farrell gave the Absolution. A lunch in Martinez' style was given the clergy. I had a religious talk with Misses Downing and Hunt at

February

their own request : it fell on the Primacy of St. Peter, and his coming to Rome. With Dr. McGlynn I visited the Gerdes and Mrs. McDowall : also assisted at his baptizing of Mrs. Contain's boy. We talked about the choice the Abp. gave him of Fr. Nilan as assistant : he asked for Fr. McGean : I told him by all means to prefer Fr. Nilan.

Fri., 9th   Omitted by the Editor.

Sat., 10th   Omitted by the Editor.

Sun., 11th   Sunday. I said 9 o'c. & sang $10\frac{1}{2}$ o'c. masses. Fr. Preston preached on the gospel : in reference to the spirit of mortification necessary for the Lenten season : showing that Protestants had rejected the spirit of self-abnegation, and that Episcopalians had a Lent in the prayer-book but not in practice : their principle of justification by faith led naturally to the rejection of self-denial, as esteemed by Christ. The boys' S. School was dismissed because the key of the room was not to be found. I talked to the girls' S. School on the 7th commandment. In the evening I attend Fr. O'Connor's lecture on the "Temporal power of the Pope" : He showed how this originated in the donations to the bishop of Rome over lands over which the owner had according to laws then accepted, great civil jurisdiction. The pope's sovereignty commenced in the 8th century : when the Greek emperors retired from Italy and left the Italians to defend themselves against their Lombard enemies. The Italians saw that self-preservation would be best attained by asking the bishops of Rome to govern them : and these only after repeated refusals took on themselves the arduous task. When the Lombards still were eager to conquer the Roman provinces, Stephen II crossed the Alps in his old age, and obtained Pepin's assistance : who conquered the Lombards and secured to the pontiff the possession of the Roman States. Charlemagne also finding the Lombards not keeping their treaty, annihilated their power, and again secured to the pontiff the sovereignty already given him by the free-will of the Italian populations. This sovereignty of the popes brought great advantages to the Roman people : and in view of their sacred office, their territory has been always held sacred in the eyes of Catholics. It insures to the Pontiff, independence and freedom in the exercise of his spiritual authority. It may be likened to the District of Columbia in these United States, whence many political privileges are withdrawn for the good of the country at large. Hence even if now-a-days the Romans were anxious to overthrow the pope's rule, the Catholics of the world who by their enriching the Roman territory and by their anxiety for the freedom of their spiritual chief have the right to take action in this matter, would be perfectly justified in opposing their desire. He thought that the Romans as a people are not anxious to be freed from the pope's sovereignty. He had lived in Rome in times of revolution : and had witnessed the earnestness with which the Romans had laboured to thwart it's designs, when they could have had every thing in their own hands. A few active men, a circulating revolutionary committee having great influence in other parts of Europe might possibly effect a revolution in Rome : but the people is truly in favour of the popes. The pope's government has it's rights from the free-will of the Italian people, from the conquest of Pepin and Charlemagne, from long possession : and had never forfeited it's rights by misrule : and therefore the Roman people would have no right, even if it wished, to overturn it. The interest of the Catholics of the world demands that it be preserved. This is the shield with which Providence chooses to cover the pope's independence in our day : hence it is a practical necessity for us to preserve this shield. If God in his inscrutable designes should deprive the pope of his temporal power : He will know how to give a substitute. But we must defend

February 232

the only means which we perceive to be able to shield the pope's independence in spiritual matters.

Mon., 12th   Omitted by the Editor.

Tues., 13th   Pat O'Connell called on me : and gave me an account of his trip through Tennesee, down the Mississipi to Texas. He found the Southerners cruel to the negroes : one widow kept them in slavery when freed by their master's last will : one whipped a negro till he was half-dead. The white soldiers cheated the negro soldiers by selling water for whiskey at $3,50 a bottle. O'Connell acted as reporter to a Pittsburgh paper : met a Catholic priest : had three Catholics in his regiment : ran the picket lines to go to Mass : refused to go to Protestant service : found the Westerners to be quite intelligent and dignified : had a Colonel habitually drunk : had a lieutenant who shut the stores of Victoria to be paid for allowing them to be opened : found the authorities quite strict in suppressing all wrong-doings of Union Soldiers, by arresting officers and men : Pat has become a strong Union-Man : would not wish to be a priest. I took a ride at Dickel's. Dr. McGlynn called in the evening : told me that he had secured Fr. Nilan as his assistant. . . .

Wed., 14th   Ash Wednesday. I blessed the Ashes : and Fr. Preston & I distributed them before the 7 o'c. Mass and after the 8 o'c. mass. It took about an hour, because we had good order : the people coming up the side aisles and going by the middle aisle. I took a ride at Dickel's : and visited Fr. Nilan who feared an attack of fever. I saw Fr. McCarthy : with the two I expressed the opinion that Abp. McCloskey was becoming very popular through his visiting families, baptising the children and standing as godfather, and inquiring of the mothers how their children were etc. and that he finding himself unable to shine among priests, sought to shine among

February   233

the laity. . . .

Thurs., 15th   Omitted by the Editor.

Fri., 16th   Omitted by the Editor.

Sat., 17th   Omitted by the Editor.

Sun., 18th   Omitted by the Editor.

Mon., 19th   I took a ride at Dickel's : went to Appleton's to inquire for the price of the American Cyclopedia, and found that to clergymen he allows a discount of 20 percent. I gave the practical instructions on the 'Sacraments in general' and Baptism in particular, following Bressani : whom I find uselessly diffuse. Dr. McGlynn called to see me at 9 o'c. P.M. and remained till 12 o'c. P.M. : We discussed whether Christ as man could have known less than we know about the Church; and if he were ignorant of the day of judgement, why could he not be ignorant of a great many other things about the Church? The Scripture positively says that he grew in wisdom before God and men: and that he had said he would not go to Jerusalem, not foreseeing that he would change his mind and go on the festival day : and that these passages cannot be explained away, by attributing to them a sense which they do not admit. St. Teresa could give a better essay on Christ and the Church, than the B. Virgin, who, we are told, was astonished at a great many things that she saw and heard about Christ's nativity and divinity : thus proving that she had not a perfect knowledge of these mysteries, and of her and of Christ as man, it is only a question of degree of knowledge : for it was metaphysically impossible for them to know all things : this belongs to the Godhead alone.

Tues., 20th   Dr. McGlynn and Dr. McSweeny called to see me. We visited Brady's Photographic Gallery, to see the photograph of St. Stephen's church as it was draped for the funeral of Dr. Cummings. We made various suggestions about the altar : and Mr. Nagle, the artist, suggested the introduction to the picture a few human figures, of sisters praying etc. We took dinner at Dr. McGlynn's. Dr. McSweeny told that Fr. McKenna, of St. Mary's, who after a begging tour in this country for a church in Ireland, finding that in this country he could have a better living than he had had before, came to settle in New York, is now aspiring to the pastorate of Yorkville, and is backed by his patron Fr. Quin of St. Peter's : this would be an injustice to the priests ordained for the diocese. Dr. McGlynn and I took a stroll through the Central park to Manhattanville to see Mad. Hardie : but reached the place so late, that we preferred returning to entering. On our way we stopped at the restaurant, which has superseded the Central park Hospital where Dr. McGlynn resided for three years. The restaurant is under the care of   and Radford : the latter we met with Mr. Ryan who lives next door. They took us through the building : no brandies are allowed to be sold : the doors of the rooms are removed to prevent ruffianism : the house's peculiarities are preserved because it is a mansion of the revolutionary era. The large chapel, is reserved for a museum under charge of the commissioners of the Central park. We visited Mr. Ryan's family : it was the first time that Dr. McGlynn had visited them, though he had been three years next door to them! We took supper at Dr. McGlynn's : and went to the debate at St. Francis Xavier's college. The subject was: 'National festivals indicate National Character'. We arrived to hear the third discourse by Henry P. Baxter showing that the celebration of St. Patrick's showed that the character of the Irish people was fidelity to it's faith and to it's country: proved through centuries of trouble and persecution, during which the Irish clung to the faith which St. Patrick had given to them, and to the country whose fate Providence had inseparably interwoven with their faith : that the two had

February 235

been persecuted together : and now seemed to be the time of both shining forth most gloriously (an allusion to the Fenian movement). He spoke quite moderately and well. Thomas J. Campbell sought to prove that the character of the Romans was devotion to the pope because of the festival of SS. Peter and Paul : the Romans' love for the pope had banished Constantine to Constantinople, and had in the 8th century made him a temporal Sovereign : in the middle ages they clung to the pope, as the cause of their greatest glory. In our century alone has the Roman lost in part his devotion to the pope. His delivery was very good. James T. Casey gave a grand eulogy of our forefathers Washington & Co. in their struggle for our Independence : concluding that our 4th of July celebration shows the love that Americans have within them for liberty. The discourses at which I was not present was the Chairman; Edward F. McGee's address : and Joseph F. Mosher's whose subject was : France = 'Military Glory' as it's character. There was solo singing by Mr. Colliere : and the college choir sang several choruses : Mr. Dessane being the director. The Abp. thanked the young men for the 'privilege' afforded the audience of attending their debate : which instructed, amused and delighted us all. Their discourses were creditable to themselves and to their professors : though he being in the vale of life, had not been able to follow the flights of their imagination, he admitted that to youthful orators was to be extended the privilege, granted according to Horace to painters and poets : Pictoribus atque poetis audendi.

Wed., 21st   I dined with Dr. McGlynn and Fr. Gamboville : who ridicules the Canadian pronunciation of French, and says that their language has been Anglicised : though the Canadians pretend to have the pronunciation of Louis XIV's time : yet the settlers were country people, whose language was not very pure. Dr. McGlynn and I walked to the Manhattanville Convent

February   236

of the Sacred Heart where we saw Madame   , to whom Dr. McGlynn recommended an ex-Jewess who is persecuted by her parents for Christ's sake, she having become a Christian. She had been protected before in one of their Canadian convents through Mad. Hardie's influence. Mad. Hardie was not home. Our conversation on the road was principally on our personal defects : I acknowledged my deficiency of the knowledge of English : my poor style of writing : my bashfulness in talking which makes me at times appear illogical in reasoning and not intelligible because of my not sufficiently articulating my words : which however does not occur in public speaking. Dr. McGlynn has an immense power of language, yet he has not read many books. He is deficient in animation. We met Fr. Huet who called me Chrysostom on account of my tooth filled with gold. Talking of St. Augustine's 'opera' Dr. McGlynn told that a French priest to get them cheap at a book stand stated that these operas were no longer played on modern theatres : but discovered the seller to be a priest : whence Fr. Huet denied that there were many such priests, and said it was a blessing to have the bad ones suspended rather than to let govern the church. I recited the beads and gave the benediction of the B. Sacrament : Fr. Preston preached on Hell a very frightening discourse : describing the fire that impregnated the bodies of the damned, and the horrid remorse produced by the memories of the facility of salvation and of the opportunities lost.

<u>Thurs., 22nd</u>   Washington's birthday. I went to St. John's college to hear the debate of which the subject was 'whether the term: 'Materialistic' specifies the character of this age.' Leopold Laflamme of Montreal, as chairman, clearly explained the nature of the question. Edward C. Monk of Montreal in a manly discourse praised the great progress of the natural sciences, and showed of what great profit their study was to the welfare of man : but

regretted that our age allowed itself to be absorbed in this study to the neglect of the intellectual culture of man : he thought that commerce and love of wealth withdrew men from the deep study of law, and philosophy, and theological questions. Paul J. Roberts of New Orleans said that there was no comparison between the civilisation of our age and that of past age : our's is essentially productive of intellectual culture, as the very study of nature gives us grander ideas of God, new arguments for admiring his wisdom. William F. Brady thought that in our age the love of materialistic progress had so turned the brains of nations, that revolution was constantly disturbing society : and prevented all deep researches into the moral wants of men. Cornelius J. O'Donnell of Brooklyn showed that the love of knowledge was now in the people, the press gave means of intellectual culture to all, that the forms of government developed the intelligence of the people, & our common schools were the best proof that our age is not materialistic essentially, but uses nature to develop man. Leopold Laflamme in a neatly delivered discourse thought that though idealism had great sway over men's minds, yet now-a-days materialism seemed to have the greater number of partisans. Fr. McNierney regretted the absence of the Abp. : who is now much pressed with business : and thanked the young gentlemen for the entertainment they had given. From their fresh hearts had gushed forth streams of fancy and intelligence, which refreshed even our more matured hearts : He admired their anxiety to avoid the materialistic tendencies of the age, but reminded them that they should tread the path of progress, which was secured by the laws of God and of the Church. He afterwards told us that the Abp. had remarked after he had delivered an exhortation in favour of the orphans, that one who spoke so well should never read his sermons (as Fr. McNierney always does) but he did not like to learn the sermon off once

February 238

because this would cause him to learn it off always (he prefers being lazy always). We had a poor dinner. I met Mr. Cahill : with whom I was at college at Montreal : and Mr. Devlin, the Clothier. Very few priests were present. With Fr. Larkin, I went to visit Fr. Nilan who had been sick for a week. I met Dr. McSweeny who equivolently called me heretical and blasphemous for this proposition: 'No grand plan for the freedom of a nation or a class originated with the external authorities of the Church,' though revelation and Christianity were the cause of all good reforms. I got angry because he threw out this imputation before Fr. Larkin : and I protested against this untheological way of acting. He cited the 'Truce of God' as a fact against me : Balmes expressly ascribes it's origin to Charlemagne. He recalled the Crusades : Peter the hermit had no external authority in the Church. When Fr. Larkin left, he gave in. Fr. Tom McLoughlin and he walked home with me. I endeavoured to witness the meeting in favour of Johnson's veto of the Freedmen's bureau bill : but the crowd was too great at the Cooper Institute. I visited the Burtsells of 4th Ave. The Doctor is constantly throwing out petty jokes about other women's beauty to tease his wife : she is the smarter of the two.

Fri., 23rd   Omitted by the Editor.

Sat., 24th   Omitted by the Editor.

Sun., 25th   I sang H. Mass & said 9 o'c. We gave notice to-day of the fair. Fr. Preston preached on the gospel of to-morrow : showing that faith in Christ is necessary : since Christ said : 'You shall die in your sins because you do not believe in me' : and he proved that indifferentism, expressed in this now popular expression 'Tis no matter what a man believes, as long as his heart is right, is 1. self-contradictory inasmuch as it supposed the question whether a man's heart can be right, if he does not accept

February   239

of God's revelation. 2. contrary to reason, which knows it must receive God's teachings, if their authority is made clear. 3. contrary to Christ's life, who being God became man, performed miracles, and died and rose again and established a church to insure the acceptance of faith in him and in all that he ever taught. I explained the 7th commandment to the boys' S.S. : and gave a few theological riddles to the girls, to be solved. Fr. Preston spoke in the evening on the words of the Saviour to the good thief: 'Behold thou shalt be with me this day in paradise.' He described the blasphemies of the Jews and of the thieves : one of whom repented and was forgiven perhaps in answer to Christ's prayer: 'Father forgive them.' Thus repentance is never too late : and sin can be forgiven by God. Yet to differ repentance till the hour of death is foolish. Mr. Dachauer dined with us. I talked against the practice by which a poor singing priest must sing the preface etc. at High Mass and also against our saying the Mass in a language not understood by the people : which makes them lose great benefits of it. At least the epistle, gospel, collects etc. which are sung should be in the language understood by the people.

Mon., 26th   Omitted by the Editor.

Tues., 27th   I acted as subdeacon at the Requiem Mass for Mr. Carroll the deceased Fr. Carroll's father; Fr. Gambosville was celebrant, Dr. McGlynn deacon. Mr. Carroll had a monomaniac's hatred for Abp. Hughes whom he accused of killing Fr. Carroll by imposing on him too hard work. Dr. McGlynn explained the doctrine of the church on the utility of prayers for the dead, saying : the Church confessed the sins of her children and asked God's mercy for them. Frs. Thos. Farrell and Thos. Quin stayed for dinner. We cut up the Jesuits frightfully on account of their love of 'the Order'. Fr. Quin told that B. McFarland had declined the bulls for Florida for ill-health. Abp.

February

Kenrick replied that the only good quality of Florida was the salubrity of it's climate. B. McFarland has no talent. Dr. McGlynn and I paid a visit to Fr. Nilan : with whom we met Fr. Thos McLoughlin. I met the altar class in the evening.

Wed., 28th   Omitted by the Editor.

March

Thurs., 1st   I took a ride at Dickel's. I visited Miss Pardow, Mrs. Pardow not being home. She thought the pope should elect his successor, because the cardinals having human passions might each be anxious to become pope! She thought the life of a secular priest to be quite comfortable since he had a fine house and good meals, whilst the regular clergy is more mortified! She has a brother a Jesuit. I suggested that the pope's selection of a successor might not be as good as that of the cardinals : and that a fine carpet does not make a secular priest perfectly happy! I visited my mother in the evening : and read a letter from Mrs. J. E. Burtsell stating that my brother John had had a severe attack of ulcerated sore-throat.

Fri., 2nd   I gave the usual instructions to tne girls' school - 'on lies'. I took a ride at Dickel's. Between confessions after Mass and of the girls in the morning, and of the boys in the afternoon and of the grown up people, I heard six hours' of confessions which I considered to excuse from reciting Matins & Lauds. Dr. McGlynn called to see me. He is quite depressed. He has been doing all the duty of St. Stephen's parish for the last four months : at least Fr. Gambosville does not do more than one sixth of the work : and that very perfunctorily. He thinks of writing to Dr. Conroy to get five or six import priests.

Sat., 3rd   I heard six hours of confessions : in the afternoon about one man's to two women's. I attended Mrs. Murphy between Houston & Bleecker

March 241

Sts. in Laurence St. I protested to Fr. Preston against Abp. McCloskey's interfering with the Fenian mass-meeting of to-morrow. The Abp. writes a letter to each pastor, that he may warn his people against this desecration of the Sunday.

<u>Sun., 4th</u>   At 7 o'c. Mass I read the Abp's letter : stating that he had thought fit to apply to the Fenian political meeting the general law of the Church which prohibited all "contentious causes." Fr. Preston stated that the Abp. did not condemn the Fenian movement but merely the holding of a meeting on Sunday. I preached at 10 o'c. Mass. I had not had time to write a sermon : but had read several sermons : but drew principally from Musso's of the 3rd Sunday of Lent and Gahan's of the same day. I was more instructive than usual. Fr. Preston congratulated me on the sermon : it was more emphatical because I had to select ideas on the spur of the moment. I preached to the boys' SS. 'on lies'. I visited the girls' SS. giving difficult questions to be solved. I sang Vespers : and read the prayers at the Stations of the Cross : Fr. Preston preaching on the words of Christ : Son behold thy mother. Woman behold thy Son. 1. He described the sorrow of the Virgin during the passion, and her dignity of mediatrix when she willingly made the sacrifice of her child for our Salvation. 2. He rejected the foolish Protestant idea that Christ showed disrespect to his mother, by calling her= woman. She was the woman who was to be united with the seed in crushing the serpent's head : the Second Eve, the Mother of the Living. 3. He showed how the Virgin was given to us as a mother : we were represented by the disciple St. John : and thus we have a right to recur to her, knowing her influence with her child Jesus. Mr. Dachauer dined with us. Remi, our basso, has left us, because Mr. Dachauer called him to an account for not being present at the rehearsals. Fr. Preston wrote to Remi reproaching him for

March

leaving, against all his former promises : saying that he was thus confirmed in his little appreciation of musicians' honour.

<u>Mon., 5th</u> I wrote my fourth letter to the Catholic Standard : one of the four was not published : they are over the signature of Excelsior. I took a ride at Dickel's : with Fr. Preston. I visited Dr. McGlynn : with whom I found Fr. Venuta. We discussed the Fenian question. Fr. Venuta had once openly denounced the Fenians and broke up a Fenian meeting. He now thinks Abp. McCloskey's letter foolishly worded, and his discourse at the Cathedral denouncing the Fenians as poorly argued. We showed him the absurdity of refusing the sacraments to the Fenians : because the question of their guilt, is, to say the least, very doubtful : they have sufficient intrinsic reasons and extrinsic authority in guaranteeing a probability to their opinion : which gives to them a right to act upon it : and no confessor can impose his opinion, even though more probable, as a condition for absolution. Dr. McGlynn had had a long conversation with B. D. Kilian : in which he learned much about secret service men set to watch the movements of the British consul here and S. Fred. Bruce (the British Ambassador) in Washington. Fr. Tom Quin, O'Mahony and Kilian had long consulted on Saturday on the propriety of postponing the Fenian meeting of Sunday, but O'Mahony had decided that if the Fenians admitted the Abp's direction once, it would make him abuse his power again. It was arranged that B. D. Kilian alone of all the speakers should take notice of the Abp's letter. Fr. Preston tells me that the Abp said : 'that he did not expect to prevent the meeting by his prohibition : but that he had intended to put in his protest, that when the Fenian scheme had failed, the Irish people might not accuse him of not having warned them against it.' Why then did he make it appear sinful for them to be present at the meeting on Sunday? If it succeed, where will his admirable

March 243

shrewdness be found? If it fail, it is to be feared that the Irish will accuse him in company with other bishops and priests, of being the cause of the failure! At dinner I met M. Remi, to whom Fr. Preston says plainly that Remi to trouble Mr. Dachauer, but gave trouble to Fr. Preston and acted dishonourably with regard to the Church. Dr. McGlynn and I walked to 40th St. I then attended the altar class : gave the instruction on Confession in the Church and attended the literary class, which performs 'the Toodles' quite well. I told Dr. McGlynn several items about Abp. Hughes known beforetime but lately confirmed by Fr. Preston's authority....

Tues., 6th   I took a ride at Dickel's : after which I visited Fr. McCarthy with whom I found Fr. Tom Quin. We talked about the Fenians : they were both disgusted with the account of the Abp's shrewdness, in not expecting to prevent the meeting, but in putting in his protest against the movement. Fr. McCarthy had been told that Card. Antonelli was accused commonly in Rome of keeping an English lady as his mistress & asked me whether it was so. I knew, of course, nothing about it. I consider Pius IX to be weak minded : having given reforms in '48; the Italian revolutionists knew and shut him up in his palace & intimidated him : he on his return to Rome confirmed all the old ways of administration : and during his tour in the Marches, as I know on Dr. Cummings' testimony, when his true friends asked for reforms in the administration, he replied: 'I shall have no more reforms : I had enough of them in '48.' Card. Antonelli has a great mind, but I could never like him. He dominates over Pius IX : who is good-hearted but is old and peevish, and never had any great strength of mind. I dined at home : Fr. Nilan and Dr. Parsons visited me : we discussed the Fenian question : they found Fr. Preston afraid to commit himself openly, though he said he would not have written the Abp's letter. We discussed McMaster's

March

late article about Mr. Hassard's life of Abp. Hughes : in which McMasters shows a good appreciation of the Abp's character. They both approve of Hassard's life. I attended the Sunday School Association : at which we made arrangements for a division of the Sunday School into four departments. 1. of boys preparing for confession 2. of those preparing for 1st communion. 3. of those preparing for confirmation. 4. of those who have received confirmation. We made a law fining the absentee-member from the Sunday School. We admitted Mr. O'Toole to the Association. I appointed Mr. O'Neil as 2nd assistant to the superintendent.

Wed., 7th   Omitted by the Editor.

Thurs., 8th   I went to visit Miss Jones at Mrs. Macaulay's school. She had the measles; Mrs. Macaulay would not let me see her, as she was in the sick-room with other young ladies. I visited Dr. McGlynn : with whom I found Mrs. & Miss McGlynn : and Fr. Tom Quin. I dined there. Dr. McGlynn and I went to Jersey City to scold Dr. Brann for his malice in speaking about Fr. Pat. McGovern, whom Fr. Senez has engaged to keep on trial. Dr. Brann told a Mr. Harlan that Fr. Senez took Fr. McGovern to show that an Irish priest cannot keep straight! because he would be lying drunk in the gutter in a few days. Dr. Brann was not home : I disapproved of Dr. McGlynn's speaking to him, because he would only begin to malign Dr. McGlynn. We visited Fr. McGovern : who thinks that Fr. Senez treats him kindly. We visited the church, which is quite large, having a very finely arched roof, beautiful stained glass windows, with saints, or religious symbols marked on them. The Altar is in Gothic style : the roof is well adorned by the ribs that unite in semicircles near the edge, and in arcs in the middle. The side altars are defective because a statue is above the tabernacles. We saw Fr. Senez who is quite indignant with Dr. Brann : to whom he wrote

March

a letter about Fr. McGovern, a copy of which with Dr. Brann's reply he sent to the bishop. We saw Fr. De Concilio too. We met McMasters : who is angry at the publication of private letters of Abp. Hughes.

Fri., 9th   Omitted by the Editor.

Sat., 10th   Bishop Martin of Nachitoches said mass in our church : as also Fr. Janeau. They breakfasted with us. Bp. Martin is a prejudiced man against the Yankees. He denounced the U. S. troops in Nachitoches, who, he said in gangs of 200 & 300 went robbing the neighbouring plantations and houses : and were constantly drunk. He thought the Freedmen's bureau, a nuisance, because it interfered with the civil Southern Courts in questions pertaining to the negro. The negroes would not work till the U. S. troops are removed that the planters may compel them to work. He thought serfdom would benefit the negroes : and hoped that soon a Southern militia would take the place of the U. S. troops. Fr. Janeau is more reasonable : he says he was always opposed to the Confederacy. Bp. Martin says that the pope intends to die rather than leave Rome, that the Mazzinian party will enter Rome as soon as the French troops leave it in September, that Mazzini thinks it lawful to kill the pope, bishops, etc., but not prudent, that Garibaldi will not be dissuaded from this pleasure by such prudential motives, that the monks of Italy are bad men, and would do it if the Garibaldians didn't, that it would be better if all the monasteries in Italy were abolished, that he read in a French infidel paper of a monk of Milan who laughed at the title of Vicar of Christ and said that Garibaldi and Mazzini were two Christs (Vicars of Christ?) !!! Bp. Martin was in Rome three days : and nowhere else in Italy!!! and says there are too many bishops, and too many cardinals in Italy, and would wish an American Cardinal! I visited Mrs. McLaughlin, who gave me letters from Pierina Romano, her sister, nee

March   246

Avezzana. Both on the part of their husbands, who are wealthy, propose to
J. McLaughlin to act as commission-agent for wines, fruit such as figs,
oranges, etc. and for 'paste'. They both complain that the jealousy of
their husbands prevents them from going to balls. Pierina has a son and
daughter. General Avezzana had been elected a deputy from an electoral
college of Naples. I visited my mother who gave me a letter from J. M.
Burtsell and his wife : in which they announce John's recovery : and that
John intends commencing business on his own hook as commission-agent for
provisions. My mother also gave me a letter from her sister Jane Sussarello,
nee Morrogh : giving news of her children Faustino who is a lieutenant in
the Italian army, and Giuseppina who is happy, but has had two miscarriages.
Of course I heard confessions in the evening.

Sun., 11th   Omitted by the Editor.

Mon., 12th   Omitted by the Editor.

Tues., 13th   . . . .Fr. Thos. Farrell told me that he had a long talk
with the Abp. about the celebrated circular concerning the Fenians. The
Abp. thought that his not having read the circular showed disrespect. He
expressed his joy at being placed in circumstances in which without disrespect to the Abp. he could omit the reading of the circular : (it did not
come till too late on Sunday : the messenger had come at 12 o'c. Saturday-
Midnight : but had been told not to leave it at the door). He told the
Abp. that he had no right to interfere. The Abp. told him that the bishops
of other places were writing to him, saying that he was accused of sympathy
with the Fenians, because he said nought about them : that he was anxious
to warn his people against a foolish scheme : that he thus showed the
Protestants that the Ecclesiastical authorities did not endorse the profanation of the Sabbath. Fr. Farrell showed him that Irishmen would now accuse

March   247

him of causing the failure of the scheme : to which he asserted, because they did not throw the blame of their failure on the bishops in 1848 : that the Irish had seen their own bishops guilty of what the Abp. considered to be a profanation of the Sabbath. Fr. Farrell is trying through Fr. Hecker, who has the ear of the Abp., to induce him to have a meeting of his priests : but Fr. Hecker says that the Abp. does not wish to meet his priests. Fr. Farrell suggests a monthly meeting of the priests to propose new church buildings : in the erection of which all the churches will concur. But the Abp. is afraid to meet his priests.

Wed., 14th   . . . .We visited the addition to St. Stephen's in which Dr. McGlynn has enlarged the plan of the Sanctuary : he intends to have the altar removed five feet from the back-wall : and a high pinnacle some 20 feet above ground, in which the B. Sacrament will be placed for exposition, the way to reach it will be a staircase behind the altar. Near the altar will be a fresco of Our Saviour in the midst of little children : and another painting. The whole church will be painted on a new plan. Dr. McGlynn has to raise $68 000 before a year : the brown stone on the back of the church will cost $13 000. I don't suppose there are more than 130 pieces of brown stone. The mason is paid by instalments of about $2000, on an average, after the completion of each coating. In 2 months he will have to pay about $40000. St. Stephen's is already mortgaged about $50000. Dr. McGlynn expects that the members of his congregation, some of whom are reputed millionaires, will soon toe the mark. He introduced us to a Mr. Canefield, who acts as organist in a Brooklyn Presbyterian Church, and is anxious to come to St. Stephen's. We heard him play on the organ without becoming enthusiastic in his favour. I went to Maximilian's to arrange about the curtains to be used at the theatrical performance of the

March 248

St. Ann's literary Society at our fair after Easter : For scenery he recommends me to Mr. Juguet, the manager of the French theatre. I preached in the evening on 'Scandal' having read the discourse on 'Bad Example' in the Catholic pulpit' 'on Scandal' of Fr. Gahan's : and Musso's discourse on the 'bad examples of parents.'

<u>Thurs., 15th</u>   Omitted by the Editor.

<u>Fri., 16th</u>   . . . .I went to confession to Fr.   the Redemptorist rector : who was the first to say a word of exhortation to me during my confession. . . .

<u>Sat., 17th</u>   St. Patrick's day. I assisted at the Pontifical High Mass, by the Abp., at the Cathedral. There were but three priests, besides those serving at the mass. Bishop Lynch preached the panegyric of the Saint. Taking for his text the 1st verse of Eccles. 24 chap. : 'Let us praise men of renown, and our fathers in their generation.' He remarked that the true history of a man is not given by him who tells where or when or of what parentage a man is born, how successfully he advanced in the estimate of his fellow men, what honours, what distinctions he gained in society, what statesmanship or military skill he displayed, and then how and when he died : nor is the true history a nation given, when it's advance in temporal prosperity is announced, or the wars described in which it has been victorious, or the acquisition of physical comforts or all those things which are known under the name of civilisation. This is what human historians must record. But the true history of the individual and of the nation is that which is recorded in the book of life : which tells of the merits or demerits in the eyes of God acquired by the individual and the nation : this is the history of St. Patrick, of which we have the privilege of repeating a part to-day : to praise him, who has gained the approval of

God, and by imitating him, to deserve a similar reward which is the greatest that can be given for virtue. His great work was performed in the island that forms the utmost boundary of Europe. A people truly great had inhabited that island. It was of Celtic origin. It had peopled this island many centuries before the Christian era. It was known to all the nations that were given to commerce : yet it had never been overcome by any nation : attacks against it may have been made, but were futile as it is certain that for ten centuries a constant succession of rulers of their own race governed this prosperous people. Their form of religion was less removed from the truth than any other pagan system : Druidism, by which name the ancient religion of this people was known, acknowledged a Supreme Mysterious Deity, though it was superstitious in attributing a divine character to the forces of Nature. The people had a literature and books and a writing of it's own : their poets or bards were always in high honour. Patrick was a native of Lower Brittany, from which he was taken captive and sold in Ireland : When he gained his freedom, his heart led him to join the priestly order, that he might bring to the truth those for whom even in bondage he had taken a great affection : and after mature preparation, he went to Rome that from pope Celestine he might receive the mission, which he as sovereign pontiff and successor of the prince of the Apostles was most entitled to give. The great characteristic of this mission of St. Patrick was that the Irish people accepted at once the Gospel : and no martyr's blood was required to seal it's truth : and before St. Patrick's death, there was no spot in Ireland, from which the call to prayer from some church, or monastery of monks, or convent of holy nuns could not be heard. Ireland henceforth sent forth teachers of the gospel to the nations of Europe : and there is no people of Europe that does not acknowledge among it's principal benefactors, Irishmen.

A time came too when Ireland should undergo as the first Christians a persecution of three centuries. England had trampled on Ireland : but the Irish people has parted with every earthly good to cling to it's faith. The Irish now are accused by England of being ignorant : who caused their ignorance : but England herself that made it a penal offence for Irishmen to teach or to be taught : England accuses the Irish of not working : but who deprived them of their natural energy but England that stripped them of their own lands and of all chance to win them back again. And we see that when they have a fair opportunity as they have in this country they display at once their quick ready genius : and they acquire for themselves very high positions. It is not for us to plan schemes for the remedying the defects which still in great measure oppress this people in their own land : no scheme for their temporal welfare of the country should ever detach them in the least from that faith and church to which they clung so nobly during centuries of persecution. St. Patrick is a powerful intercessor for them in heaven : his prayers are most earnest that the faith which he planted in Ireland, should never be snatched from Irishmen. I introduced myself to Dr. Lynch, as a propagandist. He speaks in a rather pompous manner : but his delivery though not polished was good : he shows a philosophical mind. Fr. McAleer was quite astonished to hear that I was Dr. Burtsell : he mistook some other man for me! This is good version of the personal letter he intended to write against one whom he did not know! Fr. Malone dined with me and we went together to see the procession of the Irish Societies : it was a repetition of what is seen every year : and therefore I shall not describe what every one will see for at least 20 years to come. By that time I hope Irishmen here will not celebrate purely Irish feasts. We heard confessions in the afternoon : though of course there were

March   251

not as many as there would be if it were not St. Patrick's day. I just
heard 5 hours in the whole day.

<u>Sun., 18th</u>   Omitted by the Editor.

<u>Mon., 19th</u>   I wrote my 6th letter to the 'Catholic Standard'. I
took a ride at Dickel's : and bought my third batch of tickets for $25.00.
Fr. Preston told me that Fr. Hecker has already commenced his publication
Society to belong to which as an honorary member $100, as a life-member
$30, as an annual member $5 must be paid, entitling the payer to the productions of the Society for the time for which he paid. Fr. Hecker called
Hassard's life of Abp. Hughes : a photograph of his mind : and McMaster's
review a squirting of the essence of ten years' bile compressed. A priest
who spoke against Abp. Hughes always (behind his back at least) said that
converts have not the delicacy of reared-Catholics and therefore Hassard
did not know what to conceed. The greater part of the documents must have
been given by Mrs. Rodrigue : the letters to her, to Seward who told Hassard
he had no letters which would be of any use to him, to Dr. Smith : of which
duplicates were had, as the Abp. dictated his letters in his late years,
and the rough draft was kept. I gave an instruction on the Eucharist in
the evening and attended the literary class : at which the 'Photograph' was
rejected as being too dull and stupid. It is by Fr. Gambosville : and Box
and Cox substituted in it's place. I heard Mr. Tiers' confession : he had
another slight attack of paralysis.

<u>Tues., 20th</u>   I went to see Dr. McGlynn : he had gone out with Dr.
McSweeny. I visited Frs. McCarthy and Nilan : who were both chuckling over
the Abp.'s failure on St. Patrick's day to have a great gathering of priests.
The Abp. had gone prepared to denounce the Fenians, and got quite heated
on the subject : but had about eight priests to whom to display his vehemence.

March

He accused the Fenians of bending the people from their love to the Church : and teaching infidelity. He had a letter of a priest who argued that many priests were infected with Fenianism because they read the Abp.'s celebrated anti-Fenian circular with evident dissatisfaction. I met Fr. McCarthy's mother : to whom I was introduced, she is quite old though intelligent looking. With Fr. Nilan I went to see Fr. O'Hare : he as well as Fr. McAleer was out. Fr. O'Hare had been presented with a fine sofa : and he had bought a large piano from Gonsalez. We went to Fr. Thos. Farrell's where we met several priests and warmly spoke against Abp. McCloskey's anti-Fenianism : and Bish. Bayley who had been vanquished in a debate on the subject by Dr. Parsons. Bishop Bayley remarked that all Romans were insubordinate : but was glad to hear that they did not sympathise with Dr. Brann's conduct in regard to Fr. Pat. McGovern. Bishop Bayley had another time said that if pastoral rights were given in this country, he would count himself out of the episcopacy. I dined home at 5 o'c. with Fr. Preston : attended the literary class and went with Dr. McGlynn to his place, discussing the state of religion in our diocese : and concluding that the only chance of redemption was in our young clergy but more especially in the converts. At St. Stephen's we discussed Fr. T. Quin's of Transfiguration Church conduct with M. Brady the servant girl : it had been too free: he went to the garret to eat and converse with her : when many others were in the house.

Wed., 21st	Omitted by the Editor.
Thurs., 22nd	Omitted by the Editor.
Fri., 23rd	Omitted by the Editor.
Sat., 24th	Omitted by the Editor.
Sun., 25th	Palm Sunday. I celebrated High-Mass, blessed the palms

March

and distributed them to all the boys and girls of the parish SS. : only boys in black cassocks served : about 30 girls were dressed in white. During the reading of the Passion, the organ played and there was singing to relieve the tediousness! What an absurd ceremonial which would be quite interesting if the service were in English! In Latin it does not explain itself! Fr. Preston gave quite an appropriate sermon on the inscrutable ways of Providence. Had man designed his own creation, he said, man would not have wished a free-will, which he would abuse : but he would have secured himself against the possibility of losing his happiness. Yet God ennobled man by giving him free-will, that he might merit happiness : though he foresaw man's abuse of his free-will. God chose to repair the damage done by this abuse of man's free-will, and chose to be man's redeemer and become man. Had man thought of a redeemer, the possibility of God's becoming man would never have entered his mind. And if it did, he would have expected him to come to be surrounded in his birth by the pure and holy, having power and goods of earth which were his already : and that he should never come in contact with the filth of sinful men. Yet he was born in a stable, known to shepherds and heathen magi, hated by Herod, going to Egypt a land of filthy idolatry. Man would have imagined for the Redeemer great earthly glory : God destined a life-long humiliation. Not even an easy bed, but a cross is given to the Redeemer. God's design was to separate our hearts from earth by this model. Let us then consider the sufferings of our Redeemer to love suffering that we may be crowned with him. I visited the boys' SS., and spoke on the two last commandments to the girls' SS. We had Rossini's 'Stabat Mater' instead of Vespers, followed by Benediction of the B. S. Miss Wells soprano : Miss Gomien, contralto : Mr. Tamaro tenor : Mr. Remi, basso. The Music was truly grand : the voices

March 254

were in excellent time. Fr. Langcake, Mr. Hudon and Mr. Regnaud, all three Jesuits were in the Sanctuary. The Church was packed. At 7½ o'c. we had the Stations of the Cross. Fr. Preston took for his text the words : 'It is consummated' and gave quite a life-like account of the passion to show what Christ had consummated for man's salvation.

Mon., 26th   Omitted by the Editor.
Tues., 27th   Omitted by the Editor.
Wed., 28th   Omitted by the Editor.
Thurs., 29th   Omitted by the Editor.
Fri., 30th   Omitted by the Editor.
Sat., 31st   Omitted by the Editor.

April

Sun., 1st   Easter Sunday. As soon as I awoke I united myself in spirit with the crowd in St. Peter's piazza receiving the pope's blessing! I said 7 o'c. mass and bade all to come to the fair : making it a matter of conscience for them to encourage us. Fr. Preston celebrated, I officiated as deacon, Mr. Renaud as subdeacon. I preached a sermon, which was reported in the Daily News miserably : I have a sketch among my papers. The mass sung was Mr. Dachauer's, with Gounod's Agnus Dei. I attended the boys' SS. : the girls had none. Instead of Vespers, we had an Oratorio of the Resurrection, Manzoni's words, and Tanassi's music : We had Benediction of the B. S. In the evening I accompanied my mother and Mrs. McLaughlin to the Morroghs of 26th St. . . .

Mon., 2nd   Omitted by the Editor.
Tues., 3rd   Omitted by the Editor.
Wed., 4th   Omitted by the Editor.
Thurs., 5th   In the morning Fr. Nilan called to see me : we visited

April

the Cooper Union hall to see the fair : and walked to 42nd St. He had spoken about his letter to the Editions of the Catholic Telegraph to the Archbishop : who used simply the argument of authority : reminding 'Mr. Nilan' that he was a young priest : that he acted very imprudently and was surprised to hear that the priests with whom Mr. Nilan associated sympathised with the Fenians, whilst all those he met condemned them, that a gentleman told him that persecution was already planned by the loyal league against Catholics, which was postponed by Lincoln's assassination : but will be called forth by this Fenian movement. He would not allow Fr. Nilan to give his arguments, even impolitely interrupting him : and showing himself angry : but Fr. Nilan showed that his opinions were not changed, though the Abp. told him that if he did not stop before going too far, he would fall into difficulties & though the Abp. expected that the Fenian movement would be condemned in Rome, he feared many priests would still be pro-Fenian. It would have been better, had Fr. Nilan not spoken with the Abp. who had resolved not to speak to Fr. Nilan, not thinking the letter sufficiently important. Fr. McCarthy is very sick with plurisy and is allowed to see no one. Fr. Nilan is bursting with anxiety to paint the church of the Holy Cross : the congregation is most anxious that it should be done : he wishes also to build a school : the parochial girls' school being now in the basement of the church. We went to see Fr. O'Hare : but he was out. He had sold $700 tickets for his concert : which came off yesterday at Dodworth Hall. The fair was crowded. 150 persons were present at Toodles. We had a rehearsal of Box and Cox.

Fri., 6th   Omitted by the Editor.

Sat., 7th   We had a Matinee at 5½ o'c. of Toodles. About 20 persons were present, among whom were the O'Reillys, to whom Mr. Hassard asked me

April

to give complimentary tickets : which they accepted if they could use them for Tommy Maitland. In the evening I superintended the performance of Box and Cox : in which L. Tessier acted as Cox, E. Burns as Box, Robert Burns as Mrs. Bouncer. All three did admirably. We had minstrels afterwards : in which the boys succeeded beyond my expectations. About 150 persons were present. There was a slim attendance at the fair : little work was done. We heard no confessions.

Sun., 8th   Omitted by the Editor.

Mon., 9th   Omitted by the Editor.

Tues., 10th   With Frs. McSweeny and Nilan I visited Fr. McCarthy who is now recovering from a severe attack of pleurisy. It made it difficult for him to speak. Fr. Nilan accompanied us homewards : We talked about the Triduum to be given in honour of the B. Berchmans. We agreed that B. Berchmans is hardly a model for priests or seminarians of now-a-days : on the general principle that I am being more and more convinced of every day that is that the absolute obedience inculcated in religious orders retards the individual activity of the members, and the utmost energy is required here in this country from every individual to enable the church to keep apace with the progress of the country and the times. Fr. Nilan wants me to explain this idea in my discourse. I fear it would be betraying the Jesuits with a kiss : throwing discredit on them whilst apparently honouring them. Dr. McGlynn called to see me : he is to engage Berge as his organist. Miss Philips intends to sing for him. Mlle. Carozzi Zucchi cried because illness would prevent her from singing at St. Stephen's : Mr. Braun, his organist, was displeased at his asking Berge for Dr. Cummings' funeral, and this concert. Dr. McGlynn was introduced to Mrs. Hassard : he does not like her or Mr. Hassard, whom he met now & before. I had invited all

April 257

the children of the school to a Matinee of Box & Cox : but one of the principal performers Edward Burns failed to come. I had all the monies returned: and pretended to break up the theatre for the rest of the fair but allowed myself with apparently great difficulty to continue it. In the evening we had the play of 'Toodles' : The Archbishop came with Fr. McNierney. The Abp. went to Mrs. Livingston's table and the O'Reillys' and a few others. With the O'Reillys he sat down for quite a chat! Admirable taste! At the S. School table he spent $1,00 : I suspect because he saw a Fenian chair and Fenian boots and a Fenian bond on it. I had presented the last mentioned article. He came to see a part of Toodles played. He was shocked when he heard Charles Fenton & Mr. Toodles say 'damn me' but especially when he saw Mary come out (he took John E. Burke for a girl) till Fr. Preston told him that it was an altar boy. Otherwise he laughed heartily at all the jokes of the play. The fair-room was packed : the ladies seemed to be more than usually satisfied!

Wed., 11th   Omitted by the Editor.
Thurs., 12th   Omitted by the Editor.
Fri., 13th   Omitted by the Editor.
Sat., 14th   My 26th birth-day. I visited my mother to whom as a tribute I gave $26.00. I met with her young Henry Morrogh : whom she is packing off to St. Vincent's college Latrobe. Westmoreland Co. Pa. Mrs. Archibald Morrogh was most anxious to get rid of Peter and Henry to curtail her expenses. She had told Peter who his mother is, stating besides that she had a mixture of black blood : to whom he was persuaded to write thinking She was his nurse, but whom Mrs. A. Morrogh persuaded him to address as 'dear mother'. Peter is to live with a Mr. Dwyer, husband of the widow Mrs. Smith, who had had formerly charge of Henry. Dr. Archibald Morrogh

April   258

left $4,500 in bonds : and a house in 92nd St. : one third of the revenues
of this go to Mrs. Morrogh. The will is that Lawyer Morrogh, Rev. Dr.
Morrogh and my mother hold the property of which each share is to be given
to the boys as they come of age : if one dies, the property goes to the
other : if both die, Mrs. Burtsell is to have one third : the rest is to
be divided among his other brothers & sisters. I met Rev. Dr. Morrogh :
who was quite pleasant. I did not get to the fair before 7 o'c. We had
the performance of Toodles. There was a great crowd. The auctioneering
created great excitement as well as the raffling. The billiard table was
auctioned for $400.00. The piano reached about 400 chances; after the
chances on the billiard table and bugler's clock were placed on it. Fr.
Preston won the piano : It's worth about $700.00 one of Steinway's best.
Yet the dearest objects did not raffle well. Toys sold better than any
thing else. I won a picture by Mr. Henry of a torch-light funeral procession of Capuchin into the city of Milan. I bought several articles :
vases of porcelain etc. I got home at 1 o'c A.M. The moral to be deduced
from a fair is 1. that it creates a congregational feeling : 2. that the
ladies take great pleasure during the fair, though very eager to make much
money : 3. that a great deal of flirtation takes place, which very probably
would go on elsewhere just as well : 4. that young girls become excessively
bold, because having to make free with young men to induce them to take
chances. This is true of the girls of the middle classes, more than of
those who are better educated and are never bold.

Sun., 15th   Omitted by the Editor.

Mon., 16th   Omitted by the Editor.

Tues., 17th   . . . .Fr. Thos. Farrell told me he would soon call his
friends to form a new theological society. We spoke severely about the

April

inactivity of our bishops : as if they were guilty of all the deficiencies to be found in the church of this country. . . .

Wed., 18th   I met Dr. McSweeny and brought him to dine at Fr. Malone's where several priests were at dinner : Frs. Mullane, Donnelly, Farley, Fitzpatrick; Dr. Parsons, Mr. Charleton and Mr. Malone M. D. We spoke in favour of the Fenians : and debated whether freemasons in this country are to be denied the sacraments : I maintained that we cannot consider them a secret society, as condemned by the church, for they do not seek the overthrowal of religion or of government. Dr. Farley was the subject of the post prandial chat. I attended the altar class : and the literary-class, in which Rob. Burns, Albert Burke, Thos McCabe, and Jas McKenna did not make returns for their sale of the Theatrical tickets : the three last having spent the money received at the fair. I went to the Concert in aid of Seton Hall college at Delmonico's music-hall : admittance $5. I met the O'Briens and O'Reillys. I heard all the 2nd part. Mrs.   , and Miss Brooks sang best according to my taste. . . .It was quite a fashionable affair. Abp. McCloskey, Bish. Bayley, Frs. Starrs and McQuade were in front seats. The hall was filled. I met Fr. Hecker at our house, and promised him $100 for his publication society : for which he has collected $7000. I took exception to his making rules without the consent of the priests : he said they could be amended by the priests. I disapproved of the appointment by Abp. McCloskey of the priest to review the tracts : he might appoint his Vicar : this priest ought to be chosen by the priests.

Thurs., 19th   With Dr. McSweeny I took a walk to see Fr. McCarthy : who is now quite well. We talked about the Latin prayers used in the administration for the sacraments and at Mass : It's useless to excuse it by saying that the faithful have the translation for 1st they haven't, as they cannot

April

follow the 'Ordo'. 2nd how absurd for a Jewish Rabbi to read to Jews in Hebrew with the excuse that they are reading at the same time a translation! Fr. Nilan walked homewards with us : he and Dr. McSweeny approved of the style of Excelsior's letter to the Catholic Standard : both suspect that I am the author of them, judging from their subjects and style. Dr. McSweeny suspects me of writing the two leading articles in the Freeman's Journal on the scarcity of churches : not being shrewd enough to remark that I spoke of some parts of them as unsound and untheological : where they say a Catholic cannot hear mass remaining outside the church when the church is crowded. I walked back with Fr. Nilan : and he, Fr. Preston and I took a ride on horse-back in Central Park : this is my first ride in the open air in America : the third in my life. I rode on donkeys several times. I rode on 'General Meade' : We exerted ourselves too much to enjoy the ride : it was very warm & dusty : Fr. Nilan's horse has the pace, which it acquired by being attached to a wagon. Fr. Preston's mare = Gussy = has the defect of shying constantly. In the evening I attended the 337th Anniversy of Luther's protest against the Catholic Church. The Harmonic Society sang. Rev. Mr. Dowling called it the anniversary of the declaration of independence of the human mind from the superstitions of popery : without which the declaration of 1776 would never have taken place in this country. He was anxious to promote Christian union not by denouncing the doctrines of any denomination, but on those doctrines on which all are agreed. 1st. There is but one head of the Church, Christ : and no pope : 2nd. That faith alone justifieth, without good works. 3rd. That every man must judge for himself what he will believe. To persuade Xtian Union he told how the Welsh and natives of Bretagne once met in battle in a war between France and England, and as soon as they heard the war-cry, their language being the same, they threw down their arms and fell to embracing each

April

other. The conclusion seemed to be that as the common war cry of Protestants is 'Down with Popery' they should all embrace. The three principles on which they could unite were reduced to practise by Luther, so Mr. Dowling said : for the 1st when he burned the Canon Law, the Extravangelists, the Clementine and the pope's bull against himself saying that his own works contained more gospel truth than all the pope's works together. I don't remember how Mr. Dowling illustrated Luther's application of the other two principles : but it is quite easy : for the 2nd he performed no good works : for the 3rd he was not very clement towards the Anabaptists or Calvinists, or Zwinglians. Mr. Dowling has quite a fine look : but is rather popular, not deep in his discoursing. Another minister spoke of course denouncing popery but in a more abstruse style : which did less harm as more unintelligible to the audience which was evidently of the fanatical type, few of the best educated class being present : which however set me more to thinking than Mr. Dowling's talk. I met there Mr. Churchill an Ex-Unitarian now a Catholic : who expected to hear better speakers.

Fri., 20th   . . . .I went to confession to a Redemptorist of 3rd St. after a delay of a month!

Sat., 21st   Omitted by the Editor.

Sun., 22nd   Omitted by the Editor.

Mon., 23rd   Omitted by the Editor.

Tues., 24th   I took a ride at Dickel's : visited Frs. McCarthy and Nilan with whom I dined : Fr. Nilan and I visited Fr. Farrell with whom we met Dr. Parsons and Mr. Charleton. We discussed how many states had published laws against the education of negroes : and Kent and   show that at least Georgia, Virginia, Alabama, Missouri, Arkansas and Louisiana express laws against it : the last severer than all. I went in the evening

April

to a family party of the O'Briens at 19. E. 26th St. : where were Abp. McCloskey, and Bishop Lynch, Mayor Hoffman, Capt. Reilly, Dr. Gilbert and a few others besides the several branches of the O'Brien family, viz : the Pardows, and Lummises. I talked with Misters John and Joseph and O'Brien, old Mrs. O'Brien : Mrs. Joseph O'Brien who came to the church when 13 years old, was confirmed by Abp. Hughes at the Convent of Mercy, was advised by him to return to Protestantism if her family opposed her action, did so, when she married Mr. Jos. O'Brien had too many objections to Catholicity to return to the church, but before 9 months became a Catholic. I talked with Mayor Hoffman about a clergyman going to see the cholera-patients on board the Virginia : he said all power was taken from his hands : but he could see no objection, and would favour it as far as he could. He spoke with interest about the society against cruelty to animals : about 50 very respectable persons are associated with him in the society. He is quite tall : has marked and handsome features. I chatted with Bishop Lynch about his diocese. He has repaired the boys' school and the Sisters' convent : & is building a chapel, which will be turned into an orphan asylum. There is one church in Charleston, St. Patrick's, under Dr. Moore : and a German Church. Dr. Corcoran has been called to Baltimore to prepare materials for the plenary council. Abp. McCloskey was surprised that our fair made $12 000 : he said I had immortalised myself by the theatrical performance. We had quite a grand lunch. I admired several pictures by Edmunds in their parlor : especially 'the preparation for Xmas.' and also a statue by Benzoni of 'Innocence' being guarded from a viper's bite by a dog, from the child had drawn a thorn. The evening passed off very pleasantly indeed. The Abp. led Mrs. O'Brien to supper on his arm.

Wed., 25th   Omitted by the Editor.

April

Thurs., 26th	Omitted by the Editor.
Fri., 27th	Omitted by the Editor.
Sat., 28th	Omitted by the Editor.
Sun., 29th	I preached at High Mass :

my ideas were principally taken from Musso's explanation of the gospel of the 4th Sunday after Easter. I commenced catechising the children in both Sunday Schools in preparation for confirmation. They seemed to be much pleased by this method which excites their ambition and creates emulation. In the evening I attended the services in the Dutch Ref. Church cor. 5th Ave. & 22nd St. The minister explained the article of the creed 'He descended into hell' showing "that his means that Christ's love went to the place of the departed. Hell comes from a German word which means 'lower regions'. It is a translation of   which is simply a place of departed spirits equally of good or bad spirits. The Hebrew words 'Sciol' or 'Geenna' have the same general meaning. Christ did not go where the incorrigibly wicked are." This was followed by hymns and by an explanation of Naaman's visit to Elisha to be cured of his leprosy : Naaman would have loved a pompous ceremony in which he should take part, and expected some hard work to do as a condition for his cure : but was disappointed at being told to wash in Jordan. Hence the minister deduced that we are to be saved by God's power alone, not be our works. I would have drawn the conclusion that our cooperation to God's grace is necessary for our salvation. I met Mr. Ives : who was surprised and relieved from scruples at seeing me in a Protestant church. I called his notice to the fact that I did not join in the service. The congregation was not very full : but there were about 2 woman to one man and all appeared very attentive. I liked the minister's manners : and his plain, common-sense way of talking. I visited the Morroghs where I found my mother and Mrs. McLaughlin and Peter Morrogh : whom Mrs.

April   264

Archibald Morrogh declined keeping with her any longer for economy's sake.

<u>Mon., 30th</u>   Omitted by the Editor.

<u>May</u>

<u>Tues., 1st</u>   Fr. Killeen and I went to hear Fr. Healy on B. Berchman's.
He commenced by showing the honour we pay to the Saints to be lawful : the
Saints gained heaven by avoiding mortal sin. He would therefore talk on
mortal sin. We then went to the funeral of Rev. J. Kelly of St. Peter's
Jersey City. Bps. Bailey & Loughlin and a large number of N. Y. & Jersey
priests were there. Dr. Brann sang mass in a very tremulous way. Fr.
McQuade made an eulogy stating how Fr. Kelly, had come when young from Ireland and become a priest (this he remarked, is no new story, for is told of
many), that he showed his untiring zeal in St. Louis, Albany &c. A key to
his character was his going to the mission of Liberia with Bishop Barron;
till broken health forced him to retire. He lived in Jersey for the last
25 years : has been building lately in Jersey a new church. His last act
of zeal was making arrangements with Abp. McCloskey to send his assistant
to attend the cholera patients at Quarentine, though he was of another diocese (Fr. McQuade made this remark quite pointed). He died suddenly of disease of the heart on Friday morning : being found dead in the morning : and
was last spoken to at 11 o'c. : he had gone to bed the day before for slight
illness. We could not go to his funeral because in Newark diocese : only
six carriages are allowed at a funeral. Our driver, I remarked, shrewdly
told us he would reach the cemetery by another road before the burial. I
dined with several priests at Fr. Farrell's. He told us that Bish. Barron
was well a-do in the world : and accepted the bishopric of Liberia in a
spirit of self-sacrifice. Fr. Kelly being sick promised on his recovery to
devote himself to the poorest of the poor. He followed therefore Bishop

May

Barron to assist the poor blacks. When in Liberia at Mass, when turning to the congregation he would shut his eyes : for all were stark-naked. He left Africa sick. We discussed the question whether the Latin litugy should be abolished. Fr. McCarthy was quite surprised at our calling the Latin liturgy an absurdity, and at our saying that the Pastors of the Church could mistake in making a liturgy which was useless to the people. We argued that the apostles said mass in the language of the people among whom they were dwelling. Dr. McGlynn told that St. Bernardine was the first to preach in Italian : when even the people were no longer familiar with Latin. So his biography says. The Council of Baltimore prohibits the vernacular being used at High Mass : French, Italian, Latin, any language is allowed which is not understood by the people. Dr. McSweeny gave me an open rap for going to the Fenian fair thinking I would do more good by not being openly opposed to my Ecclesiastical superiors, even in politics. I replied I simply did it to do away with the idea, which the Fenians have, that they are under the ban of the church. In the evening I presided at the Sunday School Association : at which I talked very sharply on the necessity of improvement on the part of teachers in their attendance at Sunday School. We are disorganised because Mr. Kelly the superintendent absents himself and the responsibility is shirked by every one else. Mr. Griffin became quite enthusiastic in responding to my appeal for the pushing forward the interests of the SS. I told them that the Sunday School was in great measure the work of laymen : the priests here are so few as not to be able to get along without the effective assistance of the laity.

Wed., 2nd   Omitted by the Editor.

Thurs., 3rd   I dined with the other preachers of the Triduum at the Jesuits'. I was near Fr. Perrault the sub-provincial whom I found very

May 266

uninteresting. I after dinner had a conversation with Fr. O'Shea : who accused me of being an ardent Fenian, as report had told him. . . .

Fri., 4th   Omitted by the Editor.

Sat., 5th   I visited Susan McCauley a relative of the McKnights who is dying of hasty consumption. I met Fr. Maguire of the Cathedral there : and Fr. Donnelly of St. Mary's. Fr. Preston had been there in the morning : Fr. C. Farrell had given all the sacraments the day before.

Sun., 6th   Omitted by the Editor.

Mon., 7th   Omitted by the Editor.

Tues., 8th   Omitted by the Editor.

Wed., 9th   Omitted by the Editor.

Thurs., 10th   Ascension-day. I sang High-Mass at 9 o'c. : went with Fr. Preston to ride in the park : left my card at the O'Briens' and Pardows' who were all out : Dr. McGlynn called on me and described the German plan for an altar which Sand, Renwick's partner, designed for St. Stephen's : in which he carried out the German theory of positive colours, ex. gr. a combination of red and yellow, of which the contrast affords pleasure to the eye. Renwick is the architect, but is now in Europe. Pellegrini gives a more chaste and simple design. Dr. McGlynn finds it far cheaper to send to Rome for oil-paintings than to have the church frescoed : here oil-painting costs twice as much as frescoing or rather wall-painting. Dr. McGlynn calls a meeting of the male members of his congregation to devise means for raising $50 000 for his church. He began to visit : but failed on the 1st day to see any of four gentlemen to whose residence he went. He sends circulars to every pewholder in the church. He intends showing them the several plans more to flatter their vanity than to ask their advice : the advice that will alone be acceptable will be money. After Benediction I went to the fair of

May

the Immac. Conception held in the School-house : which is very close. There were not many visitors. I met Mr. & Mrs. Duani : who are very generous. Mr. Duani told us he had not been to confession since Fr. Martin's death : I suppose at least 15 years ago. The ladies were not importunate : some young men were too rough in their dealings with the girls. Fr. C. Farrell has the management of the fair and it is good policy on the part of Dr. Morrogh to allow his assistant a fair chance for developing his powers in pushing ahead the affairs of the Church. A fair however is a dangerous field for C. F.'s zeal. Dr. Morrogh is anxious not to interfere with C. F.'s plans. There is plenty of room for all of us : and it would be shrewder on the part of many pastors that they should not dwarf or pull out the zeal and energies of their assistants. Fr. Preston is a perfect model in this.

Fri., 11th   I catechised the girls' school on the Holy Eucharist. I stayed home almost the whole day : I went in search of Metastasio's works to all the book stores from 8th St. to Canal St. in Broadway : but could not find them. I heard confessions after the Month of May Devotions. . . .

Sat., 12th   I paid a visit to my mother : My brother John has invented a cipher for telegraphic despatches of which the object is to lessen the expense : it holds much in the fewest possible words. . . . .

Sun., 13th   Omitted by the Editor.

Mon., 14th   I wrote a letter to the Catholic Standard : took a horse-ride in the park : took a walk in the afternoon to the Central Park with Dr. McGlynn. He has found a deficit of $5000 in the church building fund : he thinks Mr. Lehens is accountable for it, because through his hands a great deal of small currency passed of which an irregular account was kept. He is a broker : and asserted that he had a right to 10 percent for brokerage. Dr. McGlynn is anxious to dispense with the services of Mr. Thoron, the treasurer

May

of Mr. Dutton the accountant, a lubberly stupid fellow who set the sexton
and organ blower to strike for higher wages, that he might have his salary
raised from $800 to $1000 : for keeping the accounts of $17 000 the revenue
of St. Stephen's, and collecting the rent of one pew per diem. Dr. McGlynn
yesterday held a meeting of the principal men of his congregation from whom
he received subscriptions of $5000. A Mr. Foley showed anxiety to have a
committee appointed to advise the Dr. in the prosecution of the building :
he declined by preferring the way appointed by the Legislature of incorpor-
ating Catholic Churches in the name of five trustees viz : the Abp., the
Vic. general, the pastor, and two laymen appointed by the pastor. I gave
the instruction at the Month of May devotion on the capital sin = Wrath.

Tues., 15th   Omitted by the Editor

Wed., 16th   I went to Devlin's Grand St. & Bway to order a suit of
clothes. I met Mr. Dan. Devlin, the clerk, who thought that Catholic
churches were built in too stylish a manner, that there was no accomodation
for strangers; and our churches do not hold our own population. I pointed
out to him that the 70 priests we have can only embellish what they have,
as they cannot bilocate and be building other churches, whilst they have
the work of a parish to attend to. Fr. Nilan called in the afternoon : he
was very favourably impressed with Stephens, whom he thinks a man of extraordinary parts : and perfectly truthful. He had quite a chat with Stephens,
who was glad to see a priest at the Jones' Wood meeting. He took tea with
us and listened to my discourse on Lust and the Chastity of the B. V. M., at
the Month of May devotion. He thought the discourse very fine. I took it
from Piano's and Liguori's. I attended the boys' rehearsal of Metastasio's
play of Joseph.

Thurs., 17th   I took dinner with Fr. Thos. Farrell and a few friends who met to debate on the propriety of reorganising a theological Society. Fr. Thos. Farrell, Fr. McCarthy and Dr. McGlynn thought it would appear like opposition to the Abp's plan of a conference. Dr. Parsons, and I maintained that as the conference had for it's object practical moral cases, and was to be directed by one master of conference who probably would be Fr. Daubresse S. J. for the Abp. said he would chose a man fitted by experience, and Fr. Daubresse is the presiding genius of the Jesuits conference and yet is assistant of the parish : and finally before the Abp. certain questions could not be brought up before him, (sic) we should in the theological Society treat of speculative questions, and create our own president, and be free in our opinions, and on account of the difference of the plan no opposition could be suspected, which would be reasonable if projected after the conferences commenced. Fr. McLoughlin proposed the adjournment of a decision till the 11th of June at his place at New Rochelle. Frs. Nilan, Malone, and Tom Quin were at dinner. I attended in the evening Bishop Lynch's lecture on the History of America before it's discovery by Columbus. He thought that the difference of features in the races of men was owing to the divers influences of climate on the men after the deluge who were migratory till the time of Jacob's descent to Egypt. Passing from place to place the climate was severe on them, till even the years of men decreased in comparison with their ages before the deluge. At this time America must have been settled, because only during this period of migration were the various casts of features formed : and the Americans have a distinct set of features. Whence did the Americans come? Of course the opinion that they had an Adam & Eve of their own is opposed to Scripture. Some thought to find a resemblance between the Americans and Malays : thus these might have been wafted in their barks from China or the South East of Asia : but we find no tradition here of such migration : nor much resemblance of American to the Malays.

tells of an island called Atlantis known to the Phenicians : The Fenicians certainly passed the Pillars of Hercules and coasted along Africa, till they after a three years voyage found themselves in the Persian Gulf known to them. Tacitus says that the migrations were always by sea. In fact they established Carthage against the proud Roman senator hurled his anathema at the end of each speech on whatsoever subject 'Delenda est Carthago'. They landed in Spain and in Ireland : and it is probable that Irishmen first came to America : and therefore their descendants are so fond of America. He spoke of a monument discovered in Virginia showing that there were inhabitants in America : of which he remarked that 'it raised many questions, but of it's meaning is given to no man to speak'. He lectured in a very poor manner : hemming and hawing : now stooping over his manuscript whilst reading, now raising it in his hands : now stammering out a few sentences extemporaneously. I left disgusted with this lecture. It was for the benefit of our Destitute Children. The Abp., Frs. McNierney and Quin were present with Dr. Ives etc.

Fri., 18th   Omitted by the Editor.

Sat., 19th   Omitted by the Editor.

Sun., 20th   Omitted by the Editor.

Mon., 21st   Omitted by the Editor.

Tues., 22nd   I visited the Pardows : I saw only Mrs. & Pauline Pardow. The latter is thinking of becomeing a nun of the Sacred Heart. She speaks quite frankly of the division of heart, which her having a husband would make between heaven and the husband : whilst as a nun she could serve God alone. All her lay friends seek to dissuade her mother from letting her go. The Jesuits encourage her. Fr. Preston was quite surprised to hear of her intention. She is 21 years of age, and was always gay in society. Robert Pardow is engaged to Miss Carrigan : whom Mrs. Pardow describes as a plain good pious girl, on whom her choice would not have fallen : He is now on a business tour in the west. To-day I felt my responsibility as a priest forced upon me, when my advice was asked as to Miss Pardow's vocation. I approved of her trying. Fr. Preston and I went to the Immac. Conception fair : where Dr. Morrogh though in a mandling state was determined to point to Fr. Preston the design followed in building the school-house. The fair is a failure. He says the principal parishioners have united against it. He insinuates that Fr. C. Farrell's management is unacceptable to them.

Wed., 23rd　　　Omitted by the Editor.

Thurs., 24th　　Omitted by the Editor.

Fri., 25th　　　Omitted by the Editor.

Sat., 26th　　　Bishop Duggan came to stay with us a few days before going to Europe. His first act was a visit to the B. Sacrament. His health has been failing : dyspepsia troubles him. He is quite an entertaining talker : does not hesitate to make himself the topic : and gives out his opinions freely. He was thrown out of his carriage a few days ago. He is an earnest unionist. He carps at the ignorance of Roman authorities about this country, in fact, about every thing except perhaps abstract Theology : and was incensed at the Irish bishops and priests' sympathies with the South during our late struggle. We heard the confessions of the children preparing for confirmation.

Sun., 27th　　　Bishop Lynch of Charleston said 9 o'c. mass and preached at 10½ o'c mass on the B. Trinity : a few ideas of his sermon may be found on the margin. Bishop Lynch repeated the several formulas of the Athanatian creed about the Trinity : remarking that it was above our comprehension, but

May   272

that we were to adore even as the Jews adored God in the fiery cloud that
appeared on Mount Sinai : where they trembled at the outward display of
God's majesty. What would have become of them, if they had seen him more
clearly still? At both masses he made an appeal for money to build the
many institutions : which, he says, were destroyed by the sad events of the
last few years. His Cathedral, and house, and boys orphan asylum are not
to be found. And the 'cruel shells' have so pierced the convent of Mercy as
to make it untenantable : and the Ursuline Convent in Columbia was razed to
the ground by fire. He wilfully leaves the impression that all this was
effected by the Union troops : whilst really only the Convent of Mercy was
damaged by the war. Bishop Duggan at dinner called his attention to Sherman's indignation at the Sisters of the Ursuline Convent, of which a sister
of Bishop Lynch is superior, sending out a circular which states that their
convent waa burned by Sherman's army, implying that it was done by Sherman's
order. Sherman had first given a guard to protect the convent : and denies
having given any order to burn Columbia : and asserts that Wade Hampton had
given an order to burn Columbia, as soon as the U. S. troops should enter it :
that Hampton's troops were seen on the outskirts of the woods near by as the
fire commensed. Bishop Lynch exonerates Sherman : but states that his own
brother and Dr. O'Connell saw the Union troops set fire to several houses.
Bishop Duggan told him that if he wished to collect near Chicago : the less
said or insinuated about damages done by the war, the more copious would his
collections be. The two bishops were present at High Mass : the day being
stormy, the congregation was not large. We heard confessions in the evening.
At 9 o'c. Dr. McGlynn asked me to go to hear Mr. Witcher lecture on 'Why he
became a Catholic.' We heard a few sentences : but it is ridiculous to see
Witcher for the sake of a few dollars winding himself to a great pitch of

enthusiasm about his becoming a Catholic. The enthusiasm is artificial, not to say verbal. We called in to see Frs. Boyce and Ferrall who appeared disgusted at having to give Witcher their basement as a lecture-hall : it is ammunition wasted which could be used to better purpose for the church. We were caught in a thunder storm as we were near our house.

Mon., 28th   We had confirmation by Abp. McCloskey : about 210 persons were confirmed. The Abp. gave quite a pleasing discourse : a synopsis may be found below on the margin. (The Abp. spoke about the regeneration of baptism : considered that at confirmation we renewed our baptismal vows. The girls recited a formula of renouncing the devil etc. He spoke of first communion and told an anecdote of a French girl who became infidel but on her death bed was converted by being reminded of the joy of her first communion.) The ceremony was over by $10\frac{1}{2}$ o'c. I took a ride in Central Park alone. We had a grand dinner at 5 o'c. The Abp., Bishop Lynch, Bishop Duggan, Frs. Starrs & McNierney, Misters Pierce, Hildreth, Dachauer and Judge Wright were the guests. The principal subject of conversation was the right of the Southern States to secede. The Abp. maintained that it was foolish to give the right to any state to secede from partnership without the consent of the other partner states : but according to ideas prevelent among our people, they had the right of revolution : on which it is true they did not act at first but adopted when in confederation. Bishop Duggan said that they had no grievance to give them the right of revolution. Bishop Lynch suggested that they had as great a grievance as the United States had in 1776 against England. I asserted that then it was the principle of taxation with representation that was violated by the imposition of the tax on tea. Bish. Lynch then argued that now the Southern States were being taxed without representation. I then put in that the prisoners

May 274

in Sing-Sing had not the right of voting : the Southern States on account of their rebellion were in a similar state with regard to the Union : and therefore excluded from representation. Judge Wright maintained that they had the right to leave the Union whenever they took the whim. He had been in Fort Warren for treason : there he became a Catholic. Mr. Pierce and Fr. McNierney though unionists thought emancipation a great disadvantage to the negroes : for their masters as a rule took care of them. I replied that this care was like that given to the horses of the 3d Ave line. I had to preach during the dinner : I spoke on envy following Piano's instructions.

Tues., 29th   I attended Dr. Pise's funeral at St. Charles Borromeo's church in Brooklyn : the church was not well adorned. Bishops Loughlin, Lynch and Bayley were present. Abp. McCloskey preached the eulogy : of which a synopsis may be found in my next letter to the Catholic Standard. Fr. Malone sang High-Mass : assisted by Dr. Freel and Fr. Goodwin : Bishop Loughlin gave the final absolution. Fr. Malone, Dr. McGlynn & Andrew McGlynn and I went in the same carriage to Flatbush cemetery, where the burial took place. Fr. Malone scandalised And. McGlynn by speaking lightly of Bishop Loughlin, who had forbidden priests to act as pall-bearers. Flatbush cemetery is neatly arranged with very plain chapel. I dined at Dr. McGlynn's.

Wed., 30th   I saw Bishop Duggan off to the steamer Java on his way to Europe : he expects to be away three months. Mr. Hassard came also to the steamer. There the bishop introduced us to the McCartys of Syracuse on their way to Europe. Dr. McGlynn called : we went riding to Macoomb's dam : Dr. McGlynn was thrown from his horse : he had not ridden more than twice in 13 years. I preached on Gluttony & Sloth at the Month of May

May

devotions.

Thurs., 31st   Corpus Christi. We had solemn High Mass : Fr. Preston celebrant, I as deacon, Mr. Regnaud S. J. as subdeacon : and procession of the B. Sacrament : about 40 girls joined in it and 14 boys. In the afternoon the girls' school had a May-festival. Fr. Preston and I, Mother Angela and another sister of Charity were the only visitors. Miss Waters directed the music. We concluded the Month of May devotions with solemn Benediction. The B. Sacrament was exposed the whole day. I visited the Burtsells : we spoke principally about the necessity of Peter applying himself to the study of law. Dr. Thos Burtsell is still moody over past events. I peeped in at the Cooper Union exhibition : but did not tarry because there was too great a crowd to allow me to see or hear much.

June

Fri., 1st   Omitted by the Editor.

Sat., 2nd   Omitted by the Editor.

Sun., 3rd   We had solemn High-Mass with the B. Sacrament exposed. I preached an old sermon on the Eucharist and acted as deacon, Mr. Regnaud S. J. as subdeacon, and Fr. Preston celebrating. At dinner Mr. Dachauer remarked to Mr. Regnaud that the Jesuits were hated by a great many good Catholics : Mr. Regnaud thought that the friends of the Church loved the Jesuits, the enemies of the Church hated the Jesuits : who have always been the most persecuted body in the Church. Mr. Regnaud being a Canadian says that there is too great a hatred between the French Canadians and the Irish in Canada, for them ever to agree in expelling the British. In the evening I heard Dr. Cheever maintain that the refusal of the ballot to the negroes is a violation of the natural law by which the consent of the governed is required to give validity to the government : he ridicules those who say that white skin is requisite for the right of suffrage : because then the suffrage would not be given to men as men, but to skin beautifully painted white! I do not agree with those who denounce ministers talking of politics in the pulpit, when they are connected with a great moral truth.

Mon., 4th   Omitted by the Editor.

Tues., 5th   Omitted by the Editor.

Wed., 6th   Bishop Lynch, Dr. McGlynn and I went together to a dinner gotten up by Mr. Fagan the superintendent of Ward's Island in honour of Fr. Coyle. Mr. Fagan is a handsome man, quite intelligent and shrewd, and witty. There were some 10 priests : Frs. Malone, McGean, Walsh, Hassan, Quin, Larkin & Mooney. Mr. Fagan showed us the hospitals : the wards are all well ventilated : they have the contagiously diseased separated from all others. We noticed one girl of 7 years just come from Ireland having charge of her brother. We visited the lunatics : and also the new hospital lately erected to which the patients will be admitted within a month. It is considered the finest hospital in the world : the rooms are quite spacious and airy : a grand fan exposed to the winds constantly sends through the house a current of fresh air : which is heated in winter by passing over the fire. We had a merry dinner. At first politics were the subject. Fr. Malone told B. Lynch that they could not agree : as he (Malone) maintained the truth, and the bishop falsehood. The bishop offered a toast to all who had nobly fought on both sides North and South. Fr. Mooney introduced a toast in honour of the dead at Manasses : where his fame reached it's zenith. Dr. McGlynn interpreted the toast as a wish of health and long life to those who died at Masasses. Mr. Fagan gave a history of the Board of Emigration. It's establishment had been opposed, especially by the Irish and Germans who were bent on deceiving their countrymen. Injunc-

June

tions were placed on it's operations : because the landing of emigrants was said to produce disease in the quarter where they landed. The Emigrants are taxed $2, per head : hence the fund which has built the magnificent institution of Ward's Island. The United States are not taxed at all for them : the authorities have misappropriated part of this fund for the Blind Asylum to which emigrants are not admitted without paying : for the Medical College at Geneva : for the Juvenile Asylum, where the names of emigrants are changed and they are sent West. Mr. Fagan expressed great joy at seeing the various political opinions of the priests present. He is a republican : which by many Irish Catholics is deemed equivalent to a renunciation of the Catholic faith. He says he could be a Know-nothing and still be a Catholic : for the policy of Know-nothings is simply to keep out of the land European paupers, and those too ignorant to appreciate our institutions. Dr. McGlynn, Fr. Mooney, Mr. McSorley quite a witty man, Fr. Mullane, Fr. Malone and Fr. McGean entertained us with songs. Dr. McGlynn and Mr. McSorley gave life to the party. I was for the first time to-day on one of the 2nd Ave. steamers. I met only the literary boys for a rehearsal.

Thurs., 7th   Dr. Sinclair of Rochester came to town to order a bell for his church : and to get two metal statues of Sts. Peter & Paul for niches on it's facade. Serf near St. Alphonsis has made them. We went to Diest's 132 William St. to buy glasses for his candlesticks. He thinks Bish. Timon the most leaned man in Buffalo diocese though his memory has failed. He works very hard in his parish : has a school of 500 children : a nice church, which he is completing : finds his neighbor-priests neglecting to hear confessions : the other priests were ready to help him when he had no need of them : but not when he wanted them. He spoke of Fr. Cannon's

June

condemnation of all priests ordained here. I attended a boys' and girls' rehearsal of their peices.

<u>Fri., 8th</u>　　I gave instructions to the girls' school on the vestments worn at Mass. Dr. McGlynn and I took a walk together. Mandit was our text book. We debated the question of celibacy : a more systematic community life was considered as the best means to avoid it's disadvantages. We thought that the prohibition of whiskey etc. would be more fashionable than that of meat on Fridays. Fr. Preston showed us the photographs of his mare and it's groom Joseph. It is well taken. We visited the new Italian church of St. Anthony of Padua : bought from the Methodists for $11 000 : $6000 being paid at once : the other $5000 to be paid in three years. It is simply a hall about ten feet above ground : lightly frescoed by Pellegrini, so that it looks much higher than it is. It will seat about 600 persons. It is on lease ground, which they may have for $16 000 = two lots. We met Fr. Leo Pacilis an intelligent but remarkably sycophantic Franciscan. . . .

<u>Sat., 9th</u>　　I visited my mother : and confessed to Fr. Reidouit (?) of 3d St. I find the redemptorists a gawkish set. I have gone through them all, and can't find a good confessor. . . .

<u>Sun., 10th</u>　　Omitted by the Editor.

<u>Mon., 11th</u>　　Fr. Malone called in to see me and complained about Fr. Grundner's ridiculous eulogy of the repentance of Probst the murderer of the Deering family at Philadelphia. I dined at St. Joseph's with the usual Black Republican set, invited by Dr. Parsons to commemorate his ordination. Fr. Moroney just returned from Rome was there : and being toasted failed completely in his reply through shame. There was no subject of interest debated. Dr. McSweeny and I took a walk together. We discussed whether the Jesuits and other regular orders are better than the secular priests.

June

He prefers the regulars': of which he considers the primary object to be to preserve priests from fornication, enrichment of their families, and ambition. I thought their object to be an union of the individual strength of many to gain ends, which an individual could not reach : for which purpose, they threw into one heap their earthly goods, they submitted to the guidance of one head, and gave up family relations. I thought that practically the superiors of regular orders were prudent & safe men, inactive : and thus the members were left inert : that regulars and Jesuits in particular are not infrequently led on by ambition : and that if they are freed from occasions of fornication (though a well-known story makes two of the Fordham Jesuits sodomists) they are given to calumny of secular priests, and grasping after money, of course, for the good of the Order. Their vow of poverty is a vow to be fed well, clothed well, and have as many country seats as possible to which they may retire to recruit their health when impaired. Dr. McSweeny supped with me. I attended the girls' rehearsal : where I discovered a jealousy between Miss Cody and Miss Kelly, about directing the girls' gesticulations!!! I also attended the boys' rehearsal.

<u>Tues., 12th</u>   Omitted by the Editor.

<u>Wed., 13th</u>   I visited Fr. Lafont to get some costumes, L. Tessier had told me that Fr. Lafont had : but it was simply paper muslin he used, cut up for the different costumes required. Fr. Lafont was quite excited at the mention of L. Tessier's name accusing his mother of ingratitude in taking her son away from his school without even thanking him for having received him on lower paying terms than his other scholars. I went to dine with a party at Fr. Malone's invited to meet Dr. Brownson and his son the major. Dr. Brownson is very self-sufficient, engrosses the whole conversation, expects his decisions on politics, religion, in fact every subject,

June   280

to be final. He considers it impossible for Irishmen to govern themselves : in the United States they are a disturbing element, in fact, they are such in every country. There was never an Irish Catholic statesman. In response to a toast from Fr. Malone about his efforts to defend Catholics in the U. S. he said he was glad to see around him a nucleus of young priests who would continue this work to which he had devoted all his energies. Many of the priests present paid him such deference, as they would show to no other mortal : he is puffed up. Dr. McSweeny says pride will bring him to a bad end. The Major involved himself in a discussion on the infallibility of the pope with Fr. Farley of Jamaica!!! I attended a dinner given by the Dachauers to Frs. Preston & Gambosville, Mr. O'Connor and myself before their departure for Europe : it was served in neat French style. I attended the boys' rehearsal : as well as the altar class.

Thurs., 14th   Omitted by the Editor.

Fri., 15th   I explained to the girls' school the reasons why the Church has the liturgy in Latin : why the faithful now receive the Eucharist under one kind, though formerly they received under both : and the meaning of the word mass as derived from Missa. . . .

Sat., 16th   Omitted by the Editor.
Sun., 17th   Omitted by the Editor.
Mon., 18th   Omitted by the Editor.
Tues., 19th   Omitted by the Editor.
Wed., 20th   Omitted by the Editor.
Thurs., 21st   Omitted by the Editor.

Fri., 22nd   I said mass at 9 o'c. for Mr. Augustus Tellion : the organ alone played during the mass : the expense was $27,00 : ten for the celebrant, ten for the organist, five for the sexton, two for the bellows-blowers. I gave to the girls' school an instruction on the mass from the credo to the Pater Noster. Fr. Nilan called to see me : he had spoken to Fr. Starrs about the church in 37th St. who said it was an admirable idea that he would suggest to the Archbishop. He heard no more about it : but seems much inclined not to go further with it. He read all 'Mandit' through: and thinks it true to life. I bought three pairs of shoes at O'Neil's for $23. I visited Dr. McGlynn. We walked to Central Park. He engaged me to read the Canticle of Canticles that I might give my idea of it's inspiration. He has been reading St. Teresa's work : and is amused at her saying that the nuns may fall in love with their confessor if he is not vain, and also about her explanation of the Canticle of Canticles. I heard confessions in the evening for an hour : and visited Dr. Morrogh and my mother : who were both in remarkably good spirits.

Sat., 23rd   I acted as godfather for Mr. B. Woods' newly-born girl and baptised it. To-day on account of the Men's Sodality, I heard confessions for 5½ hours. I took a short walk to 23rd St.

Sun., 24th   Omitted by the Editor.

Mon., 25th   Omitted by the Editor.

Tues., 26th   . . . .Fr. Jas. O'Connor arrived at our house in the evening. He says that Dr. Keogh has done nothing during this year for ill health. Drink is at the bottom of it. He has gone West : a rather dangerous place for a drinking-man. Fr. O'Connor had met with great opposition in getting in a seminary for 200 students. Frs. Carter, Cantwell and O'Hara formed a building committee with three laymen. Bishop Wood is good and sensible, but jealous of being controlled, went with the priests in opposition to Fr. O'Connor, who however by a calm explanation gained his point. He states a diocese must have one priest for 1000 souls. To give to a

June

diocese 15 priests a year, there must be 200 seminarians : Eight per cent of priests disappear each year in a diocese. Their seminary gave for 4 years 15 priests a year, but of 2 years' Theology : without education the priests soon go astray in the midst of many temptations, and are a hard class to deal with. The bishop's council did not meet for 4 years! Fr. O'Connor introduced into the Seminary the Roman System of Concursus and a public dispute of 25 theses. The students studied much harder. He had intercepted a letter from B. Kelly to his cousin boasting of having been jolly over drink!

Wed., 27th   With Fr. Jas. O'Connor I went to Dr. Morrogh's where I acted as deacon at a Requiem Mass : with the alb thrown over my shirt, instead of the cassock, on account of the heat! The music was long and good enough for this congregation. We visited the school-house, which will cost $105,000. Fr. Jas. O'Connor thinks a school of the utmost importance more than churches. I partially argued him out of this idea. He thinks this school to be perfect in it's arrangements. The ventilation is good : the privies are below ground outside the school : places for washing and romping are below ground. A fine chapel is on the first floor. One side of the school will be reserved for boys : the other for girls. Each floor may be turned into one large room. Fr. O'Connor and I went to Dr. McGlynn's. We visited St. Stephen's church : of which the design is Byzantine of rather poor make. The decoration is shabby : the pillars are too light for the weight they seem to bear. The organ-loft too heavy. The new addition is poor. Dr. Cummings for pew room sacrificed a fine sanctuary. Dr. McGlynn has partially remedied this defect by extending it's area : and will extend it even more by Fr. O'Connor's advice. There are many spare rooms but no large one for a vestry. The back part of the church protrudes too far on the side-walk, the stoops are side-ways against the spirit, if not the letter of the law. Fr. O'Connor recommends oil paintings from Italy : and a marble altar. We met Capt. Churchill at Dr. McGlynn's. Fr. Jas. O'Connor went to Manhattanville Convent of the Sacred Heart to see the graduates, whom he had feted in Philadelphia : who want him to say mass for them on their leaving the Sacred Heart. Fr. Preston, Dr. McGlynn and I went together to the exhibition of the Sacred Heart. Only priests were admitted. A decree has come from France, recalling them to their rule of not having public exhibitions. The poor girls went through their exhibition mechanically, without enthusiasm : their audience was 20 priests! The dramatic composition of 'The field of Hastings' was tastefully performed : The singing was not good : the playing was agreeable. The valedictory by Miss Kernan was too fulsome in it's praises of the Sisters. The Abp. thanked them for the 'privilege' given us : remarked that the reality and poesy of the exhibition were so well blended as to make us regret it's end : and gave his good wishes for the welfare of the graduates. He then gave his blessing. The Sisters of the Sacred Heart are haughty in their ways : and too cool towards common priests to be popular among the secular clergy. They only think Jesuits worthy of their esteem. They present the Archbishop with a gift on exhibition-day : last year they gave him a $1000 cross. The 'Children of Mary' are a sodality under charge of the Sacred Heart, having a meeting at the 17th St. Convent on the 1st Saturday of the month : they only admit the 'aristocracy' of this city. Fr. Preston tells me that a real lady was excluded lately because not very wealthy. All the members of the Sodality vote. (?). Fr. Preston was the chaplain of the Sacred Heart. A bishop, vicar-general, or Jesuit was invited to say mass on any extraordinary festival. Mad. Hardie pretended not to know Fr. Preston after five years that he had been to see them. Fr. Preston considers them haughty sisters without religious spirit : he found them otherwise at Trinita dei Monti in Rome. On the way back Fr. Daubresse S. J. was in the carriage with us : who advised Dr. McGlynn not to preach long in Summer : gave me St. Augustine's definition of Predestination, without being asked for it : and advised me to read Bourdalone's and Bossuet's panegyric of St. Augustine, to prepare mine for the 28th of August. We got home at $10\frac{1}{2}$ o'c.

Thurs., 28th   Omitted by the Editor.

Fri., 29th   I gave the instructions to the girls' school on the 3rd part of the mass : we heard their confessions in the morning. In the evening Dr. McGlynn and I went in a carriage to Manhattan College. The last part of the examination took place. The college boys gave the music, singing, orchestra and band. Fr. Breen examined several of the graduates in their Philosophy. Dr. McGlynn examined one on the natural law, and got wretched answers. I examined one on the origin of civil law and got no answers at all. An extemporaneous debate on 'whether radicalism or conservatism is most beneficial to society' was rather lagging : five of the six graduates intend to become priests. Dr. McGlynn gave the address to the graduates : the principal idea was that the U. S. people was destined to be a gigantic race proportioned to the gigantic lakes, and mountains and valleys of the country : and they were to help to push it forward. I missed hearing confessions : we got home at 11 o'c.

Sat., 30th   Omitted by the Editor.

July

Sun., 1st   Omitted by the Editor.

Mon., 2nd   Omitted by the Editor.

Tues., 3rd   Omitted by the Editor.

July

Wed., 4th   Omitted by the Editor.

Thurs., 5th   I got a check of deposit for $50 for Fr. Adam from Eugene Kelly. I visited Mr. Kehoe : he is an agent of many bishops for orders of books etc. He delays the publication of tracts till they are numerous enough to be sent in packages, which cost as little as one tract, when sent by post. He is slow in action : has a good store in Willoman St. near Beekman. I met Fr. Moriarty of Chatham four corners : who had been reproached by Bishop Conroy for wearing a white straw hat, a thing not allowed in his diocese, and only introduced by innovative young men. Fr. Moriarty considers his bishop good, but rather capricious : it took him some time to calm after the storm. Fr. Moriarty tells me that a seminarian at Troy was expelled for letting in at 11 o'c. P. M. two other seminarians, one of whom was a subdeacon, who both were also expelled : the three have been absolutely refused ordination. We had a dinner of the assistant pastors of the city to celebrate Fr. Peter R. Farrell's ordination day : he is a priest of seven years' experience. Fr. C. Farrell gave a foolish toast to Fr. P. Farrell who answered by calling the assistants the slaves of the pastors! Fr. Boyce said there were pastors who were not slave-drivers! Fr. McKenna and Fr. C. O'Callaghan gave wretched specimens of priest's talent! Fr. Ryan was wordy to a toast given to the foreign assistants! Miserable jokes were cracked! No intellectuality was found among them! Oh! poor rising generation of New York priesthood! I attended the St. Francis Xav.'s Exhibition. I got in for the Master's Oration, which was a tedious review of Balmes' Comparison of Catholicity etc. Fr. Healy of St. Peter's gave the address to the graduates of which the principal idea was that the mind of man is fathomless! Who can define it's limits? It has controlled the elements of nature! They must cultivate their intelligence which makes them resemble

July 286

God! They have had their hearts cultivated in this Catholic institution. The Abp. congratulated the audience on it's privilege of being present. He never speaks after a good speaker. I did not attend the dinner at Delmonico's. I met John   who seems most anxious to know whether the clergy were pushing ahead the Roman loan.

Fri., 6th   Omitted by the Editor.

Sat., 7th   Omitted by the Editor.

Sun., 8th   Sunday. It was so warm that we had no sermon and the last mass was only a Low-mass with singing by the choir. At Vespers we left out the Litany of the B. V. M. I visited the Navarros at 25, Washington Place, who are very good people. They are going to Europe this week. We talked about the pope's temporal power : I showed my idea that it would cease to exist. The Abp. had sent a letter to the pastors asking them to recommend the Roman loan to the faithful. I declined doing so. Fr. Preston recommended it as a good security : but my protest made him drop all other reasons. I had said 7 o'c. mass at St. Ann's and 8 o'c. mass at the Immac. Conception : Dr. Morrogh being attacked with cholera morbus. I visited the Morroghs of 26th St. : where we laughed at the security of the Roman loan. Mrs. Belcher was there : Mr. Morrogh accused her of praying for my conversion to Episcopalianism. Mrs. McLaughlin and my mother and P. Morrogh were there.

Mon., 9th   Omitted by the Editor.

Tues., 10th   Dr. McGlynn, Fr. Nilan and I went by 2nd. Ave. cars to Harlaem, where we got into a row-boat and went to High Bridge, where we took a swim. We talked on the celibacy of the clergy. I maintained that marriage would give more solidity to the men in the priesthood around us. Dr. McGlynn had heard of a priest of N. Y. buying from a Catholic doctor venereal medi-

July

cines! and of other priests taking liberties with girls of a well-ado family and to the conundrum from the lady 'why are married people like the 1st of May? answered : because they go to bed together and go it while they're young!! I maintained that the seal of confession is not practically preserved, more through stupidity than malice by regular or secular clergy : having met with cases where it was broken. We debated especially on the intrigues that Abbe   attributes to the Jesuits in the 18th century under Ponibal in Portugal and Charles III in Spain. In the cars on our way homewards, we met Mr. O'Brien, who is owner of the 2nd Ave. line who stated that when he got possession, the line was bankrupt, in two years the stocks were at 134, during the war the price of provisions made it fruitless, last month the proceeds were $41,000. 1,000,000 people ride on it per year. The dumbies are useful where there are not many stoppings. Mr. O'Brien says that as a contribution to the pope, he might take some shares in the papal loan, but not as a good security. Mr. Eugene Kelly declined becoming banker for the papal loan, before it was offered to Sherman, Duncan & Co. Dr. McGlynn on Sunday made known at 10½ o'c. mass the Abp's recommendation of the loan. Fr. Nilan says he let it be a-lone (a-loan).

Wed., 11th   I read a great part of 'Le Jesuite' by Abbe
I took a ride on horseback in the Central Park. I attended the first general meeting of the Sunday School Union in the basement of Nativity Church. Fr. Starrs had declined giving St. Patrick's school room because it would be a bad precedent for similar societies. Fr. Preston thinks of offering our church. Mr. Lumuns, the president, made quite an appropriate address, stating how a similar organisation was commenced and failed at the first meeting in 1844 under Fr. Varella at St. Andrew's : this same happened in 1855 : and it is hoped this effort will be more successful. It described

July

the various purposes of such a meeting : the first social, giving the members Catholic books, and place where various plays may be inaugurated, and good company secured : the 2nd religious, because it is to train the teachers in the system of teaching the Sunday School children. About 100 members were present. Frs. Hecker & Preston and I were the only clergymen present. Fr. Hecker thought the reading room impracticable, because of the size of the city. He wants to make of the Union a lever for his Catholic publication Society. He would not speak till it was firmly organised. Fr. Preston had too much to say to begin to say anything. The young men were of quite an intelligent class.

Thurs., 12th   Omitted by the Editor.

Fri., 13th   Omitted by the Editor.

Sat., 14th   Omitted by the Editor.

Sun., 15th   Omitted by the Editor.

Mon., 16th   With Dr. McSweeny and Fr, Nilan, I started for Saratoga : We took the Albany boat. . . .and arrived at 7 o'c. and went to the Clarendon Hotel :. . . .Of course we at once drank of the Congress and Empire Waters!

Tues., 17th   We stayed about the hotel all day, except when we were at the Springs : I patronised the Empire Spring, because it communicates iron to my system : my sister died of absence of iron. I took two glasses of Congress water each day before breakfast : and six glasses of Empire water during the day, two before each meal. . . .

Wed., 18th   Omitted by the Editor.

Thurs., 19th   Omitted by the Editor.

Fri., 20th   Omitted by the Editor.

Sat., 21st   We took the boat for New York where we arrived at 4,30 P.M.

July

During our trip, we discussed the propriety of letting the clergy marry : and we agreed on it's propriety : we talked of an English liturgy, and Dr. McSweeny disagreed. We talked against bishops making laws about dress, beards etc. and Dr. McSweeny said that the laws would be binding though unreasonable. The celibacy never allows priests to become men, marriage sobers men at once : Celibacy brings lonesome hours to the priest : marriage would give him a perpetual object to be loved : Celibacy makes priests selfish : marriage would make him more social. Now any one, however vulgar or untalented becomes a priest, if a celibate : so few choose celibacy, that few smart and good men become priests. The Protestant clergy has more social influence than the Catholic : A Catholic priest has to fly a woman as the very devil : hence he cannot exercise a true influence on society. His influence proceeds from a superstitious reverence for his clerical character created by his separation from his fellow men. But few priests exert any direct influence on men. On arriving home I met Dr. McGlynn and Fr. Jas. O'Connor who came to tell me that Dr. Morrogh was dangerously ill. I gave him the sacraments of Eucharist and Oils, at his own request. He had confessed to Fr. Meagher S. J. He showed his disgust at Fr. C. Farrell's pious talk : in which he has no trust. I had Lawyer Jas. Morrogh called in to draw up his will. He leaves 500 dollars in trust to the Abp. for the new Cathedral : $500 in trust to Jas. Morrogh for the new parochial schoolhouse : $500 to the Society of St. Vincent de Paul : his library to me : his pictures divided between Dr. Clifford Morrogh and me : the rest of his possessions to my mother. His pulse has been at 120 for the week : his liver is much enlarged : he was exhausted by the heat : and tendency to typhoid, or typhus fever is manifest.

Sun., 22nd   I was called up at $12\frac{1}{2}$ o'c. to attend a cholera-morbus

July.

case at Clarendon Hotel. . . .

Mon., 23rd   Omitted by the Editor.
Tues., 24th   Omitted by the Editor.
Wed., 25th   Omitted by the Editor.
Thurs., 26th   . . . .I visited Dr. McGlynn, who is indignant at Fr. Tom Quin who has a hankering after the servant girls & is a bed fellow. We walked to Dr. Morrogh's who is slightly better : and to 42nd St. and took two neopolitans at Theresa's   near 17th St. Rway. Dr. McGlynn upholds the celibacy as the divine characteristic of the Catholic clergy : and prefers allowing many individuals to go to hell than deprive the church of this beauty : We must trust in the goodness of the greater number of the clergy! After all confidence is the foundation of society!
Fri., 27th   Omitted by the Editor.
Sat., 28th   . . . .and had a sick call at 10 P.M.
Sun., 29th   I said 7 o'c. mass at St. Ann's : 8 o'c. mass at the Immac. Conception (where Dr. Morrogh had published that a Te Deum would be sung on next Sunday for the pastor's recovery): and assisted as deacon at 10½ o'c.mass at St. Ann's, Fr. Preston celebrating, Mr. Regnaud as subdeacon. Fr. Preston celebrated the Mass of St. Ann. Fr. Hewit gave a most interesting sermon on St. Ann. "As the foundations, solid, to a house, so the commandments of God to a good woman." The Chinese instead of giving titles of nobility to the children of great men, ennoble the parents and ancestry in proportion to the great deeds : because to the parents is attributable the good of the children, but the children deserve no praise for the good deeds of their parents. So Christianity has honoured the ancestry of Christ, especially his mother and foster-father : and the Sts. Joachim and Ann, the parents of the B. Virgin. Holy women have been in the hands

of God instruments of great good, in all stations of life. Some as queens and empresses, have mothers to whole kingdoms and empires, almost the principal apostles of their countries and benefactresses of the Church. Thus an Helena, a Pulcheria of Constantinople : thus the Elizabeths of Hungary and Portugal, a Clotilde of France. Others have been the educators of the great doctors of the Church, eloquent preachers, of the great saints of Christianity as a Monica of St. Augustine, as the mothers of Sts. Gregory and Basil, an Authura mother of St. Chrysostom, this last was left a widow at 20 years, with this child, and great wealth. She retired from the world to give her thoughts to God and this child : though she never saw him a priest. At 20 years John went to Labanus the great professor of Antioch, which was the wealthiest and most corrupt city of Xtendom. Labanus used his learning to corrupt the youth, and laughed at Christians because they were under the influence of mothers and wives. Labanus when he saw John and heard his mother's history could not refrain from exclaiming: What magnificent wives these Christians have! Now-a-days Christianity is said to belong to children and women : because these are weak-minded, they love it. The contrary is true : for they love it, led on by those attributes in which they are inferior to men. Children are naturally frank and artless : and therefore love to be near God. The soul withered by sin, is afraid and ashamed to commune with God. You might as well prefer the tottering gait of the old man, to the elastic bound of the child, as to prefer the calculating irreligion of a man corrupt with sin, to the artless fervour of a child. Women are said to be superstitious too. One of their superstitions is to tend the sick, without ever complaining. Another superstition of theirs is to sacrifice themselves for their children's sake. 'Tis the same sort of superstition that leads them to be religious to God. St.

July 292

Ann was long sterile : and when it was evident that it was God's gift, a child the B. Virgin was given her. She concentrated her thoughts on this child, which was her joy and consolation. And sanctified herself in fulfilling her duties of life. So can all women sanctify themselves as mothers, and wives, and daughters : even if they are not called to Virginity. Good mothers can give good priests to the church : if they do not, then we perish. Thus the accomplishment of God's will, shown by their station of life, is the most important means of sanctification. Fr. Hewit is simple in his ways, has no pretentions to pompous eloquence : stoops too much to allow his delivery to be powerful. Fr. Preston had praised Fr. Hewit showing the wants of society so plainly. With Fr. Hewit I ridiculed the idea of the B. V. M.'s milk being held as a relic as it is at Santa Croce, Rome : this throws doubt on all other relics, even the holy cross : since the same authority protects them. I also asserted that there are too many churches in Italy, too many convents, too many priests having nothing better to do, than bear the train of cardinals, bishops etc., too much wealth of the church to be good for the Italian people : to all which he agreed, though Mr. Regnaud S. J. was shocked. At dinner Fr. Daubresse S. J. was with us. I spoke of our republic enthusiastically, because it makes men noble and independent in even the lower classes : I spoke of Fr. Hewit's underrating our Catholic population in New York. He says that B. Bayley to find the population multiplies the baptisms by 12. Fr. Hewit thinks me visionary. Fr. Daubresse was shocked at my liking free institutions : he spoke of the lower classes in England as ignorant. I asserted that to result from our aristocracy. He told me 'that I should have less confidence in myself and more in God.' In the evening I went to the 4th Ave. Presbyterian church : where I heard a young minister speak miserably of our seeking the road to

July

heaven. I visited Mrs. Morrogh and Mrs. Belcher in 26th St. Mrs. Morrogh following my example, promised to go with Mrs. Belcher to hear Dr. Corbett, an eloquent methodist minister in 17th St. bet. 1st & 2nd Aves.

Mon., 30th   I wrote a letter to the Catholic Standard. Dr. McSweeny called in the afternoon : we walked to 42nd St. He tells me that Murphy the agent of the papal loan has gone to Havana, not finding it succeeding. The Abp. says that always papal loans were recommended to the faith of the people in Europe. He regrets that Austria has been whipped : since now there will be no strong Catholic power in Europe : France being only a nominally Catholic state & Italy schismatical. He might as well call a mercantile firm a Catholic concern, of which good Catholics should lament the loss! He does not see how any one can hold that the temporal power is not necessary or useful to the pope! We found Fr. Nilan and Fr. Farrell and Dr. Parsons all of whom we called upon.

Tues., 31st   . . . .Dr. McGlynn and I went to see Dr. Morrogh, who is much better : and afterwards to Dr. Beecher's church in Brooklyn. The church is shabby : the concert for the opening of the organ had commenced : The building was crowded. We heard   play improvisations to show off the new stops : but I in vain looked for the vox humanae and angelica : though they are in the new organ. I heard Morgan play William Tell, magnificently. The new organ is grand : and has great power. Mr. Miller appeared to make more noise than music on it. I met Mr. Fleming there, I remarked to Dr. McGlynn that the reading of Abbe   's works had made me a better man, giving me greater love for God and my neighbour. This did not surprise him for he had heard of a man loving Christ more after reading Renan's life, and Fr. Hecker preaching better of him for the same reason. He appeared shocked when I said they had made me a purer man.

July

We are so sensitive about purity, that the mention of it takes even the best priests by surprise. He had made me feel the dangers to which a priest is exposed, and lessened in me the idea of a priest's guilt : yet they made me feel the greater necessity of sacrificing myself for God's sake, even though I agreed with his ideas about abolishing the obligation of the celibacy.

August

Wed., 1st   Omitted by the Editor.

Thurs., 2nd   Omitted by the Editor.

Fri., 3rd   . . . .I visited Dr. McGlynn : to whom I recommended to visit his congregation more. He would not lose his influence by being known : I thought more of him, the more I knew him : so would others. Besides, our people want some one whom they love : if he is seen only at the altar, he will be revered but not loved. He agreed with me, but said that his . . . . and shabbiness of dress had prevented him from visiting. . . .

Sat., 4th   I had two sudden sick-calls. . . .

Sun., 5th   Omitted by the Editor.

Mon., 6th   . . . .I visited Dr. McGlynn who dined with me : we called at Fr. McCarthy's whose mother we met with him. She is of the old Irish type not learned, nor polished. I told Dr. McGlynn that I endorsed Abbe   's 'La Religieuse' : and thought that we should do our best to teach mothers to keep their children at home for their education : religious vowed to celibacy, to whom the word 'marriage' sounds harsh are not fit to prepare our girls for the world. . . .

Tues., 7th   Omitted by the Editor.

Wed., 8th   Dr. McGlynn and I went to a Requiem mass for Dr. Pise in St. Charles Borromeo's : Dr. Freel assisted by Frs. McGivern & Goodwin celebrated. I acted as Master of Ceremonies. Dr. McGlynn preached : 1. The church by her wailing and plaintive strains acknowledges for the first bishop as the lowest layman, that they depend on God's mercy : by praying for them all. 2. The soul after death almost voluntarily defers it's approach to God, till it is purified by the purgatorial fire or our good works : it knows it's unfitness to be near God, yet it yearns to be near him, and to be cleansed from the filth that renders it unworthy of being with him : and cries to it's friends on earth not for the mockery of praise or decent pomp, but for mercy: 'Have mercy on me, at least you who loved me' 3. Death by Christ has been made pleasant, a sleep : as the ancient Christians expressed it on their slabs : "He slept in the Lord." Before for the Jews, even for the patriarchs it was sorrowful (remember Jacob's grieving over the grave) : for the pagans it was an unmitigated evil. He had seen a pagan inscription cursing the gods that had taken a child from it's mother. Perhaps St. Paul had seen this when he recommended the faithful 'not to grieve as they who have no faith.' : 4. Dr. Pise's mind had been so refined and so noble, so intelligent : he had such grace, and noble mein that he needed no praise. God had, as is his wont, formed a noble frame for a noble spirit : his mind charmed those who approached him : his forehead and countenance resemble one of the statues of classical sculptors. A Fr. Hoffman, a German, formed the butt of all the jokes at dinner. Fr. McGivern understands himself. Fr. McCloskey is good and quiet. Fr. McSherry has no brains. Fr. McDonald is witty. Fr. Goodwin took us to his church : which was built by Fr. Francioli for $35,000. It is quite large, seating 1300 : the congregation is of about 12,000. The roof is frescoed in grey and brown, slightly relieved by blue : with a painting of St. Peter midway. The painting of the crucifixion at the high Altar is by Anegro, and has too great a contrast of colours. The altar is of poor marble. A school house is being built : by giving out bonds of the church, with coupons payable in seven years : interest yearly. The church is mortgaged for $35,000. Peter Pise relieves by his will St. Charles Borromeo's of all it's mortgage of $9,000. The Church had cost $12,000. Dr. Pise had paid but $3000. The music here was very poor : a wretched organ to accompany a wretched choir. Dr. McGlynn took tea with me. I visited the Rogers, Mrs. Rogers is very weak still. I met her two brothers-in-law and her husband. We joked a good deal especially about one of the young men getting married to a Miss Slater, who had before given me straps for riding at her store in Bway near 14th St. I foolishly told the anecdote of the Frenchman who would not be married to his beloved because he would not think now how to spend his evenings. I spoke plainly about the pope's probably losing Rome, and in favour of Italian unity, little caring for Victor Emmanuel, but for the Italian people. They seemed to believe Mr. Rogers offered to help me at our church. Miss Rogers made me pay $2 for a church of the Passionists' Fr. Kelly in Nebraska. They all seem to be favourites of the Passionists and Redemptorists.

Thurs., 9th   Omitted by the Editor.
Fri., 10th   Omitted by the Editor.
Sat., 11th   Omitted by the Editor.
Sun., 12th   Omitted by the Editor.
Mon., 13th   In rainy weather Dr. McGlynn and I started by the Albany boat : Dr. McGlynn as usual just in the nick of time. The Hudson River is beautiful even in the rain. We slept at Saratoga.
Tues., 14th   We met Abp. Spalding at Saratoga : he is quite dignified. He had with him as secretary Fr. Gibbons, I understand, quite a smart priest. We went by Morian to Lake George : the cloudy weather prevented the sun from

August

troubling us on the top of the stage. We stopped at Caldwell : and took a row and a swim on the lake.

Wed., 15th We deliberated on going to Glen's Falls to hear Mass : but were dissuaded 1st. because we did not know of what hour Mass was said 2nd. because perhaps the priest would not let us say mass 3rd. because perhaps he was attending another station and we would not find him. Glen's Falls are ten miles from Caldwell. We took the steamboat across Lake George : which is very pretty : the hills are quite high but graceful : the many islands also are a nice feature of the lake. We took the stages to Ft. Ticonderoga : where we had dinner and whence we took the Lake Champlain boat to Rouse's Point. The Lake has very fine scenery on both sides. The hotel was poor at Rouse's point.

Thurs., 16th We went to St. John's : which we ran over thoroughly and saw a large Catholic Church very roughly built, which could have been made handsome. We travelled by RR. to Waterloo : whence we took stages for a ride of 4 hours to Lake Memphremagog, which is the prettiest lake conceivable. Every hill is graceful. It has left a lasting impression on me. We arrived at Newport at 7 o'c. P.M. The hotel here is excellent.

Fri., 17th We met Gen. McMahon, & sisters, and Mrs. Dixon & daughters. The General had been very unwell. We took a row on a part of the lake unhidden to the view from Newport, but truly lovely. We took in the afternoon a walk of 2 hours inland.

Sat., 18th We took a row and a swim in the lake and drove in a light wagon to Coventry 6 miles from Newport, a magnificent country and scenery on all sides. In the evening we went to St. Johnsbury : stayed at the hotel : visited Fr. Danielou, with whom I had come from Europe : he is a boarding with private family.

August   298

Sun., 19th   We said mass in the nice stone chapel, built on Keiley's plan : Dr. McGlynn preached on prayer. Fr. Danielou had published the bishop's circular denouncing the Fenians, whom he wished to deprive of seats in the Church. His congregation is half Irish, half Canadian. The Irish built the church! He repents of his action towards the Fenians! A man Lonergan by name complained to us of him : he is the head of a Fenian circle. We saw the cemetery : which is nicely laid out and kept clean, on a hill facing the town. The idea of (Dr. McGlynn's) sermon was that prayer is a conversation with God : an asking favours of God : to which God gives a reply : prayer is the spiritual ornament of our souls which are temples of the Holy Ghost. Fr. Danielou says that the sermon gained for him $60 more than he would have made. The collection was to plaster the church : it amounted to $100.

Mon., 20th   We went to the Profile House, of the Franconian Mts, we met the O'Briens & Capt. O'Reilly & wife. I admired the profile, whence this house takes it's name : it is formed of rocks, and presents the view of man's face only from one point. There are two lakes near the hotel : the Echo lake is remarkable for the echo, which is reverberated from the mountain that forms one of it's borders.

Tues., 21st   We visited in the morning the Flume, about 6 miles from the Profile house. An astonishing fissure has been made between two mountains, by which the water comes down bounding from rock to rock. We had ourselves stereoscoped in the midst of the great water fall. The flume house near-by belongs to the Profile, but is unoccupied : the carriage fare to and fro being more fruitful than the hotel. We walked both ways. We rode on horseback for an hour in the afternoon : and rode for an half hour on the two lakes. Mr. O'Brien had cooked for us some trout, which he caught,

August

and which was very sweet.

Wed., 22nd   We took the stage to the Crawford house, in hopes of ascending Mt. Washington : the journey was tedious, of 6 hours, though we had fine scenery : We visited the several fine cascades near the Crawford house, walking about 6 miles.

Thurs., 23rd   We found that we had not time to ascend Mt. Washington and commenced our journey homewards : rising at 3½ o'c. having 5 hours of stage-travel : and 10 hours of railway till we reached Boston at 7 P.M. On our way we saw Lake Winnepesaukee : we examined the principal buildings at Concord : found Manchester made up of factories. We took an hour's walk in Boston but did not see much on account of the rain & darkness.

Fri., 24th   We stayed at the American Hotel in Boston : hence we started for Newport, 3 hours travel by railway. We visited St. Mary's Church : a beautiful building, very neat, well designed, though too heavy looking for my taste, as all Keiley's architecture is. A fine school-house is near-by : with very spacious class-rooms, and a fine hall : in which a fair was being held. We met there a Miss Vernon.& Frs. O'Reilly and O'Connor treated us very kindly : making us take dinner with them : and then taking us to see the fine cottages and villas which make Newport a splendid place. We visited Mrs. Ward : who is an invalid, but quite intelligent. She showed us a Spanish cameo and piece of gold found in their yard : hid at least 100 years ago. She talks incessantly but very intelligently. We took a bath at the beach, which is very safe because in a bay, though the surf bathing cannot be very exciting. Newport contains about 1500 resident Catholics : and receives about 1500 during the summer. The very cream of Catholic society resides there in summer : 23 carriages were on Sunday at the Church door. Fr. O'Reilly is very good, though not brilliant. Fr.

August   300

O'Connor is intelligent though not a deep-thinker. We met Dr. Norris of Milwaukee : and Fr. Nilan : the latter came with us by the Providence boat to New York. We had very good berths.

Sat., 25th   I rose at 5 o'c. A.M. to enjoy the view on the Sound which was very fine indeed. We reached New York at 7 A.M. I went to see my mother and Dr. Morrogh off on the steamer 'City of London' on their way to Europe. They both take it as a pleasure-trip. Dr. Morrogh received a testimonial accompanied by $1000, from his parishioners. I heard confessions for 4½ hours.

Sun., 26th   Omitted by the Editor.

Mon., 27th   Omitted by the Editor.

Tues., 28th   Omitted by the Editor.

Wed., 29th   Omitted by the Editor.

Thurs., 30th   I went to the Academy of West Point to attend the President's reception. I saw the cadets being drilled : their uniforms of grey coat and white pants is very neat. They received the President with due honours. Johnson is a man of firm look, of intelligent countenance, rather awkward gait. I saw Grant well : he is quite sturdy and not remarkably bright looking. Farragut is lanking, and careless in his look. I saw all the other persons accompanying the President but did not distinguish one from the other. The cadets threw down and folded their tents in the twinkling of an eye. It was the breaking up of their encampment of two months during which they are subjected to camp-rules and manoeuvres. They passed in review before the President at quick march : and double-quick march, the latter to the tune of 'Pop goes the weasel'. The President got off at 1 o'c. the precise time : at which Capt. Boynton in his order of the day stated he would leave. Fr. Caro insisted that I should go to Cold

Spring : which I did, going over to Garrison's landing, and thence by the cars. . . .

Fri., 31st   Omitted by the Editor.

September

Sat., 1st   Omitted by the Editor.

Sun., 2nd   Omitted by the Editor.

Mon., 3rd   Fr. Woods drove me with Jimmy Meehan to bathe in the Sound. We visited Fr. Kinsella, where we found Fr. Cohl, and Fr. Breen and we took 'pot-luck' together. They expressed disgust at the filth and bugs of the Seminary : were much displeased at the appointment of Fr. Daubresse to give the retreat : thought his remarks clearly personal at times. He is the most unpopular man in the neighborhood and his appointment to give a retreat to the clergy that despises him, only makes the retreat fruitless. Fr. Breen thought all jurisdiction withdrawn from other priests but those appointed by the Abp. for the retreat. I maintained that at most they alone had the extraordinary powers : any other priest had jurisdiction in ordinary cases. I gave out some radical theological ideas about the 'Temporal Power', about Religious Orders, about matrimonial impediments. Fr. Breen declared Dr. McGlynn and me very practical : and thought well of us for the same. Fr. Woods and I visited the Protectory of Destitute Catholic children. We admired the building of brick, 4 stories high, very spacious. Two immense dormitories are on the two upper floors. 455 boys are presently in the institution. Shoe-making and skirt-making are the only trades taught, at the latter boys under 13 are working for $1.75 per week. The brother Tellion says that the working-boys study more in 5 hours than the others in eight. We saw all the boys in the refectory at supper, with stools for seats and tin-cans for dishes. We saw the small boys at play : the largest boys of 15 years of age in school and quite orderly. The boys help at baking : 3 barrels of flour are consumed daily. The 'board of health', I suspect, through Dr. Ives' suggestion, has prevented the courts from sending any more boys. The present building will be but one wing of the whole. The brother director Tellion is quite sharp : I cross questioned him about the order and gleaned these items: that one can be admitted at 12 years of age : and after 13 months' novitiate make vows for one year : after 5 years of residence, and at the age of 25 vows can be made for 3 years : after 8 years of residence and at the age of 28, one can take perpetual vows, only to be dispensed by the pope. The superior is at Paris, who selects 8 consultors and the directors throughout the world : these select a superior for 3 years, and he may be re-elected for one term : but not for more than six years successively. Brother Patrick is now superior of the Northern and Western of the United States : he can change the brothers but not the directors, who may be removed by the superiors at Paris, who give to the local superiors a few drafts signed for urgent cases. The Consultors and directors in council at Paris can amend the laws : but the amendment requires the approval of the pope. The Christian brothers were the last community abolished by the French Revolution and the first restored in 1808 by Napoleon. They were only in Rome in the meanwhile. The Italian government is taking some steps against them. Dr. Ives has opposed the heating of the boys' dormitories, because he never had the dormitory heated when he was in college! Last year the sisters' house was on the brink of bankruptsy : now $15 000 are laid aside to commence their building. The boys' confessions are heard by Fr. Kinsella : this is a heavy duty : which the brother seemed to think unacceptable. With Fr. Woods I visited the family of the Majors, near Fr. Woods'. The

September 303

young ladies sing in his church, and one sang for us. Fr. Woods sang
'Rocking in the Cradle in the Deep' accompanied by Miss Major on the piano.
Dr. Major a proud young fellow was present : as were two Mr. Kennedys,
father and brother of Mrs. Major, who was also there. We met the Whitneys
on our way : Mr. Whitney is afraid of confession. I took home a girl of
15, who became a Catholic and converted her mother on her death-bed : is
now an orphan, uncared for by her step-father : depending on a friend's
kindness for support.

Tues., 4th   Omitted by the Editor.
Wed., 5th   Omitted by the Editor.
Thurs., 6th   Omitted by the Editor.
Fri., 7th   I went to Mt. St. Vincent's to attend Mother Angela
'Abp. Hughes' sister's) funeral. Fr. Starrs sang Mass, assisted by Frs.
Quin and Farrelly. The Abp. gave the absolution. The procession then was
formed to the burying ground. The Sisters and their girls sang very well.
Especially the psalms, of which one verse was sung by the priests, the other
by the sisters etc, sounded well. I met Mr. Schmidt : who asked for my
opinion about Roman affairs. I gave it quite freely : and he said that at
last he gained a clear idea of affairs in Rome. The Abp. remarked to the
Burtsells who were present, that Napoleon would die broken-hearted at seeing his plans of aggrandizement fail : I remarked Pius IX would die broken-
hearted at the loss of his states : He thought not : Pius IX had too Christian a spirit. Frs. Malone and Quin quarrelled about the political question. I came home with the Burtsells : the Dr., Mrs. Thos. & Ann Burtsell
were there, on account of Mother Angela's kindness to the Doctor last summer. Fr. Farrelly is about to buy a church, a block away from his own for
church purposes, over which he will be pastor : it will be a chapel of ease,

September   304

he will have three assistants : he will preach them every 2nd Sunday. I
heard an hour's confessions : all that came. I then went to see the Hanlon
Brothers. The 'Parterre Act' was truly astonishing : the brothers rolled
over, as if a barrell, at full length : somersaults of the most surprising
character were performed by them. Two dogs were trained to jump the rope :
one walked on his fore-legs : the other on his side legs alone. E. Collins
quite young sang a song very well, as an old man. There was quite nice
dancing. Amateurs were introduced to perform various difficult gymnastic
feats.

Sat., 8th   I heard 3½ hours' confessions to-day : this is about
as much as one should hear at one time, to attend to them properly : and
not to be fatigued for Sunday.

Sun., 9th   Omitted by the Editor.

Mon., 10th   I wrote a letter to the Catholic Standard after a five
weeks' silence. Dr. Brann called to see me and dined with us. He is at
Fort Lee : is building two churches : has a congregation of poor people,
many of whom are Dutch : is writing a book entitled 'Curious Questions',
in which are treated picked metaphysical subjects : is planning a review
of all the sects, and a refutation of their principal errors, and building
of the whole Truth from the various truths which each one admits : finds
me changed from conservatism in Rome, to radicalism in America. I told him
that I once thought rulers ought to take care of the people : in America
I have learned that the people knows how to take care of itself. In Rome
I was shocked to hear the Jesuits of the Civilta Catholica, and Roman rulers
generally maintain that it is best for the people to be poor and ignorant.
The government is wholly for the good of the people. Dr. Brann has no firmness of judgement. He has invited all the Passionists to dine with him at

September

Fort Lee : I declined going, because I don't wish to appear to be an intimate friend of Dr. Brann's. I attacked Austria as an old-fogy government. Fr. Preston and Dr. Brann tried to shield it's blunders. Dr. Brann and I visited Dr. Parsons, with whom and Fr. McGean we played billiards. Dr. Thos. Farrell expressed sorrow at Dr. Parsons' getting a billiard-table : which cost only $100, and affords magnificent recreation. Fr. Nilan called in. We supped together. Fr. McGean said snappishly that he had other books to read, besides Mandit etc. He maintained that a New Yorker going on a Friday to Jersey City could not use the Abp's dispensation from abstinence. I maintained the contrary. Fr. Nilan had been to Long Branch, of which he likes the beach very much. I visited the singing class : complained to Mr. O'Neil that there was no energy in the conferences of St. Vincent de Paul and none in the administration of the Church in this country.

<u>Tues., 11th</u> I spoke with Fr. Preston and Mr. Channey Barnard about getting the P. E. Church in 37th St. bet. Bway & 7th Ave. which Frs. Nilan and Larkin have despaired of obtaining. I found Mr. Barnard quite a good and shrewd man : he had done business for Catholics, in buying the present Transfiguration Church, & selling the old one, and obtaining our residence for us. I visited Dr. McGlynn with whom I found Fr. McCready and Fr. Poole : the latter has just arrived from Rome after a stay of 6 years. He has received a letter from his Bp., Verot of Savannah, asking him to go to St. Augustine of Florida out of the diocese : or else to canvass the diocese for Catholics. Bp. McFarland of Hartford declined receiving him. He gave us the pasquinades about the lately appointed Cardinals : Card. Cullen is antiquior : being aged : Card.   the Barnabite, is praecox : being 34 years old : Card. Mattenci is Atrox : having been minister of police :

September

Card.   from Singaglia, and careless of the Cardinalate says 'Quare conturbasus'. Dr. McGlynn and I attended the meeting at Cooper Institute to greet the Southern delegates to the Philadelphia Convention. We heard Parson Brownlow : I had expected to meet a rough,unpolished but talented speaker : and was surprised to find him quite calm, & dignified. He said that he 'the governor of Tennessee' was electioneering and wished to preserve his dignity (an ironical hint at Pres. Johnson's stump-speeches). In Tennessee he remembered a loyal convention of 450 members from every county of the state but one : presided over by one Johnson (the president) whose platform was to give civil rights to the negro : the right to sue and be sued, to give testimony in courts etc. There were in Tennessee 60000 loyal against 80000 disloyal white men. These latter said that Johnson was their leader : he, Brownlow, conceded the fact but declared that he had 30 000 federal soldiers and would arm the militia, and fight and die in the last ditch rather than enfranchise the 800000 ex-rebels, who would disenfranchise the loyal voters. He thought the U. S. Congress the best body of loyal men : and the Tennessee legislature next best. He had an engagement at Beecher's church : he wished to help in the conversion of Beecher : if he did not succeed, he would offer himself as a candidate for Beecher's pulpit at the next election. Senator Fowler of Tennessee was the next speaker and a tedious one. He maintained that no Southern State should be re-admitted to the Union, till it gave civil rights to the negro : and made the number of voters the basis of representation : otherwise a South Carolina ex-rebel : would in vote be equal to 2 and $\frac{1}{2}$ New Yorkers : for 290 000 white ex-rebels would vote for a population of 700 000, 410 000 of whom are negroes. He acted with President Johnson : and had always found him the most radical of radicals. Jack Hamilton of

September 307

Texas said, and it was evident, that he was too hoarse to make a speech. Col. Stokes of Tennessee said that he heard President Johnson declare himself a Tribune of the people, who came to unfold the constitution that had been laid aside for the four years of the war. The Chicago peace-platform had declared that Abraham Lincoln had violated the Constitution in every item. Are not the two assertions identical : and do not both accuse Lincoln of not following the constitution. Thus is not the Emancipation proclamation of Lincoln considered unconstitutional by Johnson. Again Johnson has lately said of Congress 'that it assumes to be the Congress of these United States' thus impeaching it's legality. Are not therefore it's acts illegal? Is not the Constitutional Amendment abolishing slavery illegal? It can therefore be repealed. And the Southerners now say that they can either have back their negroes or get paid for them. He, Col. Stokes, knew that he had aided in Johnson's election : but never dreamt of the possibility of such an utter change as he had effected. He knew now that the Southerners hoped to gain the independence of the South under the leadership of Johnson. Judge Walworth of Louisiana is a polished and manly speaker : who thought that there was no use in readmitting the Southern States, till the federal government had power to enforce it's laws in the Southern States. He had seen 300 loyal men murdered in New Orleans, and none of the murderers had been punished. He considered that the rebel states by rebellion had annulled their existence as states : and now they were one vast territory to be apportioned into states as it pleased Congress. The President had no right to appoint provisional governors, or call state conventions : that was the duty of the U. S. Congress. He had led a Missouri regiment to the top of Lookout Mountain, and had fought in the war for four years. He said that the Southern delegates were accused of being

September   308

representatives of themselves. This is not so. The delegates from Alabama
represent 13 000 loyal whites : the delegates from Virginia 30 000 loyal
whites : from Louisiana 5 000 loyal whites : from Texas 11 000 loyal whites:
from Tennessee 60 000 loyal whites : from   : in all 130 000
loyal whites of the South. In their name he appealed to the North to protect them before it let their representatives enter Congress. He asked
for negro-suffrage in the Southern States if the Northern States chose not
to give it. He never known a negro in the South to be disloyal. Mr.
Stewart   answered several questions of the Evening Post 'Why does
President Johnson vituperate Congress?' because it does not support 'My
Policy'. Why does Johnson detract brave men that fought for the Union?
Because they do not support 'My Policy'. Why is Johnson surrounded by those
who during the war, sought the destruction of the Union? Because they do
support my Policy. The Evening Post is a Johnsonian paper. I forgot an
idea of Brownlow's : which was that he expected a new war : when it took
place he hoped the Northern Army would come down in three divisions : the
first with cannon and small arms to kill. (Amen, cried a voice : Brownlow
replied, I hope that prayer will be heard) the second 'with torches and
turpentine to burn (Amen said another voice) : the third with a surveyor's
line to parcel out the land to those who fought for the Union. There was
immense enthusiasm displayed throughout the meeting.

Wed., 12th   Dr. McSweeny called to show me his letter to Card.
Barnabo. There were several direct charges of incapacity on account of
old age or lack of energy against the Archbishop : which I persuaded him
to leave out : as also slurs against Fr. Starrs, the other bishops of the
country, the priests educated elsewhere than Rome, which he, at my advice,
left out; as well as the supposition that it is through disgust of the

September

persons and not through love of the church, that one exposes the needs of the Church of this country to the Authorities of Rome, who unfortunately monopolise the government of the church, and then are engaged only in the care of the Temporal Power. We visited Dr. McGlynn with whom we found Frs. Poole and McCready. Fr. Poole had remained in England 2 months with his relations of the P. E. church : who declined ever being present at his Mass : because, he thinks, the Catholic Church was too poor a building. Fr. McCready had to go on a sick-call to Brooklyn : the rest of us went to Harlem bridge from which we rowed to High Bridge and back to give Fr. Poole an idea of Harlem River. I told Drs. McGlynn and McSweeny of the horrible revelation that all Fr. Preston's dispensations whilst the Abp. is at home were invalid : for the Abp. is only authorised to delegate to his Vicars General, or to other priests when he is not in town! I attended the altar class in the evening. A young man calling himself secretary of the Temperance Society of 30 members, under the direction of the Jesuits of Yorkville asked me to speak before the Society : he had heard of my efforts in the cause. I accepted on condition that he brought me a token of the Jesuits' sanction : he never returned.

Thurs., 13th   Omitted by the Editor.

Fri., 14th   I commenced in the girls' school to give a history of the Church. I follow Reeve's Abridgement of Church History. I find he cuts up the Gallicans excessively : and is too ultramontane. I visited Fr. C. Farrell, who offered to give a house for a few weeks to Fr. De Rodas : who did not gamble his money away, but was unfortunate enough to be at the Hotel where an Italian priest from Mexico, of gambling propensities came to stay and found himself cheated. Fr. De Rodas says he was always swearing. They both said Mass at the Cathedral, the other at the Convent, with

September 310

permission from the Abp. I confessed to Fr. Maguire. I bought a Greek & English & a French & English dictionary : as well as Virgil and Quackenbos' 1st English reading book at Appleton's. The rain prevented many from coming to confession. I visited the Burtsells : with whom I had some plain talk about the pettiness that at times enters convents. A sister with hard knees and a sharp tongue, I said, very easily controls a convent. Madame Tobin is rejoiced at leaving the Convent of Mercy : the Dr. was once reprimanded by Sister Beatrice for talking of Mr. Dillon's adopted daughter at the Convent, and gave to a Sister of Mercy a newspaper on the sly. Mrs. Hassard remarked to me that she had no Catholic friends : she found Catholics too inquisitive.

<u>Sat., 15th</u>   Omitted by the Editor.

<u>Sun., 16th</u>   . . . .I met the McLaughlins : just returned from a 6 weeks' visit to Long Branch. They had received letters from Italy. Cathy had been very sick : Uncle Avezzana had been with Garibaldi but in no battle: speaks highly of the Italian kingdom. I entered the 5th Ave. South D. R. Church and heard Rev. Mr.   hold forth on the text : Turn ye from your evil ways, for why will ye die? Ezechiel XXXIII.II. These are words of remonstrance, dictated by the mercy of God. How different from the ways of earthly sovereigns, that do not beg rebels to lay down their arms but force them! These words imply that man has freedom to do good or evil : for God begs them to turn from their evil ways. Does not the Sovereign God rule the world of mind and matter as he wills? How then can man have free-will? I cannot reconcile the two things. Yet I know them to be facts. The captain of a steamer may not know why the needle points to the North, but he knows the fact. We know that God must rule the world as he wills : otherwise he would not be God. I know that

September

I am a free agent. My conscience tells me so. I know that, when I sinned, I was free : the pangs of my conscience tell me so. Why would the Son of God become man to redeem me, if I were not free to receive his redemption? Men are begged to return from their evil ways : thus they had the power of selecting evil ways : otherwise they would not be their evil ways. In the 2nd part of the remonstrance 'why will you die?' is contained a word of warning : showing the termination to which their evil ways will lead them viz : to death. They are to turn from their evil ways which lead to death : to the good way which leads to life : for God says, in the same verse : As I live I desire not the death of the wicked : but that the wicked turn from his way, and live. I did not admire the eloqution of the minister : but I saw about as many men as women present in the church : and I was pleased with the singing of English hymns though in plain style. I visited the Morroghs of 26th St. : to whom and Mrs. Belcher I explained the doctrine of 'Salvation in one church' in the most liberal sense : I decried the imaginary pictures of hell and purgatory : as well as the rigidity of Protestants about the Sabbath : as the lax way in which French & Italian Catholics frequently celebrate it. I showed that playing for money is not sinful in itself : but on account of the evils that flow from it, it is frequently a grievous sin.

<u>Mon., 17th</u>   Fr. Nilan came to see me. I went with him to Dr. McGlynn: with whom we found Fr. Poole : who told us that the writer of the letter that appeared in the Herald about a year ago against Dr. McCloskey rector of the American College of Rome wrote a retractation to Fr. Chatard, and to Abp. McCloskey : the one to the latter to be published in the Herald, if thought suitable. This was done by advice of his confessor at Paris. The students of the college signed a letter exculpating Dr. McCloskey from

September 312

the accusation of teaching politics to the students. Fr. Poole declined to sign it : but yielded. Fr. Kearney refused to be connected with it at all. Many of the signers repent having signed it : they knew the first accusations to be true. Mgr. Capalti said he never knew as strange a man as Dr. McCloskey who actually left Rome without an audience of the Holy Father, because not given as soon as he needed it!!! How strange! Bishop Lynch wrote a pamphlet in Rome defending domestic slavery. We visited the site of the New Cathedral. Fr. Hecker called in at tea : and explained the displeasure of several Irish priests at seeing an Irishman introduced to one of the tracts, speaking with the brogue, though he floored a lawyer, that attacked the pope. He tells that he argued with Abp. Spalding about beards, who said that, though Religious Orders did otherwise from him, he would have all the priests, under his control, shaved. Fr. Hecker says that one question to be agitated will be the admission to minor orders, and even to the deaconate of convert-married ministers, that they may have the chance to preach the gospel, when by marriage debarred from the priesthood. He showed how he preaches to Protestants : by proving first the necessity of a certain thing ex. gr. confession to the aspirations of human nature : then showing how Protestantism does not supply it : and how Catholicity does. He has a sermon on the Invocation of Saints, in which he speaks of American relics of the Revolution, of John Brown etc. of the sentiments excited by the view of Washington's picture : and then brings in the heavenly heroes, and their relics : showing how the respect to them answers an instinct of human nature. Fr. Hecker proves that religion cannot be all in spirit or in the heart from the fact of the incarnation : which is an external religious action of God himself, to do honour to himself. I passed through Union Square and saw the immense crowd assembled at the

September 313

Johnson meeting. The speeches were of the excited style. I heard McSorley sing a song against the negroes.

<u>Tues., 18th</u> Mrs. Dillon called on me, to get a seat in our church, and ask me to visit her at 54 St. Mark's place. She knew Dr. Thos., & Anastasia Burtsell when they went to St. Peter's. I visited Fr. Thos. Farrell, who told me of a note of his published in the Tribune refusing a subscription to the 'Irish Press' until it bespoke freedom to the negro. He will give a collection to Bishop Lynch of Charleston if he promises to devote it to the education of negroes. He intends to organise a Theological Society, if the Abp. does not establish the 'conferences' immediately after the Baltimore Council : he thinks the Abp. will keep to his promise, lest he should lose entirely the confidence of his priests. I bought Abbe   's 'Le Confesseur'. I went to see Jefferson act as Rip Van Winkle at the Olympic Theatre. He acts most naturally : as the drunken man playing with children, shrewd with Derrick (impersonated by Mr. Stoddard a good player) the money-lender : as fooling his wife, (impersonated by Mrs. Saunders, who takes the double character of a young and old woman excellently) as talking with Henrick Hudson (and crew) : and as returning to his home after 20 years' sleep : he acts the old man wondrously indeed. I got home past 11 o'c.

<u>Wed., 19th</u> In the morning I called on the Abp. : who having some document to write had left orders that no one should see him. I saw Fr. McNierney who is to be master of Ceremonies at the Council : In the afternoon I saw the Abp. to whom I submitted a note from Mr. Barnard declaring that the 37th St. Church was now to be sold with house for $50,000 and church alone for $30 000 : He thought that it was a speculation : to cheat Catholics!! I asked him to authorise me to build a church in 2nd

September 314

Ave. near 20th St. He said : no church is needed there, because the enlargement of St. Stephen's and the future enlargement of the Immac. Conception will enable all the people to go to church. He wants priests more than churches. He has authorised the German Capuchins to set a church between St. Mary's and the Cathedral. I offered to build a church, whenever he thought it worthwhile to call on me. I fortunately met Fr. Larkin and explained to him Mr. Barnard's letter. Dr. Butler of Chicago came to stay with me : Fr. Nilan and Dr. McGlynn came to the house with him. Dr. Butler had received a wretched room at the Astor House.

Thurs., 20th   Omitted by the Editor.

Fri., 21st   I had a slight 'difference' with Fr. Preston who insisted on sending Dr. Butler to next door = the French House. I said he would go to Dr. McGlynn's in preference. The bishop arrived. He had been to Prussia: where Catholics are more free than in Austria : but incurred odium because they sympathised with Austria. The German bishops helped him to get German Seminarians who had finished their Ecclesiastical course to come to his diocese. He found the Irish bishops to be great toadies to the government : and thinks the 'temporal power' lost forever. Dr. Butler and I went to the Custom-House : and engaged McSorley to get the bishops' goods through. Fr. Boyce helped us. I heard confessions in the evening. Fr. Hecker visited us in the evening.

Sat., 22nd   Omitted by the Editor.

Sun., 23rd   Fr. Preston got an attack of Cholera-Morbus and could not say Mass. The bishop said 7 o'c., I 9 o'c. and Dr. Butler sang $10\frac{1}{2}$ o'c. mass. The bishop preached. He speaks nicely : no original thought but good common sense was seen. He is artificial in his delivery : perhaps queer in the way of holding his head. I sang Vespers. I had agreed to say

September

mass at St. Teresa's, for which Fr. Boyce declined sending a carriage :
when I arrived there, they had no need of me, though Fr. Boyce said I
might, if I chose, say 8 o'c. mass. I declined. I took Dr. Butler to see
the Burtsells of 4th Ave. : and the Morroghs of 26th St. with whom we met
John Avezzana. We discussed Radicalism and Fenianism as usual.

Mon., 24th   Bishop Duggan started for Chicago via Rochester. I
wrote a letter to the Catholic Standard. Dr. Butler went downtown alone.
We dined with the Paulists : whose dinner is substantial but uncomfortable
because of their postulants to the number of 8, who the whole dinner were
hanging on our lips. Fr. Hecker is anxious to have Protestant ministers,
though unmarried, ordained deacons that they may be empowered to preach
and take charge of congregations, where priests cannot be placed. They
have received several converts from Mr. Morril's Puseyite church.
The Episcopalians have a seminary in Tarrytown, which when regulated
by a Puseyite gave no converts, but repressed by a low-church-man induces many Seminarians to become Catholics. In the evening we went to
the 14th St. Circus : where we saw astonishing feats of dancing and men
climbing on horse back : almost frightful tricks on ropes. We visited
Fr. Farrell : with whom we met Frs. Boyce, Farrelly and J. Quin : with
whom Dr. Butler was disgusted. He was amazed by Fr. Nilan directly at-
tacking his bishop's Anti-Fenianism : as secretary, he is too honourable
to cut up his bishop. I played billiards with Dr. Parsons and Fr. Nilan.

Tues., 25th   Dr. Butler and I went to Berger's 15 Maiden lane :
considered the best place for Sacred Vestments : Benziger's 9 Dey St.
good for Latin books of Theology : Turgis 16 Dey St. good for Sacred
Paraphernalia in general. We dined at Fr. Quin's Barclay St. where
were Frs. Healy, Shanahan and Madden of N. Jersey. Fr. Quin and I had

a sharp controversy on clerical dress. He thought that sleeve-buttons should not be tolerated in priests!!! I thought the church should not interfere with collars, buttons, beards etc. etc. Dr. Butler in the evening went to see Hackett play as Falstaff : he was pleased with the acting but disgusted with the play. I took Maggie Burtsell to see Hartz' illusions : of which the most remarkable was the speaking wax-head : which actually smiled.

Wed., 26th   Omitted by the Editor.

Thurs., 27th   We dined with Frs. Clowry, Breen, Beecham and Barretta. Fr. Clowry laughed at Fr. Hecker's Publication Scheme as impracticable. He thought the Council of Trent not binding in America!!! He decried Fr. Hecker's scheme of admitting married persons as deacons. He thinks Abp. Hughes great because he let drunkards govern parishes. We went to see Dr. McGlynn's family. . . .

Fri., 28th   Omitted by the Editor.

Sat., 29th   Omitted by the Editor.

Sun., 30th   Omitted by the Editor.

October

Mon., 1st   Omitted by the Editor.

Tues., 2nd   . . . .Dr. McGlynn tells me that of late I have shown myself irritable when taken up in my favourite theory and too self-sufficient in my dealings with others : and too imprudent in the expression of my radical ideas. Dr. McSweeny brought me the Distribution Catalogue of Propaganda. His brother took 3 medals : besides the Doctorship in Philosophy. He too told me that I am losing my influence for good by the too bold expression of my radical ideas. Dr. McGean had commenced to lose faith in the Jesuits because Fr. Daubresse reproached him for having bought

October

a cane with a gold head for, he said 'that is not the spirit' !!! I told
Fr. Preston that the Abp. had hurt the priests of the archdiocese by selecting as his Theologian at the Council of Baltimore, Fr. Daubresse, a Jesuit
and the most unpopular Jesuit in the archdiocese, unpopular even in his own
Society : and Fr. Starrs V. G. as theologian forsooth! some excuse would
have been given, if he took a third theologian as long as he took a secular
priest. Fr. Preston says Fr. Daubresse is an excellent theologian : I
doubt it.

<u>Wed., 3rd</u>   Omitted by the Editor.

<u>Thurs., 4th</u>   . . . .Dr. McGlynn and Dr. McSweeny called and we took
tea together. We discussed the question of the Celibacy of the Clergy.
Dr. McGlynn maintains it's necessity, but after a thorough exclusion of
idle friars, well-fed and lustful. We went to his house : where he read
a note from a priest, ridiculing his anxiety about the priest's niece, a
reformed prostitute : thinking he should give attention to a less peculiar
way of winning laurels. We cut up the Roman temporal Sovereignty. Fr.
McEvoy chatted with us about Fr. Mullins, who stood an examination for a
chair at Maymooth, was a professor at Troy, and is now at the Cathedral
in feeble health (& is good & intelligent.) We talked about Fr. Pacilio
the Italian Franciscan pastor of the Italian Church. He has now an
Italian and an Irish assistant, the latter of course to take care of the
Italians! They came to New York to care for the Italians and have almost
forgotten them. Their church is not parochial. Yet the Franciscan Fr.
Pfeiffer boasts that they receive 20 Irish baptisms to 1 Italian. Fr.
Preston tells me that the Abp. authorised them to marry in certain cases
of conscience : of course if they had 20 marriages a day, they would be
under this rule! They told the Abp. that in the confessional, persons

October

came who did not have confidence in their pastors, to reveal sins committed in connection with marriage! Fr. Pacilio offered his services at the Cathedral during Fr. Starrs' absence, at the Baltimore Council. He pressed Mr. O'Connor clerk of the Chancery 4 times to take dinner with him! He ingratiates himself thus with the people at the helm of the diocesan ship!

Fri., 5th   Omitted by the Editor.

Sat., 6th   Omitted by the Editor.

Sun., 7th   I visited the remains of St. Patrick's Cathedral, which was burnt last night. Sparks came from the fire that consumed Gunther's, and Vogts' on Crosby St. Only the four walls remain, quite solid. The roof was shingled. The vaults with the bodies are intact. $40 000 are insured on the church : $6000 on the organ. The sacred vessels and vestments were removed : everything movable was saved. Dr. McSweeny and Fr. McGean went to bed after hearing the mass of Fr. Mullen at the Convent : tired out. Fr. Mullen is quite a pleasant and intelligent man, who was at Troy Seminary. I preached at High-Mass on the Necessity of Faith. I gave instruction to the boys on Church-History : and examined the girls on the Catechism. I sang Vespers : visited Mr. Jas. O'Connor at the Brevoort House to hear his confession. He is from Pittsburgh : and has with him his wife and son. I met there Dr. Dorsee : quite a pleasant talker, who cured Mr. O'Connor quite rapidly. I visited the Morroghs of 26th St. : and returned home with Peter Morrogh who attended a spiritualists' meeting where he heard Christ handled in blasphemous manner. Mrs. O'Connor said she would keep her children home as long as she could : she had been placed under the charge of the Sisters of St. Joseph Emmitsburgh when 10 years old : experience had taught her that a mother is better than a nun to educate children. I agreed with her, as also Dr. Dorsee. He stated

October

that many Protestant young ladies used to go to St. Ann's to see Fr. C. Farrell, because he was handsome.

Mon., 8th	Omitted by the Editor.
Tues., 9th	Omitted by the Editor.
Wed., 10th	Omitted by the Editor.
Thurs., 11th	Omitted by the Editor.
Fri., 12th	Omitted by the Editor.
Sat., 13th	Omitted by the Editor.

Sun., 14th   Sunday. I sang high-mass. Fr. Preston preached on the gospel (21st Sunday after Pentecost) and exaggerated the guilt of detraction: said that to forgive and not to forget was not acceptable to God! that after an injury we should treat our neighbor as kindly as before! if we had the least remembrance of it, God would forgive but not forget our sins! and that we condemn ourselves saying the Lord's prayer, if we don't forgive our neighbor! I gave the instruction to the boys' S. School : and distributed the pictures to the boys who had 4 red (for mass) and 4 green tikets (for Sunday School) I visited the girls S. school : from whom Fr. Preston had drawn in all the tickets. Mr. & Mrs. Dachauer arrived from Europe : and dined with us. Mr. Dachauer presented to me a pocket book. Fr. Donnelly paid his seminary-collection $670. We walked together to 32nd St. He is purchasing property along side of his church because it belonged to his creditors. He found that it was impossible to support the church by giving free seats : that the people is more fervent, when forced to pay for church-going. Mr. Barnard told Fr. Larkin that I was looking after property on 2nd Ave. I visited the Morroghs of 26th St. : to whom I told that I did not believe that the Immac. Conception was absolutely a dogma : because the Roman Theologians maintain that the pope alone was

October   320

the active definer : whence they argue his infallibility. But as it is
not certain that the pope is infallible : they take away the groundwork
of a dogma. Tacit consent of the church is chimerical. I thought 'temporal power' ought to be abolished.

Mon., 15th   Omitted by the Editor.
Tues., 16th   Omitted by the Editor.
Wed., 17th   Omitted by the Editor.
Thurs., 18th   Omitted by the Editor.
Fri., 19th   Omitted by the Editor.
Sat., 20th   Omitted by the Editor.
Sun., 21st   Omitted by the Editor.
Mon., 22nd   Omitted by the Editor.
Tues., 23rd   Omitted by the Editor.
Wed., 24th   I assisted as deacon at a Requiem Mass at St. Joseph's.
Fr. Farrell made quite touching remarks over the girl. He could not give
consolation to the parents other than that of religion : she had deserved
wreaths of laurel at school, and her parents and companions were proud of
her success : she has now received a never fading crown from God : should
we not rejoice at her good fortune? Only the young are prepared to die,
for they are innocent. We older in years and older in sin fear death
more, for we are less prepared. The Sodality-girls were present dressed
in light blue, with blue wreaths and the officials with golden crowns
(with President instead of Queen cut on them) over white veils. I wrote
a letter to Card. Barnabo in Fr. Farrell's name, asking dispensation for
a woman to marry her dead husband's brother, with whom she had sinned.
I met Fr. Kearney for a moment, who is exceedingly quiet. I lunched alone
& visited Mrs. & Miss Fannie Harnett. The latter had been asked in marriage

October 321

by a Cuban : she refused to go to Cuba. A mistake led Fr. Preston and me to Mr. Dachauer's to dine : he was not at home at the hour designated. I called at Dr. McGlynn's where I met Frs. Quinn and Powers of Halifax. Fr. Quinn said that Dr. White of Washington recommended separate churches for negroes : his experience showed their utility. Fr. Pucer of New Orleans thought that the present churches would hold all who wanted to come to Catholic churches. Fr. Quinn was a prominent member on the Finance Committee : but no action was taken about the tenure of Church property. Fr. Hecker told Dr. McGlynn that his Catholic Publication Society had been endorsed, the bishops promising him a collection in their principal churches: 75 percent to be sent back to them : and 25 percent kept for charity, hospitals etc. The beards have been excommunicated. The bishops of New York province decided to postpone the erection of Boston to an Archbishopric till the provincial synod after the receipt of the decrees from Rome. Rochester is to be made a see, Fr. Hecker was impressed at seeing so many thinking men (especially the bishops of New York province?) agree so well : Drs. Butler, McMullen & Norris called at our place. Fr. Poole wrote from Savannah stating that the priests continue to administer sacraments when suspended for trivial reasons by the bishop : the people bring tales to the bishop who believes old women before priests : the priests have lost all zeal to do good : 7000 Catholics are in Savannah : there were 8000 before the war. The people don't go to confession. Fr. Poole insists on leaving Savannah : and wishes to be at St. Stephen's New York. I attended the altar and literary classes. I went to the Cooper Institute and heard Mr. Durant show how the negroes would not be educated unless the Southerners depended on their votes for office. He read a Louisiana law stating that the slaves were to give absolute obedience to their masters having no rights

October 322

of their own. Mr. Shaw gave an anecdote of a negro of 70 years who learned to read Ox, by being reminded by O of a wheel without spokes, and by X of a saw : and told how one negro made other negroes learn the alphabet. Gen. Howard spoke a few words offering to give houses for schools for any denomination in the South : but telling the Relief Associations they must pray for & send the teachers. He said "No one can be truly philanthropic in his opinion, if not imbued with the spirit of God." I am shocked at finding my Catholic prejudices leading me to call hypocrites all Protestants especially laymen who say such things.

Thurs., 25th   Omitted by the Editor.

Fri., 26th   Bishop Duggan says that Abp. Spalding gave the bishops meals a la Kentucky. A collection was taken at their parting : and expenses considered quite high. He found Bishop Lynch, the promoter, very shallow : and Abp. Purcell very indelicate in his praise of Abp. Spalding : and Abp. McClosky very prudent & gentlemanly, and Abp. Alemany quite posted about the Council of Trent. I gave the instruction on Church-History to the girls' school. Fr. Preston and I dined with the Dachauers' with whom we met Mrs. Martinez. The dinner was very good : I gave my idea about heaven or hell not being restricted to any locality but being several conditions of the soul. Mr. Dachauer agreed with me. Fr. Preston was half-shocked. I drank of the Trappists' and the Benedictines' 'liqueurs' : the latter was best. Dr. Freel & Fr. Reed of Brooklyn called to induce me to go to see   : I declined because I had to hear confessions & my curiosity too had been satiated. Bishop Duggan was sick. The Boone girls called : their brother 12 years old had run away, and lived in a hotel at Boston.

Sat., 27th   Omitted by the Editor.

Sun., 28th   23rd Sunday after Pentecost. I said 9 o'c. & sang $10\frac{1}{2}$

October   323

o'c. Masses : Fr. Preston preached on the gospel : showing the necessity of faith : and approving the exclusiveness of the church saying that : "Christ was, if you will, the first bigot." I gave instruction to the boys' S. School : and was present at the singing at it's conclusion. I asked difficult questions about the Incarnation of the larger girls. I went to hear Fr. Hecker's lecture on 'Protestantism & Catholicity compared in their civilising effects,' at St. Stephen's under the auspices of the SS. Union. An abridgement of it will be found in my next letter to the Catholic Standard. Fr. Preston said that he had $100 000 of deposits in the Chancery : Bish. Duggan has $15,000 and Abp. Kenrick of St. Louis $1,500,000. I got sick at the Morroghs of 26th St.

<u>Mon., 29th</u>   . . . .(Bishop Duggan and I) went to see B. Patrick of Manhattan College : to get brothers to take charge of a college in Chicago. We visited Mrs. Hassard of Fordham. I gave some of my radical views to the bishop about letting suspended priests get married. "He saw that I was of the advanced guard' in the army of progress : "he himself is a progressista." Dr. McGlynn dined with me : we walked to 70th St. and supped : and walked again to 40th St. & back. He has found contradictions in Miss Solomon's statements though he feels that their substance must be true.

<u>Tues., 30th</u>   Dr. McGlynn and I went to dine at Fr. Farrell's. We met there Fr. Fitzgerald, bishop-elect of Little Rock, 32 years of age, intelligent not talkative, whom Fr. Thos. Farrell congratulated for his staunch loyalty during the war : and Dr. Dunne, of Chicago, who said that 20 priests, earnest and advanced in their ideas, well banded together could put the Church on the right way of progress : Fr. Riordan, who answered a toast, with a nice but evidently learned by heart speech : and Fr. Ryan,

October 324

who gave out a string of conundrums that knew no end. Fr. Malone brings a warning from Dr. Keogh, confirmed by Bishop Conroy, that Frs. Quin and McNierney have accused Dr. McGlynn and me to all the bishops of seeking the overthrowal of the pope's temporal power.

<u>Wed., 31st</u>   I went to the Archbishop to urge the purchase of the ground on 2nd Ave. cor. of 20th St. He was satisfied that I would be well backed by Dr. McGlynn, Frs. Preston, Thos. Farrell & Dr. Morrogh. He asked time to decide : and said I might call on Saturday. In the evening I attended the altar-class and the literary-class and visited the Burtsells in 4th Ave. : where the Dr. came to converse with me. I pretended not to have noticed his passing me without speaking.

November

<u>Thurs., 1st</u>   I sang High-Mass. My mother came to see me : she had taken 14 days from Queenstown : and was sea-sick & arrived yesterday. She received many fine presents from her relatives in Ireland. I received two letters from Archbishop McCloskey at the same time. In one he says : 'After duly considering the matter of the proposed purchase on 2nd Ave. I have concluded that it would not be wise or prudent for me to assume so heavy a responsibility simultaneously with that already incurred by the authorised purchase in 37th St. Should there be any failure in this latter case, I would then be free to enter into the other project. However anxious we may be for the multiplication of churches, our zeal must be tempered with discretion : else grievous embarassments might ensue.' In the second he says : 'Since writing to you this morning I have been making a more thorough inspection corner of 2nd Ave. & 20th St., as well as of a large portion of the neighborhood. I am persuaded that no such desirable site for a church could be obtained, & if the property can be secured for the price named,

November   325

and you see your way to meet payment required, I would consent to the
purchase. Even if the erection of a church would have for a time to be
postponed, it would be well to make sure of the property." Sapientium
est mistare consilium. Drs. McGlynn, McSweeny & I went to sup at Dr.
Morrogh's. He was asleep, I fear, from having imbibed too much. . . .

Fri., 2nd   Omitted by the Editor.

Sat., 3rd   I went to the Jewish Synagogue in 19th St. near 5th Ave.:
the service commences at $8\frac{1}{2}$ o'c. and ends about 12 o'c. I arrived about
11 o'c. and was present at the singing of part of the Bible in Hebrew &
at the shutting up of the Law by the minister. The men are separated from
the women : these latter do not join in the service, the men all joined
in the singing now and then : on the men was a white scarf with blue stripes
near the borders, and the four corners of blue, according to the prescription
of the Bible : about three men made offerings to the minister. A Jew told
me that two thirds understood Hebrew. I don't believe it. No discourse
is given in this synagogue. The German Jews are the wealthiest and the
most intelligent : here were the Spanish and Portuguese Jews of this city.
Talking and laughing were common during the service. I visited Mrs.
Burtsell and confessed to Fr. Maguire, and made out from a letter in Spanish from P. Andreas de Rodas that he had borrowed Fr. C. Farrell's gold-
headed cane, without his knowledge : and was held in custody meanwhile in
Montreal : where he had gone to recognise the two thieves that robbed him
of his money, and from whom he got back his clothing and $600. I heard
$4\frac{1}{2}$ hours' confessions.

Sun., 4th   24th Sunday after Pentecost. I preached on the Gospel
taking the Exordium from Gough's lecture about the search of knowledge :
the body of it was to show how the note of unity facilitated our search

November 326

after faith : and concluded that God would save the truth and independence of the church even without the appendage of the temporal power. Fr. Preston spoke very strongly in favour of the Roman loan : considering it guaranteed by the pope as a christian no less than sovereign : and saying that any foreign government possessing Rome would have to pay this debt : but saying that he did not pretend to say that the temporal power was necessary to the church by any means : on which subject he let every one follow his own opinion. Mr. & Mrs. Dachauer & Mrs. Hassard dined with us. I spoke to the boys SS. : I told Mr. Griffin the superintendent that the Sunday School Union acted foolishly in going to 16th St. Church for their retreat : since this parish ignored their Union, and they insulted the Secular Clergy that had patronised them, to go to the Jesuits for direction and sanctification. I visited Mrs. & Miss Stella Jones at the 5th Ave. hotel : Miss Jones is to go to Mrs. Macaulay's at 253 Madison Ave. : she wishes to go to St. Stephen's. I heard Bishop O'Connor lecture on the "Disadvantages of the Catholic System'. I give a sketch in my letter to the Catholic Standard to which I need but add one useful remark of his : 'that the Catholic Church bears the marks of hard struggles through eighteen centuries. She is like a warrior scarred but rugged having signs of bravery compared to the gentleman of a drawing room who cares not for battle; the Sects fear warfare which destroys them, though they are braggarts before the battle. The Church is more modest. She has too the robes of many centuries through which she passed in her liturgy : and her language recalls that she had first to battle with the Roman empire." He has not good delivery : he spoke with the brogue : and read the lecture. He is not a shrewd observer : nor did he present his ideas with the best turn of language. I visited the Morroghs of 26th St. : and walked home with my mother and the McLaughlins,

November

who are buying a house on Duane St. near Broadway (26 ft by 80 ft.) for $25 000.00 where Mr. McLaughlin expects to have a liquor store to shut on week-days at 4 o'c. and entirely on Sundays. Another liquor-dealer made his fortune, next door.

Mon., 5th   Omitted by the Editor.

Tues., 6th   I voted the whole Republican ticket : at the polls a man who recognised me offered me the 'Regular Democratic ticket' ! I dined alone : and went to St. Joseph's and played billiards with Drs. Parsons & McSweeny & Fr. Nilan. Dr. McSweeny was too lazy to take out his naturalisation papers : the other two voted the Republican ticket. The Abp., so says Dr. McSweeny, suspected Dr. Brann of reviewing his own work in the N. Y. Tablet. I attended the meeting of the SS. Association : at which Mr. Moan asked me to shorten my remarks at the S. School, and thought that Church History was not understood by the boys. I told him that I alone intended to be judge of my subject : and recommended the Association to extend the time of Sunday School : which it did ¼ an hour.

Wed., 7th   Omitted by the Editor.

Thurs., 8th   Dr. Brann dined with me : Bishop Loughlin and Fr. Starrs spoke harshly of the Roman Students that wish the downfall of the temporal power. Fr. Starrs said Dr. McSweeny was slightly tinged with this idea : Dr. Parsons was openly denounced. Dr. Brann teaches Philosophy to the young ladies and sisters at the Visitation convent Brooklyn (about 60 in number) every Monday. Dr. Brann accepts my arguments, calls them logical, and says he dares not accept my conclusions. He could have, he says, as truthfully given in his 1st chapter of 'Curious Questions' a fine picture of the Age : but as he was to be radical in the middle of his book he thought well to be conservative in the beginning & end. Dr. McGlynn and I walked to 50th St.

November 328

and visited Fr. McMahon : a crabbed, spiteful man. We went to hear Fr.
Everett lecture on his pilgrimage to Jerusalem. He gave a minute description of the valley of Josephat, of the garden of Gethsemane, surrounded
by walls 12 ft. high : of the Dolorous way to Calvary : and the Holy
Sepulchre. The tomb is dark almost hidden by the lights of the chapel.
The place of crucifixion is in a dark place, lighted by vary-coloured
lamps. The Greeks were the most numerous pilgrims. 2000 families came
last year, with children from Candia : because they believe one pilgrimage
necessary if possible : 15 European pilgrims were present at Easter : Fr.
Everett was the only pilgrim from North America. This does not include
sight-seers. He found many dogs fighting together but useful as street-
cleaners and devourers of dead beasts. He spoke of the dress of the women,
as being of two sheets : and the face covered with thin dark veils, some
variegated as to screen the sores of small-pox and making themselves loath-
some. The Jewesses did not wear this veil. He saw three Jewish children
spit on the stone where Christ was said to have leaned when weak on the
way to Calvary. The Turkish soldiers never sneered at the devotions of
the Christians. He considered the Greeks as not praying but using only
external devotion, such as making 50 signs of the cross in a minute. The
Jews assemble to bewail over the loss of Jerusalem. The Armenians are a
grave set of Men. The Arabs are manly and feared. He hopes that the Turks
will be swept off the face of the earth. Their system of fatality prevents
progress : for they say they can't die as long as God wishes them to live.
Since the Crimean War, they respect the Christians. The tickets were $1
each : about 20 priests & Bishop Hennessy were present.

<u>Fri., 9th</u>   Bishop Bayley slept at our house and said Mass. He did
not ask for me when he came, but ordered a room to be prepared for himself,

November 329

though Fr. Preston was not home! Fr. Preston returned from Fordham, having been ill since Monday. Fr. Ferrall of St. Teresa's called, quite reestablished in health. Their choir costs $600 for McGrath the organist, $500 for Mr. Molini Tenor, $400 for Mrs.   Soprano, and $500 for Mrs. Colletti contralto : but at the concert Fr. Boyce had to pay them : the expenses were $400 : they realised about $1000. The Abp. expressed to Fr. Preston approval of the locality and cheapness of the property on 2nd Ave. : but sent me word not to collect till Fr. Larkin had a start : Fr. Larkin is timid, and troubles the Abp. who consequently is timid too. I visited Fr. Nilan : and met Fr. O'Reilly of Middletown who speaks of all the principal men in his vicinity as intimate friends of his, Democrats, Republicans, and Secessionists. He is a Republican. I met Fr. Farrell & Dr. McGlynn with Fr. McCarthy. Fr. Thos. Farrell was told a few days ago by the Abp. that the priests that gathered at his house had the reputation of being dissatisfied & rebellious as a group : and fame as well as the Abp. gave Fr. Farrell the credit of being the leader. Fr. Thos. Farrell maintained stoutly that they were earnest, religion loving, and whiskey-avoiding priests : and accused the Abp. of believing malicious people. Fr. Nilan found Fr. B. O'Reilly, Ex-Jesuit, to maintain that the 'Status Naturas Purse' was impossible : and the contreary could not be maintained!!! I heard confessions for $\frac{1}{2}$ hour : and read Griffith Guant $2\frac{1}{2}$ hours. Fr. Nilan told me that Fr.   an Italian priest at St. James' wrote to the Abp. stating that he would not remain in the uncertain position of an assistant; he would take a country-parish, but would prefer to be a professor in a seminary : if this arrangement could not be made, he would seek elsewhere for a position! The Abp. replied he could not make such an arrangement, and released him from his connection with New York.

November   330

Sat., 10th   Omitted by the Editor.

Sun., 11th   Omitted by the Editor.

Mon., 12th   I wrote to the Catholic Standard. Dr. McSweeny and I walked to see Fr. Nilan : whom we took in tow back to our house : where we dined. We went to St. Joseph's : where Dr. Parsons gave us an account of a serious dispute with the Abp. yesterday. The Abp. told him that he came with the design of giving a rebuke to Dr. Parsons : that he was imprudent in treating lightly vital Ecclesiastical subjects to the laity : that he had no right to have an opinion on any subject whatever, he being a young man : that he was a poor Catholic, having little faith : that he would prefer having no priest than a bad one in his diocese. Dr. Parsons asked the Abp. to appoint the age at which he would have a right to have an opinion : that he differed from his Superiors on vital Ecclesiastical subjects, which were free in the Church : that he could not deem the Abp. unjust in using his power : that to browbeat was not to convince. Fr. Farrell confirmed this account. A Fr. Wiseman who has lately left Louisville diocese was present and confirmed this account. Fr. Wiseman spoke ill of Bishop Lavialle, the smallest and pettiest. and most formal of Sulpicians : and Louisville is poorly provided with Catholic schools. Fr. Wiseman maintained that marriage by natural law was dissoluble!! and proved it by St. Paul's exception in favour of the Christian who had an infidel partner!!! He laughed at Abp. Spalding for holding the contrary!!! He applied to Abp. McCloskey for a place but was rejected! He goes now to apply in Albany! He was enthusiastic in his reception of me, though unknown to him : he knew Dr. Jas. Martin intimately, who was wretchedly off at the Seminary, hardly having food enough!

Tues., 13th   Omitted by the Editor.

November 331

<u>Wed., 14th</u>   I went to the Convent of Mercy to witness the reception
of Miss Mercy of Detroit a convert having a Protestant father, of Miss
of Cork who takes the name of Patricia, in religion : a
The ceremony consists in placing in their hands a candle in sign of the
new light of perfection that dawns in them. They were till then robed in
white : they put on the sisters' robe : and then first a cincture, saying
in Latin : "when thou wert young, thou didst gird thyself : but when thou
shalt be old, thou shalt stretch forth thy hands : another shall gird
thee. Joan. XXI.18." He then put the veil on them : using a formular of
words : and the cloak saying "Accipe stolam immortaletatis quam perdistam
per perdionem primi parentes etc." The Sisters prostrated themselves at
full length during a hymn, an ugly ceremony! though . . . . They were
then sprinkled with holy water by the Archbishop. They then made a reverence to and kissed the Mother Superior. The Archbishop addressed them,
reminding them that though they were to leave behind father, mother etc.
they were to be far happier than those who living in the world don't satiate themselves with their wealth, or their dissipation in pleasure. The
regularity of convent life apparently a burden would aid them to distribute their time for the glory of God and the good of their neighbour.
Their friends were to be the poor, and ignorant and sick. We had a neat
repast. The Cathedral priests were all present, besides Frs. Clowry and
Biretta. In the afternoon I visited Mrs. D'Enbranches and Mrs. O'Neil at
22 Union Square. Mrs. O'Neil spoke to me of Dr. Nugent, once my prefect
in Propaganda, whom she had met in St. John's New Brunswick, who was considered very polished and yet was thrown away in the midst of half wild
people. I promised Mrs. D'Enbranches the tickets for Mr. DeCordova's
lecture. Dr. McGlynn and I took two long walks. We agreed that Spirit-

November 332

ualism is not sinful in itself : and that we had a right to gain all the possible knowledge from spirits : that it was even lawful to deal with the devil. We doubted whether it would be an advantage to the refined church organisations of this country to accept Catholicism with all it's medieval and barbarous practises. I attended the Altar-class; finding great difficulty in making the boys acquire the right pronunciation of the Latin responses!!! Dr. McGlynn told me of Dr. Moore's impressions of Bishop Lynch : whom he considers selfish and lazy, who gives no account of the money collected at the North : has bought a house on speculation, instead of a church for his people : wishes to force Dr. Moore to give $4,400 the result of a fair for a parochial school, to be funded in an orphan asylum, a mile away from the designed location : and is never willing to take advice about his diocese : is disliked by clergy and laity.

Thurs., 15th .....Dr. McGlynn and Dr. Moore of Charleston called to see me. Dr. Moore maintains that the negroes are worse off than when slaves! He was vicar general of Bishop Lynch during his absence in Europe as ambassador of Jeff. Davis. Dr. Moore says his business was to obtain the interference of European governments to get better terms for the South when forced to give in. I attended the singing-class and called 'foolish, obstinate & pig-headed' three girls Kate Fox, Mary A. Parnell & because they would not sing when told to do so by Miss Waters and me.

Fri., 16th   Omitted by the Editor.

Sat., 17th   Omitted by the Editor.

Sun., 18th   I preached on the gospel (6th Sunday after Epiphany). I spoke at the boys' Sunday School. I attended Fr. Nilan's lecture on 'St. Vincent de Paul & his times' : a synopsis will be found in my letter to the Catholic Standard. Mr. Dachauer dined with us. I had a dispute with Fr. Preston on the Union of Church & State. I held that the State had no right to take cognizance of the revealed law, but of natural law and civil law and enactments. It has no more right to tell a man what God has revealed : than the Atlantic Cable Association. He thought heresy the greatest civil crime : and punishable with death in a country where all were Catholic.

Mon., 19th   Omitted by the Editor.

Tues., 20th   The Abolition-Roman priests met to organise an Ecclesiastical Society. Fr. Farrell, Dr. McGlynn & Fr. Nilan were appointed by the chairman Fr. Thos. McLoughlin to make a draft of a constitution. Only Fr. Hecker, besides the above-mentioned, will be asked to be present at it's formation. Fr. Thos. Farrell told the Abp. he was making a mistake to attack the young priests. The Abp. thought that it was good to check them and that Fr. Farrell treated them too kindly. Dr. McGlynn and I walked to Central park & back & again to 40th St. We talked of the state of the church : he gave me an account of his lecture on Godless versus Xtian Education : the idea 'was that God gave us our faculties to develop for God's Glory.'

Wed., 21st   Omitted by the Editor.
Thurs., 22nd   Omitted by the Editor.
Fri., 23rd   Omitted by the Editor.
Sat., 24th   Omitted by the Editor.
Sun., 25th   Omitted by the Editor.

Mon., 26th   I went to New Rochelle : where a number of priests gathered to celebrate Fr. Tom McLoughlin's 40th birthday. The dinner was good. Fr. Malone toasted Fr. McLoughlin : who toasted the Church for the next forty years : to which Dr. Parsons responded toasting the Pope. Dr.

November

McSweeny replied and asserted the temporal power to be hurtful to the Church : and many customs of the church to alienate intelligent people from her. This excited an animated discussion in which Fr. Venuta backed by Frs. Curran & McCarthy held this to imply heresy that the church was not infallible in it's discipline. I held that the church's discipline was not secured from error or imprudence : in matters of fact the church did err as in the case of condemnation of the opinion about the motion of the Sun, the existence of the Antipodes, the boundary of the two worlds. So it could err as to the best means of adapting itself to any age. The discipline of the church must adapt itself to various ages and countries. Hence now it ought to overthrow the temporal power 1. because the union of church and state entails on the church the abuse deserved by the state's control over the church. 2. because it prevents any but an Italian from being chosen pope. 3. because it prevents practically any but Italians from being sent as nuncios etc. 4. because it makes nuncios etc. agents of the kingdom not of the church; as Mgr. Bedini whose primary office was to compliment the president, and the secondary to visit the churches of the United States & Canada. 5. because it prevents Rome from keeping an agent in various countries, as in England and the United States : because he would not have the 1st diplomatic rank. 6. because it makes a great distinction in Rome between the clergy that has parochial duties, a respectable body in general : and the clergy that is attached to the temporal power, than which there is not a more selfish, intriguing or contemptible body of men : the 'cahiera' is synonymous to 'professional politicianism.' Fr. Venuta gave no reply to these remarks : but brought out the arguments for the necessity of the temporal power. I was backed by Drs. Parsons & McSweeny, Frs. Malone, McLoughlin, Fitzgerald, Donnelly; Fr. Boyce maintained neutrality. Fr.

November   335

Fitzgerald told me that Abp. Purcell gives dispensations ore tenuit which Benedict XIV declares invalid. There are five religious communities in that archdiocese, each one having a different county as it's limits. The Sisters of Mercy are known to specualte with Masses : in a few years they have made $70,000.

Tues., 27th   Omitted by the Editor.
Wed., 28th   Omitted by the Editor.
Thurs., 29th   I sang 9 o'c. Mass, this being Thanksgiving-day : offering it for the conversion of this country. I made a few remarks asserting "that God carved out this country on a gigantic scale, to prepare it for the gigantic moral growth of our people produced by our free government & it would be a great gain to have it's energy and ability directed to the propagation of the Truth." Our Catholic population needs to be taught the first page of the Patriot's catechism : the Irish-born consider themselves aliens, and in fact accustomed to rebel against the British government, they hardly recollect that they have another government over them. I dined at Fr. Thos. Farrell's where Drs. McGlynn & Parsons & Frs. Boyce & Nilan were. Fr. Farrell said that Fr. Mariani of Philadelphia excited the people's superstitions to believe in his miraculous power of curing women's diseases. Fr. Daly the Franciscan does the same. Dr. McGlynn, Fr. Nilan & I walked to Holy Cross. We talked over the power of dispensations of Abp. McCloskey in the impediments of marriage : and proved them to be in great measure invalid either because unless he is absent from town he has not the power to delegate to the vicar-general or other priests, or because he does not say in the dispensation that he gives it by the authority of the Holy See. Vide Gury. Pag. 602. Edit. Paris 1858. Fr. Nilan showed one dispensation granted last week without such form. Dr. McGlynn supped with me.

November   336

He had received an anonymous letter accusing Miss Kearney of imperious manners. He suspects Mrs. Darcy of intention to defraud St. Stephen's fair. I visited the Gallaghers, Decoppets & Miss Ann Burtsell in 32nd St.

Fri., 30th   Omitted by the Editor.

December

Sat., 1st   Omitted by the Editor.

Sun., 2nd   Omitted by the Editor.

Mon., 3rd   Omitted by the Editor.

Tues., 4th   Omitted by the Editor.

Wed., 5th   Omitted by the Editor.

Thurs., 6th   Omitted by the Editor.

Fri., 7th   I gave the instruction to the girls' school : heard their confessions & in the afternoon heard 1½ hour for the members of the sodality who made a 3 days' retreat under Fr. Preston : few of them come to me. I confessed to Fr. Maguire : and dined with him and my mother : to the latter I showed it to be our advantage if the Burtsells did not sell the property on Wall St. : for as long as it lasts, we have a fixed security for Aunt Eliza's share, which is due to us by her will after her brother and sisters' death and is now worth $60,000. Dr. McGlynn and I took a walk in the evening together.

Sat., 8th   Omitted by the Editor.

Sun., 9th   Omitted by the Editor.

Mon., 10th   I wrote to the Catholic Standard. Drs. McGlynn, McSweeny and I walked to St. Stephen's : where we lunched at the fair, met Drs. Moore & Brann, and all five supped at our house : where we discussed the temporal power and the Latin language of the Church : Drs. Moore & McSweeny and I went to the Sunday School Union : where Fr. Quin of St. Peter's spoke, saying that the young men had excluded from the Sunday School the old faithful men who formerly attended the Sunday Schools and assumed the responsibility of teaching the children in their stead. Dr. McSweeny told them that they were performing a charitable work and that he considered young men to be those who had mental energy and physical strength sufficient to carry out the purposes of the Union. The report spoke principally of the coloured children : for whom Sunday Schools are to be inaugurated. St. Stephen's registered number of children is 1250, 152 teachers : St. Peter's 800 : 25 teachers : St. James' 650 : Nativity 270 boys 335 girls, 75 teachers. St. Andrew's 208 boys : St. Patrick's 190 boys not under Christian brothers. St. Ann's 208 boys, 17 teachers always punctual : St. Teresa's 5.

Tues., 11th   Omitted by the Editor.

Wed., 12th   . . . .I heard Fr. O'Connor, S. J. lecture on Catholic Ceremonial at Cooper Institute. He said "that the rites are the universal language, known to all men, in which to show honour to God. As the word 'home' by conventional acceptation contains sentiments most endearing; so the sign of the cross, the blessing of holy water, the incensing of the altar recall to the mind of the faithful the mystery of the Incarnation, purity of heart, and prayer to God. He thought that it was good to use Latin in the Liturgy. The Apostles he said used three languages. "The Hebrew and it's offspring the Semitic dialects in homage to Jehovah's selection of the Jewish people : the Greek, the language of the learned of the day : & the Latin, the language of the dominant race : Since then only the Armenian has been adopted and probably after a time of Schism to readmit the Armenians : the Coptic for the same object : and the Slavonic was admitted by the weak-minded John, the pope that deserved to be called Popess Joan; who acceded to the request of Sts. Cyril and Methodius. He

December   338

would nôt use the usual argument that the faithful have the translation :
he did not at all consider it necessary, or useful that the faithful should
recite the same prayers as the priest, for the part of the priest is to
sacrifice : the part of the faithful is to adore and to pray to Jesus there
present : and it is better for them to have other prayers according to their
dispositions of joy or melancholy from trouble. In Protestant service the
people must follow in prayer the leader's sentiments and have no opportunity
to pray according to their present dispositions. It was proper to preserve
the Latin, because the Clergy must have a language in which to communicate
with each other throughout the world : to preserve unity of faith. The
clergy then can teach more easily the precise doctrines of the Church. The
faithful love the symbols of the Church, as the soldier loves the flag.
Both have a conventional meaning which excites in the heart sentiments of
enthusiasm : and as the soldier cares not for the price of the stuff of
the flag per yard, so the Christian cares not whether the cross or picture
be of the most refined workmanship." He is a poor lecturer. He told two
anecdotes one of an old man who asked how the Eucharist could contain Jesus
Christ, if the bread had been mixed with arsenic, replied that the arsenic
would not change and could still poison : and of a woman who asked why the
priest didn't give the blood of J. C. asked if there ever was a human body
without blood? These had no direct connexion with the lecture. About 700
persons were present.

Thurs., 13th   Omitted by the Editor.
Fri., 14th   Omitted by the Editor.
Sat., 15th   Omitted by the Editor.
Sun., 16th   Omitted by the Editor.
Mon., 17th   I wrote to the Catholic Standard & to Fr. Cannon & to

December

Fr. Danielou. Dr. McGlynn and I walked to Central Park. He promised to give Dr. Moore a collection for his schools, though he protests against having schools of his own, deeming churches more necessary! Bishop Lynch took $5000.00 made in a fair for a school, to be used in building an orphan asylum!! I went to see Zampa played at Winter Garden. The plot is that Zampa a pirate deceives a young girl : then attempts to marry Camilla her sister : but in a drunken spell promises to marry a marble statue representing her sister on whose finger he places a ring : which he cannot withdraw. His brother is his rival for Camilla's hand : whom he marries, but he is suddenly spirited away by the marble statue : and his brother marries Camilla. . . .I was mortified at a boy challenging a dollar bill of mine as bad & at my unneat appearance.

<u>Tues., 18th</u>   Omitted by the Editor.

<u>Wed., 19th</u>   For the first time I borrowed books at the Astor Library, Bailey's Liturgy, which shows the antiquity of the prayers of the Anglican, liturgy. I couldn't find Mont's 'Horae liturgicae'. I looked at the Mozarabic liturgy : all to get ideas for my essay on the Liturgical languages of the Church. I visited the McLaughlins : and Dr. Morrogh & my mother. I attended the altar and literary classes.

<u>Thurs., 20th</u>   Omitted by the Editor.

<u>Fri., 21st</u>   I heard the girls' confessions : gave instruction to the girls' school : and heard 1½ hours' confessions in the evening. Drs. McGlynn and Moore dined with us. The latter asserted that Thad. Stevens maintained that according to the constitution of the United States the leaders of the rebellion cannot be proved guilty of treason. I denied the assertion. We found that Stevens says that as a jury would have to try them at Richmond: and no jury there would find them guilty : so they cannot be convicted : but

December

yet if the jury were impartial, it would find them guilty. We visited Dietrich's Silver-ware Store : he had two Sanctuary lamps for sale at $58 : candlesticks at $7. We visited Sturgis & got gilt-candlesticks, 32 inches, for $13 each : 18 inches for $9 each. At Bensiger's we bought a sanctuary lamp for $21. We found no good vestments at either place but at Berger's there were some good chasubles at $150 to $200 each.

Sat., 22nd   Omitted by the Editor.

Sun., 23rd   Omitted by the Editor.

Mon., 24th   Omitted by the Editor.

Tues., 25th   Christmas-Day. I celebrated High-Mass at $5\frac{1}{2}$ o'c. A.M. the children singing. I preached the sermon I gave two Sundays ago at High-Mass : because I had another congregation entirely. I sang $10\frac{1}{2}$ o'c. Mass : Dr. Moore and Mr. Jardine S.J. as deacon and subdeacon. Dr. Moore preached on the gospel of the 1st Mass. He showed how man had after his fall into sin a great fear of God. Our first parents feared the sight of God, and hid themselves in the groves. The Jewish people at Mt. Sinah asked that God should not speak to them lest they should die. Jacob after his vision of God (Genes. XXVIII.17) says : How terrible is this place! and Genes. XXXII.30 "I have seen God face to face and my life has been saved!" Samson's parents (Judges XIII) "We shall certainly die because we have seen God." Thus though they could be saved by faith in the future Redeemer, men feared more than loved God. But after this day, men have learned to trust in God's mercy. He comes poor, suffering and humble into the world, 1. to give us confidence in him, lest we should fear his Majesty. 2. to teach us not to love this world's riches, to bear suffering and not to fear ignominy. Fr. Preston was too hoarse to take part in the ceremonies! We had a grand dinner, but very dull : the Cornells, Hassards, Dachauers, Dr. Bayard were

December 341

present besides four clergymen. Drs. Moore, McGlynn & I walked to the Central Park : discussing the inspiration of Scripture. We visited Fr. Nilan : and gave out our usual radical views. I vomited at his house. Dr. McGlynn had grand orchestral Mass. Mme. Gazzaniga sung at our church : Miss Wells returned to our choir. Dr. Bayard advises no stimulants till one is 70 years old : Dr. Moore states that Bishop Lynch and Dr. Corcoran ridicule the inspiration of the Canticle of Canticles : and Bish. Lynch believes that the loss of the temporal power will do no harm. Abp. Kenrick didn't approve of new definitions of faith : and to Passaglia would not admit the infallibility of the pope in interpreting Scripture, especially Gen.III.

Wed., 26th   Omitted by the Editor.
Thurs., 27th   Omitted by the Editor.
Fri., 28th   Omitted by the Editor.
Sat., 29th   I heard 4½ hours' confessions.
Sun., 30th   Omitted by the Editor.
Mon., 31st   I wrote to the Catholic Standard. Fr. Hecker called

in search of Dr. Keogh. He thinks that the Jesuits have lost the great spirit that gave them life formerly : he thinks St. Ignatius wanted an army to hurl against Protestants : and asked for corpses not men, machines not reasoning beings : hence blind obedience was his highest quality : good for soldiers! He also denounces that system of direction which takes away from the faithful the use of their reason : and teaches them to lean entirely on their director. He wants them to judge for themselves whether there is danger in going to theatres, dancing etc. He considers Luther's Psychological history a revelation of the worst traits in a man. Dr. Corrigan of Seton Hall visited me : he is very shy. I visited a Mrs. Webster in 48th St.

1867

January

Tues., 1st   I sang 9 o'c. Mass & visited the Archbishop : with whom I met Mr. Theband, Mr. Frith, Mr. Girand a seminarian, Fr. J. Orsenigo. I visited the Decoppets, Gallaghers, and Miss Ann Burtsell with whom I saw Mr. Richard, and Goulay. I visited Dr. McGlynn with whom I found the German George Keck : and Fr. Duranquet. Dr. McGlynn and I visited my mother, Dr. Morrogh & Dr. Keogh : the two latter having signs of imbibing. I received the altar & literary classes : giving them cakes, candies & fruit about $6 worth.

Wed., 2nd   Omitted by the Editor.

Thurs., 3rd   Bishop Bayley said mass in our church & gave an account of his expulsion from Amherst college, for rebellion in school against the professor of Greek who detained the boys after dinner-hour. Dr. McSweeny and I walked to Fr. Nilan's : where we dined. We discussed the extent of knowledge of Christ's human intellect : the doubtful veracity of the history of Adam & Eve & the serpent : Fr. Nilan thought St. Paul's words 'You are the body of Christ' parallel with 'This is my body.' I showed the contrary because of the different pronouns 'you' & 'this' which make a great difference. I gave a reception to the singing-class : at which we had Miss Waters to play and the children to sing : I gave them $5 worth of eatables.

Fri., 4th   Omitted by the Editor.

Sat., 5th   Omitted by the Editor.

Sun., 6th   I said 9 o'c. Mass. Fr. Lovejoy of Halifax sang mass. Fr. Preston preached on the good use of Time. In the world, he said, there was a constant struggle between life and death. Every day separates us from a friend. The love of God, which is the life of the soul, and sin, it's death, struggle for it's possession! How ungrateful it is in men to reserve to the honour of God the last hours of an enfeebled old age! In the boys' SS. we had a distribution of cakes, candies, apples, pictures, books : bought by the S. S. Association. Miss Waters played the piano, and the singing class was present. Dr. McSweeny and I went to the Christian Union meeting at the M. E. Church Cor. 22nd St. & 4th Ave. Dr. McClintock thought we could have Christian Unity not through unity of form but of faith in Christ. Different forms are suited to different tastes. Dr. Adams said that the words of Christ "Lo! I am with you all days to the consummation of the world" signified a personal union : which St. Paul felt when before the tyrant he said : Christ Jesus strengtheneth. Henry Martin the missionary felt the presence of Christ, when he died in the East, extending his Kingdom. He knew a little boy who speechless pointed to his hands & feet to signify that he placed his confidence in Christ crucified! This personal presence of Christ in all denominations was the true source of Christian Unity. Dr. Dowling, Baptist, argreed with the coloured preacher who said that Christianity was like a wheel : of which the hub is Christ, the spokes the various denominations, which were nearer to each other the more they approached Christ, as the spokes approach the hub. He wished the unity of the marble in which are variegated veins, but the substance is one : not the unity of compression, as that of sticks and stones, and dirt, by frozen water. I visited the Morroghs of 26th St. : with whom I met the Belchers, my mother & P. Morrogh. I argued against the use of Latin in the Liturgy to the perfect satisfaction of the Protestant Belchers and to the surprise of the others. P. Morrogh has taken up

January 344

some foolish ideas against prayer-books and in favour of Methodistical groanings!

Mon., 7th   Omitted by the Editor.

Tues., 8th   A meeting of the Ecclesiastical Society was called; but a quorum was not present at St. Joseph's : Drs. McGlynn, Moore & I dined with Fr. Farrell. The board of Managers of the Male Orphan Asylum rejected on Sunday a proposal to sell the orphan asylum. The 8 lots on 5th Ave. : are estimated at $450 000. The new female orphan asylum is to cost $225,000; they have on hand 119,000 : a Mr. Boland left a bequest to the orphan asylum of $90 000 : for a farm. The Protectory had a farm of 114, acres for $40000 : on which is a building for 400 boys at $50 000. The Abp. thought the Legislature would not permit the sale : but it is in the interest of the city to sell to get the taxes. We walked to Central Park to see the skaters : and took coffee etc. at the casino. At a sick-call I met a Dr. McQueone, who had heard Card. Mezzfacti answer a Welshman in Welsh though he had but once spoken it : and had not seen a Welshbook for many years. He took two weeks to learn a language : a faculty he called 'vacita.' The Doctor says that very many lunatics are children of cousins. In Rome he visited the lunatic asylum, where he saw many priests. One he guessed was there for impurity! This the Doctor expressed by pantomine. He thought that many priests, not the best, gained the best positions in Rome. He was in Rome twice.

Wed., 9th   Dr. Moore called, and endorsed my essay on the Liturgical languages of the church : wishing me to publish it. With Fr. Preston I had a sharp debate on the infallibility of the pope. I maintained that the condemnation of Pope Honorius in the 6th general council proved that the general idea of the bishops was that the pope could err in matters of faith,

January 345

though they erred in asserting the fact that Honorius did teach error. Mrs. Hassard dined with us : but would not speak to Mr. William Preston!! I visited Mrs. Webster, and saw Mr. Webster a cashier of the   Bank : who says that he caused the fall of a priest, both skating in Central park. I attended the altar-class : and visited a performance of Toodles by Fr. O'Hare's 'Madonna Society' of 40 members : yet they used Rob. Burns, J. McCabe, and J. Burke for the principal characters! Mr. Witcher called and told us that when he went to the funeral of his sister-in-law in the church of Utica, of which he had been Protestant rector, the present rector sent him a note "forbidding him the entrance to the holy house of God". Mr. Witcher went and afterwards made this letter known to the Vestry : the congregation was divided, many being indignant at such an action. Bishop Coxe also at Fire Island asked the hotel-keeper to force Mr. Berrian because a Papist, to give up his place at the head of the dinner table!

Thurs., 10th   Omitted by the Editor.
Fri., 11th   Omitted by the Editor.
Sat., 12th   Omitted by the Editor.
Sun., 13th   Omitted by the Editor.
Mon., 14th   I delivered an address before the S. School Union : giving figures to show that we had church room for 160 000 Catholics, which we have 600 000 in the city; hence all the clergy's exertions are to build churches not schools : hence the great need of Sunday schools. The teachers here are an academy in which to learn how to attend to the children. They must instruct themselves in Christian doctrine : and before going to S. School read an explanation of the truth inculcated in the lesson of their class, in order to give the explanation to the children. In our best parish-schools not more than one third of the children of the

January 346

parish are present. Fr. Bodfish endorsed my address. Fr. Griffin gave two startling facts for the consideration of the young men : 1st. that 3000 children gathered yesterday at St. Stephen's; 2nd. the discovery by Fr. Duranquet of two tenement houses holding 30 & 20 families (coloured) : 6 of which went to church on Sunday : none of them had been baptised.

Tues., 15th   I read my essay on "Liturgical languages" before the Ecclesiastical Society : which almost unanimously (except Fr. McCarthy) requested me to publish. Fr. Farrell solved the moral case : which was that Benjamin a Jew married a Jewess : and becoming a Catholic resolved to take another wife, because the Jewess would not turn Catholic. Fr. Thos. Farrell approved of his doing so. Dr. McGlynn and I dined together: and went to the Passionist Monastery of W. Hoboken to ask Fr.   , to allow Fr. Gallagher to make a two weeks' retreat at the Monastery : he consented if Fr. Gallagher would follow the rules of the house. He stated that the building, quite a solid one, cost $60 000 and that they have not many subjects. The novitiate is in Pittsburgh : the Philosophy class of six students in Dunkirk, where there are six fathers : and the Theology class at W. Hoboken with six students and eight fathers. In Italy many Passionists are secularised. I visited the Garricks : with the children I played a newly introduced game; Mrs. Garrick's father 75 years old is sick : her mother died a few weeks ago 69 years of age.

Wed., 16th   I visited Mr. Joseph O'Brien about 29 Wall St. to get him to inquire about the property Cor. 26th St. & 2nd Ave. : on which would be erected a private residence and for some time a garden. He understood my object. I saw Mr. Barnard who told me that the seven lots Cor. 23rd St. & 1st Ave. could probably be had by May for $40000; the present lessee pays since 1858 $1300 a year. The property is 75 per 94 on 1st

January

Ave. besides 94 by 98 attached to it on 23rd St. Mr. Barnard says old Styvesant will advise his son to build private residences : hence is the hope of our getting it. I visited Dr. McSweeny : to whom the oculist Dr. Noges says that he had had a ____ in his left eye since his birth: which makes him give the oval instead of the circular form to objects. His right eye is being cured from the cold. We took a walk to 23rd St. and agreed that we could believe Christ's humanity inferior to that of other great men. I stopped at the McKnights & saw their mother. I attended the altar and literary classes.

Thurs., 17th   Omitted by the Editor.

Fri., 18th   I gave instruction to the girls' school on the Iconoclasts and the 'temporal power'. Dr. McSweeny told a couple to live together though the woman had married long before to a man, who three days' after said he had only done so to satisfy his desires, and neither thought the marriage to be valid because performed before a protestant minister. Drs. McGlynn, Moore & I approved of his course. Fr. Robert Seton is now Monsignor! on his way home! Peter Burtsell called to see me : he has never received pay at the Surrogate's. He is quite self-complacent & thinks every word of his oracular : he has brains but no great power of conversation. I heard 1¼ hours confessions.

Sat., 19th   Omitted by the Editor.

Sun., 20th   Omitted by the Editor.

Mon., 21st   Omitted by the Editor.

Tues., 22nd   Dr. McSweeny showed me a letter from Card. Barnabo in which he deplores the scarcity of priests and says : 'Io farò quanto è in me per rimediare a questo difetto', and hopes the cathedral will rise from it's ashes with greater glory. Edward McSweeny writes that Bishop Lamy

January

told the pope that "he would not send the decrees of the Baltimore council to the palace, but would deliver them into his own hands, according to orders received." Dr. McSweeny says that Fr. McNierney expressed sorrow that Dr. McGlynn, Parsons, Fr. Nilan & I think him unfit for his position. He thinks Dr. McGlynn has great abilities : but thinks nothing of Nilan, Lalor Burtsell or Parsons : whom he knew as boys. The Abp. gave a decisive opinion that the ladies wear silk stockings in winter and don't feel cold! . . . .

Wed., 23rd   Dr. McGlynn and I walked to the Central Park. Fr. McEvoy had told him that Fr. Starrs' had the Doctor removed from St. Ann's in 1862, because he had gone to Europe without permission, merely announcing that he was going! and called his brother a corner-boy, implying that he died through drink! Fr. McEvoy also accused Fr. Dillon C.S.C. of keeping money, which had been given him for Fr. McEvoy's brother in the army : from which he absented himself when on the field of battle! Fr. Larkin had said Dr. McGlynn's lecture at his church to run in a circle! Fr. McEvoy accused the cook there of stealing and having strangers fed at their expense : and her daughter's washing also. We agreed that the story of Eve's creation as an afterthought to keep Adam company is ridiculous! and that in the primitive Church the material integrity of confession was not much prized : and that in our circumstances, a priest could validly absolve a whole church full of people, by exciting them to outward confession of guilt in general! it is absurd for a priest to be listening for five hours to the tomfooleries of servant-girls! If anyone wishes special advice, let him confess that special sin privately! We met a Mr. Guiard son of the Brasilian consul, who, brainless, stuck to us till we changed our route to rid ourselves of him! I attended the altar and literary classes.

January 349

Thurs., 24th   Omitted by the Editor.

Fri., 25th   I heard the girls' confessions and gave the instruction on the Schism of Photius to the day-school. Fr. Nilan and I took a walk and at last ended in a Russian bath in 27th St. : We discussed the Inspiration of Scripture, which Fr. Nilan considers inspired as Dante's Divina Commedia etc. I have, since reading Colenzo, lost the idea of inspiration generally received and doubt the authenticity of Genesis. All the inspiration to be found is the impulse to write for the sanctification of others and preservation from positive error in maxims of faith and morals, when these are the direct object of the author : this second part being about the same as the infallibility of the Church. The Church practically depreciates the Scriptures : and wisely since much of them is unto destruction rather than unto edification. Who can imagine that God Exd. XIII commanded a slave's ears to be bored and him to be kept in perpetual slavery because he refuses to purchase his liberty when unable to obtain the liberty of his wife and children, when God had decreed : 'They shall be two in one flesh'!? We need a revision of the fundamental principles of our Theology: and I am commencing again 'ab ovo' my Theological studies : which were narrowed down by Roman prejudices. I read my essay on Liturgical languages to Frs. Hecker and Young who approved of it : and wish it to be published in the Catholic World : in such a tone as to be a wedge for the change of language in the Liturgy : though now only asking for the adoption of the vernacular in voluntary devotions. Fr. Young has designed a congregational form of service to be used in Lent : in which all the prayers are in English and the hymns to be sung by the whole congregation before and after the Sermon : he instructs the choir, the students, and the Sodality, hoping that the rest of the congregation will be enabled to chime in afterwards.

January 350

I heard 3/4 of an hour's confessions. Bishop Demers came to ask Fr. Hecker for a collection : he showed him Shantyopolis as a reason for refusing.

<u>Sat., 26th</u>   Dr. McSweeny and I took a walk together and called at the Calvary Cemetery office : where Mr. Carolin told me that in one year 13 170 burials took place in Calvary. Of these little over 7000 were children. All above 12 yrs. pay $7 for the interment : between 7 & 12 $5; those under 7 $3. About 3500 burials were gratuitous. About 2,270 bought ground. One grave costs $10. A plot 16 ft. per 10 ft. is $300 : 8 ft. per 8 ft. 75; 6 ft. per 8 ft. 50$: The charge for interment is not included in the cost of the ground. Formerly by contract the Catholics dying at the Alms house were buried in Calvary for $800 : within one year the city separated a patch of ground for the Catholics, which was consecrated by Abp. McCloskey. There are now 75 acres : of which 22 acres were purchased within two years : and their charter authorises them to purchase 75 more in Queens Co. Germans frequently apply for free burials : sometimes the undertakers cheat and keep the money for the grave. Sometimes German protestants have thus been buried. Mr. Carolin complained that many Catholics take the body to the receiving vault in Calvary; even buy graves there to have the suffrages of the Church : and then take the bodies to Greenwood. Thus the law of Abp. Hughes is justly eluded! What right had he to make a monopoly of Calvary! or why should a man be kept in purgatory, because his relatives don't choose to bury him in consecrated ground! especially when the relatives are Protestant. About 20 burials take place per year in St. Patrick's and 11th St. cemeteries : some from Brooklyn and Williamsburgh are buried in Calvary. I heard 4 hours' confessions. We took a look at the Cathedral of which the building is advancing slowly. $33,000 are to be the cost of the roofing and plastering. It was to be ready for roofing

January   351

by the 15th of February : and the slating would take 21 days, but in winter no one will bind himself to penalties for non fulfilment of building contracts. I made a bet of $100 with Dr. McSweeny that Mass would not be said there before Pentecost.

Sun., 27th   Omitted by the Editor.

Mon., 28th   Omitted by the Editor.

Tues., 29th   Omitted by the Editor.

Wed., 30th   Dr. McSweeny and I examined the report of Calvary Cemetery : the gross receipts are over $91 000 : the utmost expenditures are $63 000. We and Dr. McGlynn walked to Central Park. I attended the altar and literary classes.

Thurs., 31st   Omitted by the Editor.

February

Fri., 1st   Omitted by the Editor.

Sat., 2nd   Omitted by the Editor.

Sun., 3rd   Omitted by the Editor.

Mon., 4th   I copied marriage & baptisimal records at the Chancery Office : & wrote to the Catholic Standard. Fr. Farrell & I went to the Emigrants' Savings' bank and learned from the comptroller Mr. Ledwith that the Bank is called upon by depositors on account of 'hard times' among the poor : and that it would not lend more than $50,000 on $100000 worth of property. I attended the girls' rehearsal for the exhibition.

Tues., 5th   I attended the Ecclesiastical Society. Dr. McGlynn gave out some thoughts on the Incarnation : which I transcribe elsewhere. Fr. McLaughlin decided that a woman married to a man, who had sought to seduce her, and was married to her before a protestant minister, merely to gratify his criminal desire, as he declared a few days after marriage when he left

February

her, and continues to declare many years afterwards, saying that he never intended to marry her, could remarry again with a safe conscience in another marriage which she contracted, considering the first to be invalid. The Society agreed with him. Dr. McGlynn and I lunched together & walked to Fr. Nilan's : where we discussed the correspondence about Dr. Brann's lecture's prohibition by Bishop Bayley. Bishop Bayley told me that he had the suspension made out to be sent in case Dr. Brann delivered the lecture. Dr. Brann is a fool! though Bishop Bayley had no right to prohibit his lecture! Bishop Demers called at Dr. McGlynn's and annoyed us by the history of Vancouver's island. He receives $660 from St. Francis Xavier's and $240 from Nativity. I attended the Sunday School Association : where we discussed the utility of Tracts as distributed to the boys. I visited the Waters, to engage Emilia for a tableau in our exhibition. I met Messrs. McCahill and O'Toole there : the latter seemed to be on very intimate terms there and I guess will run away with one of the young ladies.

Wed., 6th   Omitted by the Editor.
Thurs., 7th   Omitted by the Editor.
Fri., 8th   Omitted by the Editor.
Sat., 9th   Omitted by the Editor.
Sun., 10th   I preached on the Resemblance of the Church to the Incarnation in the union of the divine and human elements : my sermon was principally grounded on our ideas of Christ's human nature, well exposed by Dr. McGlynn before the Ecclesiastical Society. Fr. Preston told me that it was the most original and on the whole the best sermon I had ever preached. I spoke to the boys' S. school on the heresy of Berengarius, the deposing power of the popes, and the bad popes. I visited the girls' S. School. . . .
Mon., 11th   Omitted by the Editor.

February

Tues., 12th   I received a note from the Archbishop to this effect. "Rev. dear Sir, I write to-day that you need not give yourself any further trouble in the matter of seeking to secure a lot or lots for church building purposes. With best wishes, I remain, very sincerely yours in Xt. John Abp. of New York." I showed it to Dr. McGlynn. I take it quite coolly : but cannot guess the real motive of such an unexpected communication.

Wed., 13th   Omitted by the Editor.

Thurs., 14th   I despatched my letter to the Archbishop. Bishop Bayley said Mass at our house. Bishop Bayley said before several priests & Fr. Kearney that the bishops had to put down the Romans, otherwise the Romans would put down the bishop. He is particularly denunciatory of Drs. Brann and Parsons : with whom the other Romans have little or no sympathy. With me, he acts pleasantly. Till a short time ago, he thought me quite a conservative. Dr. Parsons called in to see me for a few moments. I gave the programme for the exhibition to be printed by Mr. Coddington. I assisted at the girls' preparation for the exhibition.

Fri., 15th   ....I received an answer from Abp. McCloskey to this effect. Rev. dear Sir, I am quite willing to acquaint you with the reasons which induced me to come, not without reluctance, to the conclusion which was expressed in my brief note. I shall be happy also to receive any explanations you may wish to make. If you call either on Monday or Tuesday morning before 10 o'clock you will find me at home & at your service. Very sincerely yours in Xt. John Abp. of New York" dated 15th Feb./67. We changed our dinner hour to 5 o'c. I heard one hour's confessions : and then assisted at the boys' rehearsal for the exhibition. I went to see Dr. McGlynn but did not find him at home. I wrote to Dr. Keogh and Fr. J. O'Connor inquiring whether Excelsior was known : news to be telegraphed.

February 354

<u>Sat., 16th</u>   I visited Dr. McGlynn : though it rained we walked to Fr. Nilan's, but he was not at home. We discussed the probable motives of Abp. McCloskey's last determination : so that I might be prepared to give the necessary explanations. I hit upon Excelsior's letters : Dr. McGlynn thought it would be the financial difficulty : or Dr. Parsons' compromising us in his difficulty. Of course in this doubt, I am unprepared to answer objections. I heard confessions for five hours : I received a telegram from Dr. Keogh stating that Fr. McConomy had told Fr. McNeirney that he thought I was Excelsior : but nothing authentic was known:

<u>Sun., 17th</u>   Omitted by the Editor.

<u>Mon., 18th</u>   I wrote very early to the Catholic Standard : after which I received two letters from Dr. Keogh with a letter to him from Fr. McConomy showing that the latter had told Fr. McNierney in Baltimore that the general impression was that I was Excelsior. Dr. Keogh states that Abp. McCloskey complained of me as correspondent to Rev. M. O'Connor S. J. at Baltimore, because I published private talk of his to the clergy at the retreat : Fr. McNierney told Fr. McConomy that the Abp. was annoyed at some things published by Excelsior. Fr. McConomy did not remember on what authority he told Fr. McNierney but said that it was the general impression that Dr. Burtsell was Excelsior. Dr. Keogh and Fr. Jas. O'Connor advise Excelsior to continue his attractive correspondence, though without treading on +J. Abp. of N. Y.'s corns for some time at least, though in this he is to use his own judgement. I went to the Abp. at $9\frac{1}{2}$ o'c. He said that he thought I would have guessed the motive of his determination, but as I had not, he desired to tell me that he had taken a great interest in me personally; he had known my family well from his earliest days, and had

esteemed them very highly; I belonged to one of the old New York first Catholic families; I was a New Yorker, and he had thought me to be a good, zealous priest on whose discretion he could safely rely : but this opinion had been changed by his discovery that I had taken upon myself the office of Inquisitor general of his diocese, giving to the Catholic papers details that were secret, thus publishing his discourse to the clergy after the retreat, giving the news that the Capuchins were to erect a church, which I had learned from a private conversation with him, though I might have learned this news elsewhere; and denouncing the agent of the papel loan, thus throwing discredit on the agent of the agents of the papel loan, who had been recommended to the bishops of this country by the nuncio of Paris, and thus both our superiors were aspersed by my denunciation : and when he gave an explanation, I did not withdraw my protest. These reasons had persuaded him that I had not sufficient discretion for him to trust me. He would have wished to give me one of the highest positions in his diocese; he had intended to make me pastor of the new parish, as it would be unfair to allow another to reap the fruit of my labours : he understood of course that he was not inflicting a penalty on me in stopping my project, since this was a great burden : but that he had come to a fixed decision about my indiscretion. I told him that I was unprepared to answer him : I supposed he had sufficient proof on which to found his assertion that I had communicated these pieces of information to the papers : As he seemed to charge me with what he seemed to deem a criminal correspondence, I was not willing to criminate myself or any one friendly to me by affirmation or denial. He replied that he did not mean to charge me with a criminal correspondence : he did not doubt my good intentions; he believed that I had done it for a good purpose : nor did he think that my conscience accused

February 356

me of any impropriety. He had sufficient grounds to consider Excelsior and Dr. Burtsell one and the same person : this was the general impression in Philadelphia : He had been advised to put a stop to the correspondence : he had prevented strictures from being made on it in the N. Y. Tablet : he had kept his own decision to himself. He thought the correspondence might have done great mischief, and has done mischief; but no good has come from it, though I might have expected it to do good. He remembered what Abp. Kenrick had told him, when perhaps he was a younger priest than I am now, about writing in papers, he feared that he would fall into a difficulty! This had been my case : though I was of course free to write in the newspapers, if I thought fit to do so. I replied that in any thing of mine printed in the newspapers, I had never wished to give private conversations, but facts spoken of by many; that I never was anxious to figure in the papers, since only once did I put my initials to an article 'on Anglicanism' because the editor wished to make me responsible for it : at other times I have appeared under a 'nom de plume' : I never wrote any correspondence, without being directly asked to do so; my principal object in accepting any thing of the kind was to supply a defect, incurred by my education in Rome, in my knowledge of the English language. He laughed at this idea, remarking that I should not have chosed as my subject for experiments, his diocese : and that he would have preferred to see me write over my own name. I called his attention to the fact that he has overrated my control over the correspondence to the Catholic papers : that I was not responsible for much that he attributed to me : and that I was anxious that he should not consider as mine opinions with which I had no sympathy, or make me responsible for the doings of persons, with whom I had never any sympathy, though they might have used my name in conversation or writing; (I alluded to Dr.

Parsons); I had uniformly used my influence lest any friend of mine or any person that asked my advice should say or write anything dis-respectful to the Archbishop. I felt that it was not right for me to be on disagreeable terms with my bishop, because this would lessen my influence for good : nor should I do this to obtain any good : since to do one good, I would disable myself from exerting myself to obtain a good equally important. He said that he understood what I meant : He knew that I was the Philadelphia Excelsior : He himself did not think that I was the Baltimore Excelsior, though that was the general impression : yet their news was ground in the same mill, and had the same source : that I had liberty to give in my own circle my ideas of the temporal power and such subjects; that I should not publish them to the laity : and that he was anxious to be on cordial terms with his priests. On the subject of the 2nd Ave. property he had given his decision and did not wish to recall it. I asked him to give the project over to some other priest, to whom I promised to give all my information : as I had not the power to change his decision, and it is really unimportant whether the property is acquired through me : that I was not ambitious of being pastor; I hoped that I would be able to remove his impression of me, that my influence for good may be lessened : and I should consider his advice as a guide, which I should be glad to follow : and I hoped that he would continue the project, when I should send him more papers concerning the terms of the property. He showed unwillingness to give the project to any one else : hoped that I would give him proof that I was not so indiscreet as he had concluded I was; and that he would let me know, if he wished me to take any more active step to secure the property. I visited Dr. McGlynn : we walked to 90th St. in Central Park, discussing my interview with the Archbishop. My calm conclusion is that I can do no good by maintaining an attitude apparently hostile to the Archbishop : it prevents my doing good. I shall be honest; I shall not shut my eyes to facts : but I shall not do what will lessen my influence for good. Mr. & Mrs. Hassard dined with us : I attended the girls' rehearsal for the exhibition and excluded the tableau in which boys and girls mingle.

I have learned this day to hold Abp. McCloskey in contempt : he never suggested to me a spiritual motive for my future conduct : he sought to bribe me by half-promise of a good position from a course, which, he professed to believe, was prompted by a desire to do good; he showed that he cared for me more on account of my family relations than my personal goodness or my priestly zeal : he pretended that he did not know me to be the author of Excelsior's communications, when he commited to me the project of purchasing the property on 2nd Ave. : This he did on November 1st 1866 : whilst at the Council of Baltimore he complained to Rev. M. O'Connor S. J. of me as communicating improper news to the Standard. I went fully determined that I should by no act of mine show opposition to him, even though he should be induced to speak harshly to me : but I intend to have a better guide than him. Dr. Keogh writes to me that Mr. Murphy, Blount & Co.'s agent, wrote to Fr. Kelly that the writer of the protest against him was a priest and a Red Republican : and that Fr. Kelly says he sent this news to Cardinal Barnabo. The Archbishop said that he would make no inquiries about the Baltimore Excelsior : and that he had kept to himself all his decisions and judgements about me, seeming especially to show that he had not communicated them to Fr. McNierney. Dr. McGlynn told me that Fr. Nilan had a difference with Fr. Preston : who accused him to the Abp. of not conforming to the Chancery rules 1st by dispensing from the publication of the banns. 2nd by asking the dispensation 'in form pauperum'. The Abp. wrote

February

a note to Fr. Nilan : who answered that he had dispensed 3 or 4 out of 40, when the case was urgent : and that the poverty of the applicants was the motive of the 2nd. He got a 2nd sharp note from the Abp. telling him to leave dispensations to his pastor, if he did not conform to the rules.

Tues., 19th   I wrote to Dr. Keogh. Dr. McSweeny & I took a walk in the afternoon. We discussed again the material integrity of confession : we concluded that especially in our circumstances of crowded confessionals we are not bound to ask questions to make the confession exact. God requires people to confess according to their knowledge, not according to our theological acumen. Mr. Carleton paid me a visit : he is quite unwell & probably consumptive. I heard Miss Anna Dickinson speak on 'Something to Do' of which lecture a synopsis will be found among my papers. Mr. Greeley made a few remarks about women's rights in a monotonous sing-song tone. John Richmond called for a moment.

Wed., 20th   Omitted by the Editor.

Thurs., 21st   Omitted by the Editor.

Fri., 22nd   Omitted by the Editor.

Sat., 23rd   Omitted by the Editor.

Sun., 24th   Bishop Demers of Vancouver's Island preached four times today at all the masses and at Vespers. I sang High-Mass and Vespers. He talked for $2\frac{1}{4}$ hours between the two : describing the difficulties of travel to Oregon, before roads were made well : the bad effect of the whites' example on the Indians. These call baptism a medicine, to which they attribute the death of their children. They call God the Great Master, and think the whites read his book. The chapels were roughly made : the windows were of deer skins : eaten at times by the dogs. He eat horse-flesh. He bought an Indian child-slave who immagined himself a civilised being because bought

February   360

by a white man for $40 worth of trinkets. Once an Indian Tribe of Ukatans stopped a warfare by all making a sign of the Cross to another tribe showing their wish to see the great man of prayer. The whites at times tell them that God and religion are humbug. One Indian made knots every day for fifteen years, to indicate how long since he had seen a man of prayer another joined little sticks together for the same purpose. One Indian having ten wives complained that the man of prayer had made him lose all his power, because he reduced him to three wives; and thus he was deprived of the other wives' slaves who toiled to let him to give a feast of deer, & berries & fish to a whole tribe. It is more difficult to convert them now since the whites have met them. One Indian was kicked and whipped and beaten and ready to die rather than break the Temperance pledge. The bishop got $660 at St. Francis Xavier's, $280 at St. Gabriels : about $200 at Transfiguration : $220 at St. Columba's.

Fr. Preston lectured in Newark. Fr. Hecker told me that Baltimore Excelsior inaccurately stated that all of their students are converts, two not being so, out of six. This fact would raise prejudices among many. I told him I did not know the correspondent. I heard O'Gorman lecture at Cooper Institute : and chatted with Mayor Hoffman. I visited the Morroghs & the Belchers.

<u>Mon., 25th</u>   I wrote to the Catholic Standard. I went to Daniel Devlin's funeral & heard the Abp. give a very tame and formal eulogy of him. Dr. McGlynn & I took a walk in the afternoon. We discussed the Abp's decision about the 2nd Ave. property. Fr. Preston after hearing my account of my interview with him said that he would get the Abp. to relent. I attended the girls' rehearsal : went to Mr. Dachauer & Mr. Villanova's concert & heard Miss Kellogg sing magnificiently. Miss Sterling, contralto's

February

low notes are almost a man's voice. Baragli is a weak tenor. I confess that I did not enjoy the playing on the piano; simply because I have not a good ear.

Tues., 26th   Dr. McGlynn and I walked. The Archbishop dined at our house to-day with Bishop Bayley, always pleasant in conversation, Fr. Starrs always stupid, who was much ridiculed by Dr. Gunning Bedford, Fr. McNierney quite stiff with me, Mr. Hildreth of New York Hotel who expressed surprise that the pope expelled the Protestant service from Rome, with which sentiment I agreed, to the dismay of the other churchmen present, Mr. Gibert who had a moving cartilage in his knee, which Dr. Carnochan told him to catch if possible, & Mr. Navarro. I attended Archdeacon McCarron's funeral. See Catholic Standard. Fr. McSherry accused me of being Excelsior of Baltimore Mirror which I disclaimed. Several priests had thought Excelsior disrespectful. Dr. Ives stated that his father-in-law P. E. Bishop Hobart was inclined to Catholicity. The Abp. related a defense by him of Catholic ceremonial. Bishop Hobart gave a tone to P. Episcopalianism in this country.

Wed., 27th   Omitted by the Editor.

Thurs., 28th   I dined at Fr. Malone's with our radical friends. We laughed at Fr. Quin's sermon : We doubted the inspiration of the history of our first parents' fall : and thought that many Adams (?) may have been created, as long as the whole human race fell from original justice. The reasoning Rom.V. about sin entering by one man, is not of faith : as the theological reasoning of General Councils. St. Paul's reasoning there is very illogical. I attended the girls' rehearsal.

March

Fri., 1st   Omitted by the Editor.

Sat., 2nd   I heard 5 hours' confessions.

March   362

Sun., 3rd   Omitted by the Editor.

Mon., 4th   Omitted by the Editor.

Tues., 5th   I attended the Ecclesiastical Society. Dr. McSweeny
gave an essay on Religious Toleration : maintaining that the Church had
never defined it's right to punish corporally heretics except where they
sought to hem in her liberty : though the prelates in Rome, Spain and elsewhere practically acted on the assumption that she had the right to inflict
corporal punishments for heresy itself. Fr. Malone said a bounty jumper
of New York had to restore to the federal government his $600 : and the
priest that burned the said $600 incurred the obligation of restitution.
I held that he was obliged to restore to the city of New York : but if the
federal government took upon itself the state war debt entirely, then the
burning the notes cancelled the obligation of the U. States to redeem the
$600 in greenbacks and was sufficient restitution. We attended a festival
of St. Joseph's academy : where I saw two nice girls' pieces 'The Peasant
Queen' and 'Christmas Gambols'. I attended the Sunday School Association :
Mr. O'Toole was appointed librarian.

Wed., 6th   Ash-Wednesday. I blessed the ashes at 7 o'c. Mass :
they were also distributed after 8 o'c. mass. We dine in Lent at 2 o'c. :
yet I intend to fast as long as I can bear it. In the afternoon I visited
the McKnights : I wanted to see Addie about a note sent to me by one outside of the church, who wishes that I should speak seriously to her about
some bad company she has been keeping of late. In the evening I met the
Altar and Literary classes.

Thurs., 7th   I visited my mother in the afternoon : and the Garricks
in the evening : with the excuse of being unable to see them again during
Lent. Mrs. Garrick told me of the admirable influence Fr. Preston's

March 363

funeral oration over a sister of Mr. Garrick's brother, had upon the last and his wife, both careless Catholics. Mrs. Garrick is a fine, intelligent lady. Bishop Bayley stayed with us. Robert Murphy wrote to him threatening to complain of him at Rome, because he refused to publish the Papal Loan in his diocese, which, he said, could not bear this burden. Dr. McCloskey of Rome writes to Fr. Preston "Bish- Bayley, rumour has it, has put his foot on the "American Idea". Deo Gratias!" Fr. Preston tells me that Fr. Starrs', and Fr. Hart's names were given for the bishopric of Albany, besides B. Conroy's.

Fri., 8th   I instructed the girls' school about the Greek and Western Schism of the 13th & 14th centuries. I saw Addie McKnight : she promised to avoid the girls, with whom she had been keeping company, of doubtful character. I visited Mr. Dachauer, who starts for Europe tomorrow : and who leaves me Mrs. Dachauer's gold-finches to take care of. I walked with Dr. McGlynn to Central Park. He had returned yesterday from Washington where he had gone to lecture on the "Christian School.' The lecture had been postponed from Sunday to Wednesday : on both days it rained : he had about 50 listeners, in the Jesuits' shabby hall. He was more pleased with Sister DeChantal's (Dr. Cummings' sister) conversation than with anything else at Washington.

Sat., 9th   Dr. McSweeny and I took a walk together. He is afraid lest the pastoral duty in a city parish might bring on consumption. He complaines especially of the confessional! I heard 5 hours' confession.

Sun., 10th   Omitted by the Editor.

Mon., 11th   Omitted by the Editor.

Tues., 12th   Fr. Nilan & I attended the episcopal evening service at St. Alban's which was the 'usual evening service' of the Prayer-book.

March 364

Fr. Nilan tells me that Fr. Quin expressed great indignation at the misrepresentation of the Standard Excelsior of his discourse over Fr. McCarron where he speaking of the St. Mary's Institute is stated to have said 'that he reserved it for the education of the poor' :'and that since it's foundation (within ten years) have sprung from it some of our noblest and greatest Catholic families'. One priest at least called my attention to this saying of his. I attended Mr. J. F. Maguire M. P.'s lecture on American and European education. He upholds the denominational system as carried out in Prussia, where there are three classes of schools, normal for teachers, elementary for the poor, and academical for the better classes : all paid for out of the government taxes, and yet under Ecclesiastical control. In England the same system is follwed. In the North of Ireland (Ulster), the mixed system is adopted : and the mutual religious animosity is greater there than in the South : where the schools are under the charge of the priests. There are 5500000 inhabitants in Ireland : one million are Protestants according to the census of 1866. Of 700000 children attendant on the schools in Ireland 350000 are regular. Of 2300; in Cork at the Xtian Brothers' schools, 2100 attend regularly. He denounced the Proselytising institutions in the U. States as teaching children to dishonour their parents and religion. He is a poor speaker : has little true humour & as Dr. McGlynn says is a cross between an Cork gentleman and a London cockney.

Wed., 13th   Omitted by the Editor.

Thurs., 14th   Omitted by the Editor.

Fri., 15th   I heard the confessions of the girls : spoke to the school about Wicliff & Huss & the reunion of Greeks in the Council of Florence. Fr. Hecker declines any essay on 'Liturgical Languages' thinking that those who for twenty years have considered him a shaky Catholic would derive an oppor-

March

tunity to oppose his progress, since my essay reaches the ultima 'Thule' on the liturgical language question. He showed how necessary it is for us to adapt our sermons to our age and times : and to bring our Theology into the streets, as Ripley said that he had done in the "Questions of the Soul." And that we must use our present position to do all the good that we can : and not grumble at the defects that we find. As giving fresh air to the body, will chase the particular trouble that may affect any limb, so giving positive health to the church body will remove the obstacles in the way of good. I engaged Miss Cody to get the girls to sew covers on our library-books. I heard 2½ hours 'confessions' in the evening. Fr. Hecker had proposed to the conference of St. Vincent de Paul to facilitate a Catholic congress in the United States on the model of the Malines Congress etc. : and the establishment of mission-houses in the poorer parishes.

Sat., 16th   Omitted by the Editor.

Sun., 17th   Omitted by the Editor.

Mon., 18th   I felt so unhappy at being accused of detraction about Fr. Quin's eulogy of Archdeacon McCarron, that I could not sleep long : and in the morning wrote to the Catholic Standard, asking to have inserted the report as given in the Freeman's journal. Dr. McSweeny and Fr. Nilan called; I read to them all the documents about the Abp's rejection of me for the purchase of the 2nd Ave. property. Dr. McSweeny says that Fr. McNierney said that I had no chance for St. Mary's because I could not sing well : and my preaching was not liked : hence it was necessary to keep me in a small parish. Bishop Bayley dined with us and told us many anecdotes. Dr. Freel called. I cannot bear him; he seems to be always intriguing. I gave the instruction on Confession : which I extracted from Seguiri's 'Il Penitente istruito'. The audience was wretchedly small. The girls undertook

March

the covering of the library books. I have felt exceedingly unhappy for the last few days caused by my letter about Fr. Quin's sermon : I hope that this trouble will teach me wisdom, and make me attend more earnestly to my parochial duties.

Tues., 19th   In the afternoon I visited Dr. McGlynn with whom I met Dr. McSweeny. We talked of Fr. McKenna of St. Mary's, who had wilfully neglected a sick-call till twelve doctors were in consultation over a case of cancer. He rudely entered and told them they could either leave the room or kneel; which they declined. He heard the woman's confession and pompously gave the instruction on Holy Oils, causing a titter when he explained it's efficacy to remit the sins of smell. A French Doctor who was taking the cast of the cancer said : damn this priest, who spoils my job. Dr. V. Mott thought it not prudent to thwart the priest who had such influence over the poor, that they would not listen to the doctor who slighted him. Fr. McKenna once asked the congregation to pray for the conversion of a pewholder whom he named who had obstinately insisted on bringing his boy, 5 years old, to $10\frac{1}{2}$ o'c. Mass. I preached an old plain sermon on the Eucharist at St. Joseph's, and told Fr. Farrell of my disgrace with the Abp. because identified with Excelsior.

Wed., 20th   Omitted by the Editor.

Thurs., 21st   Omitted by the Editor.

Fri., 22nd   Omitted by the Editor.

Sat., 23rd   Omitted by the Editor.

Sun., 24th   Omitted by the Editor.

Mon., 25th   Omitted by the Editor.

Tues., 26th   Omitted by the Editor.

Wed., 27th   Dr. McSweeny called in the morning and afternoon. He

March 367

calls Fr. Preston another Acksherhilian : and doesn't like his old ways. Dr. McSweeny told the Abp. that he never knew so industrious a person for writing sermons, as I am : a good antidote to Fr. McNierney's late bickerings at me. The Abp. was surprised! Dr. McGlynn and we two walked to 43rd St. Neither would sup with me for fear of meeting Acksherhilian. Fr. Preston preached on 'Intemperance' a practical sermon.

Thurs., 28th   Omitted by the Editor.

Fri., 29th   Omitted by the Editor.

Sat., 30th   . . . .I received a telegram from Dr. Keogh asking Excelsior's letters to be sent to him.

Sun., 31st   I preached on Alms-deeds and Correction of our neighbour : as taught by the gospel. I attended both Sunday-Schools. In the evening at the Stations of the Cross I came near vomiting : some old woman thought I was affected to tears and began to whimper.

April

Mon., 1st   I wrote to Dr. Keogh stating that as Excelsior had been made universally known, he would no longer write a regular correspondence....

Tues., 2nd   I attended the Theological Society. Fr. Nilan gathered a number of facts concerning the Liturgy : Fr. McCarthy solved the moral case which supposed a man to have taken a barral of smuggled gin from the dock, when the officers were in pursuit of the smuggler. He obliged the man to restore to the government. Fr. Nilan & Drs. Parsons & McSweeny allowed him to keep it if he paid the revenue : I could not see what title he had to it; it belonged to the government or to the smuggler. Dr. McSweeny & Fr. Nilan dined with me : we then walked to Central Park. I attended the S. School Association where Messrs Fogarty & Preston entered a complaint John Martin & Mr. O'Toole's class generally for insulting conduct

April 368

towards the teachers.

Wed., 3rd   I preached in the evening on 'Love of Enemies' following Tornielli's Lenten Sermon but made a very poor hand of it.

Thurs., 4th   Fr. Nilan & I met at St. Alban's at 9 o'c. A.M. : where the Episcopal Matins were recited by Rev. Mr. Morrill. He explained to us that the St. Alban's 'mass' or 'Eucharistic sacrifice' was like the Roman Mass : it was the Communion Service of the Prayer-book. He believed in the 'real presence' : and for the sick consecrated at their houses. The people received communion generally at 11 o'c. hence the fasting was not obligatory. Too many exceptions would have to be made for the delicate. An Irish woman asking alms said that she had been to mass there often : Catholics have gone in and said their beads : which Mr. Morrill calls a mechanical help for prayer and noways objectionable. He thinks that the Low-church party represented by old Dr. Tyng etc., is dying out : in Maine it could not appoint a bishop though offering to endow richly the diocese. He says there is no real doctrinal difference between the Roman, Anglican and Greek Churches. The two articles against the Roman doctrines of purgatory etc. and the Sacrifices of the Masses were hurled against popular practices & not against the doctrinal belief of the Church : and were couched in such terms to satisfy the High and Low parties : as the Trenten decrees. Even in the Roman Church there are extremes, ultramontanes and Gallicans. He considered the Latin tongue of the Liturgy to have impeded many Protestants from entering the Roman church : and considered it wretched policy in this country : for Protestants have a queer idea of the Mass : if they understood what was said and done, they would see it to be reasonable : now their prejudices are confirmed. He understood Doellinger, Darboy, and the Abp. of Paris to favour the introduction of the modern languages.

April 369

He considered Liberius and Honorius to have erred. I called his attention to the fact that Liberius had at most signed the formula of with the word 'Homousios' : and Honorius in his letter taught one will 'by conformity of the two' not of one nature alone, and Leo II wrote to the bishops of Spain that no predecessor of his had ever erred : the 6th Council erred in a fact calling Honorius a heretic. He had no objection to make the pope 'ecumenical bishop' as he was called in the first six centuries : but limited it to a primacy of honour. Fr. Nilan & I were pleased with Mr. Morrill's frankness, humility and theological knowledge. We walked to Central Park : dined at our house and with Dr. McGlynn walked uptown again. I attended the altar class : and was present at the death of the 'Catholic Library Association' which made over the Library of 700 vols. to Fr. Preston.

<u>Fri., 5th</u>   Omitted by the Editor.
<u>Sat., 6th</u>   I paid a short visit to my mother. . . .
<u>Sun., 7th</u>   Omitted by the Editor.
<u>Mon., 8th</u>   Omitted by the Editor.
<u>Tues., 9th</u>   Fr. Nilan and I visited Blackwell's island : saw the Lunatic Asylum, the Alms-house, the Penitentiary and Charity Hospital : doing them in $1\frac{1}{2}$ hour. Mr. Nicholson lent us his carriage. We visited Dr. McSweeny : and in the evening I made a fiasco before the Cummings Library Association, to which I was invited to give a lecture, on Sunday : I talked in a rambling manner for 20 minutes.
<u>Wed., 10th</u>   Omitted by the Editor.
<u>Thurs., 11th</u>   Omitted by the Editor.
<u>Fri., 12th</u>   Omitted by the Editor.
<u>Sat., 13th</u>   I heard $5\frac{1}{2}$ hours' confessions.

April

Sun., 14th   Omitted by the Editor.

Mon., 15th   Omitted by the Editor.

Tues., 16th   I went to hear Rev. Mr. Morrill of St. Alban's say 'Mass' as he calls it. It is the 'Episcopal Communion service' with Catholic ceremonial of bows, and elevations, and crosses! The English service is grand! The language is beautiful! The congregation was about 20 quite devout : three young men received communion with great devotion! They profess belief in the real presence! 'Tis a pity Mr. Morrill has no orders! It is downright idolatry! I drilled the boys for ceremonies of Holy Week.

Wed., 17th   Omitted by the Editor.

Thurs., 18th   Omitted by the Editor.

Fri., 19th   Good Friday. We had the solemn ceremonial. Dr. McGlynn and I went to see Mr. Marshen, Stock-broker to borrow $6000 : he said he had lost a million since Fall and had not to lend. I visited my mother. Fr. Preston preached at Tenebrae on the Passion in connexion with the sorrows of the B. Virgin.

Sat., 20th   Omitted by the Editor.

Sun., 21st   Omitted by the Editor.

Mon., 22nd   Fr. Nilan called : we took Dr. McGlynn in tow, dined at 42nd St. with Fr. Lawrence McKenna and walked to the Central Park.

Tues., 23rd   I went to the Hassards' at Fordham : where Fr. Glackmeyer S. J. dined. He feels like a boy let out of school & is cramped by the Jesuitical life, especially under Fr. Moylan S. J. who is an Irish Frenchman or a French Irishman.

Wed., 24th   I visited my mother . . . .

Thurs., 25th   I dined at St. Joseph's where I met Dr. O'Leary, Dr.

April 371

Brann & Dr. McGlynn. We had a discussion on Freemasonry. I maintained that the oath, unless wrong in itself, bound those who took it, and they could not reveal it's nature even in confession, if they promised to keep it secret; and that in this country they were not technically a secret society, because they did not design the overthrowal of religion or government. Dr. O'Leary upheld the contrary under both respects. Dr. McGlynn & I walked to Central park. I gave a treat of cakes etc. to the singing class.

Fri., 26th   Omitted by the Editor.

Sat., 27th   Omitted by the Editor.

Sun., 28th   Fr. Preston preached on the gospel. Dr. McGlynn lectured in Cooper Institute on 'Our Religious Destiny'. 'The 1st page of the Catechism tells us that man is created to love & serve God in this world & enjoy him in the next. A nation is composed of individual men : hence it's destiny is the same; God has created this continent on a gigantic scale, and fashioned it in a gigantic mould to prepare it for a gigantic race of men not in physical but moral stature : of enterprise, intelligence & vitue. Hence this nation ought to be Catholic to fulfil it's destiny. The Catholic Church praises the works of nature. A religion that reviles or curses the work of man is not fit to exist in this country. And though we do not pretend that Catholicity is directed to bring greater comfort to the world : for it teaches individual men to sacrifice their comfort for the good of others : yet it does praise the development of every talent implanted by the Creator in man : and applauds human progress, and sanctifies it's every new invention, directing it to the intellectual & moral perfection of man : The Catholic Church does not wish to stay the oar of Progress : and he is insane who in her name dares stop it in it's onward march, whither it will

April   372

tend inspite of his feeble efforts to prevent it's advance. The Catholic
Church is not foreign to this soil. It is true that the Irish and German
have transplanted Catholicity to this country. But did not the Jew bring
it to Rome and to the ends of the world. It must Americanise here : and
it will be inspite of us. Let not the Irishman combat what is inevitable.
The Catholic rejects the idea of totally depraved human nature, which is
inconsistent with the improvement of the human mind : and believes human
nature even as it is at present to be such as God could have created it
from the beginning. The Catholic Church with it's tendencies to Unity
shows itself the only powerful link which may unite together as many states
as may enter into this Union, for the preservation of which God has implanted in the American people an instinct, which has overcome immense obstacles to it. The Catholic Church too alone can reach the inmost recesses
of the human heart : and can purify and keep pure the mysterious source of
the propagation of men. Population is the wealth of this nation : more
than the mines of the territories. Every emigrant's value is great. And
hence Catholic morality especially through the confessional keeps the father
& mother & daughter chaste : and eschews that prudery which would not teach
this important branch of morality, lest it should shock the over-nice decency of respectable persons.' The Doctor spoke for two hours to about
700 persons. Fr. Preston remarked that he had never heard the Doctor lecture
as well. I thought that he lacked his usual inspiration.

<u>Mon., 29th</u>   Omitted by the Editor.

<u>Tues., 30th</u>   I went to the assessor's office to state that I had no
income-tax to pay : as I did not receive $1000 a year : I stated that I had
$800 a year and a gold watch. Dr. McGlynn received a letter in Greek-
Italian style from Dr. Sasiriaga of Corfu : asking for intentions. I wrote

April

to Card. Barnabo. Frs. Nilan & O'Hara visited me : Fr. O'Hara had been spoken against publicly by his pastor, Fr. McAleer, for employing an old maid to prepare children for first communion. Fr. O'Hara has received a chasuble worth $630 in gold as a present : and received presents to the value of $2000.

May

Wed., 1st   I visited my mother. . . .

Thurs., 2nd   Dr. McGlynn & I took a walk to Central Park and saw Mme. Restoro act as Mary Queen of Scots. She has not true dignity : and her acting does not excite enthusiasm. Schiller's play is not correct historically : her supposed interview with Elizabeth was well represented. The other actors were only tolerable : Italian players are childish, as they are in every-day life.

Fri., 3rd   Omitted by the Editor.

Sat., 4th   Omitted by the Editor.

Sun., 5th   I preached on the gospel. Sig. Errani took Mr. Tamaro's place as tenor in our choir. Mr. Remi dined with us. I visited both Sunday-Schools. In the evening I heard Dr. Bellows lecture on the 'Evil of Poverty'. He showed that the words: 'Thou shalt till the earth in the sweat of thy brow' though a curse on the earth, were a blessing to man: in as much as labour brings forth to development man's faculties. Adam through his transgression thus passed from moral infancy to moral manhood. Whilst he was in the self-producing garden of Eden, he had nought to develop him. Now his labour helps him to gain moral and physical wealth, by taxing his faculties to their last healthful energies.

Productiveness in Society is the source of all happiness. Hence there are two extreme classes miserable in Society, the poor who have no work to

May 374

alleviate their hunger, & the extreme wealthy who don't work because having no object. These are physical & moral paupers. We do not admire communism, tried by the first Christians and resulting in failure. Take away the fruit of individual labour, and you stay productiveness. The selfish principle will force men to work to provide for themselves but not for others. When they have enough, the love of privilege, of ease & comfort will spur them to produce more. But make them distribute the fruit of their labour, and they cease to produce. In France Mr. Chevalier states there are 10 000 000 000 francs of produce : which for 35 millions of Frenchmen leaves 13 3/4 cents a day for each one. 15 millions have less than that : what is taken from them makes up the fortunes of the others. Hence what misery there must be. Near the Alps the peasants bake their black bread once a year on a fire made of the dung of their animals. The whole earth does not produce more in one year than would support the whole race for three years : how little man has learned in 4000 years! How near the bone is the whole human race gnawing! If the crops failed for three successive years man would starve! Hence we can tell how dreadful are the effects of a partial failure of the crops; how damaging is warfare which draws so many from producing. Hence the necessity of productiveness : hence the evil of communism which would draw away the most powerful stimulus of labour : the selfish desire of saving one's individual life and the love of privilege, which prompts a man to tax his energies even when he has enough. Communism could only be useful, if the members were forced to work and hence can be carried out only on a small scale. We should not seek to relieve poverty, so as to take away the stimulus of work. Hunger is the most powerful stimulus. Yet there are occasions in which we must depart from the strict rule of political economy. This would induce us to leave the poor to starve, that they might be compelled to work or be an example to the next generation of the necessity of work. Yet Christian charity forbids us to allow them to starve, even though the need had been brought on by their criminal acts as at present in the South, or though their criminal indolence had now rendered it impossible for them to be productive. Thus Charity conflicts with best interests of Society as a whole : yet it must deal assistance to the needy, not so as to take away self-respect. It is foolish to say that poverty is necessary to Society, or that because Christ said 'the poor ye have always with you' therefore poverty will not disappear, or that Xtianity is for the poor. We must in our institutions of charity see this self-respect maintained otherwise they would do more damage than good to Society. Here we should encourage Mission-houses, where the children of the poor are taught to sew, schools where they are educated to take care of themselves. I saw Peter Morrogh at the lecture quite wearied. I visited the Morroghs of 26th St.

Mon., 6th   I took a Turkish bath at Guttman's in 4th St. : though the thermometer showed 158° Fahrenheit, I did not perspire much. I was more exhausted than by a Russian bath : the man says that the perspiration in the Turkish is greater, because in the Russian the vapor settling on the body appears sweat. After the bath they sent me to a room to cool off, where there was a draft which gave me a cold. I heard Sam. Clements (Mark Twain) give his serio-comic lecture on the Sandwich Islands, in which he has some good & some bad & some very vulgar jokes. He gave some facts worth noting. Ten years ago there were 200000 inhabitants, now there are 60000. The king is despot : the priests his slaves, the nobles their slaves & so on till the women are degraded. The Protestant Missionaries he said were the civilisers. I preached at the Month of May Devotions.

May

<u>Tues., 7th</u>   I attended the meeting of the Ecclesiastical Society at New Rochelle. Fr. Thos. Farrell gave a rhapsody on the law of abstinence as his essay, which seemed to be a part of a sermon. I solved the Moral Case on Freemasonry showing that absolution may safely be given to the Freemason in this country, whose object is not the overthrowal of religion or government, or bad in itself; hence they substantially differ from the European Freemasons, that were condemned by the Church. At dinner we had a lively discussion on Mr. Murphy the papal loan agent's dishonesty. I forgot to attend the meeting of the S. School Association, where however there was no quorum. I preached at the Devotions of the B. Virgin.

<u>Wed., 8th</u>   I was unwell the whole day. . . .

<u>Thurs., 9th</u>   Dr. McSweeny called & read a letter from his brother Edward at Rome, who is quite smart and a good thinker. We went by invitation of Dr. Malone to Fr. Malone's to dine, but the whole dinner-party of ten was disappointed, as no dinner was prepared. The remarkable event of the meeting was an intelligent reply to a toast by Dr. O'Leary : who admired in America the mixture of young priests on a par with the old ones if intelligent : whilst in Ireland the Lord's echo was passed down the table from vicar to canon to P.P. to curate etc. He spoke of Rome as being a place where all nations met, and thus a thinker could chose the good qualities of all nations : and where Ecclesiastics did not consider individual bishops as Interpreters of Revelation but only as channels of jurisdiction. No one has a right to the distinction of an Authentic & Absolute Interpreter who is not infallible. I preached at the 'Devotions' of the evening & gave Benediction of the B. Sacrament. I heard Col. Roberts, the Fenian, try to prove that the Freedom of Ireland was necessary for the Freedom of the World. He dwelt on the grievances of Irishmen : and showed that their enslavement

May 377

had brought slavery on the English people, among whom in 1770 there were 250000 property-holders, and in 1815 only 32000. In 1840 one in every eight Englishmen was a pauper supported by the government. The Irishman would never be respected until he had a nationality. He protested against all Irishmen being reproached for all the crimes of which individual Irishmen are guilty : every row gotton up by Irishmen is considered a disgrace to the Irish people, whilst the New Orleans riot or the Know-nothing riots are not attributed to the American people, but to a few rough characters.

<u>Fri., 10th</u>   I gave an instruction to the girls' school on the 18th century from Gaume's 'Catechism of Perseverance'. In the evening I preached in honour of the B. Virgin : and heard an hour's confessions. Dr. McGlynn & I took a walk to Central Park. We discussed the propriety of writing clear statements of the wretched condition of this diocese to Card. Barnabo, and let the consequences be what they may.

<u>Sat., 11th</u>   Mrs. Hassard dined with us. I visited my mother. . . .

<u>Sun., 12th</u>   . . . .In the morning I had a sharp talk with Sister Delafina. She refused to give seats to the coloured girls, and says she will not give them seats. The white girls, she says, have no objection to sit with them, but she will make it her business not to allow them to mix. I told her that I insisted on their getting seats if they were before the white girls' : I approved of the separation not for the white girls' sake but for the black girls' sake. She told Fr. Preston that I wished and insisted on the mixture! She told thus a deliberate falsehood, and could not have misunderstood me! I attended the Altar Society. Fr. Preston went to Fordham with the Hazzards. Mr. Villanova dined with us. He has a weak childish mind but is gentlemanly. In the evening I heard Dr. Washburne deliver a sermon to the Law-class : there is one lawgiver, was his text.

May 378

He showed the necessity of morality & conscience in the administration of law. He spoke in an indistinct manner so that I could not frequently gather the sense of what he said, though I was about midway in Calvary Chruch. I visited the Morroghs of 26th St.

Mon., 13th   Omitted by the Editor.

Tues., 14th   Dr. McGlynn and I took a walk to 50th St. We met Fr. Hecker at his house : who wished to excite a rivalry for the collection for the pope. I told him I did not see what need the pope had of our money. We all agreed that if the pope realised our wants here he would be man enough to send back the money to us. Fr. Hecker thought that instead of grumbling, we should use the materials we have to build the Church in the U. States. He showed how two years ago Abp. Spalding had refused to give the Paulists jurisdiction for a mission in his diocese, and to-day is the first to endorse him publicly in his late pastoral. Fr. Hecker is honest, but knows how to keep his tongue quiet : he never speaks ill of anyone. He does not think the pope a great but a disinterested man. He was opposed to Fr. Hecker : once Card. Barnabo advised Fr. Hecker to leave Rome till the pope's passion had gone by; he was excited at Fr. Hecker's abandonment of the Redemptorists.

Wed., 15th   Fr. Nilan & Dr. McSweeny dined with me. The latter told us how the Abp. hearing from Dr. McSweeny that an exemplary priest (Fr. Thos. Farrell) had spoken to Dr. Forbes who was moved by this, laughed at such a priest being called exemplary, and remarked that now-a-days a class of young priests had arisen which pretended to know more than the church. When directly asked by Fr. Kearney : 'whether it was a mortal sin to speak to Dr. Forbes', he replied first that the good faith of the priest might excuse him and secondly that the Canon law did not strictly bind in this country! I preached in the evening on the virtue of faith as exemplified by the B. Virgin following Segueri's Cristiano Istruito and Liguori's Glories of Mary. I attended the altar and literary classes : to the latter I distributed the characters in 'Sebastian' for the S. S. Exhibition.

Thurs., 16th I read my solution of the Moral Case on Freemasonry before the Theological Society to have it subjected to criticism. Dr. O'Leary was the only opposer : who maintained that Freemasonry raised a code of morals : which no authority but the Church has a right to do. 2. that a grand master told him that a revealer of the secrets of Masonry would infallibly be done away with. 3. that a priest as judge in confession has a right to judge whether the mason's secrets are evil in themselves. I maintained 1. that Masonry did not establish a code of morals. 2. that if it did, we could follow it, if it did not contradict the Church's code. 3. that a Freemason's oath is taken with the explanation that it is not to affect his religion. 4. that some masons exaggerated the obligations of the Society and believe it to claim the right of punishing with death but wrongly as my essay proved. 5. that a priest must be satisfied with the declaration of the penitent that there is no evil design in the Society, but has no right to make the mason reveal his secrets, which he has sworn to keep; which I proved to be merely the grips, passwords etc. We dined with Fr. Farrell. Frs. Ed. O'Reilly & Kenidore called in after dinner. Dr. Nelligan was there to bring two documents of the popes to refute my theories on Freemasonry : but we got through the meeting before he arrived, and agreed to make no further mention of it, because he would spread everywhere that we endorsed Freemasonry and would tell lies about us. We discussed the laws of our National Councils, whose decrees prohibit Penance & the Eucharist to be given to those who publicly are known to frequent the Masonic lodges, and

May 380

all those belonging to secret societies : the 1st lest scandal should be given, for they did not decide that U. S. freemasonry was condemned by the papal decrees : to the 2nd we proved that freemasonry in the U. States is not a 'technical' secret society as condemned by the Church, that is a Society for the overthrowal of government or religion. Dr. McGlynn & I went to see Fr. Hecker, who engaged to lecture for St. Stephen's Conference of St. Vincent de Paul. At the Paulists' Church the congregation takes up the Latin & English hymns sung by their students : we were present at the Month of May Service : which commenced with a hymn & the Litanies : then a hymn, a prayer in English and a Latin hymn. . . .

Fri., 17th   I heard the girls' confessions : & gave the instruction to the girls' school on the 'French Revolution' from Gaume's Cate. of Perseverance. I visited Bish. Duggan at the St. Nicholas' : he complained that some of the bishops complained of those who had sought to regulate the Baltimore Council canonically, as opposed to the Holy See & it's delegates. He had opposed a motion that the decision about the Fenians should be taken from the bishops and left to the Holy See : on the ground that the bishops were judges in their own dioceses, and knew the facts better than Romans : and the Holy See was only a Court of Appeal. He spoke of the Dominicans in the West as a lazy set : they had actually to get a superior from Europe, Fr. O'Carroll : who is a very small man. He had not been able to obtain the Oblates or Marists in France, because they demanded too many privileges from the bishop : he wanted them to take charge of the French missions. Fr. P. Butler was with him & in his presence a cipher. Bish. Duggan is great in making ladies' acquaintance : if a lady met once asks him to call on her, he is sure to continue the acquaintance. Bishop Elder called to make arrangements about saying mass : he is on his way to

May 381

Rome. The bishops seem to be so many school-boys rushing to Rome, lest they should incur the pope's displeasure or taking excuse, from his invitation, to take a pleasure trip under pretence of fulfilling a duty to the head of the Church.

Sat., 18th   I saw Bishop Duggan : he is very egoistic, talking only of himself & nothing else. I heard $5\frac{3}{4}$ hours' confessions. The bishop received 3 telegrams from Chicago in 2 days! The diocese will be unable to exist without him!

Sun., 19th   Fr. Boyce had invited Fr. Butler to sing mass at St. Teresa's, and actually sent a carriage for him! Fr. Butler heard Fr. Rogan preach very timidly! I preached at High-Mass. Fr. Preston begged of me to make an earnest appeal for the pope : he did not want St. Ann's to lag behind other congregations. I called the congregation's attention to the distinction between this appeal and the papal loan : this appeal was a personal one for the pope, not for his government & would help the pope even if he lost his temporal power : and was for the aid of the head of the church, who in the government of the universal church had necessary expenses to incur, which no one particular people should bear but all the faithful : it was but just that we should contribute our share to these necessary expenses. I suspect that if these collections succeed throughout the world, they will be the worst blow against the pope's temporal power and the heavier because coming from his friends! For the scheme of Napoleon a few years' ago was to have the pope supported by monies sent from the faithful throughout the world as also by contributions of the Catholic governments : the Roman Ecclesiastics said this scheme was not feasible : but here is a fact which they cannot easily gainsay : especially as much more zeal is universally shown in favour of a personal contribution to the head of the church, than in subscribing to the papal loan. . . .

Mon., 20th   Fr. Butler and I visited Dr. McSweeny. Fr. Butler thinks that Dr. McMullen is the greatest man in these United States, all his lectures & discourses being original : but as yet is unknown in the East & West. We visited the Protectory fair. . . .

Tues., 21st   Dr. Butler & I went to the Imm. Conception. Dr. Morrogh was taking a sleep after a journey to & from Boston in 2 days after school-furniture. I took Dr. Todd's essays on fashionable murder who shows how Catholics do not commit abortion, owing to the confessional : and also do not use means to prevent the growth of their families : whilst both are common among Protestants. He says that the average of births among Protestants is 3 to a family : which will not suffice to keep in existence the American races, the ratio of deaths being greater. We visited Dr. McGlynn; and went to the Protectory fair.

Wed., 22nd   We commented on Dr. McGlynn's letter in the Tablet about his lecture on 'Our Religious Destiny' : which is stinging to Mrs. Sadlier's vanity and calls out a flippant reply with the exception of one gustation from his lecture where he used the expression 'to Americanise the Catholic Church' to which she gives the most unfavourable meaning. She declares ultra to be an adjective, whilst Dr. McGlynn said it meant excess : she says it means 'extreme'. She had accused him of denying his corporal and spiritual ancestry because he told the Irish & Germans & French that they ought to become American in feeling : He replied that then he might be accused of telling the spouse to hate her father and mother because he told her to love her husband. . . .

Thurs., 23rd   . . . .The Abp. came this evening & made a tour of inspection having a policeman as forerunner. A woman (dressed as a lady)

May 383

threw herself on both knees before him : he angrily said : 'don't worship me'! Except for the scene, he would not have objected to this performance! He seated himself at St. Ann's table, because Miss Mullen, his niece, attends it. Mr. O'Neil invited me to an ice-cream. He & Mr. Griffin have determined to defeat St. Peter's chance to the cope at the S. S. Union table : Mr. O'Neil resented the insulting way in which Fr. Quin treated the officers of the conferences, at a meeting called at the fair. The Council seems to consider itself owner of bodies & souls of all the members. All the officers agreed with Mr. O'Neil in the indignation against Fr. Quin. Fr. Butler started for home : I accompanied him to the depot at 10 P. M.

Fri., 24th   I met Miss Sanderson at Dr. McGlynn's. She was indignant at Mrs. Sadlier's article. Dr. McGlynn read a defense of his lecture by Capt. Churchill directed to the Tablet : and an anonymous letter to this effect : "As a priest I give my blessing and God's to the writer of what you got in last week's Tablet. Imprudent puppet, and other little brats, like Brann, who couldn't be educated in Ireland, and not in this country except at the public expense, deny & revile the Irish people, whilst your mother is so Irish that she hardly knows any other language; give us a little more of the 'American Idea'." We took a long walk to Central park: at dinner at our house we met Mrs. Hassard. I got the Herald of the 29th of April & the Tablet of the 11th of May from the Mercantile reading-rooms that Dr. McGlynn might write a reply to Mrs. Sadlier. Sister Germana sent one of the 1st communion girls away 1. because she had brought a white wreath, but a green one with which the Sister said she couldn't receive the B. Sacrament : 2. when she borrowed one, she must go home and buy one: 3. when this was not deemed sufficient, because she had dirty hands, Sister Delafina stating that Fr. Preston had required the girls to be clean!!!

May 384

I remonstrated with Sister Delafina who admitted these facts but thought them providential because Katie McKittrick, the girl, was habitually careless, and last year when she was prepared, she actually drank a glass of water inadvertently : thus God showed that she shouldn't go! I thought perhaps the devil sought to prevent her from reaping the fruits of communion! The mother & child came to me crying thinking that the girl was rejected because poor. I went to the fair : Fr. Quin had told Robert Byrnes that he would do any thing desired to accommodate St. Ann's literary Society.

Sat., 25th   Omitted by the Editor.

Sun., 26th   Fr. Preston preached on the infallibility of the Church proving it from scripture : and unfortunately held as equally certain, proved the infallibility of the pope. As many Catholics do not accept the latter his equal positiveness in both cases detracts from the value of his proofs of the former. . . .

Mon., 27th   Omitted by the Editor.

Tues., 28th   The Tablet announced that it would not publish Cosmopolitan's (Capt. Churchill) letter about Dr. McGlynn's lecture on 'Our religious destiny.' Dr. McGlynn dined with us. He had not completed his reply to the Tablet's attack. The Tablet editors were not shrewd in declining Mr. Churchill's article : they could have escaped with a semi-apology! We visited Fr. Tom Farrell : with whom we met Fr. Boyce. We complained of Fr. Quin's rudeness at the fair : and at his folly in having the S. S. Union committee sworn to secrecy. Fr. Tom Farrell agreed with me that a sharp reply to the Tablet's second attack would produce more good, than Dr. McGlynn's too good-natured reply, though it is complete. We went to the fair.

May

Wed., 29th   Omitted by the Editor.

Thurs., 30th   I sang High-Mass, to-day being Ascension-day. I visited Dr. McGlynn with whom I met Frs. Thos. Farrell & McLoughlin and Dr. Ryan of S. Carolina. We commented on Channing's assertion that the Apostles tolerated polygamy in the Jewish converts to Xtianity, if already having several wives. I attended a rehearsal of Toodles by the literary class, and walked to the fair with Dr. McGlynn.

Fri., 31st   Omitted by the Editor.

June

Sat., 1st   I heard 4½ hours' confessions.

Sun., 2nd   Omitted by the Editor.

Mon., 3rd   Omitted by the Editor.

Tues., 4th   Omitted by the Editor.

Wed., 5th   I wrote to Don Filippo Tancioni, and spoke severely of Frs. Starrs & Quin, Bishop Conroy & Abp. McCloskey : Drs. McGlynn & McSweeny approved of the tact of the letter. I wrote to Cannon advising him to write to Card. Barnabo, Bp. Rosecranz and Don F. Tancioni to protest against Quin's appointment to the see of Buffalo. I wrote to the editor of the Tablet, 'to stop my paper' since the editor had wilfully misrepresented Dr. McGlynn's lecture 'Under your narrow-minded policy, I added, which impels you for your temporal interests to excite, if you could, in the hearts of Irish Catholics an Anti-American spirit, you have foolishly aimed your first blow at one of the most devoted friends of the Irish. Dr. McGlynn is notorious for his sympathy with the Irish : and I have not heard any one plead more earnestly in their behalf.' Dr. McGlynn & I visited his mother who told us of a surprising recovery of a large sum lost by Andrew at his office, but found at the Church. We went to a picnic of the

June

Cummings' library Association in Funk's garden at 63rd St. I met a Mr. Breen who was quite intelligent and a Mr. Kavanagh who informed me of the existence of St. Vincent de Paul Societies and of the utility of the libraries!! At dinner Dr. McGlynn toasted Dr. Cummings : I toasted the Cummings' library Association. At the beginning I hesitated exceedingly, but by degrees became fluent and showed that these literary associations were developments of our common school system, to fit the people to govern themselves!! My debuts before this association have been rather unhappy! We attended the fair. I bought five books of dialogues for our exhibitions.

Thurs., 6th   Omitted by the Editor.

Fri., 7th   Omitted by the Editor.

Sat., 8th   Omitted by the Editor.

Sun., 9th   . . . .In the evening I heard Rev. Mr. Dutton lecture on the 'Midnight Mission'. 24 girls have been reformed : and 45 are encouraging cases since the opening of the house of Mercy. The girls fear 'so-called institutions' : and therefore a private dwelling has also been hired where they may stay temporarily : and thus have a good chance to reform their lives. Once Greene St. was frequented by the wealthy debauchees : now the railroad has made it too exposed and fear of recognition keeps many from it. Thus public opinion is proved powerful to condemn this sin of impurity : and if those guilty of it were rejected from good Society it could be vastly diminished. Now men do not hesitate to let their sisters and daughters associate with the greatest sensualists. Good men are wanted to help this new work; pure-minded, self-confident, and not over-nice men can do a great work of charity. Women too who will not look with sternness on other women's crimes, but will breathe the word of sympathy to and delicately probe the heart-wounds of these unfortunates. Money is required to main-

June   387

tain a work of so great charity. I visited the Morroghs of 26th St.

Mon., 10th   Omitted by the Editor.

Tues., 11th   Omitted by the Editor.

Wed., 12th   I attended the altar and literary classes.

Thurs., 13th   Omitted by the Editor.

Fri., 14th   Dr. McSweeny called to discuss with me Card. Barnabo's letter stating: 'The letter you sent to me concerning the state of life, of the Catholic people, of the clergy & in a special way of the Seminary I have received and am grateful : be assured that I will do everything in my power to further the good of religion and work to its advantage in the bad situation you have described." This was in answer to a letter from me on the 1st of May : in which I had said: "I say most sincerely in this parish (of St. Ann) and in 7 other parishes in the city of New York in which there are more than 20,000 souls in each parish, each is given to the care of three priests. The problem is not a difficult one; there is not really a shortage of young men who feel they have a call to the Ecclesiastical state, but not a few at the beginning of the scholastic year were rejected by the Abp. (wishing to enter the diocesan priesthood) because he said he had no place to receive them in the Seminary and did not have the money to train them in their Ecclesiastical education. Indeed this is a high handed way to treat the Catholic people who never appear to shrink from giving money for those things necessary for the church and who find themselves in the U. S. shown only a mediocre energy to correct these defects. In the provincial seminary there are 36 students for the Diocese of New York while there are 35 for the Diocese of Albany which is not as well off as is New York. Moreover Albany has one-fourth as many Catholics as New York, and one-fourth as much money as does New York." I begin to question the policy of writing complaints to Rome : it seems to me to foster the miserable system of centralisation which is doing so much harm to the Church already. Would it not be better & more honest to fight our battles out here in the best possible manner? Yet it is necessary to use the centralising power to give us reasoning bishops, who will begin to break up the system of centralisation. I heard an hour's confessions in the evening and went to the fair where Fr. Larry McKenna insisted on giving me an ice-cream.

Sat., 15th Omitted by the Editor.

Sun., 16th Omitted by the Editor.

Mon., 17th I ordered a suit of clothes at Brokaw's for $52 : and took another for $16.50. I dined at Fr. Thos. Farrell's with Dr. O'Leary & Frs. Malone & McCarthy. We discussed the infallibility of the pope & the definition of the Immac. Conception : neither is sufficient to prove the other. Dr. O'Leary is very antagonistic to Roman Claims : and shows great intelligence in his reasoning. I read, at my mother's, Kathy Avezzana's letter to Mrs. Vic. Richmond. I attended a rehearsal of 'Sebastian'. To a request from me to open the school, upstairs, Sister Delafina answered she couldn't because the girls' premiums were there. I opened the school myself. I attended the meeting of S. School Union towards it's close.

Tues., 18th I attended the girls' rehearsal for the exhibition.

Wed., 19th Omitted by the Editor.

Thurs., 20th Omitted by the Editor.

Fri., 21st I wrote my sermon for Sunday. . . .

Sat., 22nd Omitted by the Editor.

Sun., 23rd Omitted by the Editor.

June

Mon., 24th   Omitted by the Editor.

Tues., 25th   I attended the Exhibition at the Convent of Mercy. . . .

Wed., 26th   Fr. Killeen and I went to Seton Hall. . . .

Thurs., 27th   In the evening I called at Dr. McGlynn's and Fr. Nilan's : but they were not in. I went to hear Fr. Bodfish speak to the S. School Union at the Paulists'. 'As the Captain of a vessel studies his charts, and morning, noon and evening calculates his precise position, so a S. School teacher must study his religion, and his class-boys to guide them properly. In the last yacht race, the Henrietta won because guided by an experienced seaman : so the best S. School class will be that of the teacher who knows well the way over which he is to lead the boys. They should question a great deal; because this develops the boys' minds. They should work and not think too much of their dignity. They should be fatherly. The dullest brain can be developed. He read of an idiot, who by patient care was taught to know who made him, after seeing bread & clothes & shoes made by men, and then was told that God was his 'Creator' : whom he said he wished to kiss, meaning he loved him.' Fr. Hecker is going to Europe to witness the Malines Congress. Fr. Huet tells me their young men study hard : they went through half of Perrone's Compendium this year. They have a dispute every Thursday evening between the students and professors. Fr. Deshon is considered their metaphysician.

Fri., 28th   Omitted by the Editor.

Sat., 29th   Omitted by the Editor.

Sun., 30th   Fr. Preston gave quite an interesting discourse on the Primacy of St. Peter : unfortunately teaching as positive the infallibility of the pope. I engaged the S. S. teachers to act as ushers at the exhibition. I had a general rehearsal in the evening for the exhibition.

July

Mon., 1st   Our exhibition was a perfect success : Cooper Institute was packed with the people. . . .

Tues., 2nd   I went to St. John's Fordham : the discourses were poor. I was restless. . . .

Wed., 3rd   . . . .I called to condole with Dr. McGlynn over the loss of his brother Andrew who died of nervous exhaustion at Dansville West New York.

Thurs., 4th   Omitted by the Editor.

Fri., 5th   Fr. Healy dined with us. He maintains 'that no one need fear excess in mortification when he follows his confessor's guidance.' I thought obedience could be carried too far! He thinks the Sulpicians to be without defect : I thought they attached too much importance to the exterior, and did not adapt themselves to the country. He thought the pope could declare himself infallible, with the tacit consent of the Church : in fact he believes anything taught by the pope, as much as what is taught by the Church : He considers the definition of the Immac. Conception to have emanated from the pope only, with the tacit assent of the church. I thought the church only certainly infallible and able therefore to define, if true, the pope's infallibility. It is sinful to place the pope's decrees on a par with the church's and that the Immac. Conception is a dogma only if it received the positive assent of the church. He is very narrow-minded, always comparing Boston to New York, preferring the former evidently from petty prejudice. He says his model paper is the 'Giornale di Roma' : that his faith was undermined by reading newspapers in New York for two years : that in N. York he had hardly succeeded in going to confession. Dr. McSweeny called. I heard an hour's confessions.

Sat., 6th   Omitted by the Editor.

July

Sun., 7th   Omitted by the Editor.

Mon., 8th   Dr. McSweeny, Fr. Nilan & I started for Saratoga by the Hudson R. boat & Athens' train. . . .

Tues., 9th   Omitted by the Editor.

Wed., 10th   Omitted by the Editor.

Thurs., 11th   Omitted by the Editor.

Fri., 12th   Omitted by the Editor.

Sat., 13th   We came to N. York by the Athens route starting at 8 A.M. and arriving home at 5:30, P.M. I heard two hours' confessions of all that were in the church.

Sun., 14th   I said two masses. Judge Wright & Mr. Villanova dined with us. We had a discussion on the right of secession, which the judge deemed lawful but inexpedient. I visited Dr. McGlynn : we called at the Morroghs of 26th St. : and at Fr. Tom Farrell's. The Doctor has commenced a poor-school giving bread, coffee and soup as the principal enticement to the school.

Mon., 15th   Omitted by the Editor.

Tues., 16th   Omitted by the Editor.

Wed., 17th   Omitted by the Editor.

Thurs., 18th   Omitted by the Editor.

Fri., 19th   Omitted by the Editor.

Sat., 20th   Omitted by the Editor.

Sun., 21st   I said 7 o'c mass. The literary boys invited me to a picnic for next Wednesday. The larger girls are invited under Miss Cody's direction. In the evening I was present at the ordination of a Baptist minister Mr. Frazer at the 5th Ave. & 46th St. Church. Dr. Armitage presided : and mentioning in his prayer the grace conferred by the imposition

July   392

of the hands of the presbytery, whilst four ministers in dress-coats held
their hands on the head of the kneeling subject, he went on to invoke the
spirit of Mr. Frazer's father who had been a minister, saying : 'If it be
allowed to the holy departed spirit to watch over the beloved ones left
behind, may thy father's spirit watch over thee and imbue thee with zeal
similar to his own'. Is this not invocation of saints? Rev. Mr. Pendleton
gave a sermon on the ministry : dwelling on the great mission of winning
souls to Christ. Rev. Mr. Day of Indiana, rather uncouth gave the charge:
the ceremony is awkward : the newly ordained was brought face to face with
the charger : who said : 'I charge thee 1st. to be a man, a man. There
are few men in the church. A short time ago I went to a church in Philadelphia, where there were 6 or 7 ministers : I found few men. Here I
find several assistants to the pastor : I really find one man. I charge
thee 2ndly. to be a work-man. There are few work-men in the church. I
charge thee 3rdly. to be a workman anxious to win souls!' The juveniles
kept up a tittering throughout the charge : which was a compilation of dry
anecdotes each commencing with the formula : 'A few years ago'. Rev. Mr.
            gave the right hand of fellowship another awkward ceremony; the
two standing holding each other's hand, whilst the elder gave the welcoming
address of 5 minutes to the younger minister. I left before the new minister
gave the blessing.

Mon., 22nd   Drs. McGlynn, & McSweeny, Fr. Nilan & I started by the
Hudson R. boat for Catskill Mt. House where we arrived at $7\frac{1}{2}$ o'c. P.M.

Tues., 23rd   We walked to the Kaaterskill falls : where we amused
ourselves by jumping over the rocks below. The falls are 260 ft. high :
but are of a thin sheet of water : which is increased by volume.

Wed., 24th   Dr. McGlynn went home to raise $5000 : which he expects

July 393

to get from the Comptroller as the portion of the tax-levy alotted to St. Stephen's schools by the Legislature. He has organised a ragged school : to which he has administered daily, bread, soup, arithmetic and catechism. He went by the 'Thomas Powell' S. boat in a good state-room. Mr. McCuskar our S. S. teacher visited me to-day.

Thurs., 25th   We went to Haynes' falls about five miles away, enough to make the afternoon's rest very pleasant. The fall is about 180 ft. high: I alone went to the bottom.

Fri., 26th   We fared rather poorly at meals, not finding fish or eggs in sufficient quantity : to-day is Friday.

Sat., 27th   We started for home : where we arrived about 6 o'c. P.M. I heard about two hours confessions.

Sun., 28th   Omitted by the Editor.

Mon., 29th   Omitted by the Editor.

Tues., 30th   Omitted by the Editor.

Wed., 31st   Omitted by the Editor.

August

Thurs., 1st   Omitted by the Editor.

Fri., 2nd   Omitted by the Editor.

Sat., 3rd   The weather again prevented a bath. I came home with Dr. Morrogh & my mother. I heard 3½ hours' confessions.

Sun., 4th   Omitted by the Editor.

Mon., 5th   Dr. McGlynn called after returning from Elizabethtown where he had preached last evening on Temperance : showing how even a moderate allowance produces anger & murder or lust etc. Frs. Nilan & McCready called whilst we were at St. Stephen's. I dined home. Mrs. Hassard was there and asked for my ideas about the temporal power. Her son had been

August

influenced by suggestions of mine ex. gr. 'Would we like Abp. McCloskey to be mayor of New York?' I visited my mother & Dr. Morrogh. I confessed to Fr. Byrne O.S.D. who is collecting at the Imm. Conception parish. He finds the people willing to give, more than at the West : where he says churches are built by speculations in church property. I visited the Garricks : whose daughter Lila shows symptoms of decline. They showed me some oil paintings of theirs of which they are proud, & which I criticised!

Tues., 6th   Dr. Loughlin just arrived from Rome called to see me : I had Dr. McGlynn & Dr. McSweeny to dine with us. Dr. Loughlin is quite intelligent, thinks that the subject for the general council will be 'Pantheism & Liberalism' as condemned in the syllabus : and not 'papal infallibility' which in his opinion can never be defined! He told of immoral books having been introduced into Propaganda by Sabungi, a Syrian and Tommasi an Egyptian! He gave a good deal of news of Propaganda. Drs. McSweeny, McGlynn & I went to Fr. Farrell's where we had a confab on 'papal infallibility'. I argued that if it were defined we would have to swallow the 'indirect power of deposing sovereigns' which Gregory VII arrogates to himself as of divine right coming from the power of binding and loosing & of the keys. I visited the Pardows' where I met the O'Briens. Mrs. Pardow addressed me as a 'lay-priest'! Since her son's becoming a Jesuit, she has regulars on the brain.

Wed., 7th   Omitted by the Editor.

Thurs., 8th   Dr. McSweeny & I went to Long Branch : we met Fr. McNulty who was determined to believe Dr. McSweeny to be in bad health! . . . .

Fri., 9th   Omitted by the Editor.

Sat., 10th   Omitted by the Editor.

Sun., 11th   Omitted by the Editor.

August

Mon., 12th   I sent a pair of beads blessed by Pius IX as a wedding present to Miss McGlynn. I dined at St. Joseph's with Frs. Farrell, McCarthy, Drs. Parsons & O'Leary. Dr. O'Leary & Fr. Nilan supped with me and went to the S. School Union. Dr. O'Leary recommended the teachers to instruct the children 1st by memory, 2nd by the senses, 3rd by the intelligence, 4th by engaging them to bow their reason before the authority of the Holy Ghost, who uses them as well as the pope, bishops, & priests. The new merit card was the principal subject of consideration. Fr. Nilan had been refused by the Abp. a dispensation of marriage for two cousins living in incest. The Abp. scolded him for his dealings with Fr. Preston : though he admitted that Fr. Nilan's defense was plausible. He maintained that he sought to find out the usages of the diocese, but found every priest having a different one. He asked Fr. Preston for the Chancery-rules, who said these were for his own, not for others' guidance : he asked if he was vicar-general to know his right to refuse to grant him dispensations at his pleasure : unless he sent the parties to the Chancery : In doubt he had to follow the rules laid down by Theology. The Abp. recalled his dealings with Fr. Purcell : but Fr. Nilan said he supposed that forgotten long ago. The Abp. was quite angry : though he allowed Fr. Nilan's attendance to his Ecclesiastical duties to be unexceptionable; however he was hypercritical! It is a pity to have to deal with so narrow-minded a man as the Abp!

Tues., 13th   Omitted by the Editor.

Wed., 14th   Dr. McSweeny called in the afternoon, we walked to 34th St. : and went to hear Richard O'Gorman give his eulogy of Gen. Meagher. He spoke of his attachment to O'Connell's programme and of his action in revolting against England in '48 & read his discourse before his condemnation to death :

August   396

He told of his early escape from Van Diemen's land and his part in our war as commander of the Irish Brigade.

<u>Thurs., 15th</u>   This is the 5th anniversary of my first mass : I said 7 & 9 o'c. masses. Drs. McSweeny, McGlynn, O'Leary & Fr. Nilan dined with me : We had an afternoon's discussion on the infallibility of the pope : and on the use of the Latin tongue in the Liturgy. Dr. O'Leary liked the latter, as a means of securing absolute accuracy in the sacramental forms. In the morning I visited Miss A. Burtsell where I met the Miss Mullens, nieces of the Archbishop, who have been invited to visit the Burtsells at Rockaway. This will insure my reconciliation with their uncle!! I met also my mother there.

<u>Fri., 16th</u>   Omitted by the Editor.
<u>Sat., 17th</u>   Omitted by the Editor.
<u>Sun., 18th</u>   Omitted by the Editor.
<u>Mon., 19th</u>   Omitted by the Editor.
<u>Tues., 20th</u>   Omitted by the Editor.
<u>Wed., 21st</u>   Omitted by the Editor.
<u>Thurs., 22nd</u>   Omitted by the Editor.
<u>Fri., 23rd</u>   Omitted by the Editor.
<u>Sat., 24th</u>   Omitted by the Editor.
<u>Sun., 25th</u>   Omitted by the Editor.

<u>Mon., 26th</u>   I started by the Albany day-boat for Troy; meeting about seven priests on board among whom Fr. Nilan was the most acceptable. I was surprised that we were not more remarked! on the way we received new accessions from the country-parishes on the river. We reached Troy by 8 o'c. P.M. and commenced our retreat at once. Fr. Thebaud S. J. gave the points for to-morrow morning's meditation. My room was quite small,

August

though high : the bed very hard of straw, the quilt and sheets too short.

Tues., 27th   We rose at 5½ o'c A.M. The 1st. meditation was on the utility of the retreat : the 2nd. on the End of Man : the 3rd. on the use of creatures. In this he exhorted us to imitate Christ in the use of earthly goods : for he used food and clothing and his fists! He gave a conference on practical instruction on 'our religious exercises'. Fr. Quin was director of the office, not knowing how nor having authority to direct. I was shocked at Fr. And. O'Reilly's wretched reading of the Latin! We retired to bed at 9 o'c. P.M.

Wed., 28th   The 1st. meditation was on 'the sin of the angels & of Adam' : the 2nd. on 'Our Sins' : the 3rd. on Death. The conference was on Study. He recommended the priests to study five hours a day!!! at least, two hours! He showed how necessary it is to study to keep pace with the activity of the men of brains of this century, especially in Europe! Fr. Thebaud cautions us against reading Fleury's Eccles. History!! & recommended Darras' as perfect!!! Fr. Hughes had almost to spell his office.

Thurs., 29th   The 1st. meditation was on 'Hell'. He insisted that we would contradict Scripture by denying it's material fire! The 2nd. was on the Prodigal Son. The two sons represented the priests : the servants were the faithful. Otherwise it was the old explanation. The 3rd. was on Xt's mission to the twelve : as described in Matt. X. v. 7 : 'Preach : the kingdom of God is at hand. Heal the sick etc. : v. 16 'Behold I send you as sheep among wolves etc.' In the conference he told us we had to visit! but not in the morning : in the afternoon we would only meet ladies, and it would be improper to visit them especially if young, even when with their mothers : in the evening it would give scandal to visit!!!

Fri., 30th   The 1st. meditation was on the priesthood established

August 398

for the Eucharist. The 2nd. was on Christ's self sacrifice in his passion.
The 3rd. on his Resurrection. The

Sat., 31st   We made the meditation by ourselves on Christ's ascension.
The Abp. said mass & gave communion to all the priests. Thirty seven attended the retreat. Fr. Thebaud did not express one original idea. His broken English was a constant distraction. The priests preserved silence well. The confessors were chosen poorly viz : Frs. Thebaud S.J., Regnier S.J., Pfeiffer O.S.F., Wm. Quin, & Lewis. I went to Fr. Thebaud. We paid $20 for our 4½ days' board. They gave ale only at dinner, and wine on Friday. A Mr. Mullen seminarian for New York said that we gave great edification, in comparison with the Albanians who talked & carried on every day. We took the 9,40 train by the Hudson RR. Fr. Nilan & I got out at Poughkeepsie & took the day-boat from Albany. I heard 2½ hours' confessions.

September

Sun., 1st   Omitted by the Editor.

Mon., 2nd   Omitted by the Editor.

Tues., 3rd   I began 'Deus Homo' : D'Aubique's 'Luther' : and ended Storer's 'Why Not'. Dr. McGlynn called to see me. His interview with Mrs. F. Harry McDowall had been unenthusiastic. Abp. Purcell at the Slevins' had impressed him as eccentric & mopish. Bp. Rosecranz had been uncommunicative though pleasant. Drs. Berry & O'Leary had discussed the Maynooth oath at Fr. Malone's to the disadvantage of the latter. We visited Fr. Nilan. I attended the 1st. regular meeting of the S. School Association but there was no quorum. I proposed four divisions of S. School : quarterly promotion, system in classes, visiting of the children, that all independent teachers join the Association : and that Challoner's 'Catholic Christian' be read at the meetings.

September

Wed., 4th   Omitted by the Editor.

Thurs., 5th   Dr. McGlynn called early in the morning. We lunched
at his place : and took an airing in the Central Park & dined at his place
with Bp. Quinlan of Mobile who thinks Italian religious require a reform,
as also the seculars. They have no missionary spirit. The people are
grumbling over the taxation. He thinks the bishops showed independence
at Rome, by excluding an eulogy of the Romans in the address to the pope
& in requiring the address to be in Latin & not in Italian : and that many
cardinals are anxious to adapt church-laws to civil progress. . . .

Fri., 6th   I heard one hour's confessions. I visited Mrs. Whelan,
lately Miss Mary C. McGlynn : her husband was not with her. They reside
at the Hoffman House, Bway & 24th St. : which is on the European plan viz :
ordering the meals from a restaurant. She has the family-gift 'of the gab'.

Sat., 7th   Omitted by the Editor.

Sun., 8th   Omitted by the Editor.

Mon., 9th   I visited Mrs. Carolin who has been attacked with the
dysentery. The daughter though ugly is very good and intelligent. I bought
$25 of books at Kehoe's viz : Manning's Essays, Newman's development, Power's
Instructions etc. I met Fr. Byrne O.S.D. there. I assisted at the Baptist
S. School Association at the Abyssinian Chapel, 165 Waverly Place. The
blacks were mingled with the whites. The report of the last meeting showed
that the greater number of teachers approved of S. school excursions, many
children otherwise never seeing the country. Brother Goodwin spoke on the
necessity of punctuality in every business : one boy can stop a whole factory
engine. Brothers Sheridan & Phelps advised not to have teachers who were
habitually unpunctual at every business, and thought the superintendent
can correct the others by calling their attention to their tardiness.

September 400

Brother   presided over the hymns : and Scripture reading : stating that as the Savior raised the son of the widow of Naim, so the teachers raise from spiritual death the children they free from sin by their instructions. I assisted at the monthly meeting of our S. School Union & exhorted the teachers to love the children, to be in good humor at S. School, to be punctual : and to consider this charge their most important duty after the direct sanctification of their own souls. Fr. Healy sought to interest them in the newsboys & bootblacks.

<u>Tues., 10th</u>   Omitted by the Editor.

<u>Wed., 11th</u>   Omitted by the Editor.

<u>Thurs., 12th</u>   Dr. McGlynn & I took a walk to the Central Park. We decided that the future general council ought to abolish Latin in the liturgy, introduce the representative system into the church from the priesthood to the Papacy, change many of the rites, make laws by which the priests' right would be respected, allow marriage to perpetually-suspended priests, overthrow the church's dependence on the state.

<u>Fri., 13th</u>   I commenced my instruction to the girls' school : I intend to follow Fr. Power's 'Catechetical instructions'. Fr. Nilan came in whilst I was at the school : I asked some difficult questions : he was pleased with the answers. With him & Dr. McGlynn, I walked to Holy Cross : where we dined, and discussed many theological questions. In the evening I heard 3/4 hour's confessions. We commenced in the morning to hear the confessions of the girls' school : who, a dozen at a time, confess every Friday. At 8:30 P.M. I was called to attend Col. DeFleury, Baron de Lisle, whose confession I heard. He could not speak distinctly but answered my questions. He seemed a good man, not afraid of death : his Italian companion said he attended to his religious duties. The physician stated that there was no

immediate danger. I absolved him. During the night I was called again : but he died before I could get there, though I hurried. He had been in Maximilian's army.

Sat., 14th   Omitted by the Editor.
Sun., 15th   Omitted by the Editor.
Mon., 16th   Omitted by the Editor.
Tues., 17th   Dr. McGlynn, Fr. J. O'Connor & I visited Dr. O'Hara at the Metropolitan. We called at St. Joseph's : but Fr. Farrell was away. We went to see Dr. Morrogh. I had a discussion with Fr. O'C. on the infallibility of the pope : which he holds as absolutely certain : he would not ordain any one who disbelieved it.

Wed., 18th   Fr. Thos. Farrell & Dr. McSweeny called. We discussed the propriety of annulling the church impediments. Fr. Jas. O'Connor believes me excessively radical because I thought we ought to allow marriages of third cousins! Fr. Farrell stated that Fr. McQuade has suspended about ten priests, among whom Dr. Brann, giving them the option to submit to his judgement or be tried by the priests! Fr. McQuade says that at Rochester he will suspend any priest who refuses to submit to his directions : he would suspend a priest that had a requiem mass for one who would be buried in a non-catholic cemetery! Fr. Farrell showed him his absurdity! Fr. Kandor called and spoke against Fr. Briady of Rondout, who on an excursion quarrelled fiercely with a man : and his people were exasperated against him as a 'damned black republican' because he called all democrats rascals. I attended the altar class and walked to St. Stephen's with Dr. McSweeny.

Thurs., 19th   Dr. McGlynn and I visited Bishop Wood at the Metropolitan. He admired the Romans for their providence in God. I thought it excessive because they expect God to do every thing. He considers the propositions

September

submitted to the bishops about mixed marriages, removal of parish priests etc., etc. to be of small importance. At the council (oecumenical) he expects some propositions of the syllabus to be presented and disciplinary ruled : I saw Fr. O'Reilly, and Fr. Shanahan who is quite young though on the list for Harrisburgh. Fr. Jas. O'Connor receives the doctorship directly from the pope! We walked to 39th St.

Fri., 20th   Omitted by the Editor.
Sat., 21st   Omitted by the Editor.
Sun., 22nd   Omitted by the Editor.
Mon., 23rd   Omitted by the Editor.
Tues., 24th   Omitted by the Editor.
Wed., 25th   Omitted by the Editor.
Thurs., 26th   I dined at St. Joseph's with Drs. Parsons & O'Leary. Dr. O'Leary & I visited the fair of the American Institute. We took a cursory glance at the machinery : Dr. O'Leary busied himself with tobacco & cigarettes and forced me to eat some oysters. We took a ride on the Pneumatic railway. In the evening I visited the McKnights : I met with them a Mr. Meeks. I attended the singing class.

Fri., 27th   Omitted by the Editor.
Sat., 28th   I bought the 'Mysteries of Neopolitan convents' in French: and began the 2nd. volume, which narrates the petty squabbles that women tired of each other's company will inevitably get up, when their time weighs on their hands, after they have lost their first fervour! I heard $3\frac{1}{2}$ hours' confessions.

Sun., 29th   Omitted by the Editor.
Mon., 30th   Omitted by the Editor.

October

October

Tues., 1st   We had a meeting of the Theological Society at St. Joseph's. I read a few notes on the 15th century giving events which prepared for the Reformation. Dr. McSweeny in his moral case affirmed that we could baptise a dying man in good faith, though he hated the Catholic Church; if he believed as much as he knew of the Xtian religion, especially the Trinity & Incarnation. We had a long discussion whether a pagan who knew nothing of Xtianity could be saved. Dr. O'Leary denied : because Christ had required positive conditions : Dr. McGlynn affirmed because belief in God as a rewarder according to men's merits is sufficient faith. He could conceive however a pagan keeping the natural law, and not having sufficient grace to save his soul. I maintained that all had sufficient grace to save their souls, according to the text : "Christ wishes all men to be saved". We dined at St. Joseph's. Fr. Farrell told us that a pastor (Fr. W. Quin) asserted that the young priests of this diocese were going to the devil because they had too much money. This was at a private council of the Archbishop's! Fr. Farrell said it was because they had no intellectual pursuit. He forgot to deny the supposition! The Abp. is anxious to raise the salaries. Dr. McSweeny & I walked to 43rd St. I attended the meeting of the S. School Association.

Wed., 2nd   Omitted by the Editor.
Thurs., 3rd Omitted by the Editor.
Fri., 4th   Omitted by the Editor.
Sat., 5th   Omitted by the Editor.
Sun., 6th   Omitted by the Editor.
Mon., 7th   Omitted by the Editor.
Tues., 8th   A meeting of the pastors of the diocese took place in our Church, to provide for the building of the 5th Ave. Cathedral. The

October

churches were ranged according to their wealth : St. Peter's, St. Patrick's, St. Stephen's, & St. John Evang. etc. to pay $5000 annually. St. Francis Xavier's, Immac. Conception etc. $4000, St. Andrew's etc. $3000. St. Ann's, Nativity etc. $2000, Manhattenville $1500, St. Francis Ass. (German) $1000 : some of the country churches at $400. The Archbishop expressed his displeasure at the publication of his conversation with the clergy in the Baltimore Mirror & Phila. C. Standard. He would have to ask those who violated his confidence to absent themselves, as newspaper reporters are excluded from private meetings. A Catholic layman had told him that a spirit was growing among the clergy of his diocese which would give him trouble! And the opinion was prevailing outside New York, that there are here clergymen holding opinions condemned by the Holy See! These were not however the pastors! Dr. McGlynn & Fr. A. O'Reilly were the only two that spoke at the meeting : the former to ask how long the Cathedral would take to build, & about how much money would be absorbed by it, and whether the plans were changed : to which laconic answers were given viz: 1. about ten years. 2. $1000000. 3. yes. : the latter asking exemption from the imposed tax because he had to build a church in his parish. He was exempted till he had built it. The Abp. promised soon to establish moral conferences. A lunch was given after the meeting. Dr. McGlynn and I went to Brooklyn and saw the plan for St. Stephen's new altar, by Keilley : which is very fine and to be executed in white marble by Bird & Fisher. Muller has made excellent drawings of the angels to adorn the altar. Keilley lives at 89 Hudson Ave. : or just opposite the Jackson St. Ferry.

Wed., 9th   I visited my mother & Dr. Morrogh. . . .
Thurs., 10th Omitted by the Editor.
Fri., 11th   Omitted by the Editor.

October

Sat., 12th	I visited my mother. I heard 3 hours' confessions.
Sun., 13th	Omitted by the Editor.
Mon., 14th	Omitted by the Editor.
Tues., 15th	I attended Dr. Ives' funeral. . . .

Wed., 16th   I attended the altar and boys' literary classes. At the latter the first act of Richelieu was well performed.

Thurs., 17th   Fr. Nilan & I walked to the Central Park. Mr. Salt supped, with me.

Fri., 18th   I gave the instruction to the girls' school. I heard their confessions. I met Fr. Hughes, who has a mania for Catholic day-schools.

Sat., 19th   I heard $4\frac{1}{2}$ hours' confessions. Bishop Bayley came on me unawares when I was preparing to take a nap after dinner.

Sun., 20th   Omitted by the Editor.

Mon., 21st   Dr. McSweeny and I took a walk to 54th St. Dr. Henry Preston arrived with his son from N. Brunswick.

Tues., 22nd   I walked to Fr. Nilan's : he was not at home. Fr. Hecker showed Dr. H. Preston that he must become a Catholic. Mr. W. Preston & son stayed with us.

Wed., 23rd   Omitted by the Editor.

Thurs., 24th   I took a short walk. I have been of late quite busy with writing my lecture on Martin Luther.

Fri., 25th   Omitted by the Editor.

Sat., 26th   Fr. Nilan and I walked to 42nd St. and back. I heard $3\frac{1}{2}$ hours' confessions.

Sun., 27th   I sang High-Mass. Fr. Preston preached quite earnestly on the gospel : deducing the necessity of faith to please God, showing how

October

the Bible is not a suffecent rule : since Protestants do not admit the literal sense of Matt. XVI.18 (Peter's primacy) John XX.22 (confessing) John VI.53 : Matt. XXVI.26 (The Eucharist) : and showing how simple a rule of faith the Church is : & what rewards come from faith. I attended both S. Schools. I lectured in the evening on 'Martin Luther'. About 400 persons were present : 50 cents was the admission-fee : the proceeds to be devoted to the poor of the parish. The lecture lasted two hours. A child, about midway, suddenly cried out: 'Ma, I want to pea.' Fr. Preston had it taken away. Dr. Morrogh says at his church the child would have done it. Ours are well-educated.

Mon., 28th   Omitted by the Editor.

Tues., 29th   Dr. McSweeny dined with me : we visited Dr. McGlynn with whom we found Fr. Coyle and with whom we walked to the Central Park.

Wed., 30th   Omitted by the Editor.

Thurs., 31st   I visited the McKnights. They were in expectation of the return of Mr. & Miss M. McKnight from Europe. These had been sick at Mt. St. Bernard and were delighted with their treatment by the monks.

November

Fri., 1st   I sang High-Mass. In the evening I heard 1 3/4 hours' confessions. I had a long talk with Dr. Morrogh & met my mother.

Sat., 2nd   Omitted by the Editor.

Sun., 3rd   Omitted by the Editor.

Mon., 4th   Omitted by the Editor.

Tues., 5th   I voted the Radical Republican ticket & heard confessions for an hour at the Immac. Conception of the children. I assisted at the Ecclesiastical Society at Fr. Malone's. Dr. Parsons read an interesting essay to show that the bishops do not derive their jurisdiction from the

November

pope but from Christ directly, though subordinate to the pope. Dr. O'Leary hesitatingly conceded that it was not impossible for a pagan to be saved. I showed that pagans have sufficient grace to save their souls. We had a long dinner with speeches by almost all of the party. I attended the meeting of the S. S. Association.

Wed., 6th   I dined at Fr. Farrell's with Gen. Sickles : who had seen negro children of about 14, make maps at dictation or sums of algebra as well as any white children of the same age. The negroes had raised money : and were economical beyond expectation. I dined also at Dr. Morrogh's with Abp. McCloskey. The Abp. thought it doubtful if a Catholic magistrate could give a sanction to a marriage between relatives, without the Church's dispensation. I stated that their marrying before him did not make him concur in the marriage : and that the difficulty had been practically decided where Catholic magistrates presided at a marriage of parties who, where the Council of Trent was published, did not go before the parish-priest. Fr. Farrelly said he would not give the children to the missionaries' care, as was done at St. Stephen's! They could not provide sufficiently for children! Fr. Quin thought St. Stephen's heating-apparatus an useless expense! Fr. Quin asked Dr. Morrogh if he were obliged to take the pledge as president of the Temperance Society! The Doctor had drunk too much! I attended the altar and literary classes.

Thurs., 7th   Omitted by the Editor.
Fri., 8th   Omitted by the Editor.
Sat., 9th   Omitted by the Editor.
Sun., 10th   Omitted by the Editor.
Mon., 11th   Dr. McGlynn called to borrow my chalice : we went to the Convent of Mercy to borrow an altar-stone, and to St. Joseph's to borrow

November

a chalice. We saw Mother Catherine, Mother Seton's daughter. Fr. Farrell doubts the good results of a mission sensation! I heard Mrs. Janaus check play in two selections from Schiller, one from   , the other from Don Carlos. She acts quite well : though the recitations being in German were not very interesting!

Tues., 12th   Omitted by the Editor.

Wed., 13th   Dr. McGlynn called : we walked to his place where I heard Fr. Weinrich C.S.S.R. preaching to married women only on their duties to their children in a very plain practical way, showing how their daughters lost their chastity frequently because the mothers did not discourage their keeping evil company etc. Dr. McGlynn had been on the witness stand in the Surrogate's office about a child whom he anointed in the House for the friendless in spite of the directors. He gave an account of absolution etc. Mr. Parsons was a bitter cross-examiner. Mr. Glover said that the Dr. had made an excellent debut! I attended the altar-class and the girls' literary Society.

Thurs., 14th   Omitted by the Editor.

Fri., 15th   I heard the girls' confessions : gave the usual instruction to the school : and heard 3/4 of an hour's confessions in the evening. I engaged Mr. F. O'Neil to look after the property Cor. 2nd. Ave. & 20th. St.

Sat., 16th   Omitted by the Editor.

Sun., 17th   Omitted by the Editor.

Mon., 18th   Dr. McSweeny & I compared Mulbach's account of Clement XIV's death with Muratori. The latter rejects the poison-story. We went to Fr. Nilan's : as he was not at home, we dined at the Imperial Restaurant, in Union Square for $3.20 besides $1.25 for wine, having good soup, good roast beef, potatoes, peas and apple fritters & coffee. We visited Fr. Barry at St. Columba's. We talked on the temporal power. He upholds it : he is quite pleasant & intelligent : but calls Fr. McAleer a fish-woman. Fr. O'Hare is to have a fair for Goshen in that parish in spite of Fr. McAleer! In the evening I heard Fr. Weissel C.SS.R. preach at St. Stephen's on the text 'God so loved the world as to lay down his life for it.' He remarked that Christ had a body & soul capable of suffering and made to suffer. He then spoke of the agony in the garden brought on by our sins : Christ's mockery before Herod is in atonement for our pride : The shout 'Give us Barabbas, away with Christ' is repeated by us when we say 'away with the law, give us that sinful satisfaction.' He portrays with such practical conclusions the scourging, the crowning with thorns, the crucifixion : and dwelt especially on the desolation of Christ 'My God, why hast thou forsaken me' : even his mother's presence was a new torment rather than consolation. He drew as conclusions 1. we must never commit another mortal sin which would alone crucify Jesus. 2. we must suffer patiently as Christ suffered. During the sermon one woman began to cry aloud : twenty others joined in as a chorus : and the whole congregation showed similar symptoms when the preacher said : 'Don't cry now but cry at your confession : then bewail your sins etc.' The church was packed.

<u>Tues., 19th</u>　　Omitted by the Editor.

<u>Wed., 20th</u>　　Omitted by the Editor.

<u>Thurs., 21st</u>　　Omitted by the Editor.

<u>Fri., 22nd</u>　　I gave the usual instruction to the girls' school & heard their confessions, and I heard confessions in the evening for 3/4 of an hour. Fr. Nilan called : we walked to 42nd. St. We agreed on the proposition 'that we want a centre of unity in the church for faith & morals alone, not

November 410

for discipline'. This proposition needs many qualifications & modifications: it is the opposite extreme to the centralism now the policy of the church, by which the minutest item of discipline emanates from Rome.

Sat., 23rd   Omitted by the Editor.

Sun., 24th   I sang High-Mass. Fr. Preston preached on the Final judgement from to-day's gospel. I visited the three S. Schools. In the evening I heard Dr. Thompson speak at the Bway Tabernacle 'on the mistake made by Protestants & the lessons to be learned from the Roman Church.' He reviewed a lecture in which he had shown that though the success of Prussia, the defeat of Austria and the revolution of Italy were political movements only, yet the result was to make a Protestant compact country in the heart of Europe, to overthrow the right arm of the R. Catholic Church viz : Austria, and to open Italy to the Bible. Protestantism had not been a failure : if it had not extended it's influence since the Reformation, this was owing to the political circumstances. In the petty divisions of Italy as well as in Rome a bible-class would be dispersed at the point of the bayonet : He personally knew a woman imprisoned in Rome for reading the Bible. In Spain thousands would appear that had read the 'good-book' if the present infamous dynasty were overthrown. In France more than 15 or 20 persons cannot meet for a religious purpose except the national church, without permission of the government, hard to be obtained : otherwise half of France would soon be Protestant. The 1st. mistake of Protestants was the union of Church and State. Luther &Ulrich Zwingli & Calvin maintained theoretically the separation of Church & State : but practically they sought the help of the government to defend the reformation and allowed it to punish false doctrines, schisms : thus making it judge of the church. This Union has some advantages viz : it makes the revenues stable : it gives all

November   411

an opportunity of enjoying equally the religious care, if all the subjects
wish this religion. But it also induces to a spirit of intolerance, and
tends to secularise the ministers of religion, and creates injustice in
taxing people for a despised religion as the people of Ireland are taxed
for the P. E. Church... The 2nd. mistake was the retaining of certain errors
of the Roman Church. Thus Luther rejecting transubstantiation believed in
the Real Presence : and considered the Sacramentarians as heretics. This
divided the Protestant camp. The English Church retained so much of the
Romish ritual, that her rubrics are interpreted by her 'ritualists' of to-
day as pointing to the Romish Mass. The Apostolical succession by digital
manifestation has made the Lutheran & English Churches bend the knee to the
Romish church, through whose immoralities this succession is traced. The
3rd. mistake of Protestants is the intolerance shown to those churches who
differ in ideas of religious practise. The bishop of Oxford has said that
John Wesley could have much better been retained within the Episcopal Church.
Thus the Roman Church here admits the Paulists as independent revival-
preachers. They are intelligent, some being sons of Protestant clergymen :
and have free scope for their energies. The lessons to be learned from the
Romish Church are 1st. to seek the masses of the people. Their churches
are opened to all. We have the pew-system which has certain advantages.
It gives a surer revenue : a fixed congregation & makes each family feel
at home in a certain church : but it requires one minister to provide the
best food for this intelligent wealthy congregation which occupies the church
twice a day. If we opened our churches in the afternoon for another congregation, having free admission we would do much more good. If they would
spoil the cushions, let us have less fine cushions : if they would spoil
the atmosphere let us make a little sacrifice for their sake. Go to the

November 412

mission at 28th. St. & see how crowds gather there = wealthy and poor together. Nor think that it is only grand ceremonies that bring the Catholic people together. In Munich I have seen a congregation of 2000 at 8 o'c. A.M. with a large proportion of men listen to a sermon and leave at the commencement of a High-Mass with grand music. In Barcelona & in Bordeaux I have seen similar meetings for a sermon : a practical sermon as we find here every Sabbath attracts a vast crowd. The 2nd. lesson is their system of Charity. They give less charity than Protestants, but they give it in the name of the Church, whilst Protestants form philanthropic societies out of the church's influence. They have adopted the Protestant system of S. Schools for children :. The 3rd. lesson is their systematic use of women for charity. The Conventual vow is a degradation, and a violation of woman's first law-the care of family : but they unite women in the great law of love for their neighbour. The 4th. lesson is the prominence of the Church in all their thoughts. We, Protestants, close our churches from Sabbath to Sabbath : and forget the church meanwhile. Whilst the poorest Catholic servant will leave wages rather than lose her church or her confession at stated periods. We too should seek to gain a greater love for our Redeemer, & make willing sacrifices for his honour. We should seek to win souls to him. I visited the Morroghs.

Mon., 25th   Omitted by the Editor.
Tues., 26th   Omitted by the Editor.
Wed., 27th   Omitted by the Editor.
Thurs., 28th   Thanksgiving-Day. I said a low-mass at 9 o'c. & made a few remarks on our praying for the conversion of our country : stating that for this purpose I always offered my mass on public holidays. . . .
Fri., 29th   Omitted by the Editor.

November 413

Sat., 30th   Omitted by the Editor.
December
Sun., 1st   Omitted by the Editor.
Mon., 2nd   Omitted by the Editor.
Tues., 3rd   I attended a reception of two and profession of three sisters of Mercy at Houston St. The profession is solemn : the vow of poverty, chastity & obedience being taken whilst the Archbishop held the host for communion. I noticed a poor formula 'In the name of Christ & the Imm. V. M. by authority and in presence of you, my Lord Abp. of N. Y. J. McCloskey and of S. M. Horan in religion Mother Austin' without mentioning the presence of J. C. We had a breakfast after it. Dr. Parsons' sister   , was professed to-day. The Abp. preached explaining the words 'If thou wilt be perfect, sell all thou hast & follow me.' Dr. McSweeny & I went to the Central Park and then to Fr. Nilan's to get Dr. McSweeny's umbrella. We discussed Doellinger's account of the obnoxious Roman laws in the 'Church and Churches'. Card.   had prohibited young men & women giving presents under penalty of 15 days' imprisonment for father & son or daughter! I visited the Abp. : taking liberty again of speaking about the 2nd Ave. property. I acknowledged that year he had a right to be displeased with me, for interfering in business not my own. I hoped this act of mine would not destroy my efficiency for good. He thought the financial states St. Stephen's & the Immac. Conception would not allow the purchase : especially as the people were poor. I hoped to raise $8000 in St. Stephen's, St. Joseph's & St. Ann's : and $12000 by hiring a public hall to have services, by collections in the neighborhood & from friends. He at last told me to go ahead on condition that I did not bring him into trouble : he advised me not to get myself into trouble. I thanked him for the good he

December								414

allowed me to do, & because he practically had forgotten all acts of mine that had caused him displeasure. I met Dr. McGlynn to whom I communicated this conference. He had set Cavanagh to look after the same property for a Catholic church : the agent pretends no objection meanwhile he prefers selling to Mr. O'Neil for residences! This will be a good way for averting the suspicion that Mr. O'Neil might be buying for the Catholics! I attended our S. S. Association : but we had no quorum. We determined to continue the merit cards. I visited the D'Enbranches at 102 E. 14th. St. Mr. D'Enbranches had lately failed in business : My visit was half of condolence though as they were in the parlor with other boarding people, we did not talk of their affairs.

Wed., 4th   I obtained from Sadliers the printed extract of the Almanac for Chicago, which by Fr. Butler's request I sent to Bp. Duggan who I believe, is in disgrace in Rome. We held a meeting of the Theological Society. Fr. McLoughlin read a tolerable essay on 'Education' : which opened a discussion on the right of the state to compel education. I desired it : several maintained it. Fr. Nilan gave the moral case about a man who failed, whether he was exempted from restoring when he regained his wealth & whether he could conscientiously avail himself of the bankruptcy law. The answer was generally affirmative. We dined at St. Joseph's. Dr. McSweeny, Fr. Nilan & I walked to 42nd. St. : we expressed indignation at Dr. Parsons' quoting Dr. McGlynn and me to endorse his ideas concerning the immorality of the clergy of Rome! I attended the altar-class and the literary Society.

Thurs., 5th   Omitted by the Editor.
Fri., 6th   Omitted by the Editor.
Sat., 7th   Omitted by the Editor.
Sun., 8th   Omitted by the Editor.

December

Mon., 9th   Omitted by the Editor.

Tues., 10th   Fr. Nilan called in the morning. Dr. McSweeny & I walked in the afternoon to 52nd. St. He says he considers himself very lazy when he finds the priests at St. Stephen's eternally busy! I heard Miss Anna Dickinson speaker on 'Breakers ahead'. She says that a party must fight or surrender. The Republican party is induced to surrender the principle of equality that created it, viz : negro suffrage. It wishes to have Grant for a presidential candidate, because of his personal popularity. She would say nothing against Grant : minds infinitely keener could find nothing for or against Grant who is a speechless sphynx having no principles for his platform.

Wed., 11th   I visited the hall Cor. 23rd. St. & 2nd. Ave. : which is able to hold about 1000 persons. It is now rented to the No. 2 T. A. B. So I applied to Mr. Donahue one of the five directors for the use of it for Mass. He will second my proposal : we visited Mr. Spilman, the president of the Society, who will also aid my design. I attended the altar-class & girls' literary society. I changed the day of their meeting to Monday.

Thurs., 12th Omitted by the Editor.
Fri., 13th   Omitted by the Editor.
Sat., 14th   Omitted by the Editor.
Sun., 15th   Omitted by the Editor.
Mon., 16th   Omitted by the Editor.

Tues., 17th   I called on Dr. McGlynn : we walked to 42nd St. : dined at our house, and then walked to the Abp.'s : to whom I proposed to take the hall on 2nd. Ave. & 23rd. St. from the New Year. He consented, though he told me I must take care not to get swamped. He advised me to fix my dwelling in the neighborhood as soon as possible : at least to get an office where the calls could be received. I told him we might have to pay about $41 000 for the property Cor. 2nd. Ave. & 20th St. He made no objection. We supped at Dr. McGlynn's where I met Fr. McEvoy and Dr. E. McSweeny : the latter's ideas are somewhat limited to Rome as yet. Catholics talk of Rome as if it were the whole world! We met Fr. Weinrick C.SS.R. who is quite intelligent. Dr. McGlynn & I heard Dickens read Six chapters from David Copperfield & the Medical dinner from Pickwick. He reads very well : but the huskiness of his voice detracts from it's excellence.

Wed., 18th   Fr. C. Farrell called : he comes to buy a sleigh. I visited my mother and Dr. Morrogh. Dr. Fox's death has occasioned great commotion there. He had been in the Amer. College : was now a medical doctor. He went to bed at 10 o'c. Sunday-morning & was found dead Monday evening : dead of apoplexy brought on by disease of the kidneys probably brought on by drink. I called in at the McLaughlins. Bishop Bayley said mass, breakfasted and dined with us. I went with Freckleton, the carpenter, to Demilt Hall, to prepare the design of an altar. I went to Mr. O'Neil, who has received an offer of the 2nd. Ave. property for $42,500.00 on condition that he builds 1st. class private residences. I attended the altar-class and the literary Society.

Thurs., 19th   Omitted by the Editor.

Fri., 20th   I bid farewell to the school, giving medals to those who had written compositions & given good answers during the previous 4 months. I told Dr. Morrogh of my taking possession of Demilt Hall at the beginning of 1868. He doesn't wish to give up the gas-house at 21st. St. & Ave. A! We arranged that 18th. St. to the East River would be my Southern boundary. In the morning I heard the girls', in the evening the boys' and

December

others' confessions : 4½ hours' in all.

Sat., 21st   I visited Dr. Morrogh, Mr. Donahue whom I intend to engage as janitor, & Mr. O'Neil who told me that Stuyvesant will sell the property on 2nd Ave. & 20th St. for $42,500, if he guarantees to build first-class buildings fronting on the Avenue. He promises to build one, perhaps two, very soon : for the others he will not be restricted to time. I heard 5½ hours' confessions!

Sun., 22nd   Omitted by the Editor.

Mon., 23rd   Omitted by the Editor.

Tues., 24th   Omitted by the Editor.

Wed., 25th   Omitted by the Editor.

Thurs., 26th   Dr. McGlynn & I visited the neighborhood of my future parish. He gives me an old suit of white vestments. I bade good-bye to the altar, & girls' literary & singing-class : giving souvenirs to all.

Fri., 27th   Omitted by the Editor.

Sat., 28th   I heard 5½ hours' confessions :

Sun., 29th   I said farewell to the 7 o'c. and 10½ o'c. congregations. Fr. Preston bound St. Ann's to give me a collection on 2nd Sunday of January. The S. School presented me with a gold-chalice. Mr. Griffin made an address : Fr. Preston & Dr. McGlynn spoke. I made a reply. Fr. Preston delivered the last of this course of lectures.

Mon., 30th   I said farewell to the girls' literary Society : I bade farewell to the Navarros, who will present me with a set of gold-cloth vestments.

Tues., 31st   I left my card at the Hubbards', visited the O'Reillys, O'Briens and Pardows.

1868

January

<u>Wed., 1st</u>   I visited the Abp. : who restricted me to Benediction of the B. S. to once a month. I concluded he would never get more information than was absolutely necessary! I visited the Gilberts, the Wards, the Colvilles, the Otis', the Alsops, the Dykers, the Ashmans, the Bedfords, the Tiers, the Spences : to propitiate them to liberaly. I visited also my mother, Dr. Morrogh and the McLaughlins.

<u>Thurs., 2nd</u>   I bought vestments and utensils of church from Wenniger.

<u>Fri., 3rd</u>   I arranged the altar, carpet etc. at Demilt Hall.

<u>Sat., 4th</u>   I was the whole day at Demilt Hall. Misses Cody & Whelan arranged the altar.

<u>Sun., 5th</u>   At 8 o'c. mass Demilt Hall was crowded : and also at 10½ o'c. mass. Drs. McGlynn & Morrogh spoke : Dr. E. McSweeny & Fr. Farrell were also there. I dined at St. Stephen's. I spoke of course! Epiphany being celebrated from to-day; the new district derives it's name from the festival. St. Ann's children's choir sang. The altar was neatly arranged.

<u>Mon., 6th</u>   Feast of Epiphany. All the seats of Demilt Hall were occupied at 7 o'c. : at 9 o'c. the hall was crowded.

<u>Tues., 7th</u>   I attended the Ecclesiastical Society : which elected officers to-day. I formed a building association with $5 initiation fee and 50 cents monthly dues : I received in ready money $202.00 and had subscribed $180.00. To-day I said mass on the ground floor.

January

Wed., 8th   I engaged rooms at 432 2nd Ave. : in Mrs. Trainor's house, the board directed by Miss McCoy : at $13 a week.

Thurs., 9th   I travelled over town to get benches and bought 20 at Mason's Cor. Pearl St. & New Bowery for $80.

Fri., 10th   Mr. Blanco gave me $500.00. He gave me some of his original ideas about religion, to which I listened so patiently that he told me to call again when I wanted more money & I should always find in him a friend.

Sat., 11th   I heard 4 hours' confessions : and distributed about 30 seats in the hall.

Sun., 12th   I preached at 7 o'c. at St. Ann's about the collection : said 8 o'c. mass at Demilt Hall, formed the S. School : preached at 10½ o'c. at Demilt Hall and then at St. Ann's : sold about 30 seats in the afternoon, blessed the hall on the ground floor, gave Benediction of the B. Sacrament: baptised three children, attended the Temperance meeting & visited the Morroghs in 26th St. & met my mother, Mrs. McLaughlin & P. Morrogh.

Mon., 13th   I received about $1000.00 from St. Ann's collection : with promises of fully another thousand.

Tues., 14th   Omitted by the Editor.

Wed., 15th   Dr. McGlynn brought me a note of Cavanagh's about the property Cor. 20th St. & 2nd Ave.

Thurs., 16th   I saw Cavanagh who thinks I have every chance, if I guarantee not to build a parochial school, to obtain the property on 20th St.

Fri., 17th   Cavanagh writes to me that he submitted my proposition to the Stuyvesants' agent Mr. Wakely who will report next week. I collected Cor. 18th St. & Ave. A $16 from a dozen families! I dined at Immac.

January

Conception : and protested against the use of my name on Dr. Morrogh's books for Cathedral-collection especially without my consent. I formed a S. School Association.

Sat., 18th   I dined at St. Stephen's where I received Communion particles. I heard 3½ hours' confessions.

Sun., 19th   I said 8 o'c. & sang 10½ o'c. Mass & preached at both. I assisted at the formation of S. School : the boys under Mr. Coddington, the girls under Miss Cody.

Mon., 20th   The Traynors spoke to me of property 75 ft. front by 190 deep on 2nd Ave. betw. 21st St. & 22nd St. Fr. Nilan called . He is quarrelling with Fr. McCarthy : because he wants to get two days of the week free of duty.

Tues., 21st   I held a meeting of the Building Association and received $150.00 for the Association, besides $256.25 in donations.

Wed., 22nd   I visited Fr. Preston at the Chancery to learn to keep accounts.

Thurs., 23rd   Omitted by the Editor.

Fri., 24th   Omitted by the Editor.

Sat., 25th   I heard 4 hours' confessions. Mrs. Whelan offered me $25.00. I asked $100.00!

Sun., 26th   I said 8 o'c. & sang 10½ o'c. mass. I attended altar-class in the evening.

Mon., 27th   I dined at Immac. Conception & visited the gas-house & visited Mr. Mc Colgan who promises me a donation.

Tues., 28th   I attended the Building Association.

Wed., 29th   I dined at St. Ann's : I found from Mr. Hildreth that the Traynors had mistaken with regard to the depth of Cameron's lots. I

January

attended to baptisms etc.

Thurs., 30th I sent baptismal records to McMasters.

Fri., 31st I dined at a French restaurant on Broadway : I visited Fr. Farrell.

February

Sat., 1st I heard 4 hours' confessions.

Sun., 2nd I said 8 o'c. & sang 10½ o'c. mass, gave Benediction of the B. Sacrament preaching on each occasion : at 10½ o'c. blessing the candles and having solemn procession, with boys in black and girls in white. I formed a conference of St. Vincent de Paul.

Mon., 3rd I dined at St. Ann's. Fr. Preston wanted my presence to urge Fr. Keogh to have a dramatic performance by the literary society. Mr. Garrick, 19 Roosevelt St. promised to provide coal for my church and my house till May! I presented the names of officers for St. Vincent de Paul's conference to the president of Council Dr. Anderson. I had a meeting of janitors.

Tues., 4th I attended the Ecclesiastical Society & dined at St. Joseph's : attended altar class, Building Association & Conference of St. Vincent de Paul.

Wed., 5th I visited the Garricks

Thurs., 6th I dined with Fr. Nilan & Dr. Parsons at Holy Cross Church. Fr. A. Donnelly promised to give me a collection in Summer or Autumn. I attended the singing-class : I also invited the Temperence men to attend the discourse by Dr. O'Leary on account of his avowed sympathy with the Irish revolution!

Fri., 7th Fr. Loyzance S. J., after consultation with the fathers, consented to give me a collection on Feb. 16th because I commenced my

February

education under them!

Sat., 8th   I received the Stuyvesants' answer equivalent to a refusal for their ground on 2nd Ave. & 20th St. : they require me to purchase the ten lots and build private residences on four of them : and make my church and houses to their liking! I heard 4 hours' confessions.

Sun., 9th   I preached at 4 masses at St. Joseph's. Dr. O'Leary took my place. I gave Benediction of B. Sacrament and preached at my hall. No. 2 T. A-B. Society agreed to get up a lecture for me on Feb. 23rd. by Dr. O'Leary.

Mon., 10th   I asked Mr. Hildreth to close the bargain for Cameron's property on 2nd Ave. bet. 21st & 22nd Sts. at $40 000.00 if necessary.

Tues., 11th   Mr. Hildreth closed the bargain for $37,500.00 making Cameron pay $375.00 to Homer Morgan the agent. Mr. Hildreth passed the contract for Cameron's property to me, when I paid him the $3750.00 which was paid to secure the contract. I dined at St. Ann's.

Wed., 12th   I dined at St. Joseph's : which gave me $591.00 last Sunday. I thanked No. 2 T. A-B. for their kindness.

Thurs., 13th I dined at Immac. Conception : and attended the S. School Association.

Fri., 14th   I heard $3\frac{1}{2}$ hours' confessions.

THE AMERICAN CATHOLIC TRADITION

An Arno Press Collection

Callahan, Nelson J., editor. **The Diary of Richard L. Burtsell, Priest of New York.** 1978

Curran, Robert Emmett. **Michael Augustine Corrigan and the Shaping of Conservative Catholicism in America, 1878-1902.** 1978

Ewens, Mary. **The Role of the Nun in Nineteenth-Century America** (Doctoral Thesis, The University of Minnesota, 1971). 1978

McNeal, Patricia F. **The American Catholic Peace Movement 1928-1972** (Doctoral Dissertation, Temple University, 1974). 1978

Meiring, Bernard Julius. **Educational Aspects of the Legislation of the Councils of Baltimore, 1829-1884** (Doctoral Dissertation, University of California, Berkeley, 1963). 1978

Murnion, Philip J., **The Catholic Priest and the Changing Structure of Pastoral Ministry, New York, 1920-1970** (Doctoral Dissertation, Columbia University, 1972). 1978

White, James A., **The Era of Good Intentions: A Survey of American Catholics' Writing Between the Years 1880-1915** (Doctoral Thesis, University of Notre Dame, 1957). 1978

Dyrud, Keith P., Michael Novak and Rudolph J. Vecoli, editors. **The Other Catholics.** 1978

Gleason, Philip, editor. **Documentary Reports on Early American Catholicism.** 1978

Bugg, Lelia Hardin, editor. **The People of Our Parish.** 1900

Cadden, John Paul. **The Historiography of the American Catholic Church: 1785-1943.** 1944

Caruso, Joseph. **The Priest.** 1956

Congress of Colored Catholics of the United States. **Three Catholic Afro-American Congresses.** [1893]

Day, Dorothy. **From Union Square to Rome.** 1940

Deshon, George. **Guide for Catholic Young Women.** 1897

Dorsey, Anna H[anson]. **The Flemmings.** [1869]

Egan, Maurice Francis. **The Disappearance of John Longworthy.** 1890

Ellard, Gerald. **Christian Life and Worship.** 1948

England, John. **The Works of the Right Rev. John England, First Bishop of Charleston.** 1849. 5 vols.

Fichter, Joseph H. **Dynamics of a City Church.** 1951

Furfey, Paul Hanly. **Fire on the Earth.** 1936

Garraghan, Gilbert J. **The Jesuits of the Middle United States.** 1938. 3 vols.

Gibbons, James. **The Faith of Our Fathers.** 1877

Hecker, I[saac] T[homas]. **Questions of the Soul.** 1855

Houtart, François. **Aspects Sociologiques Du Catholicisme Américain.** 1957

[Hughes, William H.] **Souvenir Volume. Three Great Events in the History of the Catholic Church in the United States.** 1889

[Huntington, Jedediah Vincent]. **Alban: A Tale of the New World.** 1851

Kelley, Francis C., editor. **The First American Catholic Missionary Congress.** 1909

Labbé, Dolores Egger. **Jim Crow Comes to Church.** 1971

LaFarge, John. **Interracial Justice.** 1937

Malone, Sylvester L. **Dr. Edward McGlynn.** 1918

The Mission-Book of the Congregation of the Most Holy Redeemer. 1862

O'Hara, Edwin V. **The Church and the Country Community.** 1927

Pise, Charles Constantine. **Father Rowland.** 1829

Ryan, Alvan S., editor. **The Brownson Reader.** 1955

Ryan, John A., **Distributive Justice.** 1916

Sadlier, [Mary Anne]. **Confessions of an Apostate.** 1903

Sermons Preached at the Church of St. Paul the Apostle, New York, During the Year 1863. 1864

Shea, John Gilmary. **A History of the Catholic Church Within the Limits of the United States.** 1886/1888/1890/1892. 4 Vols.

Shuster, George N. **The Catholic Spirit in America.** 1928

Spalding, J[ohn] L[ancaster]. **The Religious Mission of the Irish People and Catholic Colonization.** 1880

Sullivan, Richard. **Summer After Summer.** 1942

[Sullivan, William L.] **The Priest.** 1911

Thorp, Willard. **Catholic Novelists in Defense of Their Faith, 1829-1865.** 1968

Tincker, Mary Agnes. **San Salvador.** 1892

Weninger, Franz Xaver. **Die Heilige Mission** *and* **Praktische Winke Für Missionare.** 1885. 2 Vols. in 1

Wissel, Joseph. **The Redemptorist on the American Missions.** 1920. 3 Vols. in 2

The World's Columbian Catholic Congresses and Educational Exhibit. 1893

Zahm, J[ohn] A[ugustine]. **Evolution and Dogma.** 1896